Forging Reform in China
The Fate of State-Owned Industry

The greatest economic challenge facing China in the post-Deng era is the reform of sluggish, unprofitable, state-owned firms that threaten to drag down the rest of the economy. Banking reform, fiscal reform, and overall economic growth all turn on whether China can succeed in reorganizing and revitalizing its state industrial sector.

State-owned enterprises (SOEs), the foundation of China's industrial base, are the nation's steel makers, machine builders, auto and truck manufacturers, and petroleum producers. Despite an array of well-intentioned, market-oriented reform measures, these SOEs as a group have never truly been forced to face hard budgets, the pressure of a bottom line, or the threat of bankruptcy. *Forging Reform in China* explains how and why these measures have not been sweepingly successful to date, and what will be needed to achieve meaningful reform.

What constraints force some economic producers to shift to market-oriented behavior while others continue the patterns of the past? Edward Steinfeld answers these questions through an in-depth exploration of firm-level processes within the steel industry, an examination that reveals the institutional and systemic barriers to market-oriented performance in Chinese heavy industry.

While providing a penetrating analysis of the state sector of China's economy, Steinfeld also offers a more general framework for understanding the whole phenomenon of postsocialist reform. This book makes sense of the complex linkages between state actors, economic institutions, and enterprise performance in transitional economies. In the process, it challenges the two fundamental ideas that have shaped the debate over postsocialist transition: the belief that privatization can solve the problem of state enterprise restructuring, and the alternative view that painful economic restructuring can be avoided by maintaining high levels of national economic growth.

Edward S. Steinfeld is the Mitsubishi Assistant Professor of Management at Massachusetts Institute of Technology's Sloan School of Management.

Cambridge Modern China Series

Edited by William Kirby, *Harvard University*

Other books in the series:

Forging Reform in China

The Fate of State-Owned Industry

EDWARD S. STEINFELD

CAMBRIDGE
UNIVERSITY PRESS

PUBLISHED BY THE PRESS SYNDICATE OF THE UNIVERSITY OF CAMBRIDGE
The Pitt Building, Trumpington Street, Cambridge, United Kingdom

CAMBRIDGE UNIVERSITY PRESS
The Edinburgh Building, Cambridge CB2 2RU, UK   http: //www.cup.cam.ac.uk
40 West 20th Street, New York, NY 10011-4211, USA   http: //www.cup.org
10 Stamford Road, Oakleigh, Melbourne 3166, Australia

First published 1998
Reprinted 1999
First paperback edition 1999

Printed in the United States of America

Typeset in Times 10/13 pt., in AMS-T$_E$X [FH]

A catalogue record for this book is available from the British Library

Library of Congress Cataloguing-in-Publication data is available

ISBN 0 521 63335 4 hardback
ISBN 0 521 77861 1 paperback

Contents

vii

Contents

Contents

Figures and Tables

FIGURES

TABLES

xi

Figures and Tables

Preface

As this book enters publication, China stands at the most critical juncture in its journey from plan to market. In the early months of 1998, as its neighbors were sinking deeper and deeper into financial distress, China embarked on a daring, headlong scramble to solve its own escalating economic woes, problems that had been accumulating for years if not decades. Realization had finally sunk in that the system was severely flawed and that drastic measures were necessary. The nation's banking system was mired in insolvency, levels of nonperforming loans were astronomical, and demand nationwide was dropping. During the preceding fifteen years, policy makers had achieved growth but had resisted any serious changes to a system that showered subsidized credit upon heavy industry. Now, living in the shadow of East Asia's financial meltdown, and with the specter of a Chinese financial collapse looming, policy makers are coming to understand the accumulated costs of deferred reforms. They are coming to understand that China, for all its uniqueness and for all its phenomenal success, has failed to avoid the scourge of rapidly developing economies East and West: inefficient capital allocation and grievous misinvestment. Determined to avoid the fate of its neighbors, China swung into action.

Zhu Rongji, formally elevated to the premiership in March of 1998, ushered in the spring with a reform package striking for its scale and severity. The banking system was to be wrenched from local control, nearly half of the central government's ministries were to be eliminated, almost four million bureaucrats were to be relieved of their positions, and subsidized credit to state firms was to be summarily cut. If actually implemented, these measures are guaranteed to shake the foundations of a system that has lasted in China since the start of reform almost two decades ago. Some twenty million urban workers are expected to lose their jobs in the process, a phenomenal number for a country even as vast as China. This is the price to pay to undo years of misinvestment, years of channeling resources into sectors that produced little if any commercial return.

This book deals with the underlying cause of China's current economic troubles, its state-owned industries. The Chinese state sector has been the focus of

xiii

continual reform over the past fifteen years, but for all the apparent transformation and all the innovative policy measures, precious little has changed in two vital areas: bankruptcy-induced market exit and commercial provision of capital. Chinese state firms to this day neither go out of business nor find themselves subject to credit provision on anything resembling commercial standards. Despite years of managerial reform, inefficient firms have been kept afloat, and they have been kept afloat through heavily subsidized credit.

Economic reformers undoubtedly pursued this course of action with the best of intentions. While committed to growth and marketization, they were determined to avoid the societal dislocation associated with reform in Eastern Europe and the former Soviet Union. In practical terms, this has translated into a concerted effort to maintain full urban employment. Of course, from the start of reform, the price of maintaining full urban employment seemed relatively low. Chinese policy makers believed that they could preserve old jobs by simply freezing the existing state sector in place, and that they could create new jobs by allowing the more vibrant nonstate economy to surge forward. China, in effect, would grow its way out of the old state-dominated economy.

Well-intentioned policies, however, led to unexpected consequences. The determination to keep state firms afloat meant that substantial subsidies had to be provided to industry. Because the government's fiscal revenues from the start were insufficient to perform this function, bank credit had to serve instead. Ultimately, therefore, it was China's substantial levels of household savings that served to prop up commercially unsustainable SOEs. In essence, the savings deposits of ordinary citizens were mortgaged on the fate of state industry.

Unfortunately, as we are witnessing today, these policies have come at significant cost. In an effort simply to maintain a state sector of limited size, reformers created an institutional environment in which state firms actually faced incentives to expand. Moreover, the most deeply inefficient portions of the state sector – the largest and most capital-intensive firms – enjoyed the greatest opportunities for growth. Meanwhile, in an environment of soft credit and ambiguous accounting standards, fundamentally unsound firms year after year could show phenomenal profits, thus further justifying ill-advised expansion. Basic financial information, the information upon which fundamental business and policy decisions were made, lost its essential reliability. Numbers ceased to mean what people thought they meant.

Equally important, as long as unsound state firms were kept afloat, the urban workforce in these firms faced few incentives to leave. In the process, a dangerous cycle developed. As firms expanded, more and more workers sought employment in these firms. As more and more workers sought employment in these firms, the government could less afford the social and political costs of actually shutting firms down. But as subsidies flowed in, firms responded by expanding. For every year that this process was permitted to continue, the depth of misallocation deepened. More and more workers, and more and more capital, ended up in commercially unsustainable business enterprises. The systemic costs are now evident in the present-day horrendous condition of the banking system, the vast number of workers threatened by unemployment if state-sector restructuring is actually pursued, and the declining likelihood that the nation will be able to maintain the growth rates that have for so long fostered social stability. The strictures on policy makers are growing tighter and tighter, and the room for maneuver less and less.

No matter which way they turn, policy makers now face grim choices. That key state-sector reforms have been deferred for so long makes actual implementation all the more difficult and painful. If decisive action is taken, millions of workers over a very short period of time stand to lose their jobs, their health care benefits, and their pensions. Yet, if no action is taken, China stands to cripple not only its modern industrial sector but also its entire financial system. The nation's economic policy makers are, in the crudest sense, "damned if they do and damned if they don't." Nevertheless, with the possibility of financial collapse laid bare by the experiences of South Korea, Thailand, Indonesia, and even Japan, China's decision makers have decided to act. The architects of Chinese reform are finally tackling the greatest challenges of market transition, yet they are doing so at a time marked by a dearth of prior models and cases upon which to base future decisions. In undertaking the dilemmas of state-sector restructuring, China's reform leaders are facing the ultimate test, a test for which simple solutions simply do not exist.

Under such circumstances, it would be presumptuous of any academic to suggest that he or she somehow has easy answers for the tough policy choices that lie in China's future. It is my hope, however, that this book can provide readers a better understanding of the problems at hand, and a deeper appreciation for the dilemmas China faces at the dawn of the twenty-first century.

When writing a book, one learns a great deal about a particular topic, a great deal about one's basic world views, and certainly a great deal about one's own work habits and stamina. More than anything else, though, I have learned through the course of this journey the immeasurable importance of having good teachers. Over the past years, I have been truly blessed to have come into contact with an extraordinary array of fine educators. Some have taught me formally in the classroom; others informally through countless conversations and interactions.

All have given generously of their time and expertise. It goes without saying that if not for their unstinting help, this book would never have been possible. The intellectual origins of this research project began some ten years ago during my first extended stay in China. From the very first day of that year-long visit, I was exposed to wonderful teachers, my colleagues at Nanjing University. Two professors in particular, Liu Haiping and Wang Shouren, deserve special thanks, for their influence upon me was profound. During a particularly difficult period for their country, they took me under their collective wing and allowed me to view Chinese society through their own deeply informed perspectives. In a manner to which I have grown accustomed in China, they gave unfailingly and never once asked for anything in return.

That same pattern of interaction continued – with an even wider range of Chinese colleagues – during an extended stay in Beijing in 1994, and again during a series of shorter visits in 1997. Many Chinese academics, policy makers, and enterprise-level officials generously shared with this naïve outsider their rich experiences and insights into enterprise reform. Due to the sensitivity of the information they conveyed, I must resist the urge to thank them by name. Nevertheless, suffice it to say that I will always be grateful for the time and attention they devoted to me, and I will always be inspired by their commitment to helping China negotiate its transition from plan to market.

People whom I most certainly *can* thank by name are the dedicated individuals who taught me during my years at Harvard University. The doctoral dissertation from which this study emerged could never have been completed without the help of my advisors: Roderick MacFarquhar, Dwight Perkins, and Alberto Alesina. Indeed, it was Professor MacFarquhar who introduced me to the wonders of Chinese studies during my first year as a college undergraduate (and his first year as a Harvard faculty member). My research on Chinese economic reform was furthered immensely by the faculty I met at Harvard's Fairbank Center for East Asian Research. I would like in particular to thank Joseph Fewsmith, Merle Goldman, Ellis Joffe, Iain Johnston, Bill Kirby, Jean Oi, Ezra Vogel, and Andrew Walder. All are distinguished not only by their extensive knowledge of contemporary Asian affairs but also by the ability to communicate that knowledge to their students.

Now as a faculty member at MIT's Sloan School of Management, I have been blessed with another fine set of teachers, my colleagues. Approaching the subject from a variety of different disciplines and backgrounds, they have helped tremendously in the final stages of this project, sharing with me their extensive knowledge of enterprise behavior and forcing me to rethink issues that I once thought clear-cut. Especially helpful have been Michael Cusumano, Arnoldo

Hax, Simon Johnson, Don Lessard, Richard Locke, Bill Pounds, Ed Roberts, Michael Scott Morton, Scott Shane, Scott Stern, Lester Thurow, Eleanor Westney, Alan White, and Nick Ziegler.

One of the added virtues of being at the Sloan School is that I have been granted entree into the broader community of scholars and teachers here at MIT. Suzanne Berger, Cui Zhiyuan, Richard Lester, Ken Oye, Peter Perdue, Dick Samuels, and David Woodruff have been particularly helpful in guiding me through the final stages of this research project. I could not ask for better teachers across such a wide range of disciplines.

I would like to extend a special thanks to Lucian Pye and Nicholas Lardy for the detailed criticisms that they provided in the manuscript stages of this book. Lucian is a monumental figure in the field of Chinese studies as well as an exceptionally generous colleague and teacher. His comments on the initial draft chapters were invaluable. Similarly, Nick Lardy provided absolutely critical feedback on the initial manuscript and saved me from a series of grievous errors. Moreover, he graciously shared with me his own research findings (and a forthcoming manuscript) on Chinese banking reform. His knowledge of contemporary Chinese economic affairs is unsurpassed.

Throughout the research and writing stages of this project, a number of friends and colleagues contributed important insights and critiques. They include: Lucy Aitchison, John Glazer, Huang Yasheng, Ken-ichi Imai, Gary Jefferson, Kenneth Lieberthal, Lu Mai, Sid Mitter, Mark Nagel, Daniel Posner, Thomas Rawski, Takeshi Sugimoto, Daniel Thomas, Alan Wachman, Xiao Meng, Xu Chenggang, Xu Meizheng, Yang Jiliang, and Yi Gang.

That almost no book on contemporary China fails to acknowledge the contribution of Nancy Hearst is a testament to her critical role in the field. Nancy's unparalleled knowledge of Chinese-language research materials is widely known throughout the United States and abroad. She also happens to be an acute observer of the contemporary Chinese scene. Though she may claim only to have proofread this manuscript, she made important substantive contributions throughout the course of this project.

At Cambridge University Press, I would like to extend sincere thanks to my editor, Mary Child, who with a sure hand and patient demeanor responded to a barrage of requests from this decidedly impatient author. Matt Darnell copyedited the manuscript and moved it through the production process with great alacrity. David Youtz of the Asia Society generously provided the photographs appearing on the cover, photographs that he himself shot in China.

I began these acknowledgments by referring to teachers, and I would like to end on a similar note. Gordon Newcombe and Philip Lewerth were two educators who shaped the lives of thousands of students, including this one. Many of us passed through their classrooms; none can ever forget the experience. In the hands of Messrs. Newcombe and Lewerth, teaching truly did become a noble profession. It is to their memory, and with heartfelt gratitude, that I dedicate this book.

1

Introduction: China's Ailing
State Enterprises

$\mathbf{C}$HINA'S economic awakening will undoubtedly go down as one of the great events of the twentieth century. In the course of just two decades, the country has undergone processes of social, economic, and industrial change that in the West spanned centuries. On so many fronts today, China is a country and society in revolution: an industrial revolution as hundreds of millions of peasants leave the land for factories, a social revolution as a primarily rural populace urbanizes, and an economic revolution as a self-proclaimed socialist nation negotiates its way from command planning to the market. China in so many ways is engaged in processes for which there is simply no historical precedent. While the nation's entire system of economic organization – an inheritance from twentieth-century Soviet Russia – transforms into another arguably twentieth-century creation, the market capitalism of the West, Chinese society simultaneously lurches through a phase of industrialization on par with that of eighteenth-century England and a wave of urbanization comparable with that of post-Medieval Europe. It is no wonder that this fusion of processes, at once intensely modern and anachronistically ancient, produces outcomes anticipated by not even the wisest of observers and participants. These are incredible times in China – times of euphoria, dislocation, and, beyond all else, uncertainty.

As China's phenomenal growth rates since the early 1980s suggest, many things are clearly going right. Between 1978 and 1996, the country grew at an average annual rate of 9.9 percent, a level impressive by any standard.[1] Indisputable to even the most casual observer in China is that living standards have soared in the past twenty years. With the demise of collectivized agriculture in the late 1970s and the subsequent rise of rural industry, extraordinary forces of entrepreneurship, initiative, and manpower have been unleashed in the Chinese countryside. Small manufacturing operations have not only proliferated, but particularly when coupled with overseas capital and manufacturing expertise, have flooded foreign markets with textiles, shoes, and toys. These firms – nimble, market-oriented collectives and TVEs (township and village

1

enterprises) – may operate on a small scale, but together they account for a significant portion of the employment growth and productivity gains experienced by China over the past fifteen years. They are, in a sense, the dynamos of Chinese development.

Yet, for all these achievements and for all the talk – both optimistic and apocalyptic – of China's emergence as an economic superpower, the Chinese economy remains beset by critical problems. Chief among them is the perennial and intensely frustrating issue of state enterprise restructuring. By Chinese policy makers' own admission, this is the single most important challenge facing the system today. It impacts not just broadly on domestic growth and social stability, but also on China's foreign relations, particularly with regard to trade issues, and even on elite party politics.[2] State industrial restructuring has become the proverbial albatross hanging around the Chinese leadership's collective neck. Certainly the leadership understands that as long as the issue remains unresolved, the question is not just whether China can become a superpower in the future, but rather whether the nation can even sustain the gains it has made up to the present.

China's state-owned enterprises (SOEs) once stood at the "commanding heights" of the planned economy. Today, they seem little more than relics of an industrial age gone by. These firms, however, still constitute virtually all of the nation's heavy industrial base. They are its steel makers, machine builders, auto and truck manufacturers, and petroleum producers, just to name a few. State-owned enterprises are the firms that even today still provide basic industrial inputs for the economy, employment and social welfare for the vast majority of China's urban workers, as well as the bulk of fiscal revenues for most governmental levels. Unfortunately, these are also the firms that still suffer from habitual overstaffing, notoriously low productivity, and ever-declining profit performance – all the traditional ills of socialist production.[3] Despite the waves of reform measures directed toward them, China's SOEs have proven stubbornly resistant to market forces and frustratingly devoid of market-oriented behavior. It is upon precisely these dinosaurs of Chinese industry that this book focuses.

But why concentrate on dinosaurs when one could instead study dynamos? Why focus upon an industrial sector rooted in the past, rather than one holding promise for the future? Why, for that matter, does the state industrial sector attract so much attention in Chinese policy-making circles when China's phenomenal growth seems to depend on everything *but* state industry?[4] In terms of establishing a functioning market economy, China's policy makers have done many things right, and certainly many things that neither they nor outside observers would have deemed possible fifteen years ago. The economy has thrived, and millions of new nonstate firms have sprung up in the process. The question then is why not simply ignore traditional state industry – particularly when, as will be shown, it produces an ever-declining share of China's industrial output? Why can't China simply continue "growing beyond the plan" while the few remaining vestiges of command economics simply wither on the vine?[5]

The argument of this book is that China decidedly cannot continue sidestepping SOE reform. The situation surrounding the state industrial sector today, even a sector of diminished proportions, is economically unsustainable – not just for the sector itself, but for the economy as a whole. China today, for all the successes of the past fifteen years, stands at an economic crossroads and at the edge of a monumental economic crisis. The state sector is not simply dying; it also threatens to drag down the nation's entire economy along with it. China's policy makers have good reason to worry about SOE reform: it is arguably the single most important issue upon which China's economic future hinges.

For some two decades now, true enterprise restructuring in the state sector has been deferred.[6] Despite a vast array of reform measures – many of them well-intentioned, innovative, and market-oriented – the toughest choices in state industry have always been avoided. Chinese SOEs as a group have never truly been forced to face hard budgets, the pressure of a bottom line, or the threat of bankruptcy and market exit.[7] Indeed, as this study will show, many reform measures have actually exacerbated the situation. Meanwhile, just as the task of enterprise restructuring becomes ever more complex, the cost of deferring restructuring becomes ever more severe. A major goal of this book will be to explain just how and why this is so. Why has meaningful reform been deferred, and why have reform measures never had their desired impact? What exactly is the nature of the problem that makes it so difficult to solve? In what seems like a sweeping move toward privatization, Chinese policy makers have declared that 10,000 SOEs will be "corporatized," essentially transformed into joint stock companies whose shares trade publicly within China and abroad. What does this mean, and how likely is it to address the dilemmas of restructuring?

That the current condition of China's SOEs is economically unsustainable has been documented from the macro perspective by a number of recent studies.[8] Although this general picture will be summarized in what follows, the aim of this book is to be decidedly micro in approach. In a sense, this book provides not a bird's-eye view of Chinese enterprise restructuring but rather a worm's-eye view. Macro studies have been excellent in identifying the extent to which state industry has lapsed but somewhat less effective in pinpointing causal linkages and firm-level processes. It is that latter task which is the aim of the following chapters.

3

Ultimately, what emerges from this micro-level exploration is a particular view of what ails China's large-scale industrial producers, a view that emphasizes systemwide, institutional barriers to market-oriented performance. The argument is that China today lacks the key institutional mechanisms needed to make corporate governance – and, by extension, property rights – function for complex producers in complex market settings. The problem for Chinese state firms is not that they are state-owned per se, but rather that ownership itself fails to function for these kinds of producers in this kind of system. For these firms, reform measures like decentralization, "corporatization," and even outright privatization – measures that seek to encourage market behavior by transferring property rights – fail because property rights themselves do not exist in any real sense.[9] They cannot exist because the basic institutions needed to *make* them exist – functioning capital markets, a stable regulatory environment, and enforceable accounting standards – are simply absent. Until those institutional factors are straightened out in China, or in any other transitional economy for that matter, no amount of managerial training, firm-level technical upgrading, directed investment, or even transfers of nominal property rights is going to make these production organizations behave like market actors.[10]

State-owned enterprises – generally among China's larger firms, and certainly its more capital-intensive ones – thoroughly dominate the country's modern industrial sector. Whether in China or anywhere else, these kinds of large industrial producers are not simple economic actors, simple "economic men" that naturally seek to augment their assets by following basic market incentives. Instead, they are complex organizations involving a multitude of individual actors and an almost implicit division between ownership and control. Given the capital requirements of modern industrial firms, ownership tends to be spread across a number of stakeholders, and given the complexities of modern industrial methods, control falls to professional managers and skilled workers.[11]

This unavoidable division creates major challenges with respect to information and incentives. The individuals or agencies supplying the capital and bearing the risk do not possess the information needed to run the plant or even monitor the managers and workers who do. Those managers and workers, in turn, routinely control assets over which they have no direct ownership and for which they bear no direct financial risk. If the firm collapses, these employees can simply take their skills somewhere else.[12]

Clearly, the issue in any modern industrial economy, whether organized by plan or market, is not how to motivate some hypothetical unitary producer but rather how to manage the coordination and incentive problems of entire production organizations. It is not enough just to create the proper environment – just to "get the prices right" – and expect these producers to respond to the invisible hand of the market. These producers, after all, are not single-minded actors but instead constellations of interests that must be aligned and directed through intricate governance mechanisms. In order to ensure that societal assets are put to their most productive use (i.e., to ensure that investors direct their assets toward the most productive firms and that managers effectively employ rather than squander those assets), institutions of governance are required both within and beyond the firm.[13]

Of these mechanisms, the internal variety tend to be the most obvious. In modern corporations, for example, boards of directors are appointed to monitor managers, set managerial pay, exercise veto power over key strategic decisions, and generally ensure that owner interests receive proper representation. Arguably more important, however, are the external governance measures that operate even when internal monitoring lapses. Functioning capital and equity markets, the outside bank auditing which those markets entail, credible threats of bankruptcy and liquidation, enforceable legal obligations – all these institutions ensure that, even in the absence of internal monitoring and effective management, efficient producers will be rewarded while the inefficient will be driven out of business.

The fascinating thing that emerges from a micro study of Chinese SOEs is the extent to which outside governance institutions in China not only malfunction but also distort the internal operations of the individual firm. As noted previously, Chinese decision makers have been remarkably successful in establishing the conditions for a basic market economy.[14] They have been far less successful, however, in shaping the regulatory institutions needed to manage complex firms in an industrialized market economy. China's partially reformed state banking sector is an important example that will come up repeatedly in this book. State financial institutions in China today provide credit at ever-expanding levels, but rarely on market terms. Banks neither effectively select borrowers nor effectively monitor funds once dispersed. As a result, state firms end up with capital but with precious few incentives to direct that capital toward productive uses. Critical investment resources, basically the savings deposits of ordinary Chinese citizens, are routinely channeled into the black hole of state industry, never to be seen again. Financial intermediaries in China are simply not performing the external governance functions necessary for the operation of complex production organizations in market environments. The individual case studies in this book will illuminate, from the firm-level perspective, just why this is so. But the broader point is that, without such external governance mechanisms, property-rights reform – and most other forms of internal enterprise restructuring – become essentially meaningless.

The other interesting thing emerging from case studies is the extent to which certain systemwide, ostensibly market-oriented reforms have actually exacerbated the governance and property-rights problems of state industry. Even the most pragmatic of policy measures, including some of those hailed for generating growth in the countryside, have had unintended consequences in the industrial sector. Governmental decentralization and the concomitant downward delegation of fiscal responsibilities, for example, have perhaps broken up the old command bureaucracy and infused local state actors with entrepreneurial spirit, but such reforms have also unleashed all sorts of predation upon both state financial intermediaries and state firms. The average SOE now faces a plethora of governmental actors, from the grass-roots right up to the center, all of whom exert some sort of extractive authority over firm assets. Money, in effect, comes in from the banking sector and is then pulled out by poorly coordinated agents of the state.

Partly in response to this problem, policy makers even early in the reform period began promulgating measures to demarcate more clearly the boundary between firm and state. A historical review of such policies is beyond the scope of this study, but suffice it to say that a variety of measures – from responsibility systems and profit contracting to directed investment programs and the codification of autonomous management rights – have been implemented, often to the detriment of effective corporate governance.[15] Profit contracting, for example, has created incentives at the managerial level for overproduction and reckless investment in plant capacity. Shifts in accounting regulations, in addition to the codification of management "rights," have further encouraged this form of behavior by granting managers greater control over enterprise funds. Misuse of this control – namely, through the diversion of working capital toward plant expansion or even outright consumption – becomes feasible as long as the state banks are willing to pump in new loans while rolling over old ones. In the confusion, funds often simply disappear or get eaten up in the provision of housing, pensions, wage bonuses, or other social welfare benefits. Autonomy extended to managers in the absence of a credible bankruptcy threat not only discourages productive behavior but also emasculates ownership. No owners, whether public or private, can exert effective control under such circumstances.

Yet, a key reason why bankruptcy threats are so ineffectual – and why actual bankruptcies are so incredibly rare in the Chinese state sector – is that bankruptcy proceedings depend on credible financial information, an increasingly scarce commodity given China's current institutional environment. This is perhaps the most serious issue that emerges from the micro-level case studies. In the Chinese state sector today, managers themselves have difficulty ascertaining the true financial status of their firms. Accounting standards frequently change, banking regulations remain constantly in flux, monitoring is lax, and exceptions tend to be the rule. Operating accounts are mixed with investment accounts, production costs become distorted, and firms surviving solely on state subsidies find ways to declare profits year after year. Meanwhile, the banking system continues to infuse SOEs with liquidity, for if the loans were to stop then workers would go unpaid.[16] All of the firms discussed in this book's case studies are indeed officially "profitable." All, however, face serious financial problems. Several are essentially insolvent. Like many Chinese SOEs, year after year they amass tremendous liabilities, renege on obligations to creditors, and fail to generate enough income to cover even their most basic operating costs. Ultimately, many SOEs end up being net destroyers of assets; what they consume is of far greater value than what they produce. However, none of this is immediately apparent from the firms' financial records. Under such circumstances, nobody really knows what percentage of state firms in China are losing money. Is it one third? Two thirds? More? Less? A main objective of the following chapters will be to describe how this situation has come about and why it is going to be so extraordinarily difficult to untangle, with or without privatization.

While focusing on a particular aspect of China's contemporary economy, this book also aims to provide a more general framework for understanding the whole phenomenon of postsocialist reform. China is, of course, neither the only country trying to shed the legacy of socialist command planning nor the only one of these transitional countries encumbered with a troubled industrial sector. Quite understandably, many people – scholars, policy makers, and casual observers alike – view transitional reform as a process of liberation, a dismantling of suffocating institutions, and a freeing up of individual enterprise and initiative. The idea is that once the old order is swept away, all the positive energies of societal actors will somehow flower forth. With this assumption in mind, analysts of reform tend to focus on terms like "rights," "liberalization," and "autonomy." Economic actors, whether local governments, firms, or entrepreneurs, must be given the "right" to enjoy the fruits of their labor. Managers must be given "autonomy" from the state. Firms must be "liberated" from state planning. The underlying idea is that as long as strictures are lifted and rights granted, then everything will work out, and producers – whether individuals, firms, or even government agencies – will act for the social good. From the analytical perspective, scholars then focus on questions of how rights have been redistributed downward under reform, the degree to which power has been decentralized throughout the bureaucracy, and the extent to which old institutions of control have been eliminated.

The following study takes a decidedly skeptical view toward the whole assumption that positive behavior flows from the acquisition of such rights. The first reason for this skepticism concerns the way we view our own system. After all, in the developed economies of the West, we hardly expect producers naturally to maximize their own economic interests, let alone those of society. Just a glance at the volumes of law and regulation needed to facilitate economic exchanges in the United States drives home this point. With this in mind, why should we expect positive outcomes to evolve naturally in developing economies? Why should we expect that, with the granting of rights, local governments in transitional systems will promote business when such bureaucracies are hardly expected to do so in developed economies? Why should we expect newly "autonomous" managers to maximize return on capital in postsocialist firms when such behavior is hardly expected to occur naturally in Western corporations? Even in developed economies, actors do not always behave in market-oriented ways, and – as events like the U.S. savings and loan scandal suggest – it is a costly policy mistake to assume that they do. This is all the more true in the poorly institutionalized, poorly regulated environments of postsocialist systems. "Rights" can be expressed in all sorts of ways other than asset expansion, particularly in the weak legal environment of transitional systems.

The second source of skepticism involves the field of Chinese reform studies more directly. Scholars of the post-Mao reform period tend to place considerable emphasis on issues of decentralization, central–local tensions, and grass-roots noncompliance. The idea is that with the disintegration of the old system, new rights and liberties have flowed downward to economic actors, and then the key is to explain exactly what the new distribution of power looks like. It is over this issue that a tremendous amount of debate occurs. Meanwhile, the underlying assumption that the new distribution of power effectively explains market-oriented behavior goes unchallenged.

Why should these liberties and de facto rights really be considered new or unique to the reform period? One could just as easily view grass-roots autonomy and noncompliance as an historical constant, a common thread running across the prereform and reform eras. After all, we are well aware of the rampant local and firm-level noncompliance that plagued the command system, particularly in the Chinese context.[17] Firms hoarded resources and manipulated information flows to planners. Commune leaders fabricated harvest estimates. Peasants hid grain. Factory workers shirked labor. Localities protected their

8

own interests. One need only look at Liu Shaoqi's complaints about renegade local investment behavior in the 1960s to get a sense that the issues today are not that much different.

What *is* different in the reform era, however, are the ways in which autonomy and noncompliance are expressed, and the range of economic activity over which autonomy can be exercised. In other words, the interesting questions are not whether rights have increased or just who has these rights, but rather *why*, in the general context of producer autonomy, the aims of economic actors either change or do not change over time. Why is it that some actors engage in rent-seeking behavior while others do not? Why in today's Chinese reform context do certain localities express their autonomy by promoting growth rather than squandering central resources or beating up on local firms? Why do some government actors start and foster firms while others simply prey on firms? Why is it that, in the reform context, certain kinds of firms seem to respond to the market while others do not? Assuming for the sake of argument that a high degree of de facto local and firm-level autonomy is constant in developing economies, what other kinds of changes in the institutional context lead to behavioral changes among economic producers? What really are the key changes that can be associated with reform and the growth-oriented outcomes of reform?

In light of such questions, this study adopts a somewhat unorthodox framework, one that diverges from rights-based explanations by instead focusing on the nature of economic *constraint*. The argument is that outcomes and causality become far clearer if reform is viewed as a "clamping down" rather than a "loosening up." In other words, instead of assuming that economic actors respond naturally to certain freedoms once those freedoms are granted, this study assumes that behavior is somewhat sticky, somewhat resistant to change in the absence of a clear "push" or a clear penalty. The idea then is to examine in part the opportunities, but more particularly the constraints, that flow from a given institutional environment. What are the constraints that make certain patterns of behavior costly and others relatively painless? How does one type of institutional setup lead to different costs and opportunities from another setup? How does the general granting of rights lead to different patterns of behavior across differing institutional environments? In short, how do constraints and opportunities shape the way actors use their newfound privileges in marketizing economies? If (again for the sake of argument) we acknowledge that local autonomy has always been an ingredient in policy outcomes in China, then what new constraints have developed in the reform era that lead either localities or firms to engage in market-oriented, growth-promoting behavior? What constraints *force* some economic producers – be they governments, firms, or managers – to shift to market-oriented behavior even as other actors simply continue in the patterns of the past? How do constraints force some actors to translate their autonomy into productive activity? Can the absence of such constraints explain why other actors engage in easier, more directly lucrative patterns of rent seeking and corruption? In short, this study asserts that the real change in China today – the real driver of reform outcomes – has to do with new budget constraints rather than new rights, freedom, or autonomy.

Such an approach allows us to answer the kinds of questions that have generally eluded rights-based analyses. It allows us to understand why large state firms do not naturally respond to the market even after planning is lifted. It allows us to comprehend why such firms do not necessarily respond to privatization or other ownership restructuring efforts. Furthermore, it allows us to see clearly broader developmental patterns in China and beyond. It allows us to understand why rural industry has boomed in China while urban industry has fallen behind. It allows us to comprehend, within that overall pattern, exactly why some local governments promote business and entrepreneurship while others do not. It allows us to understand why even in the Chinese countryside, and even in resource-rich coastal areas, certain areas have lagged far behind others in the promotion and development of new firms. The constraints-based approach allows us to explain variation within the overall context of new rights, new freedoms, and new liberties. Such an approach allows us to understand just why, in transitional systems, many actors do not behave as they are "supposed to" while others actually do.

THE TERRAIN OF CHINESE INDUSTRIAL REFORM

One of the geniuses of Chinese economic reform has always been the tendency to blur semantic distinctions and sidestep inflammatory labels. China is a socialist nation, yet one with a vast nonstate sector. It is a nation with few "private" firms but millions of "nonstate" firms. The country maintains "public ownership" over industrial assets, but not necessarily "state ownership." State firms are owned by "the people," yet in many cases sell shares to individuals in Shanghai, Shenzhen, New York, and Hong Kong. Ambiguous language has been extremely useful for establishing continuity with the past and shrouding revolutionary change in a veil of normality. Such language, however, causes considerable confusion in the area of enterprise reform, even with regard to the most basic questions of firm-level categorization.

By official government count, there are currently 7,341,500 firms in China engaged in all manner of industrial activities.[18] Of these firms, 118,000 are classified as state owned (*guoyou gongye*), 1,475,000 as collectively owned (*jiti gongye*), 5,688,200 as individually owned (*geti gongye*), and 60,300 as simply "other economic categories" (*qita jingji leixing gongye*). These distinctions merit some explanation.

The 118,000 firms classified as "state owned" are the SOEs that are the subject of this book. Formally, they are owned "by all the people" (*quanmin suoyou*), a term that essentially means ownership is left unspecified. Every one of these firms, however, is affiliated with one of the four basic levels of government in China: central, provincial, prefectural, or county.[19] State-owned enterprises are also assigned to municipalities, which are themselves treated as either provinces, prefectures, or counties.[20] Some 2,000–3,000 of the very largest state firms are assigned directly to the center, but even here the distinction is blurry.[21] Most of these firms, regardless of under which category they fall, find themselves subject to control by a number of contending governmental agencies, regional authorities, central line ministries, and local ministerial branches.

State-owned enterprises share a number of other characteristics that distinguish them from their nonstate counterparts. Unlike other firms, China's 118,000 state enterprises are responsible for providing their employees with a wide range of social welfare benefits: housing, health care, child care, retirement income, disability insurance, and unemployment insurance, just to name a few. In the most basic sense, these firms provide lifetime employment and cradle-to-grave benefits.[22] They cannot casually shed labor during cyclical downturns, manipulate benefits in order to cut costs, or even substantially control the basic wage scale. Particularly among the larger firms, responsibility for running hospitals, clinics, day-care centers, and housing bureaus is virtually unavoidable. In short, the business of SOEs is not simply production.

State-owned enterprises are also the type of firms most closely linked with the old system of command planning. Indeed, these were the firms that sat at the very peak of the old Soviet-style system. Their investment resources came from the plan, their inputs were delivered by the plan, their output was set and allocated by plan, and the prices they received were determined by the plan. These, in effect, are "traditional" SOEs, China's equivalent to the industrial behemoths of the former Soviet Union and its satellites. Today, "the plan" in China is essentially a thing of the past, but traditional SOEs remain and, as will be described, still play a pivotal role in the economy. These are the firms that still receive most of their investment resources from the state, still comprise the bulk of heavy industry, and still employ the largest portion of the nation's urban workforce. These firms are also the one type of enterprise in China not generally subject to bankruptcy. Although mergers and acquisitions are becoming more frequent, it is rare indeed for an SOE to exit the market, and still rarer for the assets of an SOE to be liquidated.

China's 1.47 million collective firms, on the contrary, are not formally state-owned and do not generally behave like SOEs. Nevertheless, they are in fact "publicly owned." Collectives are formally owned not by "the whole people" but instead by specific local governments, whether at the county or village level in rural areas or at the municipal level in urban areas. An important subset of these collectives are the 228,800 township enterprises and the 689,900 village enterprises that together comprise the township and village enterprises (*xiangzhen qiye*) that have attracted so much attention in recent years. Undoubtedly, property rights over collectives are defined far more clearly than those over larger state-owned firms.[23] Also unlike SOEs, collectives tend to cluster around lighter, less capital-intensive industries, in part because collectives generally do not usually have access to central sources of credit, subsidization, and investment. Instead, operating and investment funds must come from retained earnings, overseas capital, or off-budget allocations by local governments. Credit constraints virtually ensure that collectives remain unable to challenge the state sector's monopoly over heavy industry.

Another key difference from SOEs is that collectives are not generally responsible for social welfare provision. Employees are usually hired on a contractual basis and paid little more than basic wages. They can, and frequently are, let go during business downturns. In the most general sense, the prime task of collectives is straightforward industrial production in accordance with straightforward financial objectives.

Perhaps not surprisingly, collectives behave far more like textbook market-oriented producers than do their counterparts in the traditional state sector. Indeed, unlike SOEs, collectives can (and frequently do) experience bankruptcy and market exit. The reason for the superior performance of collectives is the subject of some scholarly dispute, and has at various times and by various observers been attributed to clearer property rights, local governmental stewardship, lighter social welfare burdens, basic productivity gains in the shift from agriculture to industry, and harder budget constraints.[24] Certainly an implicit goal of the following chapters will be to shed some light on this debate.

It is worth noting, however, that although the number of collectives has increased dramatically in the last fifteen years, this sector pre-dates reform and has always shared a basic distinction from SOEs. Even in the prereform era, collectives were always, in effect, outside the plan. Frequently started by rural communes or brigades, these firms provided precisely the kind of basic inputs (e.g., cement, fertilizer, chemicals) that could not be obtained at grass-roots levels through the plan. Even prior to reform, these firms were manifestations of local self-sufficiency, operating on the marketized fringes of the command economy. They were run by local agencies with virtually no access to capital, they acquired inputs through informal channels, they had to sell outputs on local markets, and they set prices accordingly. The point is that, even prior to the sweeping changes of the 1980s and 1990s, these firms faced hard budget constraints and, to some extent, behaved like free-market producers.[25] Those tendencies became only more pronounced with the onset of reform and with the enhanced access to domestic and foreign markets that reform brought. Just as the existence of the prereform collectives reflected the incomplete nature of the plan – they sprung up in those sectors where the plan did not function – the growth of those firms since reform reflects the tendency of the country as a whole to grow beyond the plan. Collectives, although publicly owned, neither share the same basic environment nor display the same sorts of pathologies as traditional socialist SOEs.[26] They are, and have always been, different creatures.

Of the remaining categories, individually owned enterprises are small operations run by individuals or households that by definition hire fewer than seven employees. These firms, in keeping with the ambiguity of Chinese classifications, are not officially designated "private," but in essence constitute a private sector that has been allowed to emerge since 1978. Also new since the early 1980s are the range of firms grouped as "others": private firms employing more than seven people, wholly foreign-owned firms, foreign–domestic joint ventures, other forms of domestic joint ventures, and joint stock firms.[27] These enterprises round out the rich tapestry of firms that today comprise China's industrial sector.

THE ROLE OF SOES IN CHINA'S CONTEMPORARY ECONOMY

It is absolutely clear that, over the past two decades of reform, the contribution of SOEs to China's total industrial output has declined significantly. In 1978, these firms accounted for over 75 percent of the nation's industrial output. By 1995, the portion had dropped to under 35 percent. In 1978, collectives accounted for approximately 22 percent of China's industrial output value. The other categories of nonstate firms did not yet even exist. By 1995, collectives of all types produced over 36 percent of the nation's industrial output, while individual and other nonstate firms produced an additional 16.6 percent. Nonstate firms as a group were producing more than 50 percent of the nation's industrial output. Clearly, while output on the whole has been expanding tremendously

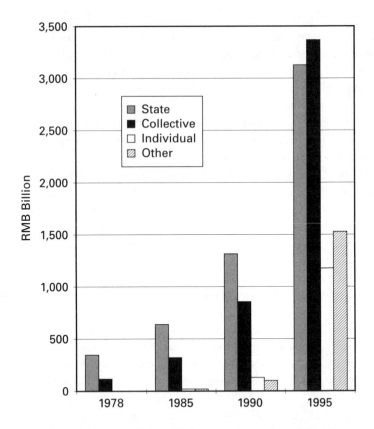

Figure 1.1. Output Value of Industry by Ownership, 1978–95
Sources: for 1978 data, Naughton (1995, p. 331); for 1985 and 1990 data,
State Statistical Bureau (1994, p. 373); for 1995 data, State Statistical
Bureau (1996, p. 401).

through the reform period, nonstate firms have been growing at a far greater
rate than traditional SOEs[28] (see Figure 1.1).

In the broadest sense, these trends convey the success of Chinese reform efforts. A thriving, market-oriented nonstate sector has basically grown up and
around the old economy, effectively dwarfing the plan. That this development
was tolerated, let alone encouraged, is a credit to Chinese policy makers, for
what it has ultimately meant is the end of command planning. Such developments have also undermined coordinated state control over the micro economy.
Goods in all sectors are now basically allocated through market transactions,
and prices for the most part have been liberalized. State-owned enterprises, in

Table 1.1. *Industrial output by size of firm
and ownership*

	Percentage of total output		
	1978	1985	1991
Large-scale sector	41.5	42.3	43.6
[State]	[41.5]	[41.9]	[40.6]
[Other]	[0.0]	[0.4]	[3.0]
Urban medium/small	49.4	38.8	25.2
[State]	[35.8]	[22.9]	[12.2]
[Collective]	[13.6]	[15.9]	[13.0]
Rural medium/small	8.7	14.6	20.6
[Township]	[4.8]	[7.8]	[10.3]
[Village]	[3.9]	[6.8]	[10.3]
Very small scale	0.4	3.4	7.8
[Urban]	[0.0]	[0.3]	[0.7]
[Rural]	[0.4]	[3.1]	[7.1]
Other medium/small	0	0.8	2.8

Source: Naughton (1995, p. 164).

the broadest sense of having to acquire their own inputs and dispose of their own outputs, have essentially been forced to operate on the same terms as nonstate firms. These are truly remarkable changes, achieved with equally remarkable speed and social stability.

However, it would be a tremendous error to think that SOEs have been peripheralized. The data charted in Figure 1.1 give a highly distorted picture, one that deserves some explanation. Despite all the changes that have swept China in the last twenty years, heavy industry still remains thoroughly dominated by the state sector. No other ownership form has penetrated large-scale, capital-intensive sectors in any significant sense. State-owned enterprises are still providing the basic inputs upon which all other sectors depend, and for that reason alone can still be considered the backbone of Chinese manufacturing. Interestingly, where state-sector output share does seem to have declined is among medium and small-scale urban firms[29] (see Table 1.1). These smaller state firms, urban units engaged in light manufacturing, have clearly been edged out in the last two decades by rural nonstate enterprises. In a sense, the rise of the TVE has come at the expense of the small urban SOE. China's most

Table 1.2. *Urban workforce employed by state-owned firms,*
1978–95 (millions of persons)

Year	Total urban workforce	SOE employment	SOE portion of total
1978	95.1	74.5	78.3%
1980	105.3	80.2	76.2%
1985	128.1	89.9	70.2%
1990	147.3	103.5	70.3%
1991	152.7	106.6	69.8%
1992	156.3	108.9	69.7%
1993	159.6	109.2	68.4%
1994	168.2	112.1	66.6%
1995	173.5	112.6	64.9%

Source: State Statistical Bureau (1996, p. 90).

impressive output gains since reform have come in the area of light industry, gains that have witnessed a supplanting of small-scale urban manufacturers by newly created rural firms. The thousands upon thousands of textile producers, sneaker manufacturers, and toy makers that today dot the Chinese countryside have thoroughly changed the competitive environment for small urban SOEs. Small urban state enterprises have proven rather incapable of competing against their rural cousins, firms that are frequently favored by Taiwanese or Hong Kong investors. The SOE monopoly over more capital-intensive industries, however, remains unchallenged.[30] Overall, therefore, while SOEs are producing a smaller share of China's national industrial output than in the past, that remaining share has become even more concentrated in such core heavy industries as coal mining, petroleum extraction, metallurgy, and machine building.

Employment levels are another indication both of the continued significance of SOEs in the economy and of the general tendency of policy makers to defer any serious restructuring of the sector. China's total labor force in 1995 amounted to approximately 623.9 million persons, 173.5 million of whom were classified as urban workers[31] (see Table 1.2). Sixty-five percent of those workers, even in 1995, were still employed in state firms.[32] In short, about seven out of ten urban workers in China are employed by state firms. That portion, interestingly, has not declined significantly during the reform period, and stands in stark contrast to the far more dramatic decline in the state sector's share of national industrial output. On the eve of reform in 1978, SOEs employed

16

Table 1.3. *Government revenue from state-owned firms, 1978–95*

Year	Total government revenue	Government revenue from state firms	State-firm portion of total
1978	113.23	98.48	87.0%
1980	115.99	100.73	86.8%
1982	121.23	103.29	85.2%
1984	164.29	136.03	82.8%
1986	212.2	166.2	78.3%
1988	235.72	168.8	71.6%
1990	293.71	209.51	71.3%
1992	348.34	248.3	71.3%
1994	521.81	372.74	71.4%
1995	624.22	444.1	71.1%

Source: State Statistical Bureau (1996, p. 226). Units: RMB billion.

78 percent of the urban workforce. By 1990, the portion still hovered around 70 percent, and even by 1995 the number had crept down only five more percentage points. In essence, employment growth in the state sector has not slowed to match the sector's declining share of national output. In terms of production, the traditional state sector may no longer dominate, but in terms of urban employment, SOEs – by an overwhelming margin – are still the primary game in town.

The Chinese government's continued dependence upon SOEs for fiscal revenue is equally striking; see Table 1.3. State-owned enterprises may constitute the slowest growing industrial sector in China, but they are still (again by an overwhelming margin) the primary sources of tax revenue for all government levels in China, from the center right down to the urban localities.[33] In 1995, SOEs produced only 35 percent of China's industrial output value but still contributed 71 percent of the government's revenue.[34] This incongruous situation reflects the persistence of prereform patterns of governmental revenue mobilization. Under the old command economy, prices were set so as to channel financial surpluses upward from the agricultural into the modern industrial sector.[35] Prices for basic agricultural and industrial inputs were set at extremely low levels, while prices for finished industrial goods were set at high levels. Financial surpluses – "profits," in a sense – were thereby intentionally concentrated in a relatively small number of downstream, state-owned industrial producers. Those surpluses could then easily be extracted as governmental revenue. The

17

system allowed a bureaucratically stretched government to capture a tremendous share of national income and at the same time obviated the need for a complex tax-collection apparatus.

The command economy may be gone, as are most state-set prices, but the old pattern of revenue generation persists. Despite significant tax reforms in 1994 and a substantial restructuring of the revenue mobilization process, state industry still remains the only sector that the government can tax with any substantial effect. This situation has many implications for policy, but certainly one of the clearest is that unless SOEs in the transitional context are revitalized, the state's capacity to generate revenue will continue to erode.

THE PERFORMANCE OF THE STATE SECTOR

Erosion of the government's tax base leads to the next issue, the overall financial performance of state industry since the inception of reform. It would hardly be an overstatement to say that Chinese SOEs, particularly since the early 1990s, have been locked in a downward economic spiral, a spiral only partially reflected in the rising number of firms that officially declare losses. In 1985, 9.6 percent of all "within budget" industrial SOEs declared losses, losses amounting to RMB 2.7 billion.[36] Ten years later, 44 percent of such firms were declaring losses, losses that had risen to RMB 40.9 billion.[37] In 1996, China officially acknowledged that the state industrial sector as a whole had posted net losses for the year, the first time this had happened since 1949.[38]

Of course, some of these losses can be attributed to structural factors such as the gradual liberalization of input prices, and others pertain to accounting shifts involving more realistic assessments of certain production costs. Nevertheless, these figures on losses actually *understate* the severity of the crisis in state industry today. Many (and arguably the vast majority) of nominally profitable SOEs in China today teeter on the brink of insolvency. In other words, even the approximately 50 percent of industrial SOEs that do declare profits are beset by problems. These firms are currently consuming monumental amounts of investment capital and amassing extraordinary liabilities, liabilities that probably exceed the true value of firm-level assets.

Again, because of the unreliability of firm-level profit declarations, statements regarding the number of SOEs that formally declare losses fail to convey the magnitude of the problem. A much better picture comes from data on the dramatically rising levels of subsidization being directed toward the state sector. Even here, though, the situation is confusing because in recent years the government has shifted the manner in which funds are channeled into SOEs.

18

Early in the reform era, subsidies to state firms generally came in the form of direct allocations from the central budget. These subsidies or directed investments constituted state expenditures, and would appear as such in the government's overall fiscal balance. Over time, however, the government slowed the growth of these on-budget subsidies, and instead encouraged funds to move through the state banking system. Subsidies would increasingly take the form of interest-bearing loans extended by the major state banks.

The change, coinciding with an overall effort to marketize the nation's financial system, was at least partly well-intentioned. The theory was that subsidies in the form of quasicommercial loans would force borrowers – namely, state firms – to bear some cost for capital, use that capital in more efficient ways, and generally operate on a more market-oriented footing. Furthermore, channeling investment funds through a commercially oriented banking sector would encourage financial deepening throughout the system and lead to a more efficient, market-determined allocation of capital nationwide. The theory works, however, only if subsidies truly cease being subsidies. In other words, in terms of changing firm-level behavior, the issue is not from whence the infusions of capital come (the state budget or the banks) but rather under what terms the capital is extended. The capital must come at a cost, and it must be extended to those most likely able to repay. The capital, in effect, would have to be the opposite of a subsidy. Of course, for such an outcome actually to obtain, several conditions would have to be met. First, credit would truly have to mean something – borrowers would have to face the threat of bankruptcy in the event they could not meet their financial obligations. Second, for lending to move forward on a commercial basis, banks too would have to be given autonomy over lending decisions and then be forced to pay a price if those decisions resulted in losses and an accumulation of bad debt. Unfortunately, for reasons that will become clearer in the case studies, neither of these conditions has been met in China.

Once again, given the complex institutional requirements of the modern industrial sector, half-way reforms can be extremely dangerous. By shifting the manner in which capital flows into state industry, the government has essentially decided to avoid fiscal deficits by increasing public-sector borrowing from the state banking system.[39] This change is clearly reflected in the data. Since 1990, the sum of explicit and implicit subsidies going directly from the central budget to loss-making SOEs has declined slightly as a percentage of gross domestic product (GDP),[40] a trend that makes sense given the overall decline in government revenue vis-à-vis GDP.[41] At the same time, lending by the state banking system, especially to SOEs, has skyrocketed in relation to GDP.[42] The banking sector's total outstanding loans on an annual basis grew from approximately

19

50 percent of GDP in 1978 to approximately 90 percent in 1996.[43] Clearly, lending was up nationwide.

Unfortunately, the vast bulk of this lending has been directed toward the least productive and slowest growing portion of the economy: the state industrial sector. By the end of 1995, outstanding loans to state industry amounted to approximately RMB 3.36 trillion, 83 percent of all outstanding bank loans that year.[44] In other words, by the mid-1990s, lending was way up in relation to GDP, and state firms were absorbing the overwhelming majority of that lending. The accumulated liabilities of SOEs (again, not surprisingly) have surged during this period. In 1988, the external liabilities of industrial SOEs stood at approximately 45 percent of those firms' book-value assets.[45] By 1994, that figure had increased to 79 percent.[46] This number is understated, however, given the tendency of Chinese firms to inflate the value of both their fixed and liquid assets.[47] Total debt in the SOE sector – whether owed to banks or other firms – had climbed by the end of 1995 to approximately RMB 800 billion, a 20-percent increase over the previous year.[48]

The problem lies not only in the fact that state industry is absorbing tremendous amounts of capital, but also in what is being done with that capital. As the case studies will illustrate, a significant portion of SOE borrowing ends up directed toward working-capital needs. In other words, a large portion of this capital is not going toward long-term productive investment – the sort of projects or modernization efforts that might yield returns in the future – but is instead being used simply to cover firms' current production costs. Even nominally profitable firms are amassing liabilities just so that they can sustain production processes that bring in no cash. In a sense, firms are decapitalizing themselves in order to stay afloat, a pattern that is increasingly showing up in sectoral liquidity reports. In the steel industry, for example, more than one third of the nation's integrated mills by the mid-1990s were running current ratios (current assets divided by current liabilities) of under 1.0, and several of those firms were reporting ratios under 0.50.[49] Without routine infusions of short-term loans, many firms simply cannot pay workers or maintain basic production. Indeed, in the tight-credit atmosphere of 1995, some 60 to 70 percent of the firms in China's industrial Northeast simply ceased production, and millions of workers went unpaid for months on end.[50] Meanwhile, firms with better connections to the banking system and easier access to credit were directing short-term loans toward ill-advised expansion projects, all as part of an effort to increase output and profits.[51]

The obvious outcome of either form of behavior is an inability on the firm's part to service its mounting debts. Since capital is devoted to uses for which there are no productive returns, firms can pay neither the interest nor principal on their escalating debts. The banks simply keep rolling the loans over, often taking the unpaid interest from one year and tacking it on to the principal for the next year's loan. As state-sector borrowing increases, therefore, so too does the level of bad debt in the banking system. Owing to a number of factors – the flexibility of Chinese accounting standards, quotas for the number of loans that banks can classify as nonperforming, and uncertainty in the classification standards themselves – estimates of the magnitude of this bad debt are admittedly rough. Nevertheless, statements by Chinese banking officials suggest that nonperforming loans in the nation's four major banks amount to approximately RMB 860 billion.[52] Other estimates have placed that figure at RMB 1.27 trillion or higher.[53] Even the more conservative of those estimates, however, implies that China's four major state banks are technically insolvent. The corollary, of course, is that a large number of the SOE borrowers are also insolvent.

Banks continue lending under such circumstances for several reasons. First, banks in many cases are expressly directed by the central government to extend "policy loans" to specific failing enterprises, loans which are themselves supported through credit from China's central bank, the People's Bank of China (PBC). Estimates in the mid-1990s suggested that such policy lending accounted for 60 to 80 percent of the loans extended by the central bank to the nation's financial system.[54] Second, banks frequently receive pressure from local governmental agencies to extend preferential loans to favored firms. Governmental decentralization and the diffusion of state authority has bolstered this trend. Third, in the overall context of financial system reform, new financial intermediaries have emerged, some of which have ties to specific SOEs or state industrial groups.[55] These ostensibly commercial banks accept regular household deposits, but in several well-publicized cases have engaged in irregular lending to their parent organizations. In other words, some of these banks have on occasion served as conduits for channeling household savings into their parent industrial organizations.

The combined data showing rising levels of loss-making SOEs, rising levels of bank lending to the state sector, and rising levels of nonperforming debt present a fairly persuasive picture. The state sector is being kept afloat through vast amounts of subsidization, whether from the central budget or the financial system. Yet, the government's decision to transfer to the financial system the burden of supporting loss-making SOEs actually has serious implications. Subsidies to SOEs continue just as they have in the past, but now the vectors for delivering those subsidies have grown far more numerous and far more difficult to control. Furthermore, the ties of those vectors to household savings are now far more direct. The central state may still be bailing out firms, but now a whole new range of actors – local governments, local branches of national banks, banks tied to specific industrial groups – have become engaged in the process, sometimes in accord with national policy but sometimes simply on their own.

The problem now is not just that the government still bails out failing SOEs. Rather, the problem is that half-way reforms in the modern industrial sector's institutional environment have actually increased the extent to which stagnating state firms capture societal resources and simultaneously decreased the extent to which policy makers can control or even monitor the flow. In 1996, over 50 percent of China's SOEs were declaring losses, but the state sector was still capturing more than three fourths of the nation's domestic credit.[56] The ultimate tragedy is that the savings deposits of ordinary citizens have become increasingly tied up in this process, and the banking sector as a whole has been effectively undermined. It is no wonder that, within Chinese policy circles, an air of utter crisis surrounds discussions of the SOE problem.

Over the short term, a number of parties suffer from this situation. Workers suffer when the government periodically cuts bank lending and leaves firms unable to issue wages. Nonstate firms suffer since they cannot easily access domestic capital. Citizens suffer when they defray banking inefficiencies by enduring negative real rates of interest on savings deposits. In the event of an immediate crisis such as a run on the banks, household depositors will certainly bear the cost. Over the long term, however, it is the whole country that suffers through the misallocation of capital. When so much of the nation's resources flow into failing state industry – in other words, when capital is forced to move from high- to low-growth regions and from faster growing industrial sectors to slower ones – there is only one logical outcome: slower growth overall.

THE SEARCH FOR EXPLANATIONS

The foregoing discussion outlined in general terms how partial reforms in the financial system and partial reforms in the modern industrial sector have combined to create an economic situation in China that is both unsustainable and potentially volatile. Untangling this situation in policy terms represents the greatest challenge facing Chinese decision makers today. Untangling this situation in analytical terms represents the challenge of the following chapters.

Chinese decision makers, like their counterparts in other transitional systems, face crucial choices: in the ways they can tackle SOE restructuring and

22

in the sequence by which they can stage reform measures. Choices, of course, are made for a variety of reasons and in response to a variety of pressures. At least in some sense, however, choices reflect implicit assumptions about the way things work, implicit visions about the nature of causation.

For Chinese policy makers today, the prevailing assumption seems to be that what really counts in SOE reform is "ownership." More precisely, in this view what really counts in driving enterprise performance is the placement of property rights in appropriate hands. Because this view is accepted, reform debates usually revolve around more instrumental issues of how to separate the firm from the state, how to extend autonomy to managers, and how to "clarify" property rights. Exactly who should hold these rights – private citizens, foreigners, state holding companies, mutual funds – is of course an unresolved and sensitive issue. That sensitivity, however, frequently overshadows the broader underlying consensus in Chinese reform circles that "who should own" is the right question to ask.

Today, we are witnessing the culmination of those ideas as China's senior leaders publicly contemplate the corporatization of 10,000 major state firms.[57] Ironically, the conclusion seems to be that state industry can be saved by increasingly turning it over to individual investors, whether they happen to be in Hong Kong, New York, or anywhere else. In one sense, these strikingly radical measures are driven by a pragmatic issue, the dire financial condition of the state sector. State-owned enterprises are hemorrhaging money, and if the banking system can no longer be relied upon to pump in capital then private investors will have to pick up the slack. In another sense, however, the turn toward "corporatization" signifies the power of ideas. Chinese leaders may steadfastly proclaim their loyalty to socialism and state ownership. Yet their actions reflect a tacit acceptance, if not of outright privatization, then at least of the causal assumptions underpinning privatization efforts.

The chapters to follow take issue with those assumptions and offer a decidedly different framework for comprehending SOE reform in postcommand economies. Chapters 2 and 3 tend toward the more conceptual side, examining competing frameworks for addressing the nature of ownership and property rights in modern industrial firms. They argue that the problem with Chinese SOEs today is not that ownership is in the wrong hands but rather that ownership simply does not function. Ownership fails to function because the external market mechanisms needed to make it function in large production organizations are at best deeply flawed in the Chinese context.

Chapters 4–6 illustrate these ideas through the stories of three very different firms in a single, extremely important Chinese industry: the steel sector.

The firms are drawn from the steel sector not because this is a book about steel per se but rather because that particular industry has been targeted by virtually every major industrial reform effort in China. Steel, in a sense, serves as a bellwether for Chinese enterprise reform writ large. Each firm discussed in this book reflects a particular style of property-rights restructuring. When taken together, these firms represent the full spectrum of reform policies in the Chinese industrial sector. As a result, they allow us to examine in micro detail exactly how transfers of property rights impact upon complex producers in transitional economies. Indeed, the firm discussed in Chapter 5, Ma'anshan Iron and Steel, has already been corporatized and currently lists its shares in Hong Kong. As an experimental test run for the more widespread corporatizations promised by Chinese leaders, it offers us a view into China's future.

In a more general sense, these case studies illustrate the firm-level behavior underlying the macro data described earlier. In doing so, they allow us to understand better some of the causal relationships driving the macro-level outcomes. At the very least, they allow us to understand just how intensely complex the task of state-sector restructuring really is. The three firms discussed in the case studies are admittedly exceptionally large by Chinese standards; in fact, they are among the largest in China. Although atypical in size, they are thoroughly typical in the behavioral patterns that they display. In short, their micro-level behavior remains quite consistent with China's macro-level outcomes.

The final two chapters delve into some of the broader ramifications of the framework introduced to study SOE reform. Chapter 7 examines the general pattern of Chinese economic reform, particularly the stark contrast between rural industrial growth and urban industrial stagnation, and attempts to provide a unified institutional explanation. Chapter 8 concludes the study with some remarks about future reform trends in China and the role of the state in managing enterprise restructuring. All of the following chapters are unified by a common desire to flesh out the complexities of state industrial reform in transitional systems. In the area of industrial reform, there have been a large number of simple, seemingly logical policy solutions put forward. Few, if any, have worked. The following chapters attempt to explain why. In the most general sense, this is a book not about how to solve SOE restructuring but rather about how to understand SOE restructuring.

Part I

CONCEPTUAL APPROACHES TO POSTSOCIALIST ENTERPRISE REFORM

2

Property Rights, Privatization, and the State-Owned Firm

AMONG scholars of reforming socialist economies, the point that "institutions matter" is taken as something of a truism. After all, the shift from command planning to the market almost by definition involves an institutional revolution, a nearly complete shift in the rules of the game for economic actors, and an extraordinary transformation of the organizational environment in which those actors operate. As the institutional environment evolves, new incentives presumably bear down upon enterprise managers and government officials alike. Behavior in the most general sense, then, can be expected to shift accordingly. Government officials should cease micromanaging the firm, and instead should move toward more regulatory roles. Managers should cease hoarding inputs, and instead should expand profits. In the broadest sense, this conceptual linkage between institutional change – changes in the regulatory environment – and economic outcomes appears rather uncontroversial, particularly in the transitional environment.

Interestingly, scholars who otherwise differ on a range of issues tend to be rather unified in their choice of the relevant institution to study: property rights and ownership. Property-rights analysis has constituted a sort of explanatory chic for the 1990s, the means by which a whole range of outcomes in the post-socialist context are spelled out. The consensus view seems to be that reform entails a process of liberation, a dismantling of suffocating institutions, and a freeing up of individual enterprise and initiative. The idea is that once the old order is swept away, all the positive energies of societal actors somehow flower forth. Economic actors – whether local governments, firms, or entrepreneurs – must be given the "right" to enjoy the fruits of their labor. Managers must be given "autonomy" from the state. Firms must be "liberated" from state planning. The underlying idea is that if strictures are lifted and rights granted then everything will work out, and producers – whether individuals, firms, or even government agencies – will act for the social good. All will presumably behave in growth-promoting ways. New rights and freedoms then lead to new, growth-oriented patterns of behavior among economic producers.

Within this accepted framework, scholars quite vigorously debate over the issues of *to whom* and *how quickly* rights should be transferred. Can property rights remain in the hands of state actors, or should they necessarily be transferred to private holders? Must privatization occur rapidly, or can it proceed gradually? How should it be brought about?

Despite these questions, the "privatization perspective" – the notion that firm-level incentives and behavior are shaped primarily by property rights – has come to represent a sort of orthodoxy, a paradigm against which other views of economic reform are measured. Yet, what are the basic assumptions and logical connections underlying this powerful framework? Should it be the conceptual guide that we adopt to understand postsocialist reform? The purpose of the present chapter is to examine just what the privatization perspective offers, to what extent it is applicable in the transitional context, and which alternative frameworks might offer more explanatory power.

PROPERTY RIGHTS: THEORETICAL UNDERPINNINGS

The exalted status of property-rights analysis is not without merit. The basic concepts underlying privatization are rooted in an intellectual tradition running from Adam Smith through R. H. Coase and on into the present day.[1] These concepts embody a powerful logic, a logic that is in many ways relevant to understanding any economy, whether market or command. Because many of the notions of property rights emerging from this perspective will be revisited in the following chapters, it is doubly important that, before challenging the efficacy of privatization policies, we take some time to understand their basic theoretical underpinnings.

The conceptual framework surrounding privatization identifies two main issues with regard to property rights and the problems of SOEs. The first issue concerns *how* property rights are allocated; the second issue involves *to whom* such rights are allocated.[2] State firms are said to have performance problems first because control and cash-flow rights – the main components of ownership – are distributed among too many different actors. Too many people have control over the firm and access to firm-level capital, while nobody clearly bears any responsibility. Obvious incentive problems arise as a result. As a manager or state official, why worry about squandering assets when you will never be blamed for any negative outcomes that result? Moreover, rights in the state firm are distributed not only to too many different people but also to the wrong people. Political people with political interests (employment maximization,

28

patronage, national pride) end up running the firm, pushing it to produce at great expense goods that nobody wants. Societal resources are put to their least rather than their most productive use. In the view of privatization theory, the people who should hold property rights are economic, rather than political, actors: people for whom return on investment, and therefore efficiency, is the only concern.

From the privatization perspective, the key to economic growth is efficiency maximization, and the key to efficiency maximization is the proper structuring of incentives for economic producers. In effect, property-rights theory asks two fundamental, deeply intertwined questions. At the individual level, how can economic actors be encouraged to create, maintain, and improve scarce societal resources? At the systemic level, how can resources be put into the hands of those who will use them best?[3] The answer provided is that property rights, the bundle of legally defensible claims that constitute ownership, must be provided in a coherent fashion to the correct people – private producers. Once that is done, once the rights are provided and the proper context created, positive outcomes should flow naturally.[4] Producers will respond to market incentives, and the market itself will reward the efficient while weeding out the inefficient.

In the most general sense, economic systems can be organized to allocate by one of two means: they can allocate via the market or they can allocate bureaucratically by plan. The reasons for the command system's appeal and its ultimate failure will be discussed later in the chapter, but what is important to note here is the privatization perspective's emphasis on the opposite mode of economic organization, the free market. The free market, operating through the price mechanism and girded by the institution of ownership, is viewed as providing precisely the incentive structure needed to achieve efficient allocation and growth.[5]

Central to this framework is a particular notion of what exactly constitutes "ownership" and "secure property rights." Proponents of privatization generally view ownership as signifying the possession of two related rights with regard to a given asset: rights of control and rights to returns.[6] If, for example, I own a piece of land – a productive asset – then I can make certain decisions regarding the disposition of that asset. I can plant crops on it, build a house on it, or simply let it lie fallow. Similarly, if I do decide to turn it to productive use – if I decide to farm it, rent it out, or do any number of other activities – I can lay claim to the revenue that might accrue as a result. I essentially enjoy secure property rights over an asset to the extent that I can control the use of the asset and lay claim to any additional returns that such use may provide.

Of course, even at this level of abstraction, it is clear that my rights are far from absolute or exclusive; they are restricted by a series of contractual arrangements. Broadly speaking, if I reside and interact in a given community, I have in effect entered into a social contract whereby I agree to live by the laws and rules of society. Therefore, I may own land in the community, but I cannot use that land in violation of the community's agreed-upon rules and regulations. I cannot use the land to produce contraband, nor can I build on the land in violation of zoning or environmental laws. I cannot casually build a factory on property located in a residential district, nor can I blithely ignore rules against emissions, noise, or toxic wastes. Similarly, I do not enjoy absolute claim to the returns from my land. Again, by living in society and enjoying a bundle of public goods, I at least implicitly consent to pay taxes on my productive returns and even on property ownership itself.

In a somewhat less abstract sense, I can personally restrict the scope of my rights by voluntarily entering into a contract with another individual. I may decide to rent my land out to another person; although I receive payment for this service, I cannot arbitrarily evict that person within the duration of the contract. I have essentially limited my control rights. In a related sense, I can invite somebody in to develop my land and agree to receive in return a fixed percentage of any profits that may accrue. Again, I have voluntarily and contractually restricted my right to claim all returns from the given productive asset.

Clearly, then, the property rights that constitute "ownership" are actually complex bundles of control and possession claims.[7] These rights, rather than being absolute, represent a balance between competing claims to a given asset, claims that emanate from the actual "owner" of the asset, parties who have entered into contractual agreements with that owner, and society at large as represented by governmental and legal authorities.

If property rights represent balances, how then can we define the "owner" of the asset? A useful approach is to view ownership as the possession of "residual" rights, residual rights of control and rights to residual returns.[8] As for residual control, the owner of an asset retains the right to make any decisions regarding the disposition of that asset which are not explicitly prohibited by law or otherwise assigned to another party by contract.[9] Similarly, rights to residual returns signify the owner's right to claim any net income resulting from the use of an asset. In other words, the owner gets to keep anything left over after taxes have been paid, debts cleared, and any other contractual obligations settled.[10] Ownership, therefore, involves the right to make use of an asset in any way not expressly prohibited by law or contract, as well as the right to claim all profits after all others (creditors, suppliers of inputs, the government) have been reimbursed.

What the property-rights perspective suggests is that the optimal situation in terms of incentives is to have the two aspects of ownership – residual rights of control and rights to residual cash flows – clearly specified and brought together in the hands of a single individual. That individual would then decide how to use the asset in question, but would also bear all the financial costs and benefits that may result. Ideally, then, just by pursuing his or her own financial gain, the owner will put the productive asset to its most efficient use. Theoretically, once rights are granted – once the constraints prohibiting a producer from enjoying the fruits of his labor are lifted – positive, growth-oriented behavior should naturally evolve.[11]

In a similar vein, the property-rights view suggests that big problems develop when control rights and cash-flow rights are either misaligned (e.g., split between several holders) or simply left undefined. For example, it is not exactly surprising that people treat their own cars better than cars they rent.[12] The renter of a car assumes residual control rights, yet bears few financial risks with regard to the treatment of the auto, provided the vehicle is not obviously trashed during the duration of the rental. Conversely, an owner – who must personally replace the tires when they go bald, fix the transmission when it wears out, and clean the interior when it gets filthy – is less likely to spin the wheels, grind the gears, and smear ketchup all over the seats. In no small part owing to the nature of property rights, cars belonging to a single owner last a lot longer than cars that have been passed from one renter to the next. Basically, the solution is to define property rights clearly and to ensure that they are placed in the hands of a single holder.

Perhaps more important is the observation that, in a free-market system girded by property rights, if the owner does not put the asset to its most efficient use then somebody else will. This is where the function of the market and its price mechanism becomes so crucial. As long as the free market is allowed to operate, assets will be transferred to those who are willing to pay the most, and willingness to pay is presumably reflective of the potential to realize returns from the asset. As long as property rights are clearly delineated and prices are allowed to float according to supply and demand, transfers become possible and efficient allocation results. This, in effect, is the Coase theorem.[13] As long as property rights are clearly defined and contracts made to be enforceable – in other words, as long as property rights are secure from challenge and permitted to be transferred to the highest bidder – the market, operating through the price system, will ensure efficient resource allocation. Goods will ultimately go to those who can put them to the most productive, and therefore most profitable, use.

31

Coase initially illustrated the point through his now-famous example of the cave:

> Whether a newly discovered cave belongs to the man who discovered it, the man on whose land the entrance to the cave is located, or the man who owns the surface under which the cave is situated is no doubt dependent on the law of property. But the law merely determines the person with whom it is necessary to make the contract to obtain the use of the cave. Whether the cave is used for storing bank records, as a natural gas reservoir, or for growing mushrooms depends, not on the law of property, but on whether the bank, the natural gas corporation, or the mushroom concern will pay the most in order to be able to use the cave. One of the purposes of the legal system is to establish that clear delimitation of rights on the basis of which the transfer and recombination of rights can take place through the market.[14]

It is easy to see why, from this view, state ownership is considered so detrimental. With regard to incentives, a basic problem is presumed to result from the ambiguity and inevitable splitting of control and cash-flow rights in the state firm. For an SOE, control and cash-flow rights are formally held by the state, but who represents the state? In reality, control rights end up being distributed among a series of governmental agencies, bureaucrats, and politicians – all of whom are supposed to serve as agents of the general public.[15] These "agent-owners" may have all sorts of competing ideas regarding how the firm should be operated; when they attempt to implement those ideas, the firm gets pushed in contradictory directions. Meanwhile, amidst this cacophony of voices, none has clear authority. None of the agent-owners has final say and, more significantly, none has final responsibility for ultimate outcomes. The state firm thus becomes an industrial-version "rental car": there are many different drivers, but none pays any cost for destroying the asset in question. In the case of the SOE, as assets are destroyed, resources squandered, and losses incurred, the government responds by pumping in subsidies. Ultimately, therefore, it is the general public that pays the price, either through inflation, higher taxes, lower living standards, or some combination of the three.[16]

As noted earlier, privatization advocates go further by suggesting not only that property rights are too dispersed in the SOE but also that those rights are distributed to the wrong kind of people. Control is granted to political rather than economic actors, to people who care more about patronage than profitability. In this view, political owners – because they can always bilk the public to cover SOE losses – freely push the firm to overemploy, overproduce, and misallocate. Basic return on investment never quite makes it into the calculus.

All of these fundamental incentive problems are then compounded by the fact that, under state ownership, assets cannot generally be transferred on the open market. In other words, because the state is generally unwilling to sell its assets even to the highest bidder, actors who might put those assets to more efficient use are shut out of the game. The state-owned asset is put to inefficient use and remains in that mode indefinitely.

From this perspective, state ownership per se is ineffective, regardless of whether it exists in a command or free-market economy. The problem is basically the same across systems, whether socialist or capitalist, but is more obvious and extreme for those systems in which state ownership represents the norm rather than the exception. In other words, from the property-rights perspective, the key question is not whether an economy is market-oriented or planned but rather the degree to which property rights are held by the state or private individuals.[17]

It is easy to understand how these concepts become translated in the transitional context into advocacy of rapid, across-the-board privatization. The privatization perspective asserts that, in transitional systems, property rights are in the wrong hands: the hands of the state. What results are distorted incentives and inefficient modes of allocation systemwide. The solution is to *depoliticize* property rights, where depoliticization is defined primarily as the clear and definitive transfer of property rights from the hands of the state to the hands of private holders. As will be shown in what follows, this focus on transferring rights is critical. In the top-down view of privatization advocates, it does not really matter to whom property rights are transferred, so long as those actors are removed from the state and so long as assets can then be transferred on the open market. Once these conditions are met – once the proper environment for economic activity is created – individual producers will presumably shift their behavior accordingly and efficient, growth-promoting allocation will result.

THEORY MEETS PRACTICE: PRIVATIZATION EFFORTS IN
TRANSITIONAL ECONOMIES

That mass privatization has been the policy of choice in postcommunist Russia and Eastern Europe attests to the power of the property-rights notions just described. The idea is hardly an absurd one, and though its proponents acknowledge that privatization on such a large scale represents "uncharted territory," mass privatization has still been the preferred course of action in most post-socialist settings.[18]

Between 1992 and 1994, Russia transferred shares in over 11,000 state companies, approximately 70 percent of the nation's industrial sector, to private hands.[19] Some five years after passing its first privatization bill, Poland in 1995 began implementing a mass privatization program, transferring shares in 415 major state firms to fifteen investment funds.[20] The Czech Republic by 1996 officially declared privatization complete, with approximately 66 percent of the economy in private hands.[21] As for the Ukraine, despite repeated attacks on privatization programs by parliamentary conservatives, some 2,650 medium- and large-scale state firms had been sold off by 1995.[22]

Perhaps most surprising, even in China, where state ownership now stands as the final sine qua non of Chinese socialism and communist party rule, the privatization rationale has quietly and subtly – and altogether thoroughly – imbued the reform process. Although advocacy of privatization is still taboo, Chinese policy makers and academics alike consistently attribute poor SOE performance to the "lack of separation between government and firm" (*zhengqi bufen*) and "unclear property rights." Furthermore, since the Fifteenth Party Congress of 1997, the Chinese government's official stance on SOE reform has become to push "corporatization," almost universally recognized outside China (and even occasionally inside China) as a critical step toward privatization.[23] Chinese policy makers may speak euphemistically only of "revitalizing state ownership" or "establishing a 'modern corporate system'," but in reality they are undertaking many of the very steps advocated by privatization experts in the West, and for many of the same reasons. In essence, although Chinese reformers may not speak the language of privatization, they have certainly internalized the logic.[24]

Despite all of these intellectual and policy developments throughout the world, the question of whether privatization measures actually *work* in transitional systems – whether they actually do change firm-level behavior – is an open and extremely critical one. Of course, answering this question empirically represents a formidable challenge. First, we really are dealing with something new here, something without any prior benchmarks or earlier cases upon which to judge present performance. Much like the initial creation of command systems, the task of shifting these systems to a free-market footing constitutes an historically unprecedented process. Never before has the entire ownership structure in a single, integrated industrial economy – let alone several economies – been subjected to sweeping, policy-driven overhaul. Second, actual mass privatization efforts in Eastern Europe have not been under way long enough to yield the sort of firm-level data needed to draw conclusions about outcomes or policy effectiveness. In short, the jury is still out with regard to the success of privatization in postcommunist Europe.

With this absence of data, an unfortunate tendency has developed in which privatization is evaluated not in terms of whether it has changed behavior or resulted in growth but rather in terms of how extensively it has spread. In other words, what initially was the subject of inquiry – the hypothesis that privatization improves enterprise performance – becomes accepted as fact, and then the only issue becomes measuring the number of firms that have been privatized. The biggest, most contentious, most intrinsically interesting empirical question simply drops out of the picture. Some of the recent literature displays this analytical shift rather clearly. There is a tendency first to hypothesize that SOE underperformance is caused by excessive politicization of the firm, second to advocate privatization of the firm, and finally to measure the success of privatization in terms of the number of SOEs that have actually been privatized.[25] The hypothesis regarding excessive politicization is never tested, and privatization subtly moves from being an object of inquiry to an end in itself.

Yet simply assuming the worthiness of mass privatization as a transitional reform measure is neither interesting intellectually nor particularly consistent with the initial indicators emerging from Eastern Europe. Again, the jury is still out in many respects, but the mass privatization programs that make so much sense on paper have not exactly lived up to their billing when put into practice. In Russia, many newly privatized ex-SOEs seem not to have shed their habits of old. They lose money, harbor gross inefficiencies, resist worker layoffs, maximize wage payments, and generally fail to look anything like corporations in the West. Even careful quantitative studies have failed to confirm the sort of positive enterprise-level behavioral changes that would have been expected after privatization.[26] Moreover, we see very little of the market exit that would mark a truly competitive environment. The firms perform poorly, but they do not disappear over time.

The story seems to hold in Poland, despite the country's sustained efforts at macrostabilization and market liberalization. Since the implementation of the Balcerowicz Plan in 1990, the Polish government's explicit goal has been to create the free-market economic structures that have "proved their worth in the West."[27] Prices and trade were liberalized, and subsidies to state firms were summarily cut off. Basically, Polish reformers "got prices right" – prices actually reflected relative scarcities in the market. And as noted earlier, Poland has successfully privatized (at least nominally) several hundred large state firms. In theory, these policy achievements, when combined with the cutting off of state subsidies, should have been enough to force firms to respond to market incentives and behave like prototypical market actors. Strangely, though, Polish firms did not respond by cutting costs, laying off workers, boosting efficiency, or otherwise rationalizing their production processes.[28] Instead, they simply increased their indebtedness, either to banks or to each other, and generally decapitalized themselves in order to remain in business at full levels of employment.

Similar patterns seem to obtain in Czech firms as well, particularly the larger, older firms symbolized by the Poldi steel works. In the case of Poldi, the firm began defaulting on past loans soon after being transferred to private hands, and accusations abounded that the new owner, Vladimir Stehlik, was decapitalizing the firm. The situation was serious enough, and perhaps emblematic enough of more widespread problems, that the government publicly signaled its intentions to shift privatization strategies in the future.[29] In essence, firms behaved much as they had under the old system of socialist state ownership – although perhaps in a somewhat less constrained fashion – despite absolutely radical changes in their environment. Just as in the Chinese case, recently privatized state firms prove stubbornly immune to the environmental changes brought on by freer markets. Something must be wrong: rights are granted, but many producers either do not respond at all or respond with rent-seeking behavior.

Of course, if market forces are allowed to prevail and if bankruptcy laws are enforced, then this sort of behavior will eventually be brought to a close by the collapse of the firm. However, the whole purpose of privatization is to alter enterprise-level behavior precisely to avoid widespread shutdowns and overall collapse of the industrial economy.[30] It is hardly a stroke of genius to suggest that SOE inefficiencies can be eliminated by bankrupting the entire SOE sector. Rather, the challenge is to privatize, reform, or restructure the SOE in such a fashion that the entire economy does not implode as a result.

The key questions, then, still remain. Why is it that state firms in transitional systems respond poorly to the new incentive structures created by free markets? Why does privatization not produce in the transitional SOE the kind of obvious behavioral changes that theory would predict? Is there something about our particular understanding of the problem that is leading us to grasp at the wrong solutions? How can we even go about addressing these questions when the formal mass privatization programs that do exist have been under way for only months or a very few years?

At this stage in the analysis, the Chinese context becomes crucially important – both for the amount of data it offers and for the conclusions toward which those data lead. In the field of SOE restructuring, China in recent years has been lost in the shadows of seemingly more radical developments in Eastern

Europe. On the surface, China appears to be the recalcitrant stalwart, clinging to the old ways of state socialism while the rest of the world moves toward privatization. Appearances can be deceptive, however, for in certain respects China has been engaged in the game of transitional enterprise reform longer and more consistently than any other country. Not only does China represent a better environment in which to test theories of enterprise reform – as mentioned previously, there is interesting variation across the state and nonstate sectors – but even within the traditional state-owned industrial sector, the country has engaged in a wider range of policy measures than any other postcommand system. The Chinese case contains all the ingredients for interesting hypothesis testing.

China's efforts at urban SOE restructuring began in a concerted fashion in 1984 and have continued through the present day. This means there is effectively a twelve-year data stream that can be used to examine enterprise reactions to changing incentive structures and market reforms. Furthermore, that data stream itself contains important types of variation. Because Chinese policy makers throughout the reform period have adopted an experimental rather than a monolithic approach to reform, similar types of enterprises have been exposed to a range of policy measures. In other words, whereas at any given moment a particular style of reform may seem to hold sway nationally, Chinese leaders have appeared reluctant to subject the entire industrial sector to any single, coordinated reform measure.[31] In effect, widely divergent policy efforts proceed simultaneously. At any given time, one can find (even in a single industry) different firms enjoying vastly different property rights or corporate governance arrangements vis-à-vis the state, all under the rubric of "state ownership." In the Chinese state steel industry, for example, some firms have been corporatized – and indeed issue stock on international markets – while others are managed according to contractual agreements with state agencies. Still others are managed according to a system of standardized enterprise taxation. Basically, a range of policy "treatments" encompassing everything from nascent privatization to traditional state control is made available for observation. Similarly, variation exists on the enterprise performance side. Many Chinese SOEs exhibit all the prototypical ills of socialist state firms, yet others have actually adapted to the new incentive structures of the market and have improved their performance accordingly. That they do in fact display the sort of growth-promoting behavior usually associated with private ownership suggests that there are a few success stories among all the failures. In a more general sense, such variation allows us to treat the Chinese state industrial sector as a "laboratory of reform" for testing the impact of property-rights reform on enterprise behavior.

37

More important than the mere existence of this variation is the puzzling conclusion that comes along with it. In China today, the state firms that exhibit behavior most associated with private enterprise in the West – value maximization, strict budgeting, rational investment strategies, efficiency maximization – happen to be among the *least* privatized in the country. As the case studies presented in Part II suggest, it is not the corporatized, partially "privatized" SOE that responds in what would be considered a market-oriented fashion but instead the firm that has, in a sense, been drawn closer to the state rather than pushed farther away.[32] Proximity to some forms of state control *is* affecting performance, but in the opposite way from what traditional property-rights theory would predict. This, in effect, is the great paradox of Chinese SOE reform, a paradox that will be examined at some length in the chapters to follow.

THEORY REVISITED: WHAT'S WRONG WITH THE PROPERTY-RIGHTS APPROACH?

If conventional privatization theory has failed to explain outcomes in transitional systems, and if economic actors have not behaved as predicted, then the next logical step is to explain why. Is the theory itself internally flawed, or is the theory simply being misapplied? The answer, no doubt, involves both factors, though this section will focus primarily on the latter explanation. Many of the fundamental assumptions behind property-rights theory – the assumptions girding its internal logic – simply do not apply in transitional systems and frequently do not apply to large industrial producers as a whole. As will be shown, these assumptions involve both the nature of the actors being acted upon and the level of institutionalization of the economic system. The point here is neither to dismiss the logic of property-rights theory nor to assail its ultimate objectives. Rather, by understanding the ways in which postcommand systems fail to meet even the basic preconditions for property rights to function, we can better understand exactly where the problems of transitional reform reside. In the process, we can begin to explore alternative modes of analysis and alternative levels of causation for understanding not just the transitional environment but also our own.

With regard to problematic applications of privatization theory, the first area of concern involves the term "depoliticization." As noted previously, privatization advocates in transitional systems (whether in Eastern Europe or China) frequently stress the need to *depoliticize* the state-owned firm, the need to detach the state firm from the state.[33] This process is generally described as one of transferring property rights from the state to the private holder.[34] Suggesting that property rights can be transferred, however, assumes that property rights in the abstract actually exist in the economic system under discussion. Indeed, the Coasian assertion that clearly delineated property rights lead to efficient outcomes is quite explicitly based on the assumption that contracts are enforceable in the given system.[35] In order for the privatization strategy to work, rights must really be rights. They must truly be enforceable claims, claims that can be defended through the legal system against any transgressions, including those of the government. In short, for the theory to work, the society in question must truly operate under the principle of "rule of law." Neither "rule by law" (arbitrary legislation by government actors) nor "rule of man" (arbitrary action by authorities in total disregard of law) fits the bill. Unfortunately, this basic precondition of "rule of law" – one so obvious in the West that it is frequently taken for granted – simply does not exist in the transitional context.

As will be discussed at length in the following section, the command economies from which transitional systems evolved did not function with any real sense of property "rights," "defensible claims," or "sovereign law." These systems were organized, however imperfectly, by vertical chains of command and rule by fiat, not law. Even if the Coasian view is correct – that is, even if clear property rights in a fully institutionalized legal setting do lead to efficient outcomes – the view is essentially irrelevant to the transitional context. In transitional economies, the institutional underpinnings for a property-rights system are nowhere to be found.

The challenge of transitional reform, therefore, is not to transfer property rights but rather to *create* them from scratch, and create as well the whole institutional underpinning necessary to make them function.[36] Only when that is done does it make sense to worry about who ultimately holds these rights – the state, citizens, foreigners, or anybody else. In terms of efficiency maximization, it may ultimately make sense to worry about who in fact holds property rights, but that cannot be the first concern; the rights themselves must be established on something more than just a nominal basis. To transfer rights in a system in which rights have little meaning is to put the "cart before the horse." Yet, by putting the cart before the horse and attempting such a transfer under these conditions – essentially by removing the firm from state control – one risks bringing about decidedly unexpected and negative outcomes. As will be shown in this study (particularly in the chapters on the Ma'anshan and Capital Iron and Steel companies), the firm in a transitional system can indeed be split from the state, but functioning property rights do not then simply materialize out of thin air. Instead, chaos materializes. Renegade agencies of the state fail to respect the transfer of rights and continue to intervene in firm-level affairs. Even with the formal splitting of the firm from the state, ownership becomes increasingly opaque and lines of authority increasingly blurred. Old patterns of intervention and rent-seeking continue, but now at less cost to those intervening and with less likelihood of attributing blame for any negative outcomes that might result. Furthermore, as responsibility blurs and the firm is split off from normal state monitoring channels, restraints on firm-level managers virtually disappear. A flawed mode of ownership is replaced, in effect, by no ownership or oversight at all.

However, once the objective is viewed as creating rather than transferring rights, the utility of tearing the firm away from the state and pursuing depoliticization becomes much less obvious. Indeed, the state, however much a source of problems, also happens to be the only organization capable (over the long term) of creating a property-rights system and (over the short term) of providing interim measures to stabilize firm-level incentives.

This brings us to the second problematic assumption of privatization theory, an assumption related to the nature of the economic actors being acted upon. This flaw actually pertains not only to the way privatization advocates have sought to apply the theory, but also to the way the theory itself is structured. The top-down emphasis of privatization – the notion that if you set the environment accordingly then proper incentives will be created and good behavior will result – depends on the assumption that the actors under consideration are individuals. In other words, the whole point of focusing on property rights, and particularly the wedding of control and cash-flow rights, is to ensure that incentives exist for an individual to maintain or expand a given asset. The logic is that, if people are rational "economic men" (i.e., if they are the self-interested wealth maximizers described by Adam Smith), then they will invest their energies in improving an asset as long as they can lay exclusive claim to the resulting returns that accrue.[37] If you view the relevant economic environment as being populated by individuals like this, then privatization makes perfect sense because the policy provides just the right incentives to promote growth.

The problem is that transitional systems are industrialized economies. Because they are industrialized economies, the relevant economic actors are firms, and often extremely large firms at that. Once firms are taken to be the major actors, however, the terms of debate shift dramatically. Property rights per se, particularly the degree to which those rights can be brought together and merged into the hands of clearly specified owners, recede in importance. Instead, a host of new issues – issues related to transaction costs, information asymmetries, and corporate governance – take precedence.

The modern industrial enterprise is almost by definition characterized by a separation of ownership and control, a separation necessitated by the nature of

40

modern industrial production.[38] Manufacturing since the early twentieth century has come to be associated with grand scale, continual innovation, and massive capital requirements.[39] Massive capital requirements generally mean that single individuals or individual families can no longer supply the financial resources needed to create, maintain, and expand the industrial firm. Instead, such levels of capital accumulation can be achieved only by an organized group of disparate individuals or, more likely, a number of financial institutions. The key point is that ownership over an industrial asset – in this case, the firm – is distributed among a series of investors, whether they are individuals or organizations. Furthermore, the complexities of modern production make it unlikely that any of those investor-owners will actually be able to manage the firm. These owners may be experts in capital accumulation, but they are unlikely to have the specialized knowledge needed to coordinate production and make day-to-day managerial decisions. Hence professional managers must be brought in, essentially as agents of the principal owners, in order to control and coordinate production. Ownership, defined in this case as claims to and responsibility for financial flows relating to an asset, becomes split off from actual control over the asset.

This splitting is not necessarily bad – it allows for highly complex, capital-intensive, and innovative forms of production – but it considerably blurs traditional notions of property rights. No longer is it patently obvious that control rights and cash-flow rights need to be wedded. Quite to the contrary, in the large firm it is clear that these two aspects of ownership cannot be merged, and it is somewhat ludicrous to suggest that they should be. Indeed, the whole emphasis on clarification of property rights as a precondition for efficient production and allocation becomes highly problematic. After all, in a developed capitalist economy, can it really be determined who "owns" a public corporation? Is it the stockholders? They invest money and assume risk, but their access to dividends hardly constitutes a claim to residual returns. As Milgrom and Roberts point out, stockholders have little if any power with regard to investment decisions, managerial hiring and compensation, or the setting of product prices.[40] Alternatively, is it the board of directors that owns? They hire and fire managers, set compensation, and often determine mergers and acquisitions, but they can neither claim residual returns nor expropriate profits.[41] Finally, is it the manager who owns? He or she, in effect, exercises residual control – albeit only with the cooperation of subordinate employees – but exercises that control under the terms set by the board of directors. Once we are talking about modern firms and complex bundles of assets, it no longer makes much sense to say that the key to efficiency is the "clarification" of property rights or the concentration

41

of those rights in the hands of a single holder. We should no more focus on this issue in transitional firms than we do with firms in developed capitalist economies. Why, in other words, should we claim that the problem of the post-socialist SOE is that control and cash-flow rights are split when we would never use this approach to explain poor performance in Western firms? The division of ownership and control, and the ambiguous property-rights situation that results, must be taken as given. The challenge then becomes to deal with the new corporate governance problems that emerge.

In order to understand these problems, not only in transitional economies but also in developed capitalist settings, it becomes necessary to depart from traditional property-rights notions of the firm as a "black box": a single, undifferentiated entity. Instead of viewing the producer (the firm) as a unitary actor concerned with converting input to output at some production cost, it becomes critical to accept the firm as an intricate system that – through the very complexity of its operations – incurs certain *transaction costs*. These transaction costs are, as Oliver Williamson has noted, "the economic equivalent of friction in physical systems."[42] They are, in effect, the costs not so much of producing an actual unit of output as of running a complex system itself. Only after we accept that coping with such transaction costs constitutes a fundamental challenge of modern production do many of the basic institutions of capitalism make sense. After all, what is the purpose of complex takeover mechanisms, strict accounting and disclosure requirements, and intricate corporate legal codes if not to deal with problems stemming from the separation of ownership and management? Similarly, only when the reality of transaction costs is recognized does it become possible to see which institutions in transitional systems are missing and to see just why it is that firms in these systems, even "privatized" firms, fail to respond to free-market incentives. In effect, to a far greater degree than the pure rights-based approach, an analysis based on transaction costs provides consistent explanations across economic systems – both transitional and developed capitalist – and allows us to understand variation between systems.

One way of viewing the modern firm's separation of ownership and control is through a particularly important source of transaction costs: imperfect information. The owner-investors who happen to have the necessary capital for starting an industrial firm do not have the requisite information or skills for managing industrial production. There is, in effect, a situation of asymmetrical information between owners and the professional managers they bring in to run the firm, a situation that exists throughout the life of the firm. Managers possess all the information about the firm's daily operations – plus the knowledge required to interpret that information – whereas owner-investors do not. Yet the owner-investors, since they are supplying all the capital for the firm's operation, assume a disproportionate share of the risk. Asymmetric risk becomes coupled with asymmetric information: the principal bears all the risk while the agent monopolizes all the information.

These asymmetries lead to a number of potential "agency problems," fundamental divergences of interest between nominal owners and managers. Since owners (at least technically) retain rights to residual returns, managers may see no reason to increase their own efforts in maximizing the value of the firm. In other words, managers, having little incentive to work harder if they are not going to be paid more, may engage in "shirking."[43] Similarly, managers may seek to maximize their own salaries and benefits over the short term – at the expense of the productivity and long-term value of the firm. Finally, even if managers and principals are all striving to maximize value, who can say whether their respective time horizons are similar? It is quite conceivable that the agent would have a far shorter time horizon than the principal, though the exact opposite situation could certainly obtain as well. In many cases, what is needed to maximize the short-term value of the firm is not the same as what is needed to maximize its long-term value. Conflicts, therefore, inevitably arise.

These issues are raised simply to suggest that, given the fact of divided ownership and control (i.e., given information asymmetries and resulting agency problems), particular mechanisms are needed to unite the interests of owners and managers and thus make the firm run efficiently. Even with the institution of private property, modern capitalist economies still need an additional set of mechanisms to ensure that managers act in the interests of owners and that firms respond to the productivity incentives of the market. These mechanisms, generally falling under the rubric of "corporate governance" and frequently operating in the firm's external environment, are designed expressly to cope with the transaction costs – particularly those related to imperfect information – that inevitably accrue in the running of modern firms, whether state-owned or private. Governance mechanisms include a wide range of institutions that have come to be taken for granted in developed economies. Strict accounting standards and financial disclosure requirements keep stockholders informed. Highly developed capital markets and specialized financial institutions provide not only independent analyses of firm-level performance information but also the capital infusions that reward effective enterprise management. Moreover, there exists a significant corpus of law to regulate these information flows and resolve disputes when they arise. If these measures fail to result in adequate firm-level performance, and if owners themselves are unwilling to address managerial errors, then another set of governance mechanisms kick in – namely, hostile takeovers or outright bankruptcy proceedings. In the former case, new owners come in and appoint new managers; in the latter case, creditors themselves may perform this function.

Unquestionably, enterprise governance mechanisms differ widely among developed economies. In Japan and Germany, for example, banks themselves sit on the advisory boards of large public corporations, serve as major shareholders, and actively intervene when the firm lapses into financial difficulties.[44] In the United States, where direct bank ownership over corporations is severely circumscribed, the hostile takeover mechanism is more prevalent. What is critical to recognize, however, is that all developed capitalist economies have these mechanisms, mechanisms that are absolutely essential for getting firms to respond to the price signals of the free market. Even with the institution of private property, markets do not function spontaneously but instead must be *made* to function, particularly in the context of the modern industrial sector. Unfortunately, the corporate governance mechanisms that make markets function are strikingly absent in transitional systems. Only by understanding this absence, particularly the ways in which certain reform policies compensate for the problem while others exacerbate it, can we hope to understand the true challenge of SOE reform in transitional systems. More broadly, only by understanding the nature of malfunctioning corporate governance – especially the conditions under which this matters greatly and the conditions under which it matters less – can we hope to understand the variation observed both within and across transitional economies.

CONCLUSION

The point of the preceding discussion is to suggest that, in order for traditional property-rights analysis to "work" in the transitional system, one must assume a degree of institutionalization that simply does not exist. The theory falls short not so much because of internal inconsistency as because the assumptions it makes are inappropriate both for transitional systems and for complex industrial producers. The task of the next chapter is to outline an alternative approach, one that does "work" in the transitional context. The challenge for any such theory is to capture the unique restructuring issues facing transitional systems and also to remain consistent with observed patterns of variation.

3

The Nested Problems Dynamic: An Alternative Approach

I N the previous chapter, we suggested that traditional property-rights analysis provides an inadequate foundation for understanding the unique processes of transitional reform. The aim of this chapter will be to begin the search for an alternative approach, an approach focusing not so much on the dissemination of rights as on the restructuring of institutional constraints on economic behavior. The overall plan of attack will be to start with the specific and then work outward to the more general. This chapter will focus on providing a new approach – the "nested problems" dynamic – for understanding the specific problem of SOE reform. The broader implications of this model for our general understanding of transitional systems will be explored in Chapter 7.

NESTED PROBLEMS AND FEEDBACK LOOPS

For large-scale Chinese SOEs, the questions that demand immediate attention are why these firms lose so much money and why they appear so resistant to market-oriented reform efforts. Answers become clearer as soon as one moves away from the question of "who owns" and toward questions of how ownership in general, and market-driven enterprise governance in particular, are undermined in the transitional context.

Chinese SOEs suffer from a particular form of corporate governance failure, a failure created by the dynamic interaction between state intervention into the firm and distorted information flowing out from the firm (see Figure 3.1). On one side of the cycle, insecure property rights – or, more precisely, the ability of state actors to override any countervailing claims of "rights" by producers – provide the context in which uncoordinated agencies of the state routinely intervene in, and extract profits from, the firm. These agencies, particularly local governments, intervene not on the basis of ownership or "right" but instead on the basis of raw governmental authority.[1] In short, in the transition from command plan to market, formal state control ends but the controllers remain. De jure control is superseded by de facto control.

45

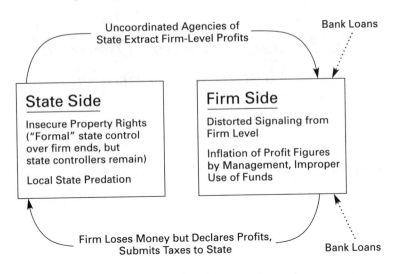

Figure 3.1. The Nested Problems Dynamic

On the other side of the cycle, the firm – for a variety of reasons to be discussed shortly – loses money but still declares profits. In essence, the enterprise broadcasts erroneous signals regarding its own financial condition. These signals, once received by governmental actors, serve as grounds for more taxation, and the cycle deepens. What ultimately happens is that the ability of local governments to override legal regulations and "rights" interacts with distorted firm-level information to create a self-reinforcing cycle, a *nested problems* dynamic that thoroughly undermines the ability of potential owners (whether public or private) to control the firm.

Driving the cycle forward and ensuring its perpetuation are the soft loans pumped in from the state banking system. As long as banks themselves have a soft budget constraint – as long as they retain access to central financing – the subsidization continues. As long as the subsidization continues, local agencies can then engage in predatory taxation and managers can distort performance data, all at no cost to the actors involved. The firm is kept afloat from outside, so it simply cannot go bankrupt. Under such circumstances, rent seeking by a variety of economic actors (government agencies, bankers, managers) never clearly affects the bottom line of the firm and can therefore persist indefinitely. The firm simply keeps on declaring nominal "profits" and amassing substantial liabilities.

Even as ownership over the firm changes hands, the dynamic continues unabated and indeed often worsens. Through repeated cycles of profit inflation, tax extraction, and bailout lending, the true financial condition of any given firm becomes increasingly opaque, a condition that suits many of the economic actors involved. Distortions in firm-level information flows then make the assigning of accountability for disastrous performance outcomes nearly impossible. Under these conditions, pressure for change – namely, pressure to shift from rent-seeking to value-enhancing business behavior – becomes negligible.[2]

The broader theme of the nested dynamic approach is that transitional reform is best seen not as a granting of rights but instead as a varying of constraints and opportunities for economic actors. Reform does not simply mean that economic actors receive more autonomy, freedom, and power. Rather, reform creates a series of new institutional conditions, institutional setups that influence the payoff structure for different kinds of economic behavior. By understanding the nature and variability of constraints upon economic actors in differing transitional contexts, we can develop a sense of why autonomy is exercised in productive ways in some environments and in unproductive ways in others.

For the specific case of Chinese SOEs, an important variable to focus upon is access to soft subsidization – more specifically, access to the state banking system. Once firms have access to unlimited bailout loans, pressure to shift over to market-oriented behavior decreases for government regulators and enterprise managers alike. Opportunities for rent seeking are created, and ultimate constraints – namely, the bankruptcy and liquidation of the firm – never quite materialize.[3] Predatory state taxation and managerial distortions of performance data can go on unabated. As will be described in detail in what follows, efforts to change the nominal ownership structure have little impact on the behavioral payoff structure for managers or government officials. The nested problems dynamic grinds on regardless of "who owns."

What does have an impact, however, are successful efforts to cut the firm off from the budget-softening, malfunctioning regulatory environment. More specifically, what seems to affect enterprise behavior is the termination of ties to the banking system. Once the loans stop flowing in, both firm-level inefficiency and outside state predation start to impinge upon the firm's financial situation. Constraints – even simply defined as basic accountability – once again start to shape behavior now that rent seeking threatens the viability of the firm. Actors are pushed to use their autonomy in less destructive, more growth-oriented ways. In short, even as ownership is held constant, varying the firm's access to the banking system shapes the degree to which relevant economic actors engage in market-oriented behavior.[4]

The remainder of the chapter will be devoted to fleshing out the causal linkages and underlying patterns of the nested problems dynamic. The following section outlines in the most general sense the bureaucratic changes wrought by reform, particularly with respect to the urban SOE. Given that background of change, the remaining sections then explore in detail each pole of the enterprise–government dynamic. The chapter concludes by examining more precisely the interaction effects between the poles as well as the impact of the banking sector as a whole.

FROM PLAN TO MARKET: THE CHANGING NATURE OF
AUTONOMY AND CONSTRAINT

China's prereform economy, particularly with regard to heavy industrial development, rather closely followed the model of Soviet-style command planning.[5] As part of China's effort to build up heavy industry, resource allocation decisions were placed in the hands of state planners rather than left up to market forces. Planners controlled a large volume of resources in the economy, particularly the scarcest and most vital inputs, and controlled the flow of those resources from producer to consumer through the process of price setting.[6] On the whole, therefore, the signals upon which economic actors based production decisions in this type of economy came from bureaucratic commands rather than market-responsive prices. As a producer, you produced what you were told rather than what you might believe any downstream consumers would ultimately consume. On the bureaucratic side of such an economy, the central planners ruled; on the production side, the state-owned heavy industrial firm occupied the "commanding heights." The state firm served both as an extension of the state bureaucracy and as the production arm of a vast state planning machine.

Of course, Chinese command socialism, at least in terms of the number of products administered by the central plan, was far less extensive and far more regionalized than the Soviet variant.[7] This was in part a reflection of China's severe shortage of trained officials, particularly in the 1950s and 1960s, and in part a reflection of the Maoist emphasis on local self-sufficiency. Nevertheless, the Chinese compensated for their relatively understaffed central bureaucracy by restricting planning primarily to scarce goods while allowing local governments or the firms themselves to market nonscarce goods.[8] In a sense, when a buyer's market existed, the burden of allocating output was shifted to the firm. For a seller's market, state planners retained strict control over allocation. Not all goods remained on the plan, but certainly vital and scarce inputs did. Because of this, systemic outcomes in China were quite similar to those in the more developed command economies of Eastern Europe and the Soviet Union. In a sense, the total number of commodities contained within the plan is far less

48

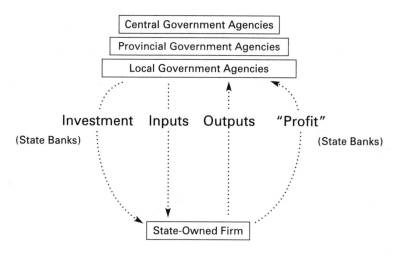

Figure 3.2. The SOE in the Command Economy

significant than the *type* of goods on the plan. Nobody cares whether nonessential commodities are allocated by plan or market – surpluses mask inefficiencies in the allocation process – but command planning becomes important when applied to vital, relatively scarce resources. At this point, a series of inefficiencies exacerbate scarcities, lead to misallocation of goods, and hamper growth. Everybody can feel it when already scarce goods become even scarcer.

To understand these inefficiencies, one must delve slightly deeper into the relationship between firm and state in the command system. As indicated by Figure 3.2, the heavy industrial firm in such a system served as the production arm of the state. State planners told the firm exactly what to produce, how much to produce, and at what price inputs would be acquired. Inputs were allocated bureaucratically from above, as were the investment funds needed to carry out production. The banks served merely as state cashiers, channeling allocated investment into the firm. On the output side, production levels and prices were again set bureaucratically. Because the state controlled the prices and output levels, it knew a priori what the surplus – the "profit" – would be. That profit could then be extracted from the firm. Those funds either went directly back to the center, where they could be reallocated downward as firm-level investment, or remained in bank-controlled accounts for later use in the firm. The key point is that the fundamental relationships and flows in this economy were vertical and hierarchical, between producer and planner, rather than between producer and consumer.

Although the system as a whole may have been strictly hierarchical, firm-level actors clearly had their own particular interests and incentives, plus enough de facto autonomy to act on those interests. In the command economy, managers were held accountable primarily for output levels. The manager knew that, in terms of his own career advancement, he had to meet the bureaucratically assigned output targets. However, the problem was that, at any given time, the manager could never be sure what sort of input and investment levels would be granted from above to meet those targets. Furthermore, he could assume that hitting the targets in one year would invite only the raising of targets in the next year.[9] The problem from the manager's perspective, though, was that goods in socialist economies, in part because of a systemwide passion for expansion and growth, always remained locked in perpetual scarcity. Chronic shortage became a fact of life for producers and consumers alike. The manager knew he had to have excess resources on hand lest output targets be raised. Yet, he also knew that resources were terribly scarce. The logical thing to do in this situation was to hoard investment and inputs.[10] Every opportunity had to be taken to maximize what you had today – whether in terms of input levels, labor, or investment – just to ensure an ample supply in the event output targets were raised tomorrow. Indeed, as the manager, you had every incentive *not* to use your factors of production efficiently, lest you exhibit surpluses that could be reclaimed by the planners. In an environment of chronic shortage, you expanded your control over inputs whenever possible, particularly since you did not clearly bear any costs for obtaining or stockpiling these inputs. You were responsible for output, not cost. Under such conditions, the hoarding of resources – keeping them in reserve rather than putting them to productive use – became an effective managerial technique and an absolutely logical entrepreneurial strategy. In short, the particular mix of autonomy and constraint in this system pushed producers to engage in rent seeking.

In this light, it is important to reiterate that, despite the hierarchical nature of the command economy, the manager did have a certain degree of autonomy to act on the incentives just described. Managerial autonomy, in other words, is not something entirely unique to the reform era. In the command system, the manager may not have had any clear property rights, but he did have a near monopoly on information flows. After all, central planning – the determination of input and output flows for the entire industrial economy – required the collection and interpretation of colossal amounts of data, and on an annual basis no less. Because the task simply swamped the bureaucratic apparatus, planners ultimately had to rely on the firm itself for the provision of vital information. Managers themselves had to estimate their investment needs and output potential, and it was upon those estimates that central plans were calculated. Firm-level autonomy, therefore, stemmed from the manager's control over information and was frequently expressed through inflated investment requirements and deflated output estimates. The manager did what he could to hoard today what he might ultimately need to use tomorrow.

Despite the overwhelmingly hierarchical and apparently top-down nature of the system, power to some extent (particularly in the area of information flows) ran from the bottom up. Managers retained certain de facto powers, certain de facto "rights," which translated into investment-hoarding behavior. Opportunities existed to maximize interests, and those opportunities were grabbed. Entrepreneurs existed in this system, yet the incentive structure ensured that their activities became devoted to value-subtracting activities.

From the manager's perspective, constraints did exist in this system but not necessarily in the area of cost. The firm did not "pay" for its inputs or investment in any conventional sense, and profitability was determined a priori by state-set prices and output levels. The socialist firm, in a sense, had no "bottom line." Nevertheless, ultimate restraints were imposed simply through the vertical nature of resource flows in the system. Managers could and did manipulate information in order to hoard investment and tamp down output targets. Planners, however, retained ultimate control over resource flows. Central officials may not have had a good idea of what was happening in the firm, but they certainly could stop the flow of inputs. Similarly, firms may have sought to hoard inputs, but they had only one real source for those inputs: the state plan. Managers, except on the margins, generally could not engage in direct horizontal transactions with other producers or consumers. In other words, even without a bottom line, at least this was a closed system: in the allocation process, the hand that was giving was in some sense the same hand that was taking. Planners may not have had control over information, but they at least understood the incentives bearing down on the managers who did control information. Furthermore, because central planners shouldered ultimate responsibility for allocation errors, these officials had some incentive to exert their authority over resource flows.

Even in the absence of reliable information, therefore, planners still took action to curtail managerial autonomy. Managers systematically overstated investment requirements, and planners systematically pushed downward the final investment grants. Managers habitually underestimated output potential, so planners habitually raised output targets. In addition, planners compensated for information gaps by developing standard operating procedures and prioritization techniques for allocation. Certain enterprises (e.g., vital military firms) were placed higher on the recipient list for scarce inputs and investments; they could always obtain resources, regardless of need. Other firms, far lower on the list, could almost never get resources, again regardless of need. The point here is not to suggest that this was an effective mode of allocation; indeed, it was an extremely inefficient way to allocate. Rather, the idea is simply that ultimate constraints existed and served to limit the extent to which planners could accommodate the soft-budget incentives of individual firms. Resources flowed, and they often flowed in terribly inefficient ways, but planners maintained final control over the tap. The mechanisms used to maintain that control may have been highly inefficient and inexact, but they served to put a cap on firm-level autonomy, particularly autonomy directed toward value-subtracting, rent-seeking strategies.[11]

The entire situation changed dramatically with the onset of reform in the early 1980s. Reform in China has been neither constant nor necessarily coherent, but certain broad patterns have emerged. These patterns, in shaping the set of constraints and opportunities facing economic actors, have had an extraordinary impact on both microeconomic behavior and macroeconomic outcomes.

In the most general sense, reform has sought to replace bureaucratic control over resources with market-based allocation, allocation that is driven by objective conditions of producer supply and consumer demand. Organizationally, this has meant that the various components of the command bureaucracy have, in effect, been cut loose and told to fend for themselves. Vertical economic transactions between superior and subordinate agencies have been gradually edged out by horizontal transactions between market actors. As indicated by Figure 3.3, state-owned industrial firms are now expected to acquire their inputs on the open market and at market-determined prices. At least in theory, firms are supposed to pay for what they use in terms of both investment capital and physical inputs. Capital is now supposed to be supplied on a commercial basis, at positive rates of interest, by state banks that have themselves been detached from the old bureaucratic hierarchy. The banks are ostensibly no longer cashiers; they are now semiautonomous market actors. On the production side, enterprises are supposed to determine their own output levels, sell their output at market prices, and retain significant portions of the profits that accrue. The general principle is that – in order to achieve societal increases in allocative efficiency, growth, and living standards – producers must be forced to pay the costs of production *and* be permitted to enjoy the rewards of their efforts.

On the bureaucratic side, the principle in theory is that government agencies will no longer directly control resources or micromanage firms. Instead, the agencies are to focus on overall regulation and the provision of social goods,

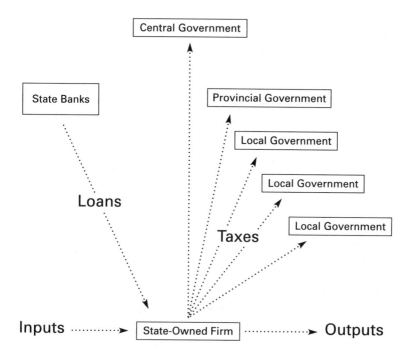

Figure 3.3. The SOE in the Reform Economy

whether defined as investments in physical infrastructure, education, public se-
curity, or other traditional governmental functions. As part of this shift, local
agencies in particular can no longer rely primarily on fiscal grants from central
coffers but are instead directed to rely on tax revenues from local producers.
Again, the idea is to couple the power to use resources with responsibility for
actually paying the costs. Local governments, therefore, are charged with a variety of new tasks, but they are also given the independent fiscal authority to
raise the funds needed to accomplish those tasks. The result is that the command
bureaucracy still exists, but it no longer commands and it no longer operates
as a unified entity. It has essentially been disaggregated, split into constituent
parts, and told to adopt market-enhancing policies.

Of course, the logic described here exists somewhat more in theory than practice. The Chinese industrial economy today operates in a vast gray area – an
area not only nestled somewhere between plan and market, but also one gripped
by extraordinarily rapid transformation and flux. Certain elements of autonomy and "rights" clearly exist for economic actors in the reform economy, just

53

as they did in the command system. Again, neither autonomy nor decentralization as a whole are particularly new in China. The new "gray area" organizational environment, however, has reshuffled the opportunities and constraints that bear down on economic actors. These new combinations then reshape the ways in which autonomy is exercised. Autonomy, perhaps, is constant, but the incentives conditioning the way it is used have shifted dramatically.

In this odd gray-area environment, one could imagine three hypothetical scenarios, each with its own corresponding set of incentives for the economic actors involved. For the first scenario, imagine a local governmental agency entirely detached from the other entities described in Figure 3.3. In other words, imagine a locality, perhaps a remote rural locality, with no access to SOEs or the state banking system. This locality must now shoulder many new responsibilities, pay for its operations, and take care of its citizens, yet it no longer receives financial disbursements from the center. The local government, in effect, suffers extreme financial constraints. It faces an inflexible hard budget constraint and therefore has little choice but to encourage the formation of firms that could function as a tax base and future revenue source: the local government can either promote business or go hungry. Moreover, just as the locality is cut off from central transfers, the firms it starts are also cut off from transfers. By default, and for lack of any other options, both the locality and the firms face a hard budget constraint.

For the second scenario, consider the situation described in Figure 3.3 – an urban context with existing industrial firms – and assume that the state banks operate on a truly commercial basis. They lend only to commercially viable firms and, when they choose to withhold credit from nonviable firms, those firms ultimately go bankrupt and exit the market. Under these conditions, the local government has the choice, and indeed the "right," either to promote business or to beat up on business. That is, the locality can invest in business in order to create a healthy tax base, or it can, by means of its legal power to tax, drive the firm into the ground. Presumably, however, if banks really withhold capital from nonviable firms (e.g., enterprises that are being taxed to death) then predatory taxation will result in an erosion of the tax base. The firm would simply be driven into the ground and would shut down. Even worse, since direct financial transfers from the center to the localities have been curtailed during the reform era, destruction of the tax base would hit the local government where it hurts most, in the purse. The point is that, under this scenario, local governments would have the right, as agents of the central state, either to promote business or to prey upon it. Indeed, reform would create all sorts of new opportunities for localities to achieve quick, short-term financial gains by directing newly acquired powers toward the extraction of firm-level profits. However, the new financial constraints imposed by reform would push the government to curtail its rent-seeking preferences – its preferences for a quick payoff – in order to stave off future poverty.

The opportunities and constraints bearing down on managers in this second scenario are similar. Managers in this situation have just as much de facto right as in the past to overstate their needs and hoard investment. Many firms squandered resources in the command era, and the opportunities for squandering have only grown in the reform era. The key point, however, is that if capital is being directed on a truly commercial basis and if bankruptcy actually looms over those firms unable to attract funding, then constraints on managerial rent seeking escalate tremendously. The manager can extract from the firm, just as the government official can, but the result for both in this scenario is the same: the firm goes out of business. In essence, this scenario assumes an ultimate bottom line, a final constraint on predatory, rent-seeking behavior. Managerial and governmental policy mistakes can be made, but those who make the mistakes will end up paying a price in the end.

Now consider a third scenario (again in the organizational environment depicted by Figure 3.3) in which the state banks do not lend on a commercial basis. Indeed, assume that the state banks have both unlimited access to central funds and significant autonomy over the choice of to whom to lend. In other words, the banks operate on a thoroughly soft budget, lend to whomever they want, and are never held accountable for losses. This then changes the opportunities and constraints for all the other actors involved. Local officials still have the right to determine tax levels, and still have the option of promoting business, but now it makes sense for these officials to prey upon the firm. After all, no matter how much tax money is extracted, bank loans will presumably come in and make up the difference. The firm will never go bankrupt but can instead serve indefinitely as a conduit for central–local financial transfers. The opportunities for governmental rent seeking become overwhelming. Why hold off and invest in business if you can instead extract today and pay no price tomorrow?

A similar set of incentives applies to managers. Once you can gain access to free capital and avoid any threat of liquidation, why should you care about efficiency? No matter how hard you try to invest in growth, governmental agencies end up beating you into the ground. You might as well pump resources into consumption (wages, worker housing, or benefits), rely on the banks to fund your basic production costs, keep on paying taxes to the government, and keep the production processes rolling along until you get promoted out. The advantage of such chaos is that you can never really be held accountable for any negative outcomes. Such outcomes can either be hidden through infusions of credit or (should they come out into the open) be explained away as products of "external circumstances." Excessive taxation would be just one of many things that could constitute such circumstances. As a manager, you might even encourage excessive taxation by the state simply to absolve yourself of any responsibility for shortfalls in production or profitability.

Once financial intermediaries enjoy both a soft budget and autonomy in lending decisions, a worst-case outcome obtains. Soft budgets in the financial sector end up creating soft budgets at both the firm and local governmental level. Because nobody – other than the public at large – ultimately pays, resources just keep getting pumped in. Although the command economy was grossly inefficient, at least it ensured that central officials would maintain the ability to "turn off the tap" – the hand that was giving could also take away. That hand may not have had a good idea of what was happening, but at least it could turn off the tap if need be.

The system just described in our third scenario is different. Here, essentially autonomous actors (the banks) pump in revenues that more accurately belong to the central government. Those resources are then misallocated and ultimately devoted to extremely inefficient uses. In effect, they end up being squandered. The costs are then borne by the public through inflation, low firm-level productivity, and declining living standards.

Over time, it becomes increasingly difficult for key central decision makers to cut off the flow. Bank lending so confuses market signaling that good firms can no longer be distinguished from bad. For no clear reason, certain firms appear awash in credit while others seem starved for cash. Unsure of which firms should be shut down and which should be allowed to persist, the center then neither pursues bankruptcy measures nor restrains the banks from continued lending. Indeed, the banks are directed in the crunch to bail out failing firms. Yet once the banks engage in bailout lending and their own books become irreversibly swamped with nonperforming loans, a "moral hazard" problem develops.[12] Because of policy directives to bail out firms, bank balance sheets become swamped with bad loans, and the banks themselves can never really be held accountable for losses. However, the banks still have access to central funds as well as the discretionary authority to lend to whomever they like. The banks, then, have a clear incentive to engage in extremely high-risk and ill-advised lending. In the likely event of losses, the bank steers clear of responsibility; in the unlikely event of repayment, the bank stands to earn substantial profits.[13]

Unfortunately, it is this third scenario that is absolutely critical for understanding the situation surrounding Chinese SOEs today. The organizational environment depicted in Figure 3.3 describes the uncontrolled lending and predatory taxation elements of the nested problems dynamic. Furthermore, it becomes clear that frequently the banking institutions, and the very presence of state banks, determine which scenarios obtains at any given time. In other words, in the Chinese transitional context, it is the availability of soft credit (supplied either directly or indirectly) that determines the budget constraint for key economic actors at both the firm and governmental levels. Economic actors, then, express their entrepreneurial instincts accordingly, either through value-adding strategies in the hard-budget environment or through value-subtracting strategies in the soft-budget context.

CONTROLLING THE CONTROLLERS: THE STATE INTERVENTION SIDE OF THE NESTED PROBLEMS

Undoubtedly, a key component of the nested problems dynamic involves insecure property rights and excessive state intervention. The problem in China, and in transitional systems as a whole, is not that property rights are poorly aligned but rather that the rights themselves are virtually nonexistent. A brief comparison between market and command economies makes this point a bit clearer.[14] In market economies, resources are assigned, by means of property rights, to the exclusive use of private individuals or groups of individuals.[15] The holders of these rights possess a legal claim over assets, a claim which – though subject to challenge and dispute – can be defended in a court and upheld by the sovereign laws of the land. Holders of private property presumably seek to maximize their own material gain and, bearing the full costs and benefits derived from use of their asset, engage in voluntary transactions with each other. These horizontal transactions between buyers and sellers, coordinated through the bottom-up market mechanisms of price and competition, and anchored in the institution of private property, presumably translate individual interest maximization into a socially acceptable allocation of goods.

However, centrally planned systems – usually adopted under conditions of intense resource scarcity and an overwhelming desire to initiate rapid heavy industrial growth – avoid leaving such vital issues as societal allocation up to the "invisible hand" of the market. In the command system, resources are not handed over to the exclusive use of individuals but are instead held communally. Rather than being achieved spontaneously through bottom-up market mechanisms, allocation is instead carefully prescribed by a group of governmental planners, officials who presumably have a privileged sense of the interests of society at large. As noted earlier, the flow of inputs and outputs throughout society, particularly in the industrial sector, is set through a series of hierarchically arranged government bureaus, with the industrial producer (the firm) sitting at the bottom of the stack. Information about capabilities flows upward, and orders for specific input and output targets flow downward to the producer. Transactions in the economy are not between autonomous, horizontally arranged actors, but instead occur between vertically arranged superiors and subordinates. Goods flow not laterally from producer to consumer but rather up and down from producer to allocating agency and back down to the consumer.

In command systems, government officials certainly do have extraordinary degrees of control, particularly over industrial producers and particularly in the area of resource flows. Yet, mighty though these powers may be, they do not derive from any right per se; they do not flow from any sort of legal claim grounded in sovereign law. Rather, these powers are simply exercised in the name of state authority. They are assigned by the highest officials of the state downward through the planning apparatus, and in no real sense can be viewed as subject to challenge, transfer, or debate. Holding a clear monopoly over coercive power in society, the government intervenes because it can, not because it is entitled. That is not to say that the powers are always clear. They may be held simultaneously by different agencies employing thousands of bureaucrats. Perhaps more important, the agencies themselves may lack the information needed to exercise these powers. Nevertheless, although it does not spell out property rights or other legal claims to ownership, the system does indeed have coordinating mechanisms. It coordinates by fiat, by direct orders from superior to subordinate agencies. It is this hierarchical coordinating mechanism that, for better or worse, substitutes for property rights in the command system.

This point about nonexistent property rights may amount to little more than semantics when the command system is at its height, but it becomes vitally important when the system begins sputtering and a shift toward the market is required. Centrally planned systems may be effective over the short term in channeling the nation's resources into industrial development, but as policy makers in the former Soviet Union, China, and Eastern Europe are all too aware, these systems get bogged down in gross inefficiencies and low productivity. As indicated earlier, planners, no matter how dedicated, prove unable to coordinate efficiently the innumerable transactions of even a relatively undeveloped economy. The information overload simply becomes insurmountable. Information overloads are compounded by skewed incentives at the firm level, economic growth grinds to a halt, and reform becomes not just an abstract goal but an urgent necessity.

When facing this situation as a policy maker, you may feel (as do many Chinese officials) that you need to improve incentives by giving producers what amount to property rights. You may also understand that you need to remove government bureaucrats from the business of micromanaging the firm. Yet how do you do this? You cannot casually transfer property rights from the state to the firm, for there are no rights to transfer. You could declare that property will be owned privately, but there is no legal system to which new owners can appeal if their rights are challenged. There is no sovereign law, no rules, and no tradition which can simultaneously protect new property owners and constrain the governmental organizations that had previously ruled by *dictat*. Meanwhile, though you may formally dismantle the planning apparatus of the state, the numerous agencies which had been part of that apparatus do not simply disappear. They continue to exist, and indeed strive to retain the powers of control and extraction they had once monopolized. It is one thing to abolish state control but another thing entirely to abolish the controllers. Formal control ends, but the controllers remain.

This pattern becomes all the more focused in the urban SOE sector. China, during its nearly thirty-year experience with command planning, developed an extensive state supervisory system over industry, a system far more complex and bureaucratized than anything found on the agricultural side. Heavy industry – whether in China, the Soviet Union, or Eastern Europe – stood at the "commanding heights" of the command system and thus became vested with nearly religious significance.[16] The industrial sector came to be seen as the ultimate expression of national autonomy and the ultimate source for the breakneck growth needed to catch up with the capitalist West.[17] More concretely, the fiscal system, operating through the state-determined price structure, absolutely depended on large state firms for revenue mobilization. In general, just as the hopes of the nation became focused on the industrial sector, so too did the bureaucratic apparatus of the state. Everything in industry would be planned and nothing left to chance. Agencies were set up to determine input and output levels for each industrial sector. Other agencies had to coordinate the plan across sectors. Still other agencies had to set investment levels, investment strategies, employment levels, wages, and a host of other basic factors. An entire apparatus was needed to handle personnel appointments all the way down through the middle levels of enterprise management. In essence, an extremely complex, integrated bureaucratic network developed to achieve macroeconomic planning through micromanagement of the individual firm. The agencies of this network each developed finely honed skills of firm-level intervention and extraction, skills that were then integrated into the entire command process. Although they may not have been particularly effective in managing the economy, these bureaucratic organizations proved extremely skillful in pulling resources out of individual production units and interfering in even the most trivial of managerial decisions.

As noted earlier, the problem is that, when the mystique of command planning begins to dissipate and a decision is made to shift to the market, the bureaucratic apparatus of the old system does not simply disappear into thin air. China may no longer have a serious state plan, but through early 1998 it still had a State Planning Commission. Indeed, there are planning commissions right on down through the provincial and municipal levels as well. All the industrial ministries, investment boards, economic commissions, and fiscal agencies that once managed the "commanding heights" of the economy are still around today, their powers of intervention and extraction diminished perhaps but certainly not dead. These agencies, though they have no clear mission, are staffed by thousands of professional bureaucrats, people who have spent their lives acquiring skills that have been rendered obsolete in the reform economy. Bureaucrats of any stripe do not just stand aside and relinquish power easily.

For reform leaders, declaring war on the state bureaucracy is neither feasible nor necessarily desirable. Political elites in transitional systems, swamped by the tasks of managing change while avoiding social upheaval, are understandably reluctant to alienate the nation's civil employees. Waging the economic battle of shifting from plan to market, while simultaneously waging an open political battle with the entire state bureaucracy, is simply untenable for most reform leaders. Furthermore, the Chinese in particular, through the grim experiences of the Great Leap Forward and Cultural Revolution, are well aware of the catastrophic results that occur when leaders lay siege to the very institutions and agencies of civil governance. Mao Zedong proved that the state apparatus can indeed be brought to its knees, but also that utter chaos ensues when alternative agencies fail to arise in replacement. Most reform leaders, whether in Russia, Eastern Europe, or China, have had their fill of making revolution and wreaking havoc upon their own people. The mission of reform is to bring change, not destruction. The agencies of the old command system may be cumbersome and trained to perform unneeded tasks, but they also happen to be the only agencies available at the moment, the only agencies maintaining some semblance of national governance. It is clear that, over the long term, the old state planning apparatus must be dismantled, many agencies dissolved, and many others reoriented toward styles of governance better suited to market economics. Governance patterns must shift from micromanagement of the firm to macromanagement of the entire economy. All of these long-term goals, though, are somewhat removed from the more immediate problem. The old agencies of the command system are still around, they will persist for the foreseeable future, and they are causing significant trouble in the industrial economy.

In the Chinese case, a sort of reform trajectory has emerged that to some extent is mirrored in the recent experiences of Russia and Eastern Europe. As reforms in the SOE sector move forward, the locus of firm-level autonomy shifts from control over information to control over actual resources. The firm becomes responsible for acquiring its own inputs, determining its output levels, setting prices, and handling distribution. Policy measures attempt to depoliticize the firm, pull it away from the bureaucracy, and provide what amounts to a set of incentives based on property rights. The planning functions formerly undertaken by the industrial ministries and related agencies no longer have any place in the national economy. Even so, these agencies still try to intervene in basic managerial decisions, still maintain an iron grip over personnel decisions, and – though no longer in control of the flow of goods in and out of industry – still retain the power to pull money out of the state firm.

Unfortunately, the reform process in some senses actually exacerbates the problem of bureaucratic plundering. Under the old system, the state apparatus pumped investment money into the firm and pulled profits out, all in a relatively hierarchical, coordinated bureaucratic process. Whether it was the municipal government, provincial government, or a central agency removing profits from the firm, at least those extractions were part of an overall effort under the state plan. With reform came the need to dismantle this system, and as certainly happened in the Chinese case, sweeping efforts at bureaucratic decentralization were undertaken. Decentralization, though, results not in the destruction but rather in the multiplication of bureaucracy. What has occurred in the Chinese case, and to some extent in the Russian and Eastern European cases as well, has been a general decentralization of authority throughout the state bureaucracy but no corresponding decentralization of accountability. With these changes, even more agencies now claim some sort of power to intervene in the firm – and especially to extract money from it – while few of those agencies bear any responsibility for their actions. The old hierarchical coordinating mechanism of the command system is gone, but government bureaus are left intact to operate on a renegade basis. Indeed, additional agencies, particularly local players, jump into the game. They act in the name of the state but serve their own parochial interests, employing powers of extraction perfected in earlier times. The sheer number and complexity of transactions between firm and state rise precipitously. In the process, accountability becomes increasingly difficult to trace.

Why do sweeping privatization or corporatization measures fail to address this problem? As noted previously, when privatization takes place in transitional economies, rights are not being transferred from the state to the firm but are instead being created from scratch and simply granted to the firm. Typically, transitional systems emerge from a tradition of extensive bureaucratization and paltry legal institutionalization. There is a great deal of government, very little law, and even less subjection of the former to the latter. Under these circumstances, a policy of simply declaring that the SOE will have property rights becomes almost meaningless. The firm is granted a "right" in a system totally devoid of functioning laws, courts, or social traditions needed to support that right. In other words, the firm gets a right in a system in which rights do not count for anything. The property title becomes a weak weapon indeed when the primary challengers to that right are state agencies themselves. After all, it is not as if the property right granted to the firm has somehow been taken away from the state agencies. The currency of the bureaucracy is authority, not rights. The bureaucratic agencies of the old system continue interfering in the firm, and they do it not as owners of the firm but as agents of the state. They could care less what sort of "rights" the firm has.

As will be illustrated by the case studies in Chapters 4–6, it is now typical in China for the municipal government of a small city to march into a major national SOE and demand huge, above-quota tax payments that will then be used to fund various ad hoc local projects. Technically, the local government should have no authority over the firm, but what is the firm to do in this situation? To whom can it appeal? The municipality, though pursuing its own policies and interests, acts under the unassailable authority of the state writ large. The firm (whether public or private) cannot turn around and sue the state or appeal to some sort of higher law. The state, as decentralized and disorganized as it is in the reform era, *is* the law. The simple extension of a property right under these circumstances is thoroughly ineffectual. When the large firm is state-owned, predatory agencies extract profit in their role as owners. If the firm is declared "private," those same agencies will extract tax money in their role as agents of governmental authority. Unfortunately, as reform becomes increasingly focused on the question of "who owns," the state intervention problem is never quite resolved. Nominal ownership changes hands, yet the institution of ownership itself remains tenuous at best.[18]

Nevertheless, as difficult as this issue is to solve, it represents only half the problem surrounding SOE reform in transitional systems, and it is only one obstacle of many in the establishment of a functioning system of property rights. State predation is no doubt destructive but, at least in theory, it should have a clear limit: the termination of the firm. In other words, local actors may plunder, but that behavior should be limited by the exhaustion of resources, an exhaustion that should indicate to central policy makers the extent of the problem. The firm should ultimately have some sort of final "bottom line" that, once transgressed, should serve as a signal to outside observers. Yet this bottom line seems perplexingly absent in the Chinese SOE. Agencies of the state keep plundering, yet the central banks keep injecting capital. Meanwhile, managers themselves frequently cooperate in the process, turning over extraordinary amounts of tax money with little hue and cry.

Why should central policy makers on one end, and local managers on the other, all cooperate in a process that seems diametrically opposed to their respective interests? Clearly, there is something far more complex going on here, something that cannot be explained just by local–state or managerial rent seeking. Although such rent seeking no doubt occurs, the real question is why the central banks keep pumping in the financing that fosters only more rent seeking. In other words, how is state predation – behavior that in theory should constitute just a one-shot exhaustion of resources – converted into a repeated cycle over time? Why do the bank loans that facilitate the cycle keep getting extended? To understand the answer to that question, one must turn to the issue of corporate governance – more precisely, to the intrinsic *failure* of corporate governance in the transitional context.

BARRIERS TO EFFECTIVE ENTERPRISE GOVERNANCE IN
TRANSITIONAL SYSTEMS

Corporate governance in any economy can be seen as a twofold issue. First, from the perspective of actual enterprise owners, there is the question of how to provide incentives for managers to maximize return on investment. In other words, incentives must be created for managers to act in the interests of owners, and mechanisms must be established to provide owners with the type of data needed to monitor managerial performance. The manager needs to know that, if resources are used inefficiently and firm-level performance declines, this information will find its way back to the owners and the manager's career prospects will then suffer.

Second, from the perspective of the market as a whole, there must be mechanisms through which unsuccessful, inefficient firms can be distinguished from successful, efficient firms and ultimately culled out. This issue is clearest in financial markets, where credit and investment need to be simultaneously channeled toward value-enhancing, efficient firms and withdrawn from value-destroying, inefficient ones. Clearly, the selection and incentive aspects of enterprise governance go hand-in-hand. The very real threats of bankruptcy and possible liquidation of the firm serve as powerful performance incentives for managers.[19] On a more subtle level, through the process of weeding out good firms from bad, functioning financial markets reinforce firm-level managerial incentives and send important signals to owners. Effective managerial behavior is rewarded with additional investment, the kind of investment that allows for growth and greater profit generation in the future. Growth then attracts more investment. Meanwhile, ineffective behavior is punished through the withdrawal of credit. As this withdrawal hampers performance, creditors become increasingly unwilling to supply more capital. In effect, efficient firms are given the means to expand while inefficient firms are driven from the market.

For enterprise governance to work in both its incentive and selection roles, firm-level performance data must actually mean something, and mean something consistently from firm to firm. It is not only that raw numbers regarding a given firm's profitability or liquidity must be available but also that the information must actually reflect circumstances within the firm. The information must actually tell you something about current firm-level performance and changes in performance over time. The data must provide a sense of whether firms are in reality destroyers or enhancers of value. Regardless of any apparent market orientation or of any perceived marketlike behavior, does the given firm actually produce assets of greater value than what it consumes, or is it simply subtracting value through the production process?

In the kind of transitional system represented by China, however, the problem is that firm-level information becomes severely distorted, and distorted in rather unpredictable ways. Once this information ceases to be a reliable indicator of firm-level performance, the selection and incentive processes so critical for making a developed market economy function never actually work, regardless of who owns the firm. The system becomes plagued with extraordinary agency problems, for there is no consistent information upon which either owners can evaluate managers or the market can credibly weed out poorly performing firms. The central government, unable to distinguish good firms from bad and fearing the effects of widespread unemployment, has little choice but to bail out any and all firms in financial distress.[20] In turn, SOE managers understand this, and their budget constraint inevitably softens. Local officials likewise understand this, tax the firm accordingly, and end up facing soft budgets at the local governmental level. The firm serves as both a conduit for central–local transfers and as an instrument for softening the budget constraint of the locality. In effect, unfettered lending lifts any effective restraints against rent-seeking behavior at both the firm and the governmental level.

64

The Nested Problems Dynamic: An Alternative Approach

In China today, the information distortions that undermine corporate governance fall into three broad patterns. First, there are the obscure financial circumstances inherited by the firm from its operations in the command era. Second, there are the financial irregularities associated with the unclear property-rights situation between firm and state in the postcommand era. Third, and arguably most significant, there are the financial distortions related to the general dysfunction of China's financial markets and banking sector. Unfortunately, the second and third areas have been unintentionally exacerbated by the series of "market-oriented" reform measures pursued over the past fifteen years. Some of the best-intentioned policies have led to unanticipated, and decidedly negative, outcomes.

Tilted Playing Fields and the Inheritance from Command Planning

The problems associated with the legacy of command planning boil down to one basic question: How should assets and liabilities inherited from the command era be valued today? In other words, any Chinese state firm that was in operation prior to the early 1980s – and that would include most of the country's state firms – inherited certain assets and debts from the command period. Yet the level of assets or liabilities inherited had little if anything to do with objective measures of the firm's performance. The reason is that, in the days of command planning, prices were set by the state at levels that expressly did not reflect relative scarcities. Furthermore, firms never paid interest on investment. What that meant was that, during the command era, some firms, namely those converting low-priced inputs into high-priced outputs, were by definition profitable, while other firms, particularly the producers of low-priced goods, were by definition unprofitable. The differences were simply made up by pumping investment back down into those firms that did not generate revenue on their own. Profitability was determined a priori by the price structure – a structure that itself reflected the state's effort to channel revenues into producers of final industrial goods – and could not be taken as any indicator of firm-level performance. Instead, output became the prime measure of performance.

Given this legacy, not all firms ended up on the same footing when command planning ceased. Moreover, not all firms started from the same footing when told to shift over to market-oriented operations. In other words, certain firms emerged from the command era with considerable assets while others were awash in government debt. These financial outcomes had little to do with firm-level performance but were instead simply artifacts of the previous era's distorted price structure. Furthermore, at least in the Chinese case, industrial prices were liberalized only gradually in the reform era, so these distortions in performance data continued even after firms were expected to reorient toward the market. Under such circumstances, it was quite conceivable that a highly efficient state firm could appear unprofitable and severely indebted, while an extremely inefficient firm might be able to show significant profits and an impressive asset-to-debt ratio.

Most important, given the confusion surrounding financial data, it becomes feasible for a mismanaged, truly inefficient firm to blame its financial difficulties on the particular situation it inherited from the command era. How is a policy maker to know the difference? How is an owner or potential investor to understand the difference? How is it possible to discern whether negative financial performance, and a firm's subsequent inability to attract capital, is the product of factors endogenous to the firm or of factors related more to arbitrary systemic and historic conditions?

The social welfare responsibilities inherited from the command era serve actually to expand the range of distortions possible in enterprise performance data. Most SOEs expend considerable resources on worker housing, retirement benefits, and medical care, all responsibilities inherited from the command era and basically alien to operations in a market economy. Such expenditures obviously impinge on the firm's financial performance, but by how much? How can you – as a government official, or a potential private investor, or an owner – tell whether social welfare costs are bankrupting the firm or just being used as an excuse to cover up losses accrued through mismanagement?

In general, because negative performance outcomes can always be blamed on factors exogenous to the firm, a key constraint on managerial behavior is lifted. As noted earlier, the interesting thing about reform is not so much the "rights" extended to managers but rather the nature of constraints that shape the exercise of autonomy. Certain kinds of constraints can encourage managerial autonomy to be used toward productive rather than rent-seeking ends. The relative presence or absence of these constraints, then, go a long way toward explaining the most interesting patterns of variation observed in the transitional context.

The Variable Impact of State Predation

Similar ambiguities are produced by the second category of information-related governance problems, those involving governmental predation upon the state firm. We noted earlier that, because of the opaque property-rights situation, large state firms are subject to financial extraction and asset stripping by a wide variety of government agencies. Yet such forms of intervention, frequently occurring on an extemporaneous basis, rarely apply consistently across firms even in a single industry. Real rates of taxation, in effect, differ from firm to firm.[21] A highly efficient and profitable enterprise may become an excellent target for ad hoc extraction, and may indeed be forced into a liquidity crisis simply by virtue of its tax bill. Many Chinese managers have become quite familiar with the governmental strategy of "whipping the fast ox" (*bian da kuai niu*), the practice of "rewarding" successful firms with higher tax levies. Rarely, though, are the cases so clear-cut. Instead, it becomes exceedingly difficult to distinguish efficient firms actually being taxed to death from inefficient firms simply using the tax issue to mask poor performance. It is frankly quite hard to establish market-oriented incentives in the SOE when managers know that the results of their efforts – whether positive or negative – will be swamped by the impact of the tax bill.

The same ambiguities inevitably apply to market selection. When the tax bill is both excessive and thoroughly unpredictable, on what basis should decisions about extending credit be based? On what performance information should questions of future solvency be determined? Which are the "good" firms, and which are truly the "bad"?

Again, and most significant, the presence of such grave ambiguity removes key constraints for a number of economic actors. As long as informational uncertainties exist, accountability becomes virtually impossible to pinpoint, while opportunities for rent seeking expand greatly. Indeed, in an environment of such distorted information flows, rent-seeking behavior becomes nearly untraceable. A manager has little incentive to fight excessive taxation by local actors. Instead, by turning over vast sums to the state, the manager can at once signal his patriotic fervor and absolve himself of any negative outcome in the firm. His own managerial mistakes can be hidden in the shadow of his firm's great financial contributions to the community. By participating in the cycle, the manager creates a safety net for himself.

The success of reform ultimately turns on the extent to which informational uncertainties can be circumvented and constraints on behavior reimposed. Key economic actors, in effect, must be forced to shift toward the market. It is not so much that they must be "forced to be free" as that they have to be forced to use their autonomy in value-enhancing, growth-promoting ways. Rights in any economy do not guarantee growth-oriented behavior. Economic actors always face a range of behavioral choices encompassing everything from pure rent seeking to pure productivity maximization. In transitional systems, the opportunities to enjoy the former are numerous and the pressures to pursue the latter severely lacking. The primary, and absolutely crucial, task of reform is to reverse that pre-existing balance between opportunity and constraint.

Financial Markets and the Impact of Uncontrolled Lending

A key determinant of the balance between opportunity and constraint is China's state banking sector. It is from the state banking sector, and from the general collapse of the "rules of the game" surrounding borrowing, that the most important informational distortions and corporate governance problems derive.

Over the past fifteen years, the role of the state banking system has changed dramatically. Under the old command system, capital was allocated directly by the state planning agencies, and banks served little more than a basic accounting function. Beijing would set credit quotas to be allocated to different firms and savings targets to be collected from enterprise profits. The banks served as "cashiers" for the state, doling out the investments assigned from Beijing and pulling in the savings represented by firm-level "profits."[22] The savings would then be cycled back down to other firms as centrally allocated investment. The banks simply kept the accounts as the state planners cycled financial resources from one part of the economy to the next. Financial institutions, therefore, certainly played no selection function – they did not determine to whom the credit quotas could be assigned – nor did they play much of a monitoring function.[23] Once ordered to release funds to a given firm, the bank no longer actually monitored the investment project at hand. Higher-level planning agencies, at least in theory, were to perform that role.

Of course, numerous incentive problems emerged under this system. Capital was on the one hand essentially free but on the other hand strictly rationed by the planners. Hence, firms with the best political connections, rather than those offering the highest potential return on investment, attracted the bulk of scarce capital. Furthermore, because capital carried no cost, there was relatively little pressure on the firm to maximize efficiency of investment. Indeed, the incentives pointed in the opposite direction. In order to guarantee continued levels of investment in future years, firms made sure they consumed fully the current year's allocation, regardless of need. Firms habitually overestimated their capital requirements simply to ensure that, if output targets were increased in the future, necessary capital would always be on hand. China's state enterprises displayed all the characteristic ills of the socialist enterprise: sagging efficiency, low returns on capital, and an insatiable appetite for investment.

Under such conditions, China surprisingly still managed to maintain fairly impressive annual industrial growth from the 1950s to the 1970s. The problem, however, was that growth could be maintained only at ever-escalating costs. Particularly by the 1970s, the levels of gross investment needed to realize incremental gains in industrial output were rising precipitously. More and more resources had to be pulled out of society at large to keep industry growing. Living standards suffered accordingly.[24] Put somewhat more simply, China was getting less bang for its investment buck, even as ordinary people were being increasingly pressed to notch in their belts.

An overarching goal of Chinese reform was to correct this problem by improving the efficiency of investment. The key to accomplishing this would be to make allocation of investment more market-oriented. At least in theory, the idea was that direct government subsidies would be replaced by bank loans that would carry real interest rates and real requirements for repayment. Once commercialized – that is, directed to make loans on a for-profit basis – banks could play a true market selection function. The banks, in effect, would pick winners and losers among firms and then channel capital accordingly. As bankers sought to maximize their own returns on investment, capital would presumably flow to the most efficient firms, and productivity-oriented incentives would arise at the firm level.

Actually achieving this outcome, however, has proven extremely difficult for the Chinese, far more difficult than any other aspect of reform pursued since 1978. Much of the problem involves the inherent complexity of capital markets and the vast information flows needed to make those markets function rationally. Unlike activities in most markets, capital market transactions involve intertemporal trades. The asset, money, is given today in exchange for a promise to pay tomorrow.[25] It is not enough that the provider of the good sell to the highest bidder, for it is never clear that the highest bidder today will actually be able to pay either tomorrow or whenever the loan comes due. The provider of capital, therefore, cannot simply sell to the highest bidder per se, but instead only to the highest bidder most likely to repay in the future. This distinction injects a tremendous amount of uncertainty into the transaction and places a tremendous burden upon the provider of the good. In general with capital markets, there are always more people who claim to have good uses for funds than there are funds available, and there are always more people promising future repayment than people who will actually be able to pay.[26] In order for financial markets to function, it is therefore not enough to set interest rates at market-clearing levels: no matter how high the rates, somebody will always be willing to promise repayment at a later date. Instead, financial markets demand that the providers of capital engage in complex selection and monitoring processes vis-à-vis investment recipients.

Selection and monitoring, however, require a great deal of information and institutionalization. Effective selection is possible only when banks can obtain reliable information about firm-level performance, information that is itself dependent on consistent reporting and valuation rules. Similarly, monitoring can be effective only if the banks have legal recourse to enforcement mechanisms. In one way or another, contracts must be enforceable if financial markets are to function. Laws must exist to protect creditors and pressure debtors.

Chinese financial markets are in chaos today precisely because they fail to perform either the selection or monitoring role coherently. They do allocate capital, but in a manner capturing the benefits of neither command nor market systems. Changes have undoubtedly occurred. Indeed, in 1983, the government fully restructured the nation's financial sector through the creation of a two-tiered, state-owned commercial banking system.[27] The Industrial and Commercial Bank of China was spun off as a separate commercial lending operation from the People's Bank of China, while the People's Bank of China itself continued on as a central bank. Nevertheless, in subsequent years, China's state-owned commercial banks have always been caught in a sort of middling position. They have achieved unprecedented autonomy and authority, the kind of authority that allows them under certain circumstances to make independent lending decisions. At the same time, they have retained their old command-era role as the cashiers of the government, channeling money from state coffers into state-owned enterprises. The result is a rather dangerous incentive environment. The banks have considerable autonomy and access to state resources but precious little accountability.

This awkward situation of autonomy without accountability is important, and it is worth exploring somewhat more deeply. State banks during the reform era have been granted access to state funds and told to lend those funds on a commercial basis. Banks are supposed to be responsible for their own balance sheets, and banking performance is supposed to be measured by profitability. At the same time, though, whenever a major state firm is threatened with financial collapse, central authorities not only provide bailout subsidies, but also elect to provide those subsidies in the form of "policy loans" from commercial banks. In other words, government officials order the commercial banks to pump in subsidy loans, loans that are counted against the books of the commercial bank. Of course, these loans would never be made if purely commercial standards were applied, and they are unlikely ever to be repaid. Therefore, the policy loans do little more than saddle the banks with considerable levels of nonperforming debt.

Once the bank's own books become awash in red ink, banking officials themselves begin to face distorted incentives. The banks have no hope of becoming profitable, but they still have autonomy in many lending decisions. Furthermore, they still enjoy a steady stream of central capital through their role as cashiers for state-sector bailouts. Once again, a serious moral hazard problem arises. Because of centrally directed policy lending, many banks cannot possibly be profitable no matter how successful their commercial operations. The undermined balance sheet, however, can then serve as a cushion for bank officials. Poor lending decisions or financial losses on the commercial side can always be subsumed under the overall losses declared on the balance sheet. In the end, bank officials have the power to make their own lending decisions but can never really be held accountable for bad loans. Not surprisingly, ill-advised and high-risk lending occurs under these circumstances, the type of lending illustrated in Chapter 6 with the case of Capital Iron and Steel. Once they have made policy loans directed from above, bank officials have nothing to lose by simply loaning the rest of their available capital to the highest bidder, regardless of the bidder's creditworthiness. After all, in the unlikely chance that the loan is repaid, the bank will make a handsome profit; in the more likely event of default, the bank can always be bailed out by the central state.

Meanwhile, as long as the commercial banking sector serves as the chosen vehicle for pumping in SOE "policy" loans, the central state cannot credibly threaten to stop bailing out insolvent banks. The government, in effect, loses the few levers it has to force ostensibly "commercial" banks actually to operate on a commercial basis. It simply cannot threaten to shut down a failing bank, for how can it tell whether bank losses are due to poor lending decisions or to state-directed SOE subsidization? The state can no more easily select banks for shutdown than it can select SOEs for shutdown. Bailing out SOEs may not be great policy, but ordering ostensibly "commercial" state banks to provide those subsidies is just plain disastrous.

At a more conceptual level, China's banking system reflects an environment in which assets have become increasingly decentralized while liabilities remain highly centralized.[28] Bank officials, in effect, can allocate nearly limitless supplies of capital that are not their own. Through all the haphazard lending that takes place, the banking system performs a selection function that is not market-oriented, and it completely abdicates on monitoring responsibilities. Meanwhile, since contracts to repay are not enforced, capital ends up being free, though allocated in a totally irrational manner. The worst state firms gain access to policy loans, and in general the worse they perform the more loans they get. Yet, as will be shown in Chapter 6, the better performers can also attract soft discretionary loans – high-risk loans that end up funding terribly ill-conceived ventures. Potentially viable firms, once exposed to soft lending, lose any incentives to maximize productivity. Meanwhile, amidst all this credit expansion, the various forms of lending (policy lending, commercial lending, gray-area lending) become indistinguishable. The only clear thing is that, in the Chinese state sector today, financial resources are allocated neither by plan nor by market. Instead, chaos reigns.

The chaos is compounded by the "triangular" debt (interenterprise lending) situation. Firm-level liquidity crises are dealt with in a variety of manners by the Chinese. In some cases, state officials themselves direct "healthy" SOEs to extend credit to, or actually take over, financially depleted SOEs. In other cases, a cash-rich SOE may, of its own volition, elect to lend to or merge with a poorly performing SOE. Finally, a poor performer may simply "force credit" on another firm by accepting deliveries of goods and then refusing to pay. Once again, it becomes extremely difficult to distinguish between these cases and their respective impact on firm-level balance sheets. This is all the more true because, prior to the accounting reforms of 1993, Chinese industrial firms were still employing more than seventy different methods of accounting.[29] There simply was no standardization and no adherence to clear rules of the game, even as autonomy was increasingly devolving down to the level of economic actors – be they banks, firms, or individuals.

The implications for corporate governance are quite serious. As long as budget constraints in the banking system remain soft – in other words, as long as banks can rely on continual bailouts from central authorities – budget constraints at the firm level will remain soft, regardless of who happens to own the firm.[30] The problem actually goes beyond soft budgets and accumulated debts. In China, and in transitional economies in general, no single selection principle ever really takes hold. Instead, a multitude of selection standards coexist simultaneously. China's malfunctioning financial markets are but one example. Some firms get loans because they lose tremendous amounts of money, other firms get loans because they earn tremendous amounts of money, and still other firms get loans because they happen to be politically well-connected. Because the selection principle is constantly shifting, firms themselves face continually shifting incentives, regardless of ownership. In other words, as David Stark has pointed out with regard to Hungary, firms in transitional economies must worry about more than whether their products will sell or whether their return on investment will be high enough.[31] In addition, they must continually ponder the possibility that proof of market-oriented success will be neither necessary nor sufficient to guarantee future credit flows and hence their survival. Even if managers know that they must maximize profits or return on investment – in other words, even if basic market objectives hold – managers cannot be sure what counts in terms of securing access to credit and other resources. Indeed, showing huge losses may be just as good a means of gaining access to resources, and ultimately of converting those resources into return on investment, as showing huge profits or high efficiency. As the case studies in Chapters 4–6 suggest, managers may want to show desperate financial need, high profits, and great efficiency simultaneously!

In an environment embodying such organizational uncertainty, clarifying ownership alone does not solve the problem. No matter who owns the firm, managers face incentives to pursue all sorts of hedging strategies, all sorts of multiple accounts of their actions, and all sorts of multiple claims to continued credit flows.[32] Even if the government were to forgive the years of accumulated debts, and even if the playing field inherited from the command era were somehow leveled out and the system permitted to restart from scratch, the fundamental incentive problem at the firm level would still exist. As long as the selection process for credit allocation remains uncertain, performance objectives at the firm level will also remain uncertain, and non–market-oriented behavior will just as likely be rewarded as market behavior. All of this will occur, and does occur, even when managerial objectives are phrased in financial terms. Over time, the debts will just accumulate once more, and societal resources will continue to be squandered – whether by private firms, public firms, or firms conveniently caught somewhere in between.

THE DYNAMIC IN OPERATION

By conceptualizing SOE reform as a deeply intertwined property-rights and governance problem – a nested problems dynamic – we can see how essentially value-subtracting, nonmarket outcomes are produced despite the best intentions of policy makers and firm-level managers. Through the interaction of the property-rights and enterprise governance problems, Chinese SOEs end up plunging downward in an ever-tightening spiral, a spiral that the government drives forward through the provision of subsidies and a number of other reform measures. With the disintegration of the command system, enterprise-level cost structures and performance information have become thoroughly unreliable and readily subject to distortion. Nobody quite knows how to correct for the nonlevel playing field passed on from the command era. Under these conditions, allocation of capital – whether directly by state agencies or through the

73

banks – cannot be based on any consistent selection mechanism, but instead moves forward rather indiscriminately. That a firm might be raking in investment ceases to be an indicator of its productivity in market terms. Indeed, it might be an indicator that the firm is in dire financial straits.

Once firms receive capital, however, numerous government agencies – agencies that have been forced to shoulder all manner of new financial burdens in the reform era – have an excuse to come in and extract. Furthermore, because most of those agencies have no clearly traceable influence on (or responsibility for) the long-term fate of that firm, profit extraction becomes all the more indiscriminate. Excessive extraction, by further distorting firm-level performance, provides managers an added excuse to go to the banks for more loans. "We need money because we are a major source of revenue to the state," or "we need money because we would be tremendously profitable if it weren't for all the extraction going on," or "we deserve money because we have made so many sacrifices for the state" replace the more standard market notion of "you should lend us money because we offer you tremendous returns on investment."[33] The system just keeps chugging on, with the banks pumping in money, government agencies pulling out money, and any funds remaining at the firm level hardly monitored at all.

Such a system, where authority is separated from accountability and control over assets is frequently detached from responsibility for liabilities, develops a logic of its own for all the players involved. Managers benefit because, no matter what mistakes they make and no matter how badly their firms perform, blame can always be placed on exogenous factors. As the following case-study chapters illustrate, managers can choose any number of systemic reasons why their poorly performing firm is entitled to investment; so long as information remains sketchy, all of these reasons appear to be plausible. Some actually *are* plausible.

The banks benefit because, as long as they maintain a middling position between plan and market, they will always be able to extract some rents from the allocation decisions they control. In other words, as long as information remains opaque and banks can excuse losses as the result of forced "policy loans," banking officials can always manage to make some high-risk loans on their own. Payoffs may be unlikely, but when they come they are substantial, and if they do not then the losses are absorbed by the center.

Governmental agencies at all levels benefit, for as long as confusion reigns they can claim assets through extraction. They can tax firms that in a more rational system would have long ago been driven into insolvency. Indeed, all actors benefit, for they can claim assets while passing risk and liability onto the amorphous "body politic." After all, it is the public that ultimately pays.

74

For the time being, the severity of this payment has been offset by growth in the "new economies," the rural collective and urban service sectors. However, with the sort of liabilities being accumulated by SOEs in the 1990s, the ability of these growth sectors to offset the languishing state sector is falling into doubt. Revenue generated by nonstate firms and individual households ends up as savings deposits in the banking system. Those savings deposits are then loaned out to state firms, the capital gets squandered, and the level of nonperforming loans in the system rises. This pattern is simply not sustainable over time. More generally, as reform continues to disperse authority while centralizing liability and as economic actors then push the process on their own, the nested problems phenomenon starts spiraling out of control.

Viewing SOE reform as a nested dynamic also clarifies just why it is that conventional privatization measures, or at least efforts to separate the state-owned firm from the government, do not work very well in transitional systems. Post-command industrial reforms, whether phrased in terms of "privatization" or "depoliticization" or "marketization," and whether they take place in China or in the former Soviet bloc, have a common theme. They all attempt to impose market-oriented incentives on managers by severing the traditional tie between the state and the industrial firm. Put somewhat differently, the reforms attempt to harden the firm's budget constraint and raise productivity by cutting its access to public funds while simultaneously granting the firm the kind of autonomy that will allow it to respond to market opportunities.

The goal is perfectly fine, but the problem is frequently misunderstood as one almost exclusively of ownership or control. The question mistakenly becomes one of asking how to remove control from the state and place that control in somebody else's hands, somebody either within or outside the firm. Only half the nested problem phenomenon is considered – the property-rights issue – while governance and regulatory issues are virtually ignored. By addressing only half of the problem, policy makers end up exacerbating the whole problem, particularly with regard to larger industrial firms. As the state is driven out, the modicum of monitoring and control that existed under the old system virtually disappears, yet nothing arises in replacement. The banking system still operates on a soft budget, and standards for credit selection remain in flux. Managers may face new owners – the managers themselves may be the owners – but firm-level survivability still remains detached from normal market-oriented performance standards. Indeed, given all the unresolved information problems (which are exacerbated by the retreat of state auditors), it becomes increasingly difficult for all parties concerned to have any real sense of what is going on inside the firm. At least with regard to the modern industrial sector,

75

the inefficient system of command planning is replaced by no control at all. As performance slackens, two options become available. Either widespread bankruptcies occur – bankruptcies that are as likely to drag down efficient firms as inefficient ones – or the government can elect once again to pump in the subsidies. The handcuffs, in effect, just get tighter and tighter.

Through its emphasis on not just the rights but also the constraints that lead to market-oriented behavior, the nested problems perspective offers a way out. It suggests that what explains market-oriented behavior on the part of both managers and decentralized taxing authorities is the existence of hard budgets at the firm level. A hard budget constraint neither precludes rent-seeking behavior nor guarantees effective decision making. It does, however, place an ultimate price on rent seeking and ineffective management. By threatening the firm with liquidation, a strict budget constraint places a final cap on the amount of resources that can be diverted away from productive use. If too much is pulled out then the firm simply goes bankrupt. Clearly, hard budget constraints must be imposed on the firm, and they must be imposed quickly.

Imposing hard budgets, however, involves actively circumventing the logic of the nested problems dynamic. In other words, the dynamic serves the interests of many key economic and political actors while passing all the costs on to the general public, which has no voice in the political process. Obviously, though, the general public's paying for this situation – through either inflation, unemployment, or declining living standards – is of concern to top policy makers. One need not search too widely in Beijing to find central officials who are utterly panicked at the prospect of failing SOEs and massive urban unemployment.

The point is that if anything is to be done about the situation then decisive action must be taken, action that runs against the interests of key players. The path of least resistance is to keep pumping in the money while allowing local players to continue extracting. The path toward effective reform, though, requires a decisive move by the center to sever the links between state banks, state firms, and local state agencies. The center must wield its authority – authority that is still considerable in contemporary China – to cut the firm off from the banks and reconstitute lines of accountability. Contrary to what rights-based approaches suggest, the state, in a very specific fashion, must actually be linked *closer* to the large SOE. The power of the central state must be brought in so that even the most basic forms of corporate governance can be restored. Only after that is accomplished can real consideration of property-rights issues even begin. Until then, further efforts to expand autonomy at the local and managerial level will only exacerbate the situation. Autonomy without corresponding constraints will just expand opportunities for rent seeking as well as the power of local actors to force financial transfers from the center. Under such conditions, the SOE, rather than serving any productive role, becomes little more than a conduit for central–local financial transfers, and an inefficient conduit at that.

Part II

ENTERPRISE CASE STUDIES: THE COMMANDING HEIGHTS IN TRANSITION

4

The Living Museum of Iron and Steel Technology

THE best way to understand the "nested problems" dynamic and related dilemmas of SOE restructuring is to delve into the operations of the individual firm.[1] This chapter will do that by focusing upon the Anshan Iron and Steel Company, a 220,000-employee integrated steel operation based in Liaoning Province, the heart of China's Manchurian "rust belt."[2]

Anshan Iron and Steel, known informally as "Angang," once stood at the commanding heights of China's planned economy. The whole point of command economics was to foster firms like Angang. Indeed, command planning was so appealing precisely because it could direct resources to heavy industrial producers in ways that markets never could.[3] Without the plan, such firms could never have survived in China. In the heyday of the command era, Angang received virtually all of its investment capital and inputs *from* the plan, and it produced virtually all of its output *for* the plan. The system set clear managerial incentives: output was to be maximized at given levels of state-allocated inputs. The clear goal was to match annual production targets.

Needless to say, staggering changes have swept across Angang since the days of command planning. Over the past fifteen years, the entire system of state allocation has essentially been dismantled, and the industrial behemoths that once served that system now struggle to negotiate a transition to the market. For the most part, goods now flow freely between producers and consumers. Prices, even for many basic industrial inputs, have been liberalized. Direct state subsidies to heavy industry have been scaled back significantly. Now that the plan is gone, firms have become responsible for obtaining their own inputs and selling their own outputs. Firms are now required to marshal their own investment capital, primarily from the state banking system and other newly emerging financial intermediaries. State-owned enterprises like Angang are told repeatedly that they must revitalize their operations, remake themselves into efficient market actors, and recast themselves as attractive investment opportunities for outsiders.

Attitudes have certainly shifted as a result. Even the briefest visit to one of these firms, the briefest discussion with managers and workers alike, confirms that the mantra of "output" has been replaced by the mantra of "profit." By dismantling the system of state allocation and fixed prices, Chinese policy makers have clearly changed the environment in which Angang operates. The question, however, is whether they have actually stimulated market-oriented behavior in Angang or in any of its counterparts in the modern industrial sector.

Unfortunately, the answer in the case of Angang is not particularly heartening. The firm has undergone tremendous transformation, particularly in the 1990s, but its performance rather closely mirrors that of the entire faltering state sector. On the one hand, there are impressive profit statements. Angang, like approximately 55 percent of its fellow SOEs, year after year displays rising sales revenue, compelling profit growth, and significant physical expansion. On paper at least, Angang is by no means the worst of China's state firms. After all, it *is* profitable. On the other hand, Angang's growth, like that of the entire state sector, has come at considerable expense. The firm has been amassing tremendous liabilities over the past five years. At the same time, it has been undermining the quality of the assets it still possesses.[4] The Liaoning steel producer often finds itself unable to fund even its daily operations and instead must rely on infusions of short-term credit to stay afloat. Not surprisingly, Angang has been buffeted over the past few years by a number of liquidity crises, some serious enough to impede the firm's ability to issue wages.

Angang, by consuming tremendous amounts of capital to produce goods of decidedly dubious value, exhibits behavior rather typical of the state sector. The firm produces in the absence of demand, undergoes physical expansion in the absence of operating funds, and, not surprisingly, decapitalizes itself in the process. The problem is not that Angang responds slowly to market forces. Rather, it responds in direct opposition to such forces. Indeed, its behavior in many respects constitutes the antithesis of market-oriented production. That a firm like Anshan Iron and Steel keeps chugging along today signifies the misallocation of capital characterizing much of Chinese state industry. Angang may be a basket case, but it is by no means a special case. Despite its exceptional size, it is in many ways a typical Chinese SOE.

In one sense, Angang is typical in terms of the static problems that it has inherited from the prereform period. Angang, like other SOEs, must provide a full range of cradle-to-grave benefits for workers: housing, medical care, child care, pensions, disability insurance; the list goes on and on. Within Angang's company confines are not only vast, smoke-belching blast furnaces and rolling mills but also schools, hospitals, day-care facilities, clinics, and housing complexes. Like many SOEs, Angang is as much a small city as an industrial producer. These characteristics are all the more apparent at large SOEs like Angang, a firm that boasts 220,000 workers and approximately 110,000 pensioners.

Extensive social welfare burdens undoubtedly impact upon the firm and undoubtedly distract managers from normal production-related activities. Nevertheless, it would be a mistake either to overstate the significance of these factors or to assume that, in their absence, the SOE would perform far better. Social welfare burdens are a static issue. They existed before reform, and they still exist today. However, as the case of Angang shows, such burdens have not prevented the industrial producer from declaring profits. Nor are these the factors inherently responsible for Angang's tendency to overproduce and overexpand. Social welfare burdens are certainly part of the explanation for Angang's ills, but they are by no means the whole explanation.

Instead, to understand the morass that Chinese SOEs find themselves in today, one must turn to newer developments in the firm's institutional environment, developments that in many cases were, ironically, pushed to encourage market-oriented behavior. Again, Angang is typical in many respects. It finds itself continually exposed to intervention by local state agencies, agencies empowered by the very policies of governmental decentralization that were intended to undermine command planning. Meanwhile, profit contracts – arrangements intended to rationalize the relationship between firm and state – fail to protect the firm from the state yet do encourage the firm to overproduce and overexpand. Overproduction is then fostered by soft credit, capital that is made available through a banking system that was supposed to be the linchpin of market reform. On top of all that, new accounting standards – intended to permit managers the kind of autonomy that would encourage market behavior – actually make the misapplication of funds or outright decapitalization of the firm even easier.

The very institutional changes that were meant to force market-responsive behavior ultimately undermine such behavior. Firms fail to behave in a market-oriented fashion not because their social welfare burdens are too heavy, not because ownership is in the wrong hands, and not even because managerial autonomy is too narrowly circumscribed. The problem is rather that, given the institutional environment in which the firm operates, governance – and, by extension, ownership – fails to function at all. Indeed, managerial autonomy extended under such circumstances leads not to the enhancement of assets but rather to their destruction. Unfortunately, this seems to be the story of Angang and many other Chinese SOEs. The nation's investment resources are pumped in, but very little of actual value is pumped out.

Table 4.1. *Angang revenue, profit, and fixed asset growth, 1990–95*
(RMB 100 million)

	1990	1991	1992	1993	1994	1995
Sales revenue	77.45	104.02	139.51	189.47	196.94	186.5
[increase from previous year]		34%	34%	36%	4%	−5%
Profit[a]	7.61	9.83	9.99	20.62	22.4	3.32
[increase from previous year]		29%	2%	106%	9%	−85%
Net value of fixed assets	86.49	91.17	147.02	156.03	156.21	168.26
[increase from previous year]		5%	61%	6%	0%	8%

[a] Profits prior to the collection of income tax and assorted nontax fees.
Sources: Ministry of Metallurgical Industry (1991, pp. 319, 331 [1990 data]); Anshan Iron and Steel Company (1993, p. 327 [1991–92 data]); Ministry of Metallurgical Industry (1995, pp. 380, 382, 385 [1993–94 data]; 1996, pp. 346, 348, 351 [1995 data]).

THE FINANCIAL PERFORMANCE OF ANSHAN IRON AND STEEL

At first glance, Angang seems to have performed rather solidly through the early 1990s, at least through 1994. Despite a climate of rapidly accelerating industrial reform and marketization, the firm seemed to weather the storm fairly well. Revenue through the end of 1994 rose steadily and indeed surged upward over 30 percent annually between 1990 and 1993. Profits also surged upward, albeit somewhat more erratically, increasing by nearly a third between 1990 and 1991 and then more than doubling between 1992 and 1993. Moreover, throughout the whole first half of the 1990s, Angang's fixed assets expanded steadily. Table 4.1 appears to tell the story of a firm successfully coping with marketization and expanding physically in the process.

The odd thing is that when speaking with officials in the Ministry of Metallurgical Industry (MMI) or when visiting Angang itself, one hardly gets the impression that the firm is in good financial health. Indeed, through the mid-1990s there was a distinct atmosphere of both stagnation and impending doom within the walls of the Liaoning steel producer. Stories of liquidity crises, production stoppages, and unpaid wages abounded. Officials within MMI privately pointed to Angang as a model for everything that is wrong with state industry, and wondered how the firm could be kept alive. Angang officials themselves routinely referred to their operation as a "living museum of iron and steel technology."[5] Although reluctant to specify the exact nature of the financial crisis at hand,

Table 4.2. *Angang consolidated balance sheet (partial), 1993–95*
(RMB 100 million)

	1993	1994	1995
Assets			
Current assets	108.87	189.18	169.94
Long-term investments	3.83	4.1	3.81
Fixed assets			
Fixed assets at cost	267.31	288.29	320.48
Net fixed assets	156.03	156.21	168.26
Ongoing construction	25.96	32.8	29.42
Total fixed assets	182	188.22	196.92
Intangible assets	0.22	0.76	5.52
Total assets	294.94	382.27	376.2
Liabilities and owner equity			
Current liabilities	142.22	195.7	210.9
Long-term liabilities	41.8	60.2	32.68
Owner equity	110.9	126.38	132.62
Total liabilities and owner equity[a]	294.92	382.28	376.2

[a] Because of rounding errors, columns in some cases do not sum perfectly, and total liabilities and owner equity do not in some cases equal total assets.
Source: Ministry of Metallurgical Industry (1994 [1993 data]; 1995 [1994 data]; 1996 [1995 data]).

they were more than eager to assign blame to a variety of factors: excessive social welfare burdens, excessive taxation, insufficient protection from imports, insufficient investment capital, unreliable customers, and so on. Clearly, there must have been something occurring at Angang beyond what the revenue and profit figures in Table 4.1 indicate.

Certainly one sign of trouble during the mid-1990s was Angang's rising level of short-term, or "current," liabilities.[6] As the balance sheet in Table 4.2 suggests, current liabilities throughout this period outstripped current assets – the firm, in effect, had no net working capital at its disposal.[7] As with many SOEs, Angang's day-to-day operations were maintained primarily through short-term bank loans and credit extended by other enterprises. In 1994, for example, approximately 95 percent of the firm's current liabilities consisted of outside debt; the remainder pertained to unpaid wages or unfunded pension liabilities.[8] It is not surprising that, under such circumstances, the firm proved extremely vulnerable to governmental macrostabilization policies. One of the few effective weapons the central government has against inflation in China is the severe curtailment of bank lending nationwide.[9] If this weapon is employed, as it was in late 1994, then credit is cut off to firms like Angang; when credit is cut, the firm can neither maintain production nor pay workers. This was the dilemma facing Angang in the mid-1990s, and it is the dilemma still facing policy makers in China today.

Contractionary policies lay bare the fact that many SOEs cannot fund their own operations. The government attempts to rein in inflation in order to avoid social unrest, but in doing so ends up temporarily shutting down major producers in the heavy industrial sector. Shutdowns and the accompanying suspension of wages then threaten to provoke the very social unrest that contractionary policies were attempting to avoid. The central government is at this point forced either to tolerate inflation or to increase the extent to which state industry can access household savings through the banking system. Greater flows of household savings to the state sector mean decreased flows of household savings toward the more efficient nonstate sector. In short, as long as the government insists upon pumping working capital into SOEs like Angang, the only real choice is between inflation or reduced GDP (gross domestic product) growth.

Moreover, the rise of short-term liabilities at Angang and many other SOEs is only part of the picture. The arguably more important part involves the declining quality of assets actually possessed by the firm. In the case of Angang, current assets through the mid-1990s became increasingly tied up in receivables (money owed to Angang by steel purchasers) and in inventories (goods that Angang was not able to sell). By the end of September 1994, Angang's current assets were apportioned as follows: 61.5 percent consisted of receivables, money that had not yet been paid to the firm for steel deliveries; 34.4 percent consisted of inventories; 1 percent pertained to unpaid expenses; and just over 3 percent consisted of cash deposits.[10] The firm's "liquid" assets were concentrated in the absolutely least liquid of categories. As will be explained later, a considerable portion of Angang's receivables are unlikely ever to be paid, and the firm's inventories are of equally questionable value. The point is that, for SOEs like Angang, the problem is not just that liabilities are rising relative to assets but also that the asset quality is eroding rapidly. Put more simply, firms like Angang seriously overestimate the value of their liquid assets and, in so doing, mask the firm's slide into financial insolvency. Many of these firms are producing goods they cannot sell, selling goods for which cash cannot be collected, and making up the difference by amassing liabilities.

A sense of the situation can be gleaned from Angang's operations in 1994. Through the first nine months of that year, the firm's revenues were up 6 percent over the previous year, and pretax income was up nearly 37 percent. Nevertheless, the firm was collecting cash for only 38 percent of its sales.[11] The steel company's chief economist noted at the time that, on a per-month basis, Angang required approximately RMB 1.38 billion to maintain normal production activities. Yet, through the end of the third quarter of 1994, the firm was achieving cash returns of only RMB 640 million per month. Hence Angang was producing output and then, in effect, giving that output away to consumers who themselves had no available cash. Angang, devoid of any liquid assets, would in turn then borrow inputs from suppliers. The result at Angang, as with most SOEs, has been an ever-expanding web of interenterprise debt. By the end of the year, Angang owed approximately RMB 8 billion to various creditors (other enterprises and banks) and was owed RMB 11 billion by various debtors.[12] The net debt levels are somewhat questionable, particularly given the reluctance – and, in some cases, the inability – of firms to write off nonperforming loans. What is clearer is that, through 1994, receivables were building up at Angang and cash was desperately short. The firm had little choice but to rely on bank loans to sustain its operations. At the same time, however, the firm was required to pay sales taxes to the state for every sale that was made, regardless of whether cash came in as a result.[13] Hence, just as the firm received cash for only 38 percent of its sales, it proved unable to pay 62 percent of its tax responsibilities. Needless to say, for Chinese SOEs in general, unfunded tax liabilities constitute a portion of the broader solvency problem.

The more important overall point is that, even in an ostensibly high-profit, high-revenue year, Angang was amassing assets – namely, inventories and promises for future payments – that were of highly questionable value. A combination of legal restrictions and firm-level reluctance leads Chinese SOEs to make inadequate provisions for bad debt and bad inventory. As a result, financial data of the kind presented by Angang in 1994 – data frequently used to describe "cash flow" problems – conceal a deeper truth. Angang and many SOEs like it are net destroyers of value. They consume investment resources but fail to produce output that has market value.

The interesting thing is that, despite all these problems in the mid-1990s, Anshan Iron and Steel continued to expand its facilities. As the balance sheet in Table 4.2 indicates, net fixed assets grew throughout the mid-1990s, even in the contractionary 1994–95 period. Levels of ongoing construction also experienced no appreciable decline. The Ministry of Metallurgical Industry's assessment of the situation was that physical expansion and ongoing construction were essentially crowding out working capital – not only at Angang but at many other large steel producers. In the case of Angang, MMI reports point out that, from the end of 1992 to the third quarter of 1994, the gross value of fixed assets and ongoing construction amounted to around RMB 5.3 billion. Accumulated depreciation and retained profits during that period amounted to approximately RMB 5.5 billion.[14] Meanwhile, levels of long-term debt remained relatively stable and short-term debt escalated rapidly. The clear implication is that Angang was diverting its internal resources to long-term expansion while simultaneously using short-term debt to fund operating costs. Again, the broader point is that the firm was operating without any clear budget constraint. Production and physical expansion could move forward regardless of prevailing market conditions and regardless of the firm's ability to generate positive cash flow.

That Angang faced a series of liquidity crises in the mid-1990s is hardly surprising, particularly as the firm had negative net levels of working capital during the period. Somewhat more surprising, however, was the tendency of ostensibly more healthy firms to run into similar problems. The Wuhan Iron and Steel Company provides a good example. Among major Chinese steel producers in the mid-1990s, this firm stood out both for its apparent revenue-generating abilities and its improving liquidity position. Unlike Angang, Wuhan Iron and Steel did enjoy positive levels of working capital. By the end of 1994, the firm's current ratio (the ratio of current assets to current liabilities) stood at 1.27, a 6.5-percent increase over the previous year.[15] On paper anyway, the firm appeared at least to be supporting its own basic production activities through sales revenue. Officials at MMI were therefore somewhat puzzled when, just like Angang, Wuhan Iron and Steel experienced tremendous funding problems toward the end of 1994, particularly as the central government attempted to curtail bank lending.[16]

Wuhan Iron and Steel's cash-flow statement from the period (Table 4.3) provides a sense of just what was going wrong.[17] According to the MMI, the Wuhan steel producer by the end of 1994 had amassed approximately RMB 2.9 billion of receivables and RMB 2.5 billion of payables. In net terms, therefore, the firm was owed RMB 400 million in overdue loans. In addition, the firm in 1994 counted among its current assets inventories worth RMB 1.2 billion. Again according to MMI reports, most of these inventories belonged in the category of "overdue loans."[18] They were, in effect, sales for which no cash had been collected. Of Wuhan Iron and Steel's RMB 1.7-billion net increase to working capital, RMB 1.6 billion actually consisted of overdue loans owed to the firm. In short, the firm's surplus current assets consisted for the most part of bad debt – sales for which the firm would likely never receive cash.

Table 4.3. *Wuhan Iron and Steel, statement of changes in financial position, 1994* [a] *(RMB 100 million)*

	Changes in circulating funds
Increases to current assets	
Monetary funds	8.31
Short-term investment	
Bills receivable	0.56
Accounts receivable	17.91
Advances to suppliers	4.62
Other receivables	6.12
Inventories	12.37
Expenses to be apportioned	8.6
Net increase in current assets	57.98
Increases to current liabilities for the year	
Short-term loans	6.96
Bills payable	1.48
Accounts payable	23.75
Advances from customers	−4.75
Other payables	6.19
Wages payable	6.66
Welfare benefits payable	0.24
Taxes payable	0.04
Other payables	0.04
Withheld expenses	0.34
Long-term liabilities due within the year	0.04
Net increase in current liabilities	40.99
Net increase of circulating funds	16.99

[a] This is a partial statement showing changes in working capital accounts.
Source: Ministry of Metallurgical Industry (1995b).

In one sense, Wuhan Iron and Steel had net working capital simply because it was not properly devaluing nonperforming loans. But in a deeper sense, whether in the case of Angang or Wuhan Iron and Steel, elevated receivables indicate a tendency on the part of the firm to produce in the absence of real market demand. Firms produce as much as possible and sell as much as possible, even when that means giving goods away to customers who are not likely to pay. Ultimately, firms find themselves with cash-flow problems: liquid assets are needed to maintain basic production, pay workers, and cover investment needs. It is the banks, then, that must step in to cover the costs of this decidedly non–market-oriented pattern of production.

As these brief descriptions of financial performance suggest, the problem at firms like Angang or Wuhan Iron and Steel is not that they are unable to earn "profit." The problem is not simply, as many managers suggest, that firms have too many historical burdens – modernization costs, social welfare responsibilities, outdated facilities – and therefore cannot hope to compete on the market. Such burdens lead to high production costs, but if high production costs were the only problem then SOEs would not be showing profits. In other words, the problem is not that Chinese SOEs are simply uncompetitive market actors or ineffective market actors. Rather, the problem is that they are decidedly not market actors. Because Chinese SOEs operate in an environment of inherently soft budgets, they can overproduce, overexpand, sustain themselves on bank credits, and all the while show profits. Historical burdens may contribute to this behavior but certainly do not cause it. Nor does the legacy of command planning cause this problem. Non–market-oriented behavior among SOEs is an artifact of the present system, not of the past one. It is a product of partial reforms that have simultaneously extended autonomy to complex producers, opened new channels of financing, and undermined governance mechanisms. The task of the remaining sections of this chapter will be to show, in the case of Angang, how these processes actually function.

GOVERNMENTAL DECENTRALIZATION AND ANGANG

Angang's complex financial problems stem not from just one cause but from many. All of these causal factors, though, proceed within a general context of muddled authority relations between firm and state in contemporary China. Throughout the 1980s, Chinese reformers aggressively pursued measures to decentralize the nation's bureaucracy. Such measures were not entirely new in China – they had been employed at several points during the command era – and the goals remained relatively straightforward throughout. Governmental decentralization, whether in the 1960s or the 1980s, proved effective in shaking up the hierarchies of the command system and in freeing up goods for local allocation. Even before the reform era, the dissemination of authority to subnational agencies and grass-roots producers was viewed as a means of improving local incentives: local actors would conceivably produce more if they were given greater control over financial or material returns. The more pronounced decentralization efforts of the reform period are, in a sense, natural extensions of these ideas.

Decentralization over the past fifteen years has had a potent impact on large industrial producers like Angang. Now that the era of firm-level output targets, guaranteed investment levels, and state-set prices is basically over, government ministries engage far less than before in firm-level micromanagement. As noted earlier, individual firms now must source their own inputs, market their own output, and scramble for investment resources. However, the demise of governmental control over asset flows has not meant the demise of governmental control over, or intervention in, the firm. Reform has decidedly reduced the scope of firm-level activities in which the government intervenes. Decentralization, however, has dramatically increased the sheer number of governmental agencies (central, provincial, and municipal) that are empowered to intervene. In other words, the scope of intervention is down while the scale is arguably up.

For Angang, the immediate result is that nobody knows who has direct authority over the firm or who has ultimate responsibility for its performance outcomes. Indeed, when asked who "owns" the company or which agencies have final authority, Angang officials offer a range of possible candidates, from central agencies (the State Council, the State Planning Commission, or the State Commission for Economics and Trade) to the local governments of Liaoning Province and Anshan City.[19] The managers' confusion is understandable, for in essence no single principal supervisory body seems to exist. Certainly, no state agency takes responsibility for Angang's financial troubles, nor do any agencies take responsibility for upgrading the firm's assets to achieve positive returns in the future. Even the central banks keeping Angang afloat make no ownership claims.

However, many state agencies are willing to extract from Angang, claiming taxes in their capacity as governmental bodies and claiming profits in their capacity as state owners. As officials at another steel firm recalled, the enterprise is in no position to deny interference or extraction by even municipal agencies. Those agencies enter the firm and demand funds under the principle, "you are a state firm, and we are the state."[20]

Industrial managers in China are fond of describing the problem as one of having too many mothers-in-law (*po po*). That stock phrase – "too many mothers-in-law" – crops up routinely as one travels from enterprise to enterprise in China. Almost every agency claims supervisory authority over the firm, but none accepts accountability. This indeed is a major characteristic of the bureaucratic reform efforts carried out in the post-Mao era. There has been significant decentralization of supervisory authority but no corresponding decentralization

91

of accountability. In the organizational chaos that has ensued, many state agencies acquire the power to interfere and extract, but none shares any of the risk or responsibility traditionally associated with ownership. There is neither effective monitoring of the firm itself nor effective monitoring of the agencies interfering in the firm.

Even before the reform period began, Angang was subject to a frequently changing bureaucratic and administrative environment.[21] During the height of command planning in the 1950s and 1960s, Angang was under the direct supervision of the Ministry of Metallurgical Industry, a central "line" agency. In 1969, during the decentralization campaigns and general disorder of the Cultural Revolution, Angang was placed under the control of the Anshan Municipal Revolutionary Committee. The balance had swung somewhat toward the other direction by 1975, when the State Council placed Angang and other major steel firms under the dual leadership of the provincial government and the MMI. In this arrangement, which prevailed at most large firms like Angang through the late 1980s, the provincial government was supposed to play the dominant role.[22] In the case of Angang, Liaoning authorities delegated supervisory authority over the steel company's party and government affairs to Anshan Municipality, a somewhat ludicrous situation given that the municipality was as much an outgrowth of the steel mill as vice versa.[23]

Throughout the 1980s, the supervisory system over Angang remained in flux. Regardless of any nominal status as a provincial firm, Angang was in most respects centrally run, a situation that applies to most of China's large-scale steel operations. As Angang managers note, the province had neither the information nor the actual authority to interfere in such issues as product mix, output levels, or investment.[24] Nevertheless, the province maintained certain authority over personnel appointments in the firm and also happened to be the primary state agent for tax collection from the firm. The province collected taxes, and was itself bound contractually to turn over a portion of those revenues to central agencies.

The situation caused Angang to be torn between the conflicting goals of its supervisory agencies.[25] On the one hand, central authorities, concerned primarily with issues of product mix, pushed Angang to produce low-profit items such as pig iron that could meet allocation demands throughout China. On the other hand, provincial authorities, who depended on Angang for the tax revenues needed to fill annual quotas, pushed the firm to move toward higher-end, more profitable production in the area of rolled steel products. Partly as a result of this confusion, Angang during the 1980s suffered from chronic inefficiency and an inability to meet either the province's profit goals or the center's production goals. There were simply too many disparate actors – within the center itself and all the way down to the municipality – interfering in the day-to-day affairs of the enterprise, all pushing in a variety of different directions. Goals were unspecified, and lines of command blurred.

Profit Contracting and Enterprise–Government Relations

In 1987, Angang's supervisory system underwent a wholesale reorganization, a sort of rationalization of the relationship between firm and state. Throughout the 1980s, Chinese economists and policy makers openly acknowledged that, in order to improve firm-level incentives, the boundaries between firm and state had to be clarified. Whereas overall state ownership would be maintained, it was felt that greater autonomy on the part of enterprise managers and a more standardized, specified division between ownership and management would re-vitalize China's flagging heavy industries. More specifically, it was believed that if the firm's financial responsibilities to the state were set at a given level and if the firm were permitted to retain any of the profits earned above that level, then firms would have clear incentives to improve efficiency and achieve self-sustaining growth. At the same time, the scope of state intervention in the firm would have to be formalized and clearly delimited. By the late 1980s, long-term contracting between enterprise and state – in the form of either profit contracting or managerial responsibility systems – was seen as the best vehicle for achieving these goals.[26]

Angang, like most other major Chinese SOEs, was swept up in the wave of contracting. Contracts differed from firm to firm, but the Liaoning steel producer's particular arrangement was set to run for nine years, from 1987 to 1995.[27] According to the contract, Angang's primary responsibility was to sub-mit profits to the state at an increasing rate of 3 percent per annum.[28] These profit submissions in effect constituted income tax, and would formally be termed as such by the mid-1990s. Any profits above the annually increasing baseline submission level would be retained by the firm. The basic point was to guar-antee revenue flows to the state while simultaneously placing an upper limit on tax extraction. In the process, firm-level productivity would be encouraged through the incentive principle of "the more you earn, the more you keep." Angang was granted the right to dispose of retained funds as it desired, but the firm's total wage bill was contractually bound to rise at a slower rate than pretax income (*shixian lishui*).[29] The idea was to prevent the entire portion of retained earnings from being directed toward wage increases or other forms of consumption.

93

While specifying rights and responsibilities for both firm and state, the contract was far less effective in determining on the state side exactly to whom these rights and responsibilities pertained. The Angang contract was formally between the enterprise on one side and, on the other side, the State Planning Commission, the State Commission for Economics and Trade, the State Commission on Economic Structure Reform, and the Ministry of Metallurgical Industry. The old concern prior to the contract was that Angang had too many supervisory agencies, many of which had conflicting interests and none of which could be held accountable for outcomes in the firm. The contract, originally intended to eliminate this situation, simply duplicated it. The contract essentially spread control rights and rights to financial returns across four major central agencies, not one of which had clear final authority.

This diffusion of power had two major implications. First, no single state party to the contract ever ended up being held accountable for what happened at Angang. None of the parties on the state side shared any risk with the firm, so they neither enforced the contract effectively nor adjusted it when it clearly seemed to be operating against the well-being of the firm. Second, since none of the state parties was held directly accountable, none defended Angang against interference by other agencies not included in the contract. This proved important because, despite the existence of a formal contract, governmental decentralization encouraged state agencies totally outside the arrangement to exert profit extraction privileges over Angang. In short, authority relations have remained muddled and governmental intervention extensive even after the advent of formal profit contracting. In the case of Angang, this situation has had repercussions in at least three areas: taxation, definition of firm boundaries, and personnel appointments.

Taxation. As indicated earlier, Anshan Iron and Steel operated through the mid-1990s with negative net levels of working capital, staying afloat primarily through the accumulation of short-term liabilities. The interesting thing is that, throughout this period, the firm was submitting rather substantial levels of tax revenue to various governmental levels. Taking the sample year of 1992, Angang's profit statement (Table 4.4) suggests that the firm submitted approximately RMB 2.53 billion in taxes and fees to various state actors while retaining only RMB 33 million for its own uses.[30] Net profit basically amounted to only 1 percent of total sales revenue. Although part of the problem related to high costs of production, another part involved high and unstable levels of taxation. As Angang managers are proud to point out, their single organization annually submits more revenue to the state than does the entire province of Guangdong.[31]

Table 4.4. *Angang profit statement, 1992*
(RMB 100 million)

Sales revenue	139.51
Less: Cost of production	106.03
Sales tax	18.49
Marketing and other expenses	2.85
Of which: Education fees	0.35
Sales profit	12.15
Add: Nonoperating income	0.09
Less: Nonoperating expenses	2.76
Total profit	9.99
Less: Repayment of construction loans	0.30
Repayment of special project loans	4.95
Income tax, adjustment tax, and profits submitted to government	4.24
Net retained profit	0.33

Source: Anshan Iron and Steel Company (1993, p. 318).

The financial flows right through the present day are actually quite complex. Money comes into the firm in the form of loans, and is partially consumed through the funding of normal production processes or long-term construction. Some of these costs need not be covered by cash loans, however, since the firm can run up its payables – money owed to suppliers.[32] Sales of output are also made, yet many of these transactions actually end up in the "receivables" column, since customers often do not pay within any reasonable period of time. Still, for every sale that is made – regardless of whether cash flows in or not – the producer is levied a sales tax. After sales taxes are paid, various governmental agencies (municipal, provincial, central) impose a series of additional levies and nontax fees. As indicated by Table 4.5, these smaller taxes come in various forms and are frequently employed by the lowest levels of government, agencies that have themselves been burdened with increasing fiscal responsibilities since reform. After these taxes are paid, or at least tallied up as unpaid tax liabilities, the firm repays outstanding bank loans. Even here, however, since the firm is frequently short of funds, loan "repayments" often constitute unpaid funds that are simply rolled over into new loans the following year.[33] Once those repayments take place, the firm still must pay the income tax or "submitted profits" stipulated by contract. Any funds left over can be termed "retained profit."

Table 4.5. *Angang submitted taxes, 1992*
(RMB 1 million)

Income tax	569.01
Sales tax	1,748.88
Education tax	33.94
Real estate tax	24.96
Transportation tax	0.74
Printing tax	6.19
Land usage fees	21.54
Energy and transportation construction tax	20.00
Budgetary adjustment tax	35.39
Construction tax	7.75

Note: Figures do not correspond exactly to declarations on company profit statement.
Source: Anshan Iron and Steel Company (1993, p. 327).

The overall picture seems to be one of significant levels of assets flowing into Angang and then significant levels flowing right back out through tax levies. In the process, the firm consumes assets and produces output of dubious value. The firm, therefore, is burning vital investment resources in its own inefficient production processes while serving as a node of financial transfers from the state banking system to various tax-collecting agencies. In a sense, this is the firm-level segment of a much broader national pattern of financial transfers from high-growth, high–household-savings regions (primarily in the coastal South) to low-growth, low-savings regions (particularly those of the industrial Northeast).[34] Money flows into the banking system in high-growth regions dominated by nonstate firms, and then money flows back out in the form of loans in low-growth regions dominated by SOEs.

With respect to Angang's situation, it is interesting to note how ineffectual profit contracting has been in stabilizing real rates of taxation. The first problem is that the contract addressed only income-tax payments. A considerable portion of the producer's tax bill, though, comes in the form not of income tax but rather as sales tax and various local levies. Indeed, it is this last category that is the most flexible and the most subject to manipulation by state actors. The second (and related) problem with the contract is that the signatories were all central agencies. Local agencies, even ones with formal fiscal authority, were not even included in the contract. Hence, major tax categories and important tax-levying bodies were simply not addressed by the formal profit contract. Blurred lines of authority remained just that – blurred.

Under such circumstances, it is not surprising that SOE managers at Angang and elsewhere frequently complain that, whenever cash is present in the firm, local agencies can be expected to follow with extractive powers at hand. For example, if a road is being built locally and firm-owned vehicles will be driving over it, then the firm is asked to pay the construction costs. Similarly, if a municipal swimming pool is to be built and firm employees are likely to utilize it, the firm is asked to pay. The firm, in a sense, becomes a cash cow for local agencies. It is no wonder that real rates of taxation, at least when measured from the perspective of the individual firm, vary so much across China. Local agencies extract to varying degrees, and firms themselves cooperate to varying degrees.[35] Blurred authority relations – despite the existence of formal profit contracts – simply perpetuate this situation.

Boundaries of the Firm. In the case of large SOEs like Angang, unclear lines of authority impact upon the very definition of firm-level boundaries. In the earlier years of the reform era, the impact tended to be more direct, as bureaucratic agencies stepped in and overtly reshuffled the firm's boundaries. In the case of Angang, certain production units were summarily removed from the firm's control and others arbitrarily added. Needless to say, the moving target of enterprise boundaries did not make the managerial task any easier. Through the later 1980s and early 1990s, the impact of bureaucratic intervention on boundaries has become somewhat more indirect. Frequent manipulation of enterprise boundaries persists, but the perpetrator now tends to be the firm itself, and precisely for the reason of avoiding predatory extraction by uncoordinated state agencies. By creating complex webs of affiliated subsidiaries, collective units, and private companies, the SOE can in some cases quite effectively shelter assets from tax collectors of all governmental levels.[36]

In the case of Angang, both forms of boundary reshuffling have occurred, though detecting such manipulations is not always easy in view of the firm's vast size. Even today, managers at Angang find it difficult to pinpoint exactly where the firm begins and ends. The formal core enterprises alone (of Anshan Iron and Steel Company, excluding subsidiaries) represent a sprawling mass. Packed into a gargantuan complex in the middle of Anshan City are coking facilities, smelting plants, hot and cold rolling operations, rail-line manufacturing facilities, several power plants, chemical plants, an automotive factory, several electronics factories, and a multitude of other production facilities. From the top of Angang's blast furnaces, one can peer out beyond the ever-present wall of acrid smoke to see Angang factories stretching out to the horizon. Also nestled into this massive complex or dotting nearby neighborhoods are six Angang hospitals, at least six different research and development companies, nine Angang secondary schools or vocational institutes, several construction firms, and several huge housing projects for workers. Finally, in the nearby Liaoning countryside are Angang's five primary mining operations, complete with sintering and pelletizing factories.

If this alone were the extent of Angang, the situation would still be quite complex. Angang's "core," as it is termed in company documents, comprises over 140 different factories or "units." Figures referring to the 220,000 employees at Angang generally include only these core companies. The same is true for Angang's social welfare responsibilities – they pertain to the workers in the core Angang facilities. Yet, even with regard to the question of how many people are actually employed here, there is confusion. The company's own year-end records for 1992 list both 216,925 and 213,000 for total employment.[37] As noted earlier, by 1994 there were also approximately 110,000 retired workers still being provided full pensions, medical care, and housing by the company.

Certainly one reason why Angang has had trouble pinpointing the exact number of workers is that bureaucratic agencies have periodically moved units in and out of the firm's organizational aegis. Through the mid-1980s, Angang's investments in facilities always ran the risk of a local agency or central ministry claiming the facility as its own, often without adequately compensating the parent company.[38] In 1980, for example, Angang's iron ore mining operation was separated from the parent company and transferred to MMI control.[39] The mines were then returned to Angang in 1982. Similarly, in 1980 Angang lost its magnesium mines to the MMI, apparently because magnesium had good export potential and the ministry sought to capture those profits.[40] The same reshuffling of enterprise boundaries occurred even within the walls of the main steel complex. During the 1950s, a cement plant was built inside the Angang compound and was originally put under the independent supervision of the Ministry of Building Materials.[41] In the early 1970s, the plant was transferred over to Anshan Municipality and then finally (in 1974) placed under the direct control of Angang – a move that made sense since Angang annually consumes a tremendous amount of cement. Nevertheless, through the early 1980s, most of the cement produced by this plant was claimed by the state plan and could not be used by Angang. Hence, the parent company had no incentive to invest in its own subsidiary facility.[42] With facilities coming and going from its organizational chart, it is no wonder that Angang has had trouble managing its finances.

98

For the most part, such egregious forms of bureaucratic intervention have given way in the 1990s to firm-led shifts in enterprise boundaries. Angang, like other large SOEs, has both created and acquired a huge number of collective enterprises throughout the reform period. Although in some cases the purpose of these acquisitions has been to ensure access to important industrial inputs, more often than not the reasons involve employment creation and (possibly) asset protection.

Acquiring local collectives – whether light manufacturing facilities, food processing plants, service companies, or even small retail stores – has several advantages. First, excess workers from the main steel operations can be dispersed to these sideline operations.[43] Second, the collectives provide employment for the children of Angang workers, employment that would otherwise be difficult to find in the somewhat stagnant region of Northeast China. Enterprises located in booming urban areas like Shanghai or Beijing are at an advantage in this respect, for the market can absorb some of their excess staff. Angang does not have this luxury and, in many cases, the collectives it runs are money-losing operations; they serve simply as employment centers.[44] Third, even though a collective may be a loss-maker, it can still help a firm like Angang economize on its social welfare burdens. Young workers are given wage incentives to move to subsidiary collectives, where they will not receive the full social welfare benefits accorded to employees of the state-owned parent company. The worker gains on short-term wages but loses on long-term benefits. In theory this should save Angang money, but the problem is that many of the collective workers are dependent family members of regular Angang employees and hence free-ride on those employees' housing and medical benefits.

Finally, there is a fourth probable incentive for expansion into the collective sector: evasion of taxes. As noted earlier, SOEs – particularly given their size and privileged access to bank loans – become prime targets for revenue extraction by a bureaucratically stretched tax system. Even if tax levels were the same between collective and full-fledged state firms, tax collection in any given region is much easier from one large state firm than from several hundred small collectives. Furthermore, until the 1994 tax reforms, collectives (firms formally owned by localities) were provided official tax advantages over standard state enterprises. The very existence of these incentives has led to allegations that large SOEs have been hiding assets – essentially, decapitalizing themselves – by funneling money into collective or even private subsidiaries. There is no hard evidence for this behavior at Angang, but the firm's extensive web of subsidiary units does create an environment of extremely turbid financial dealings.

According to company records, Angang's subordinate collectives at the end of 1992 comprised some 323 different firms employing 178,510 workers (this is, of course, in addition to the 220,000 workers employed in the core company).[45] Interestingly, women made up the majority (56 percent) of the collective employees. For the most part, Angang records never actually specify the relationship between parent company and subsidiary collectives. The firms are not listed on Angang's organizational chart, though there is a listing for the Angang Subsidiary Enterprise Company. This umbrella company is charged with "leading and managing" the individual firms, but there is no explanation of just what sort of authority is involved.

More important, it is unclear how the attached collectives are related to the parent company financially. The situation is complicated, since more than a few of these collectives are actually owned by local governments. There is apparently a profit-sharing and investment scheme by which the parent company both extracts from and invests in the collectives. Issues of actual "ownership," though, are hazy. In 1992, Angang did report that its affiliated collectives had total accumulated profits and taxes of RMB 228 million, of which RMB 146 million was termed "profit."[46] These numbers are not particularly large. The subsidiaries' "profit and tax" figure equals 7 percent of the parent company's total for that year, while subsidiary profits equal about 14 percent of the parent's total. Nevertheless, it is never explicitly stated how much of the subsidiaries' profit was actually sent upward to the parent company, or how much investment flowed downward. In short, with so many companies involved, there is plenty of room for confusion, accounting errors, and snarled financial flows.

In addition, Angang also maintains what it terms its "contract company," a division for managing, on a contract basis, seven firms across Anshan Municipality and Liaoyang City. This contract company apparently runs these seven municipally owned firms and then retains a right to extract certain profit levels. Unlike the accounting treatment of normal subsidiaries, Angang records do clearly state the profits that these seven firms actually turn over to the parent company; in 1992, the figure was RMB 5.6 million. Still, the exact financial relationship between the contract firms and the parent company is unspecified. Just as governmental agencies contract with Angang to extract taxes, Angang contracts with these seven firms to extract profit. In the first case, the system operates irrationally since bank loans continue to be pumped in by an outside source. It is conceivable that the same thing happens in the latter case as well, but the records simply do not provide enough information to draw solid conclusions.

Indeed, answers are difficult to come by for most of these issues concerning enterprise boundaries. However, that there is so much confusion regarding these most basic issues is important in itself. The financial flows in a large SOE become so complicated, and so difficult to follow, that performance data are divorced from reality. How can financial performance figures be relied upon when nobody is certain of the boundaries of the firm? How can labor productivity be measured when nobody knows exactly how many workers are involved? How can financial flows be traced when transactions within the firm blend together with, and become indistinguishable from, transactions beyond the firm? Top-level managers are flooded with statistics – Angang publishes records even for the number of chickens raised and eggs yielded annually by each of its factories' sideline agricultural operations – yet those same managers are hard-pressed to describe accurately their firm's financial status.[47]

Personnel Issues and Enterprise–Government Relations. The impact of opaque authority relations between firm and state is perhaps clearest in the area of personnel appointments. This is a particularly interesting issue because the Chinese communist party has historically relied on control over personnel as an ultimate, last-ditch source of power. Information may never have flowed very well up and down the Chinese bureaucracy, and policies may have always run in to resistance at the implementation stage, but in the end, recalcitrant officials could always be dismissed. The highest echelons of the party-state always retained the final say on any given official's career prospects. There would be no independent "mountain tops," no secure fiefdoms from which freewheeling officials could produce their own policies. Even into the reform era, the state has aggressively protected its monopoly over personnel appointments, right down to the firm level. In other words, the Chinese state, no matter how poorly it monitors its SOEs, always retains the right to fire top managers at the enterprise level, regardless of whatever particular property-rights reforms are pursued. Whether under managerial responsibility systems, profit contracting, or joint stock efforts, state officials have refused to give up the power of personnel appointment.

The problem, however, is that even as the state retains ultimate control over personnel, there remains the question of just who constitutes the state. This question becomes vitally important with all the decentralization that has taken place during the reform era. The "state" may have control in theory, but in reality, which level of the state are we talking about? The center? The provincial government? The municipal government, perhaps? Because different state actors now claim a piece of the power to appoint enterprise officials, that power itself becomes highly ambiguous. As a result, the system of personnel control creaks along slowly and rather unresponsively. All of these qualities became apparent at Angang in the early 1990s, and especially in 1994 when a major managerial shake-up occurred.

Deciphering the personnel system in a Chinese firm is never an easy task, and different answers are often provided in response to the question of just how top management is appointed. Nevertheless, at Angang there seemed to be a general consensus among respondents that the top three officials in the firm – the general manager, the party secretary, and the vice–party secretary – are all appointed directly by the State Council, the highest body of the central government.[48] Yet, as those respondents also admitted, the process is more complicated than a simple declaration from Beijing. The first issue is that although Angang deals mainly with agencies in Beijing, the party organization of the enterprise is formally subordinated to the Liaoning provincial party committee. Furthermore, the whole firm, as mentioned before, is still in some senses considered to be under the Liaoning provincial government. Meanwhile, the Ministry of Metallurgical Industry in Beijing claims a certain degree of authority in matters relating to personnel. What has evolved is a complex process in which the provincial government and the MMI both have the power to recommend candidates for top positions; those recommendations are then passed up to the State Council. Finally, it is the provincial party committee that is given the right to announce top appointments at Angang, thus preserving at least a semblance of local authority over the firm. When a new party secretary was appointed at Angang in 1994, the formal announcement was made by the head of the organization department of the Liaoning provincial party committee, though the appointee himself was serving simultaneously as a vice-minister of metallurgy in Beijing.[49] Later in the announcement, mention was made that the new personnel appointments were approved by the party center and the State Council.

It can, of course, be argued that provincial involvement in these decisions is simply window dressing on what is essentially a central matter. That may indeed be true, but even so, there are several points worth mentioning. First, it is interesting that in the whole appointments process there seems to be no involvement of the state agencies charged with administering Angang's managerial contract. In other words, a whole slew of ownership responsibilities were handed over to four different central agencies, yet none of these agencies is involved in the most crucial aspect of ownership, the appointment or dismissal of the firm's top management. Not surprisingly, dismissals do not seem carefully gauged to poor economic performance or to the firm's non-compliance with the contract. Second, the agency that does ultimately control appointments, the State Council, is the one farthest removed from the daily operations of the firm. Information regarding Angang must be filtered upward through either the provincial party organization, the MMI, or the other central commissions charged with monitoring the steel firm. As indicated in the previous section, the monitoring process itself does not work well, and this then affects the efficiency and responsiveness of the appointments system.

The managerial reshuffling that occurred in mid-1994 illustrates the way the system seems to operate.[50] In August of that year, Angang's party secretary, Cheng Xichang, was summarily dismissed and replaced by a vice-minister from the MMI, Wu Xichun.[51] Wu simultaneously retained his position as vice-minister. As part of the same reshuffling, Angang's general manager, Li Hua-zhong, was given the additional position of enterprise vice–party secretary. The appointments, announced by the Liaoning provincial party committee, were made at a cadre conference convened by the province and the organization department of the central MMI. In fact, many agencies placed their imprimatur on the shake-up. Apparently what happened was that Angang's general manager, who had been appointed several years earlier, had not been able to get along with the party secretary, Cheng Xichang. Neither individual was willing to back down and enterprise management suffered as a result. Outside government agencies, however, were reluctant to intervene. At least some people in the Chinese steel industry felt that Angang party secretary Cheng was a "Liaoning man," closely linked with the provincial party apparatus, and that the province was therefore reluctant to dismiss him. Actually, officials at other steel mills expressed a certain amount of shock that the general manager was ultimately able to prevail, a victory indicated by Cheng's dismissal and Wu Xichun's appointment. That Wu was a vice-minister of metallurgy and a member of the MMI party committee lends credence to the idea that the general manager scored a victory over a locally backed colleague. Wu, the "Beijing man," replaced Cheng, the "Liaoning man," and then the old Angang party leadership was further diluted by having the general manager simultaneously appointed vice–party secretary.

The story is interesting for several reasons. First, it suggests just how complicated the appointments process is. A number of agencies with a number of competing interests are sucked into the game. It was a common perception throughout the Chinese steel industry that this whole affair involved a battle not only within the top echelons of the firm but also between various provincial and central interests. Second, that it received so much attention in the industry

103

suggests just how unusual such high-level managerial reshufflings are. It was a big deal that the Angang party secretary was fired, and a particularly big deal because of all the personal and bureaucratic battles involved. One gets the impression that a firing like this required extraordinary measures, extraordinary forms of central intervention that would not normally kick into action when simple economic problems arise. In other words, there was a general sense that these kinds of personnel changes do not come up simply when there is poor management, but only when management is so deadlocked as to be unable to function. What that means is that the state's best weapon for enforcing managerial efficiency and competence – the power to fire managers – is not even used as such. And it is not used precisely because it is such an unwieldy instrument. Rather than being put in the hands of a single agency capable of monitoring the firm, and rather than being put in the hands of the four agencies charged with the firm's managerial contract, it is so spread out among different state actors that only the highest governmental body can step in and sort things out. This is hardly a type of ownership instrument conducive to positive managerial outcomes at the firm level.

Yet, while the state power of appointments is inefficient, it is also extensive. In Angang, as with other large SOEs, the general manager does not have the power to appoint his vice-managers. Instead, these appointments are made from outside the firm. As the company's own organizational diagrams suggest, there are ten vice-managers serving immediately under the general manager at Angang. Those vice-managers are generally appointed by the provincial government and the Ministry of Metallurgical Industry, and are not susceptible to dismissal by the general manager.[52] Only the single "assistant general manager" (*zong jingli zhuli*) is appointed directly by the general manager. In short, therefore, the general manager has very little control over his immediate subordinates. Instead, it is an opaque owner – several state agencies – that reaches into the firm and appoints midlevel management. The general manager is basically robbed of an important disciplinary tool, and can do little more than shift a poorly performing subordinate horizontally. Because the whole state appointments system must stir into action for even midlevel managerial dismissals to occur, such dismissals are rare and take place only after disastrous outcomes begin to plague the firm. This is tremendously inefficient. Ideally, a manager should be able to fire subordinates so that poor performance can be cut off early and disasters avoided. For the most part, this just does not happen at large Chinese SOEs like Angang. Personnel changes, because they are controlled from outside the firm and because they take so long to effect, are used to mop up after a mess occurs, but unfortunately they cannot serve as an effective means to avoid the mess in the first place.[53] The personnel system simply does not allow for fine-tuning.

However, it should be noted that even though the government is clearly involved in the firm-level appointments process, this involvement now stems from concerns of power rather than ideology. In other words, although a dispute between a general manager and a party secretary did occur at Angang in 1994, this episode should not be viewed as a battle of " 'reds' versus 'experts'." Within Chinese enterprises, there are indeed dual chains of command: an administrative side and a party side. Nevertheless, at least in contemporary China, this division should not be overemphasized. Within the steel industry, one gets the impression that the distinctions between the political functions of party cadres and the "professional" or "managerial" functions of administrative cadres have, for the most part, disappeared. In a sense, everybody is a businessperson today, including the party people. At least at the enterprise level, there are few if any "reds." To the extent that there is a division of labor, the party leadership tends to be more engaged in long-term strategy and development, while the general manager and vice-managers are involved in the day-to-day running of the firm. Even here, the distinctions do not always hold, especially since senior managers often simultaneously share a top party position within the firm. This really is a key point: The *same* people tend to hold top positions on both the administrative and party ladders. It is hard to conceive of a red-versus-expert dispute when the same people are sitting on both sides of the equation.

Nevertheless, large Chinese SOEs do have group leadership. There is always a general manager and there is always a party secretary, and the two positions are rarely held by the same person. As several respondents within the steel industry suggested, problems occur when there is disharmony among the two senior enterprise officials and, more directly, when a dominant one fails to emerge. In other words, in most functioning enterprises, multiple leadership usually degenerates in practice to unitary leadership as one official becomes dominant. There does not seem to be any consistency as to whether it is the party secretary or the general manager who prevails, and there is variation even among major steel mills. As will be discussed in Chapter 6, at Capital Iron and Steel it was clearly the party secretary, Zhou Guanwu, who dominated throughout the 1980s and early 1990s. Alternatively, at Angang the general manager seems to have prevailed in the struggle of 1994. In essence, it does not seem to matter whether it is the party side or the administrative side that prevails, since personnel on both sides have similar business-oriented goals. The key issue is whether any one side, or any one leader, can secure final authority within the firm. At Angang, this did not happen prior to 1994. As a result, internal enterprise management became deadlocked, and the cumbersome state personnel system had to grind into action.

Governmental decentralization through the reform period has complicated the firm's operational environment, and it has also exposed the firm to myriad forms of state intervention. Blurred authority relations, however, are not the only source of firm-level financial difficulties, nor are firms entirely passive victims of the process. As noted earlier, many ostensibly market-oriented reform measures interact in such a way as to encourage firm-level managers to engage in asset-destroying strategies. One key lesson emerging from China's prolonged efforts at enterprise reform is that opportunities and incentives for non–market-oriented behavior are frequently, albeit inadvertently, created by policy makers. These opportunities, then, are readily exploited by managers desperate to keep firms afloat and keep workers employed in an extremely turbulent environment.

Profit Contracts

Profit contracting provides a good example of a market-oriented reform measure that leads to rather destructive firm-level behavior when employed in a context of partial reforms – partial reforms of the banking sector, bankruptcy rules, and tax codes. Profit contracts linking managerial or worker compensation to firm-level profitability send a clear signal to managers: profits must be maximized. Yet there is nothing magically market-oriented about the term "profit," and indeed there are many ways – both productive and destructive, market-oriented and non–market-oriented – in which profits can be maximized. On the one hand, profits can be realized by cutting costs or streamlining production processes. On the other hand, profits can be increased by wildly expanding physical capacity and output. Unfortunately, the latter option, given the contemporary context, becomes a rational strategy for SOE managers to pursue. They expand physical facilities and output regardless of prevailing market conditions and regardless of their own investment capabilities.

What results is the sort of situation observed at Angang, a firm that shows profits year after year but which has, in the process, amassed tremendous liabilities, many of which do not even show up on the balance sheet. Certain behavioral patterns occur again and again in the Chinese steel industry, and arguably right across China's modern industrial sector. Firms both expand and

106

produce as much as they can, regardless of prevailing market conditions. In order to be recorded as profit, output is then sold to purchasers – whether other SOEs or nonstate firms – that are frequently either unwilling or unable to pay. Such "sales" result in the high levels of receivables evident in firms like Angang or Wuhan Iron and Steel. Indeed, internal ministerial reports bemoan the tendency of steel firms both to produce goods that cannot be sold and to extend loans that can never be repaid.[54]

As the case of Angang suggests, much of this overproduction distorts not only profit statements but the firm's balance sheet as well. Firm-level current assets become severely overstated, and latent conditions of insolvency may fester unnoticed as a result. Industrial producers mimic Chinese banks in consistently refusing to write off nonperforming loans extended to consumers long ago. Similarly, firms are reluctant to settle such debts at anything less than face value, even if doing so would bring in much-needed cash.[55] The firm, in other words, would rather carry bad debt than engage in any write-offs that might erode nominal profit declarations. For the very same reasons, producers are frequently unwilling to settle disputed claims with consumers. As MMI research teams have observed, for cases in which consumers complain of damaged or subpar goods, the producer would rather leave the sale unresolved – albeit booked as "profitable" – than settle the claim at less than face value.

The nonmarket nature of many of these transactions is underscored by the drop in profitability that hit Angang and other major steel producers during the 1994–95 period. It was precisely during this period that the MMI was more assiduously enforcing rules against inventory accumulation and credit-based sales.[56] The notion was that firms had to be discouraged from producing goods for which there was no market demand – in other words, goods for which there may have been "customers," but not customers with an ability to pay. Even the ministry itself recognized that these measures, intended mostly to curtail the growth of interenterprise debt, were the main reason for the steel sector's drop in profitability. Angang's profits certainly dropped through late 1994 and 1995; moreover, a number of major producers, including mills in Nanjing and Nanchang, actually became net loss makers as a result of the MMI restrictions on credit sales.[57] The firms simply could not show a profit if forced to sell on anything resembling a cash basis.[58]

Just as they seek to maximize "paper" profits, many SOEs also engage in physical expansion whenever possible. The growth of Angang's fixed assets right through the mid-1990s is but one illustration of a far broader phenomenon. Increasing both productive capacity and actual output is one guaranteed method of surpassing profit targets, particularly when the firm is essentially permitted to give away – or "loan" – output during market downswings. An internal MMI investigation of twelve major steel producers in East China consistently observed this phenomenon. Despite ministerial protests, firms proved intent on expanding capacity and output, even during market downturns and even when such expansion came at the expense of vitally needed working capital.[59] In other words, many firms were either devoting working capital to long-term investment or simply running up short-term loans for the same purpose. In some cases (e.g., the Shanghai No. 1, No. 3, and No. 5 steel companies), both practices were employed simultaneously.[60]

For Angang and many other firms – and, indeed, for many banks – short-term loans when used in this manner allow firms to expand even during periods of government retrenchment, periods when long-term construction loans are severely restricted. Again, the overall pattern obtains: firms in the state sector show profit, expand physically, run up liabilities, and repeatedly run into liquidity crises.

Financial Reform

Expansion and the running up of receivables have certainly been encouraged by profit contracting, but such behavior is possible only because of another ostensibly market-oriented measure: the government's decision to shift enterprise subsidization from the central budget to the state banking system. The original intention was to force firms to pay for capital and, in doing so, encourage market-based allocation of investment resources. The outcome, however, has been to provide firms like Angang with access to soft loans, loans that – in a manner analogous to enterprise receivables – can be classified by the banks as profitable. That is, lending institutions, as long as they are periodically recapitalized by the central bank, can continue rolling over nonperforming enterprise loans year after year. Because short-term loans can be rolled over, firms like Angang face no penalty for devoting these loans as well as any net working capital to long-term expansion.

The Angang balance sheet presented in Table 4.2 fits China's broader pattern of a nominally profitable modern industrial sector effectively decapitalizing itself through the running up of short-term liabilities.[61] As long as the central government provides mechanisms by which industrial lenders can keep infusing themselves with household savings – in other words, as long as banks continue to face soft budgets – neither the banks nor the SOEs will attempt to stop inappropriate lending practices. Calling in nonperforming or misapplied short-term loans would reveal the underlying insolvency of many banks and firms alike.

Hence, the various parties involved have little if any interest in stopping these soft lending practices.

Ironically, as firms decapitalize themselves, they become at once both vulnerable to and empowered against governmental retrenchment measures. When dependent almost entirely on short-term loans to pay workers and maintain production, firms like Angang put themselves at tremendous risk. Any time the government shifts toward a more contractionary macroeconomic stance by imposing lending freezes, the firm stands to go right out of business. In other words, when loans are cut off, the firm cannot maintain even the most basic productive functions. For precisely that reason, however, firms can turn to the government during contractionary periods and request emergency loans simply to keep workers paid. Whether they actively pursue it or not, large SOEs – simply by virtue of their vast employment and social welfare role – have implicit leverage over the government during even the most stringent of retrenchment periods. Loans may be cut off temporarily, but as soon as the number of unpaid workers begins to skyrocket, the loans start flowing again. This is precisely what seems to have happened at Angang and other Northeastern industrial producers during the 1994–95 period. Financial weakness, oddly enough, serves as an important source of strength.

Firms compound this strength by sinking resources into ongoing construction projects, the kind of projects central agencies are reluctant to stop funding in midstream. Nobody wants to see a multiyear investment effort go to waste in an unfinished investment project. For a variety of reasons, therefore, capital keeps flowing in, firms keep on investing, inventories and receivables keep accumulating, and very little of real value – at least in any market sense – gets produced. Clearly, none of this could continue if soft loans were not being pumped in by the state banks, whether under the direction of various government levels or of their own volition. Firms like Angang that consistently run working capital deficits – or firms like Wuhan Iron and Steel, whose assets are tied up in nonliquid forms – simply could not keep producing without cash infusions from financial intermediaries.

Under such circumstances, it is not surprising that state-sector output has continued to rise, even with growing recognition in China of the sector's deepening financial problems. Even immediately after the Fifteenth Party Congress, the official media was with one breath heralding output increases in the state sector and with the other breath gravely outlining the restructuring measures needed to cope with the sector's financial woes.[62] Unfortunately, there seems to be little recognition that the financial problems and output increases are in fact related.

The Impact of Changes in Accounting Standards

In some ways, the new accounting standards announced by the Ministry of Finance in July of 1993 actually exacerbated patterns of overproduction and asset destruction in the state industrial sector. This is once again a case of an ostensibly market-oriented reform that – when introduced into an environment of only partially reformed governance institutions – ends up encouraging decidedly non–market-oriented behavior.

A primary aim of the 1993 accounting reforms was to afford managers greater control over enterprise assets, the idea being that flexible asset management would encourage firms to adjust to prevailing market conditions.[63] Under China's old system of accounting, an inheritance from the command era, managers had virtually no control over the disposition of assets. The pre-reform system essentially treated firms as production arms of a broader state apparatus, rather than as economic actors in their own right. Therefore, accounting during the command era and right through the early 1990s paid a great deal of attention to flows of resources in and out of the firm but relatively little attention to describing ownership over those flows. Because the firm was but an appendage of the state industrial apparatus, concepts of firm-level liquidity or solvency had very little meaning. Nor did it make much sense to determine whether the funds being consumed actually "belonged" to the firm, the state, or any other particular units. Resources were simply being moved from one pocket of the state to another. In actuality, though, these resources emanated from a number of places: from direct central subsidies, retained enterprise profits, and retained depreciation, to name but a few.

Rather than focusing on the origins of the funds – or on the question of which funds constituted firm-level assets and which constituted liabilities – the accounting system emphasized the intended function of various funds. Each major industrial firm, as illustrated by Angang's balance sheet through 1992, had separate accounts earmarked for long-term investment, current operations, and special projects. The funds within these accounts came from a range of sources, but the key point was that the accounts were controlled and carefully monitored by the specialized industrial banks of the state. Managers had no autonomous access to these accounts, even when composed primarily of enterprise retained profits.

The system had both advantages and disadvantages. On the more positive side, separate accounts controlled by the banks ensured that funds earmarked for operations actually went to operations and that those earmarked for long-term investment were actually used for such investment. Transgressions on this front were treated as serious violations of the law. On the more negative side, though, the system severely inhibited the ability of firm-level officials to engage in any sort of market-oriented financial management. Such rigidity was appropriate in the command era but not in the reform era, when managers were supposed to have both the ability and authority to respond to market incentives. For firm-level operations to shift in accordance with prevailing market conditions, managers would need some degree of flexibility in altering the mix of long-term investment, inventories, cash savings, and other firm-level resources. Yet if this were to happen and managers were granted access to firm-level accounts, better distinctions between firm-level assets and liabilities would have to be developed. Reliable measures of firm-level assets and net changes in those assets over time would be needed to draw any sort of meaningful "bottom line" under managerial performance.

The new accounting rules of 1993 attempted to achieve many of these market-oriented objectives. From 1993 onward, firms were supposed to produce financial statements with assets, liabilities, and owner equity on the balance sheet and with profits and losses on the income statement.[64] Furthermore, taxable income was to be distinguished from net profits, thus allowing for some measurement of performance besides mere revenue generation.[65] Perhaps most important of all, the traditional boundaries between long-term investment accounts, special project accounts, and operating accounts were effectively dissolved.[66] Through the lifting of these tight restrictions on asset use, unprecedented autonomy flowed downward to enterprise managers.

The new accounting standards have been somewhat less impressive in practice than in theory. Problems are clearly evident in the area of basic asset valuation. As indicated by Angang's situation, firms do not make adequate provisions for nonperforming loans or bad inventory, and scant attention is paid to the varying degrees of liquidity among different types of assets. Receivables and other credits of doubtful value are treated more or less like cash. Depreciation rates remain extremely low – partly as a result of the firm-level desire to boost profit figures – so assets of no realistic market value still carry book value.[67] Meanwhile, firms themselves operate without being forced to service their outstanding debt obligations: short-term loans are rolled over repeatedly and long-term loans are converted into owner equity.[68] The overall effect of these factors is to inflate the enterprise's net asset holdings. Essentially insolvent firms in China today can still appear relatively healthy on paper.

Reliable estimates of profitability are as hard to come by as reliable estimates of liquidity. As noted earlier, firms throughout the reform period have come under great pressure to show net profitability. It is therefore not surprising

Table 4.6. *Angang's total labor costs, 1992*
(RMB 1 million)

Total wage bill	933.44
Of which:	
Bonus	342.93
Supplementary piece rate wage	2.61
Subsidies and perquisites	181.74
Total worker insurance and welfare	341.13
Of which:	
Retirement, pensions, disability	122.44

Source: Anshan Iron and Steel Company (1993, p. 319).

that numerous methods are employed at the firm level to inflate income statements. In addition to underestimating depreciation costs on the income statement, managers can also deflate labor costs by counting significant portions of the wage bill as "distributed profit."[69] Although difficult to document in the post-1993 period, such behavior was certainly evident at Angang through 1992.

On its 1992 income statement, Angang declared pretax profits of approximately RMB 1 billion, based on production costs of RMB 10.6 billion. Of that RMB 10.6 billion, RMB 220 million was attributed to total labor costs.[70] Given these numbers, the firm appeared to be performing rather well. Its raw materials and energy costs were substantial but, since labor costs were low, profits remained high. However, when presenting its labor payments on a separate page in the annual report, the firm came up with entirely different numbers. As Table 4.6 indicates, the independently calculated wage bill amounted to approximately RMB 933.44 million, while social welfare costs added an additional RMB 341 million.[71] Total labor costs, therefore, were approximately RMB 1.27 billion, more than five times the amount recorded on the income statement. Interestingly, the MMI in its own records of Angang's 1992 performance cites the company's higher total wage bill (RMB 933.44 million) under the category of labor costs, but under the category of enterprise profit it cites the company's profit figures based on the lower wage bill.[72] Looking at the MMI's presentation of Angang's performance, therefore, one would get an entirely distorted impression. There would appear to be high labor costs but also high profit levels. In reality, the figures bear no relationship to one another.

Whether the 1993 accounting standards can effectively deal with these distortions remains to be seen. Given all the problems involved in actually implementing the new liquidity standards, it is hard to imagine that profit measurement will fare much better. This is all the more true given the intense pressure firms face to declare profits. Unfortunately, by inflating their profits, firms expose themselves to elevated income-tax extraction. Whether at Angang or any other major Chinese SOE, managers on the one hand complain about rapacious tax collection yet on the other hand encourage just such predatory state behavior by making artificially inflated profit declarations. In a manner typical of the nested problems dynamic, distorted incentives interact with unreliable accounting standards and unchecked state power to guarantee poor performance at the enterprise level.

The greatest problem with the 1993 accounting standards, however, lies not in the issue of measurement. Rather, the greatest problem relates to the extension of managerial autonomy in an environment of only partially reformed financial markets and virtually no threat of bankruptcy. Eliminating the boundaries between separate accounts for long-term investment and operating funds proved extremely dangerous in the context of unchecked soft lending. Managers could for the first time easily access firm-level accounts and easily devote working capital to long-term investment, all the while incurring no penalty to firm-level performance. After all, the banks have continued pumping in the loans, infusing overextended firms with liquidity. The accounting changes have in effect given managers license to decapitalize the firm, and in ways that are increasingly difficult for policy makers to detect.[73] Unfettered investment shifts from being simply a matter of misapplied government subsidies to a far more complex and autonomous interaction between financial intermediaries and the firm. These developments not only undermine firm-level performance, they also deepen allocative inefficiency nationwide. Particularly given the plunging performance of SOEs since 1993, the lesson of China's new accounting standards is clear: Autonomy extended in the absence of functioning governance and hard budgets is a recipe for disaster.

Triangular Debt

China's growing problem of interenterprise or "triangular" debt contributes to many of the firm-level incentive problems described in earlier sections. By running up high levels of receivables or "loaning out" excess inventory, producers, in effect, extend credit to consumers – consumers who are frequently other industrial firms. Similarly, by delaying payment for basic inputs, firms forcefully extract loans from suppliers. When both forms of behavior happen simultaneously, complex chains of debt develop among individual firms, between firms and the banking system, and across various industrial sectors. Clearly, one byproduct of the general regulatory laxness characterizing the reform era has been a marked rise in the level of interenterprise arrears. Just as the total volume of lending has risen tremendously during the reform era, so too has the level of interenterprise lending. Virtually unheard of at the start of reform, total triangular debt by 1994 had grown to RMB 600 billion, approximately 19 percent of GDP.[74]

These aggregate debt levels are but reflections of endemic behavior at the enterprise level. When firms like Angang run up payables of over RMB 30 billion, that figure simply contributes to the triangular debt totals nationwide. When firms like Wuhan Iron and Steel accumulate RMB 2.9 billion of receivables in a given year, that too contributes to triangular debt. By the end of 1994, Angang alone was owed approximately RMB 11 billion, and owed to others approximately RMB 8.2 billion.[75] For some firms in the Chinese steel industry, receivables account for 30, 60, or even 97 percent of annual sales.[76] Such elevated levels across so many different firms suggests the presence of a serious systemic problem.

China's rising levels of aggregate interenterprise debt can be attributed to a number of factors. Most immediately, when the central government pursues policies of monetary retrenchment – often by severely restricting lending – firms simply force debt on their suppliers. The firms keep operating, but they just stop paying their bills. Meanwhile, suppliers also must keep operating, so they accumulate receivables and then turn around and borrow inputs. In a more general sense, however, triangular debt stems from an environment of distorted firm-level incentives and poorly developed legal institutions. In China today, little if any legal protection exists for creditors. Bankruptcy proceedings, particularly in the state sector, are extremely infrequent; as a result, debtors rarely face the threat of liquidation. No clear penalty exists for nonpayment of loans. Furthermore, many debtors in the state sector benefit from local protectionism. Local governments, often the very agencies charged with enforcing business law, have no interest in seeing a major local employer driven out of business. Creditors have very little recourse under existing law and very little inclination to submit disputes to arbitration by local courts.

Even so, triangular debt rarely involves clear cases of victims and victimizers. Producers may complain of having debt "forced" upon them by nonpaying customers, but those very same producers often encourage such credit-based sales. As indicated earlier, the producer's objective is generally to maximize sales and "paper" profits, regardless of whether customers can pay or not. Suppliers like Angang, therefore, are frequently more than willing to run up receivables, particularly since serious cash shortfalls can be alleviated with bank loans. Likewise, when those bank-sponsored cash infusions stop for any extended period of time, the firm's first reaction – rather than scaling down production – is to extract loans forcefully from other suppliers. Interenterprise lending becomes a convenient budget-softening device for all the firms involved, whether creditors or debtors.

The Chinese environment contains numerous barriers against successful market-oriented production: excessive state intervention, high levels of taxation, and unclear regulatory regimes. All the while, however, firms are expected to keep on producing and keep on disposing of their output. Under such circumstances, triangular debt serves as but one more means for the firm to survive without having actually to engage in value-adding activities. As long as Chinese policy makers refuse to shut down insolvent firms, interenterprise lending will continue to serve as a cushion for non–market-oriented production.

However, the key issue in this respect is not the absolute aggregate level of triangular debt but rather the distribution of debt among firms and across sectors.[77] Interenterprise lending does not in itself fuel demand, particularly if credits and debts are in relative balance. In other words, in a given firm or sector, if credits and debts are in balance then the total volume of credit remains unchanged and so no additional demand for output is induced. Alternatively, net levels of credit extended through the interenterprise lending process do induce excess final demand. Firms or entire sectors can, by acting as net creditors, stimulate demand for their rising output levels. The most interesting questions, therefore, involve determining how triangular debt is distributed and whether or not net levels of credit are actually being extended.

Although detailed breakdowns of triangular debt nationwide are difficult to come by, data from the state steel sector and the individual case of Angang are perhaps indicative of broader trends. The 1995 MMI study of twelve major steel producers found that seven of the twelve firms were net creditors while five were net debtors.[78] Among the creditor firms, credit sales accounted for anywhere between 97.4 and 7.6 percent of annual sales, with the median at 25.6 percent. The 97.4-percent figure actually applies to a particular pig iron supplier, the bulk of whose credits were extended to two of the study's net debtors. In general, though, it seems that most Chinese steel firms – particularly the largest firms – tend to be net creditors.[79]

The 1995 MMI study provides a glimpse of how these credits are distributed. Approximately 39 percent of the outstanding debt owed to the firms in the study was actually owed by government ministries. Twenty-one percent was owed by the Ministry of Electronic Industry, 14 percent by the MMI, 2.43 percent by the Ministry of Railroads, and approximately 1 percent by the Ministry of Geology and Mineral Resources. Conceivably, these line ministries purchase steel for various investment projects and do so on a credit basis. While vague on this point, the implication of the study is that the remaining 61 percent of outstanding debt was owed by individual firms, either collectives or SOEs.

By 1995, policy makers were aggressively trying to curtail the growth of interenterprise lending. Interestingly, though, officials at all levels seemed to view the problem more as one of tangled cash flows than of induced demand. In other words, there seemed to be far more concern about the absolute size and complexity of debt chains than with the effects of net credit on final demand. The problem was perceived more as one of irresponsible purchasers or inadequate legal protection of creditors and less as a natural outgrowth of overproduction. In short, triangular debt was viewed as a debtor-driven process. Only gradually, and in limited cases, have policy makers begun to understand the creditor-driven aspects of triangular debt. By the second quarter of 1995, ministries including the MMI began advocating rather general slogans such as "No production without contracts, and no delivery without cash" (*wu hetong bu shengchan, bu jian qian bu fahuo*) and "Reduce credits by one third in the next half year" (*shang ban nian yasuo ru qian 1/3*).[80]

The perception of interenterprise arrears as debtor-driven is reflected in a much-publicized method developed by Angang for dealing with its own triangular debt problem. By late 1994, as noted earlier, the firm was a net creditor of approximately RMB 2.8 billion (the firm was owed by others RMB 11 billion, and itself owed to others RMB 8.2 billion). During the month of October 1994, Angang was apparently able to "settle" approximately RMB 580 million of outstanding credits by means of a method its chief economist was eager to see disseminated nationwide.[81] The essence of the technique was that interenterprise debts would be transformed into bank debts.

The logic proceeds along the following lines (see Table 4.7). Angang owes money to the banks because of outstanding working capital loans, and steel purchasers owe Angang money due to nonpayment of steel deliveries. Banks, according to Angang's technique, would issue loans to the steel purchasers, purchasers would then transfer those funds to Angang, and Angang would transfer those funds back to the banks. In the end, Angang's debt to the banks would be reduced, the steel purchasers' debts to Angang would be erased, and the purchasers' debts to the banks would increase. In effect, net creditors like Angang would reduce their levels of outstanding bank debt by selling their outstanding interenterprise credits to the banks at full face value. The banks, rather than

Table 4.7. *Hypothetical debt-clearing example*

Initial condition: Angang owes $100 to banks; customer owes $10 to Angang. Step 1: Bank issues loan of $10 to customer. Step 2: Customer transfers $10 to Angang. Step 3: Angang transfers $10 to bank. Final condition: Angang owes $90 to banks. Customer owes $10 to bank. Customer owes $0 to Angang. Interenterprise debt has been reduced, and overall scale of credit remains unchanged. Bank has assumed the debts owed by customer to Angang.

Angang, would then take on the responsibility of collecting payments from the recalcitrant debtors.

Angang officials argued that the technique has two major merits. First, it would permit a clearing up of all the complex, messy credits that Angang had been "forced" to extend in the past. Second, transforming interenterprise debts into normal bank loans would increase the pressure on debtors actually to repay, since bank loans would accumulate interest whereas interenterprise loans generally do not. As a result, debtors would be held to more market-oriented standards.

The technique had another implicit attraction to firms like Angang. Since the process would reduce Angang's outstanding debt to the banks, the firm would likely be more able to obtain additional bank loans in the future. Any limits on the amount of loans that banks could extend to individual borrowers could thereby be skirted. The debt-clearing technique did not directly solve Angang's liquidity problems, but it indirectly created the conditions under which the firm could continue to receive cash infusions from the banks.

In a more general sense, though, the debt-clearing scheme completely fails to address the underlying behavior that leads to interenterprise debt in the first place. In the view of many Chinese officials, and certainly many of those at the enterprise level, triangular debt is just an unfortunate result of consumers who do not pay bills. Because consumers do not pay bills, producers face liquidity crises. From this perspective, firms like Angang are merely passive victims of a poorly regulated business environment. The real situation, however, is that firms like Angang, rather than being victims, often encourage triangular debt by overproducing. Firms overproduce and then, by extending tremendous amounts of credit, encourage consumers to purchase. The producers are, in a sense, inducing elevated final demand. In doing so, producers should be held responsible for the credits they extend. When such a large portion of these loans end up in the "overdue" or "nonperforming" categories, that is as much a fault of the producer as the consumer. The producer in these cases should have to pay a price for such behavior. Indeed, in more developed market economies, firms that extend too much credit and prove unable to meet their own financial obligations are thrown into bankruptcy.

In China, unfortunately, this does not happen. Indeed, the opposite happens. The producers end up transferring the detritus of their irresponsible lending practices over to the banks. In this sort of environment, when loans are simply rolled over year in and year out, why would a debtor be any more likely to repay a bank loan than an interenterprise loan? Similarly, why would a producer like Angang, after having its outstanding interenterprise credits cleared up once, not be inclined simply to turn around and run up those receivables a second time? Indeed, Angang's heralded debt-clearing technique, by cushioning the impact of such behavior, simply encourages it.

The general point is that, by misinterpreting triangular debt as a problem merely of nonpayments, policy makers ignore the more serious underlying issue. Triangular debt results from systemic incentives that encourage industrial producers to maximize output and sales. Producers then turn around and essentially give the goods away to customers who under normal conditions would never be able to make these purchases. It is only through producer-extended credit that the consumer can "buy" the goods. Precisely because key institutions like bankruptcy and insolvency do not exist, producers can continue these activities unabated. Moreover, producers like Angang then "generously" offer to have banks essentially purchase these bad loans at full face value, thereby reducing the producer's own debt to the bank. When the producer ultimately runs into a major liquidity crisis, the banks then step in and loan money if only to keep the firm afloat and workers employed. The cycle simply goes on and on.

MANAGERIAL INCENTIVES AND THE PROFIT MOTIVE

The preceding sections have referred extensively to institutional factors that inhibit market-oriented behavior in complex industrial producers, yet those barriers are significant only to the extent that they actually influence managerial incentives. Behind the financial stagnation of China's SOEs are a series of abstract causes – distorted information, improper signaling, bureaucratic predation, and excessive state intervention – but what really counts is how a manager perceives this situation and then responds to it.

118

The whole question of managerial incentives in Chinese SOEs has been the subject of considerable academic debate, both in China and the West. A wide range of views have been expressed on this issue, but certainly at one end of the spectrum are scholars who argue that Chinese SOE managers have become profit-oriented.[82] The point of this view is to suggest that, despite the state sector's poor overall performance, reform has brought about important and decidedly positive behavioral changes. Chinese managers, in this view, are coming more and more to resemble their counterparts in developed market systems. The argument is supported by extensive survey data showing that SOE managers in China hold profitability as their primary objective. When scholars interpret this data as reflective of market-oriented attitudes, the key implicit assumption is that "profit" or "profit-making" actually means something in a market-economic sense of the term. However, as illustrated by the case of Angang, profits in the Chinese context can be easily manipulated. Indeed, profit maximization can and *does* take place through decidedly non–market-oriented, value-destroying strategies.

On the other side of the scholarly spectrum are researchers who, observing China's high real rates of taxation, deduce that Chinese managers not only have no interest in profit maximization but in fact actively seek to declare financial losses.[83] Hence, the argument asserts, the number of officially loss-making SOEs rises steadily in China year after year. This view posits that what SOE managers really try to do is maximize retained earnings, and that they do this by hiding profits and exaggerating losses. The firm essentially "chooses to lose."[84] The implicit message is that China's figures for the number of loss-making SOEs are not only unreliable but actually highly overstated. Enterprises, in effect, declare losses when they are actually doing just fine.

This second view, though, fits patterns neither within the Chinese steel industry nor, arguably, within any portion of the Chinese state sector. If SOEs were actually performing rather well, it would be hard to explain the phenomenon of skyrocketing liabilities and declining output. A presumably healthy industrial sector would not be producing less and costing more. Furthermore, as the Angang case suggests, large companies that are in fact operating in the red actually go out of their way to declare annual profits. Thoroughly insolvent producers end up being counted among China's profitable enterprises! If anything, current statistics for loss-making SOEs understate, rather than overstate, the actual situation.

Ultimately then, which side of the debate is correct? Are enterprise managers the profit maximizers that questionnaire data suggest? If so, why would they maximize profits when the tax system seems to reward loss making? Finally, how does this fit the apparent fact that there are more, rather than fewer, enterprises actually operating in the red than national figures suggest? If managers hide anything, it seems to be losses rather than profits. What really is going on?

In general, Chinese survey data are not so much wrong as tremendously deceptive. Survey after survey produces the same result: managers aim for profits. But surveys fail to capture the parameters within which profit maximization takes place, or even the very definition of "profit" in the transitional context. Managers at Angang and other large Chinese SOEs know that profitability is supposed to be the primary firm-level objective in the reform era.[85] After all, the goals of market responsiveness, efficiency, and profitability are trumpeted across practically every governmental document on enterprise reform. It would be surprising, indeed, if managers did not say that they were trying to maximize profits. Nonetheless, that managers say they are maximizing profit, or even that they think they are maximizing profit, is hardly a statement about what sort of behavior actually occurs. Moreover, it is hardly a statement that the firm has actually reoriented toward the market.

As illustrated by the Angang case, managers of large SOEs face tremendous pressures to maximize employment while maintaining basic production. When asked why production or employment levels are not reduced during market downturns, managers frequently respond, "We can't do that."[86] For managers, output cuts or labor-force reductions are career-wrecking moves that must be avoided at all costs. This seems to be true even during periods in which the central government actively encourages sectorwide output cuts. Individual managers are unwilling to risk output or employment cuts during their watch, regardless of the tenor of central policy at any given time. The first (and clearly more superficial) reason is that many of the outside state evaluators who potentially determine promotions still use the tried-and-true standard of the command system: output levels. The second and far more important reason is that employment cuts, because of their potentially destabilizing effect, set off alarm bells in central and local supervisory agencies alike. Managers of major SOEs are government cadres with career ladders extending up into the central bureaucracy. As a result, few if any of these individuals are interested in pursuing managerial strategies with conspicuously negative political or social ramifications. Nobody wants to be responsible for slashing the employment rolls.[87]

In reality, therefore, managers maximize profitability only to the extent that they can meet an initial condition of full or near-full employment. Since most Chinese SOEs suffer from tremendous labor surpluses, the initial condition supersedes the profit goal.[88] Managers may say they are maximizing profits, they may wish they could maximize profits, they may even think they are maximizing profits, but there is always the primary problem of trying to dispose of excess workers. What managers really end up doing is maximizing output and employment. This partially explains why firms continue to produce and expand in saturated markets.

Enterprise managers themselves understand this situation, and they frequently express considerable frustration with it. Many are at least practically versed in market economics and are generally familiar with Western managerial concepts. Yet Chinese managers operate in a system filled with significant obstacles that often preclude profit maximization in any market sense. The great problem is that many of these institutional obstacles provide opportunities for *nominal* profit maximization through decidedly unproductive strategies. In a sense, partial reforms have created an environment in which managers can maximize "profits" while at the same time maximizing output and employment. Managers can juggle accounts, deflate real costs of production, build up tremendous accounts receivable, and pump in capital for which they are paying nothing. Cost cutting and efficiency enhancement become peripheral objectives at best. Managers, in a sense, are neither "profit maximizers" nor "loss maximizers" but rather "paper profit maximizers."[89]

Almost inevitably in the Chinese context, paper-profit–maximizing behavior involves value-destroying rather than value-enhancing business strategies. Firms, in effect, destroy assets rather than create them. Meanwhile, the modern industrial sector as a whole becomes a vehicle more for financial transfers than production. The most important aspect of China's modern industrial sector today is not what it produces, and certainly not how well it produces, but rather how terribly much it consumes. Given the institutional environment surrounding Chinese SOEs today, and given the particular brand of profit maximization frequently pursued within that environment, the state industrial sector ends up playing a key role in the transfer of societal resources from high-growth areas to low-growth ones. The implications for economic development nationwide are both clear and unfortunate.

CONCLUSION

Angang – with its complex interweaving of governance, property rights, and performance dilemmas – symbolizes the policy challenge for SOE reform in transitional systems. Over the past decade and a half, the Chinese government has attempted to effect SOE restructuring without incurring the pain usually associated with such measures. In the modern industrial sector, seemingly decisive reform policies have been consistently and frustratingly undercut by ad hoc countermeasures. Neither local governmental bodies nor banks nor firms have been forced, in any broad systemic sense, to face hard budget constraints. Half-way reform measures have led to poor enterprise-level performance and a brewing systemic financial crisis. Vast amounts of resources still flow into the state sector, but the issue is no longer whether central policy makers still have control over the tap. Clearly, in many aspects they do not. A broad range of economic actors from bankers and managers to local governmental officials now have the power on their own to channel resources, extend credit, and force debt. If policy makers cannot control the tap, then the real question is whether they will cease to support the actors who indirectly do. The question, in other words, is whether banks or firms that have overextended themselves will ever be forced to face the threat of closure.

Over the long run, market control over resource flows may be preferable to governmental control and, in a complex industrialized economy, market control may indeed be the only viable option. Yet, market control can take place only in the presence of key regulatory institutions, not the least of which is bankruptcy. Economic actors, whether banks or firms, must face the threat of market exit or closure. Unfortunately in Chinese state industry today, neither governmental control nor market control really exists. There is little possibility or desire to go back to the former, and there are seemingly insurmountable hurdles to overcome before achieving the latter.

That said, Chinese policy makers have hardly been passive in recent years. Since the early 1990s, moves in fact have been taken to try to cope with the SOE reform challenges typified by the Angang case. Interestingly, these moves in the broadest sense reflect the privatization logic driving reform in other transitional systems. In other words, China's policy makers – gradually, and perhaps quite unintentionally – have internalized the same neoclassical approach to SOE reform that motivates privatization in Eastern Europe and Russia. Although Chinese leaders may be loathe to discuss actual privatization, they do accept the notion that only by specifying property rights in the firm and by exposing managers to real capital costs can industrial firms be made to operate on a market basis. In practical policy terms, this means that firm-level assets must be evaluated, shares must be made available to private investors, and managers must be forced to deliver real returns on investment. This is precisely what is being done in China's current wave of corporatization, measures that do not look appreciably different from corporatization policies in "privatized" post-communist Eastern Europe or Russia. The wave is likely to increase in magnitude given the highly public support it received during the Fifteenth Party

Congress in late 1997. The question to be addressed in the next chapter is whether corporatization, and property-rights reform as such, goes to the heart of the problem in transitional SOE reform. What happens when a firm like Angang "goes public"?

5

King of the Red Chips:
Ma'anshan Steel and the Debacle
of the "Public" SOE in China

INTRODUCTION: MAGANG GOES PUBLIC

ON October 26, 1993, the Ma'anshan Iron and Steel Company ("Magang") completed its offering of "H" shares on the Hong Kong stock exchange, thus becoming one of the first large-scale state-owned enterprises in China to, in effect, "go public."[1] Ma'anshan Iron and Steel – a sprawling 85,000-employee integrated steel operation on the banks of the Yangtze River – by most measures represents the cutting edge of property-rights reform in Chinese industry. It is a state-owned firm whose assets have been evaluated by a Western accounting firm and whose stock freely circulates on both domestic and international securities markets. Magang is an SOE whose owners now include nonstate actors and whose internal governance structure has been made to resemble corporate models from developed capitalist economies. In the broadest sense, the newly "corporatized" Ma'anshan Iron and Steel is engaged in a revolutionary property-rights experiment that Chinese policy makers hope can save the last great remnant of state socialism in the People's Republic, the large-scale state-owned industrial enterprise.

The overseas listing of Chinese SOEs – an experiment that by 1997 included over thirty firms – aims for a series of interlinked, extremely ambitious goals.[2] Policy makers hope that corporatization can in one fell swoop depoliticize the firm, increase efficiency of asset use, and ultimately increase revenue flows from the firm to the state.[3] The underlying premise is that SOEs perform so poorly not so much because the owners happen to be governmental per se, but rather because the number of government bodies claiming ownership privileges is far too many and the actual financial stakes linking those bodies to the firm far too few. According to this logic, once policy makers provide a clear and decisive answer to the question of *who owns,* enterprise performance will then almost certainly improve. The appeal of corporatization lies precisely in its ability to specify ownership. At least in theory, corporatization – by designating shares in the firm and then divvying up those shares to a contained group of holders – creates clearly defined owners who have a true interest in maximizing efficiency and expanding profitability.

Linked with these new ownership forms are at least the trappings of a modern corporate governance system, one that includes the shareholder meetings, corporate boards, and voting mechanisms familiar in the West. The point here is to ensure that capital not only flows into the firm but is also applied by managers according to normal commercial principles. The theory is that owners, once clearly defined, must be given control over managers, and that managers must be forced to respond to market incentives. Corporatization, through its combination of ownership and governance restructuring, offers the hope that China's largest production organizations can at least be weaned from subsidies and perhaps even be converted into globally competitive dynamos.

In a somewhat less lofty sense, corporatization also offers policy makers one last hope of achieving "reform on the cheap." Over the past fifteen years, China's industrial reformers have repeatedly sought to address firm-level performance problems through rather narrowly defined firm-level policy measures. In a way, of course, this makes sense; problems within the firm should be handled at the firm level. However, as indicated by the Angang case, many firm-level performance failures are actually manifestations of broader systemic distortions. Throughout the reform period, Chinese reformers – for all their creativity and pragmatism – have been reluctant to tackle these systemic distortions in any consistent fashion. After all, doing so would entail forcing many firms to exit the market, and forcing firms to exit the market leads to unemployment. Hence, measures like profit contracting and managerial responsibility systems move forward, while banking reform, legal reform, and bureaucratic reform remain at best partial. Systemic reforms of this kind are undoubtedly difficult, costly, and potentially destabilizing, so it is no wonder that policy makers avoid them assiduously. The question, though, is whether real enterprise restructuring can be effected without substantial changes in the firm's institutional environment. Corporatization once again posits the idea that internal changes in the firm's ownership structure can foster market-oriented, "commercial" behavior. But can commercial behavior really be fostered when external regulatory and governance institutions remain decidedly noncommercial? Moreover, can commercial behavior be fostered in the absence of a threat of market exit? China's policy makers – given the unequivocal support for corporatization that emerged from the Fifteenth Party Congress, seem to think that it can.

Unfortunately, initial indications from experimental stock issuers like Ma'anshan Iron and Steel are not particularly good. As will be documented in the following sections, Magang, within a year of its debut on the Hong Kong stock exchange, began facing financial irregularities within the firm, a growing tax debt to the state, and rising levels of short-term liabilities. Magang's own managers now complain that the joint stock reforms have had the opposite effect of what was originally intended.[4] Budgets within the firm have been softened rather than hardened, links between owners and managers have been weakened rather than strengthened, and the ability of bureaucratic actors to extract has been expanded rather than curtailed. The property-rights relationship between firm and state has not been resolved, while information flows from the firm – and, concomitantly, corporate governance – have been made only more hazy. Finally, despite quite radical reform efforts, financial discipline has still not been imposed upon the firm and, indeed, has arguably slackened.

Magang's Postcorporatization Performance

Magang in many ways exhibits behavior rather typical of major Chinese industrial producers. Ownership restructuring has by no means prevented the firm from engaging in interenterprise lending, overproduction, and ill-advised expansion. In some of these areas, the behavior is actually more pronounced at Magang than at other steel enterprises in the region. Through the first quarter of 1995, Magang had accumulated just over RMB 2 billion in receivables and approximately RMB 1.1 billion in payables and other forms of interenterprise debt. Credit sales were still accounting for over 30 percent of the firm's annual steel deliveries, the second-highest rate among the region's twelve major steel producers.[5] The rate of decline for such sales was far slower at Magang than at comparable regional competitors.[6] Meanwhile, Magang's inventories were climbing during this period, despite MMI prohibitions against inventory accumulation.[7] Indeed, Magang during this time was one of the only major steel producers in East China that did not actually lower inventory levels.[8] Overall, Magang's level of interenterprise lending has risen far faster than its sales revenues. The firm, in effect, has been loaning out more and more of its output.[9]

The general point is that Magang's ownership restructuring evidently did not move the firm away from some of the same incentive patterns exhibited in the Angang case. Production is still maximized, with the result that either inventories must accumulate or credit must be extended in order to induce elevated final demand. Furthermore, despite a sagging steel market, the firm continued to engage in fairly substantial fixed asset expansion (see Table 5.1). This combination of declining cash returns on sales and increasing levels of fixed asset construction not surprisingly presented Magang with cash-flow problems similar to those of Angang. Also not surprisingly, Magang, even after its initial public

Table 5.1. *Magang revenue, profit, and fixed asset growth, 1990–95*
(RMB 100 million)

	1990	1991	1992	1993	1994	1995
Sales revenue	24.52	30.13	41.43	65.22	68.43	62.16
[increase from previous year]		23%	38%	57%	5%	−9%
Profit[a]	2.05	5.48	2.15	19.59	7.78	0.21
[increase from previous year]		167%	−61%	811%	−60%	−97%
Net value of fixed assets	18.04	21.58	24.49	40.14	72.35	84.12
[increase from previous year]		20%	13%	64%	80%	16%

[a] Profits prior to the collection of income tax and assorted nontax fees.
Source: Ministry of Metallurgical Industry (1991, pp. 320, 332 [1990 data]; 1992, pp. 99, 111 [1991 data]; 1993, pp. 101, 107 [1992 data]; 1995, pp. 380, 382, 385 [1993–94 data]; 1996, pp. 346, 348, 351 [1995 data]).

offering in Hong Kong, was still amassing short-term liabilities in order to fund both construction and daily production activities. As indicated by the balance sheet in Table 5.2, the firm's current ratio sunk steadily throughout the 1993–95 period; at the same time, asset quality arguably declined as levels of receivables increased. The overall pattern is consistent with the SOE sector as a whole: rising liabilities, declining asset quality, and expanding levels of fixed assets.

In terms of sales and profit levels, Magang's performance mirrors quite closely that of Angang's. A comparison between Table 4.1 and Table 5.1 is illuminating in this respect. For both firms, growth in sales revenue and profit peaked in 1993 – a year, not coincidentally, of relatively expansionary monetary policies on the part of the central government. Credit was still readily available, construction was booming, and the steel industry was thriving. By 1994, however, and certainly into 1995, governmental austerity measures were starting to have a clear effect upon sales revenues and profit. Both had slowed by 1994 and experienced outright declines the following year. In 1995, Magang profits basically languished.

Nevertheless, fixed assets grew throughout this period in both firms, with particularly conspicuous increases at Magang. The expansion boom, in effect, straddled the firm's 1993 initial stock offering in Hong Kong, and indeed picked up pace after the firm's oversubscribed public offering. The investments continued to grow, albeit at a slower rate, right through 1995, even after the firm's share price in Hong Kong had already sagged considerably.[10]

Table 5.2. *Magang consolidated balance sheet, 1993–95*
(RMB 100 million)

	1993	1994	1995
Assets			
Current assets	82.07	95.7	92.32
Long-term investments	2.67	17.12	2.18
Fixed assets			
Fixed assets at cost	46.22	83.38	101.06
Net fixed assets	40.14	72.35	84.12
Ongoing construction	44.28	26.63	24.51
Total fixed assets	84.42	98.98	108.45
Intangible assets	7.75	7.46	10.57
Total assets	176.91	219.26	215.37
Liabilities and owner equity			
Current liabilities	37.93	54.17	63.21
Long-term liabilities	22.15	19.45	16.02
Owner equity	116.83	145.64	136.14
Total liabilities and owner equity	176.91	219.26	215.37
Current ratio (current assets : current liabilities)	2.16	1.77	1.46

Source: Ministry of Metallurgical Industry (1994 [1993 data]; 1995 [1994 data]; 1996 [1995 data]).

To some extent, Magang's performance problems have simply reflected general trends in the Chinese market. That profits took a steep downturn following the imposition of governmental austerity measures is neither surprising nor particularly interesting. In any country, basic industries like steel suffer during downturns in the business cycle. The volatility of Magang stock in Hong Kong is also neither particularly surprising nor necessarily a reflection of internal problems in the firm. After all, the stock fluctuations probably say more about overseas perceptions of China than they do about the health and future viability of the firm itself. As shown in Figure 5.1, investors initially stormed in to buy stock, drove the share price upward, and then rather rapidly lost interest. In essence, thoroughly unrealistic expectations were brought back to ground level by Magang's less-than-stellar profit performance. Whenever mainland SOEs list in Hong Kong, the general pattern is that investors rush in to buy a stake in the China "miracle" and then just as quickly bail out at the first

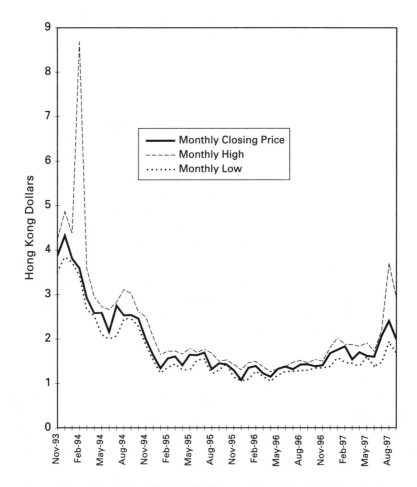

Figure 5.1. Magang Stock Price History (Hong Kong "H" Shares)

sign of profit downturns or the first news of triangular debt. With regard to investors in the Hong Kong "red chips" – Chinese SOEs listed on the Hong Kong stock exchange – their inflated expectations are matched only by their excessive skittishness.

However, a more interesting issue than downward dips in stock price or profitability is the apparent persistence of typical SOE behavior: extensions of inter-enterprise credit, decapitalization of the firm, and expansion even during periods of austerity. Although it is still too early to draw definitive conclusions, this chapter aims to examine just why it is that substantial ownership restructuring has failed to deter this sort of behavior at Magang. Indeed, the thrust of the chapter is that rather than deterring non–market-oriented and value-subtracting business strategies, corporatization actually facilitates them.

The Divergence between Theory and Practice

An important aspect of joint stock reforms is their rather uncanny tendency to attract support from widely divergent interests and for widely divergent reasons. In the case of China, key political leaders have thrown their support behind corporatization as the only means by which privatization can be averted and at least a semblance of state socialism maintained. Simultaneously, China's more radical reformers – joined by mainstream economists in the West – view corporatization as precisely what is needed both to usher in privatization and to undermine the last vestiges of inefficient state ownership.[11] In a sense, these diverging perspectives hint at the particular problems firms like Magang face today as well as the more general incongruity between the theory and actual practice of Chinese property-rights reform.

Magang's journey toward joint stock operations has been neither smooth nor rapid. The idea of pursuing stock reforms in large SOEs was first bandied about in Chinese policy circles in 1983, but only after a decade of political and intellectual wrangling did joint stock reforms for large SOEs move from abstract planning stages to actual trial runs. For ten years, Chinese economists and policy makers debated not only the potential impact of corporatization in China but also the very meaning of stock ownership in a socialist context. Could a firm whose shares are publicly traded and owned by foreigners still be considered a state enterprise? Was this to be the end of China's forty-year experiment with socialism? That the joint stock reforms were ever permitted an experimental test-run in 1992 marked a drawn-out, but ultimately successful, passage through an ideological minefield.

Nevertheless, corporatizing major state firms in China – essentially making these firms look something like Western publicly owned and publicly traded companies – posed much more than just an ideological challenge. Whenever serious efforts are made to restructure ownership in a major industrial producer, a host of issues ranging from power and governance to economic efficiency are raised. Sensitivities exist in a variety of areas, not the least of which is the political realm. When an SOE is corporatized, numerous bureaucratic interests become involved and potentially threatened. Many of the governmental agencies that exerted control over the firm during the command and early reform eras clearly stood to lose as joint stock measures gained in prominence. The opaque lines of authority and ownership under the old system conveniently allowed many disparate agencies to claim firm-level assets without ever being held responsible for firm-level liabilities.[12] The prospect of a clarified ownership structure, particularly one that includes nonstate parties, threatens not only the extractive powers of bureaucratic actors but also the very raison d'être of a state industrial bureaucracy. What does a ministry of metallurgy do if it neither owns nor controls steel firms? Why should it continue to exist? What does a state investment commission do if the enterprise controls all its own investment decisions and actualizes those decisions through funds flowing in from abroad? What does a state planning commission do if it cannot control output decisions in major firms? The list goes on and on. Reform threatens big bureaucracies in China, and those bureaucracies do not give way easily. They may accept reform – they may have no choice – but they struggle to retain power nonetheless. For this reason, even after stock reforms had received approval in Beijing, the policies met stiff resistance at the implementation stage. They came up against resistance from the bureaucratic agencies that still sought to preserve ownership claims over the firm, and they came up against resistance from elements within the firm itself. Partly as a result, the reforms led to unexpected and often deeply disappointing outcomes. Indeed, it was precisely because of this situation that Zhu Rongji – China's economic "czar" and premier-elect – moved so aggressively in early 1998 to scale back the size and power of the industrial ministries.

Yet, it should be noted that political factors were not the only – nor even the most significant – obstacles confronting joint stock reforms. The previous chapter's discussion of Angang describes what happens to large industrial producers in environments marked by the absence of such key regulatory institutions as functioning financial markets, commercially oriented financial intermediaries, meaningful accounting standards, and bankruptcy-induced market exit. China's corporatization measures were, and currently are, being introduced into precisely this environment. In other words, complex, marketlike ownership structures are being introduced inside the firm before many of the most basic institutions of an industrialized market economy are functioning outside the firm. As the experience of Magang suggests, this is not simply an issue of sequencing. Joint stock reforms provide firm-level "insiders" both new investment resources and unprecedented autonomy. In China's partially reformed market, however, that autonomy (control over resources) is extended in the absence of the very institutional mechanisms needed to guarantee that autonomous actors behave in value-enhancing ways. It should not be shocking, therefore, that the Magang experience has been marked by new claimants to firm-level assets and new modes of dodging liabilities. Undoubtedly, outside bureaucratic intervention has been a serious problem, but so too has internal mismanagement. Firm-level actors have found it increasingly possible to gain control over assets and, at the same time, increasingly easy to shift responsibility for firm-level liabilities elsewhere – most often to the state banking system. At least in the early experimental stages, corporatization – a reform agenda again motivated by the best of intentions – has led to a worst-case outcome. Old problems of uncoordinated state intervention persist, yet new opportunities for managerial misbehavior and firm-level asset stripping have been created. Rather than ending the soft budget constraint so characteristic of socialist firms, corporatization has instead perpetuated the soft budget through unprecedented and novel means.

The experience of Magang offers interesting lessons for industrial reform as a whole. Among China's largest industrial producers in the postcommand era, there has been a vast gulf between reform in theory and reform in practice. That gulf exists because new reforms are not simply draped over a blank slate; instead, they plunge into an extremely volatile mix of partially reformed regulatory institutions. Western experts in particular make the mistake of thinking that in China the issue is one of figuring out how to build a market economy or modern corporate system from scratch. Rather, the real question is how to move toward these new systems in the face of potent opposition and without the aid of even the most basic regulatory mechanisms. The question is not just one of building up, but also one of simultaneously negotiating around or even tearing down. Furthermore, the question is not just one of "freeing up," but also of "properly constraining" or "appropriately motivating." If ostensibly market-oriented reforms create merely the impression of a modern corporate governance system while simultaneously encouraging overexpansion, overproduction, and other asset-destroying strategies, then they are hardly worth pursuing. Often, the best reforms on paper – those that make the most sense from an abstract economic perspective – are the most likely to be rendered impotent when brought into contact with an established system . This indeed is the story of Magang: theoretically sound reforms that are nonetheless ill-suited to China's immediate systemic realities, and treatments leading to disease more severe than the original ailment.

THE EVOLUTION OF STOCK MEASURES: REFORM IN THEORY

The idea of joint stock reforms for large SOEs first appeared in China in a 1983 internal governmental policy paper by Wu Jiaxiang and Jin Lizuo.[13] The authors were two young economists, the former a thirty-year-old official in the

Theory Department of the Central Department of Propaganda and the latter a twenty-seven-year-old official in the State Commission for Economic Structure Reform (*Tigaiwei*). Though written at the dawn of the industrial reform era in China, the article delivered a penetrating attack on the old order, from the inefficiencies of centralized planning and investment to the distorted budgets and wasteful behavior of socialist enterprises. That Wu and Jin could have offered such an analysis suggests that at least some policy makers, even at the very start of reform, harbored no illusions regarding state ownership in command systems. The fundamental property-rights issues that Wu and Jin outlined in 1983 were exactly those that Magang's joint stock experiment sought to address ten years later. Indeed, Wu and Jin, as they discussed the potential implementation process for stock measures, hinted at many of the dilemmas Magang would face by 1994. The article is actually quite remarkable for its clarity of vision.

Wu and Jin's policy essay, although relatively controversial at the time, was disseminated publicly in 1985 as a front-page essay in *Jingji ribao,* China's most widely circulated economics newspaper. Publication in the central economic daily, albeit two years after the essay's initial debut, suggests that the Wu and Jin view – at least its diagnosis of the problems of SOEs – fit into the mainstream of theoretical debates over reform. From the start, it seems that Chinese policy makers understood the essential problem at hand. It was the solutions that proved – then and even still today – so elusive.

Wu and Jin began their analysis with the observation that investment resources are squandered in China at precisely the period of national development when efficient investment is most necessary. The young authors noted that, in the modern technological age, all nations face the challenge of amassing and concentrating the capital needed for rapid development and innovation. The Chinese system, however, was perceived to be unable to meet this allocative challenge. Because investment funds were parceled out by the central state, often the most needy firms failed to receive funding, while those that were funded often went unmonitored. Investment capital would then be wasted on nonproductive applications. This style of argumentation touches on the basic information asymmetries that hobble centrally planned economies. Planners monopolize allocative decisions, yet they have neither the information to distribute investment efficiently nor the ability to monitor firms once investment is allocated. Furthermore, the authors maintained, the centralized system is unable to capture the "societal capital" (i.e., private household savings) that in Western economies is channeled with such great effect into industrial development.

The authors argued that the inefficiencies of the system are exacerbated by unspecified property rights. In one sense, the government is encouraged to behave "irrationally" owing to its joint role as owner of some firms and macroeconomic regulator for all firms. Ministries charged with regulation or resource allocation accord preferential treatment to their own firms. Because there is no clear demarcation between state and firm, investment decisions tend to become mixed up in bureaucratic interests and disputes. As the authors suggested, there has never been an "objective," market-based source of financing in China.

Unclear property rights, according to Wu and Jin, have a secondary impact on the internal operations of the firm. Because of the overlap between state and firm, the incentive structure for enterprise managers becomes so skewed that, even if investment funds successfully reach the firm, those funds are likely to be misapplied. Since managers are all appointed by state agencies and are in fact cadres within the governmental hierarchy, managerial behavior is consistently influenced by short-term calculations. If the manager achieves poor results over the short term then he will quickly be relieved of his position, yet if he is successful then he will be promoted up and out of the firm. Hence managers, knowing they are unlikely to remain at the firm for more than a few years, are unwilling to engage in the longer-term investment strategies needed for sustained growth. They instead pump money into short-term, high-profile projects. The managers constantly seek investment funds, but those funds are rarely channeled toward applications that will allow the firm to generate higher returns over the long run.

The whole analysis – with its implicit references to the insatiable investment demand and soft budget constraints of socialist firms – bore a striking resemblance to the writings of János Kornai, articles that in the early 1980s were just starting to receive considerable attention in the West, let alone in a barely "opened" China.[14] Whether or not Wu and Jin had actually read Kornai is immaterial. What is important, though, is that they seemed to be at a similar point on the learning curve with regard to socialist systems as were economists in the West. In other words, even in the early days of industrial reform efforts, the Chinese reform dialogue was not exclusively driven by the high politics and ideological blinders that some have suggested.[15] The problems were well understood at least by some, and were certainly being raised in nonideological terms in such prominent forums as *Jingji ribao*. Again, it was often the pragmatic issue of just how to dig out of the morass of command planning that provoked infighting. Even here, though, Wu and Jin's revolutionary proposal for large state enterprises was phrased in surprisingly objective, pragmatic terms. Perhaps the only barrier that the young economists were unwilling to cross was the call for total and outright privatization.

Wu and Jin latched onto joint stock reforms in the hope that such measures would ease investment shortages by attracting capital from the public at large. Enterprise profitability would serve to signal investment by the public, and ultimately capital would migrate via market forces to the most efficient firms. A better distribution of capital would result, with the added benefit that property rights would be clarified. The firm would be separated from the government, and ownership would be separated from management. In the end, the interests of state, firm, management, and labor would all be unified once SOEs switched over to joint stock operations and began producing more profitably.

Given all the unresolved issues of corporate governance that plague firms even in the highly institutionalized setting of the West, Wu and Jin clearly overestimated the potential benefits of joint stock measures. Like many subsequent reformers, they neglected the critical role played by external governance mechanisms in market economies and instead chose to focus their energies on operations within the firm. Nevertheless, the two economists were anything but naive when it came to anticipating the sort of resistance that the Chinese system would offer toward even those reforms targeting the firm's internal operations. The young policy analysts understood that, since supervisory agencies in the state sector would not cede power easily, gradual and incremental change would be necessary. A three-step process toward joint stock restructuring was therefore recommended.

The first step was to involve the evaluation of firm-level fixed assets and the issuance of shares. The vertical chain of bureaucratic command would be maintained, but each supervisory agency would receive shares and have the power to send representatives to enterprise corporate boards. Enterprise boards of directors would then select enterprise managers, individuals who were business professionals rather than ordinary government cadres. In effect, their fate would be tied to the firm and not to the governmental bureaucracy.

Wu and Jin admitted that this first stage would at best only partially resolve the property-rights issue. The firm would still be an administrative arm of the state, and state agencies would still share the conflicting roles of overall macroeconomic regulation and internal enterprise management. The next step, therefore, would be to transfer stock ownership from individual government agencies to special state holding companies emanating from the financial and banking sectors. The idea was that holding companies would manage firms on a purely commercial basis. The members of enterprise boards would presumably come from the financial system, and those boards would then have the exclusive right to appoint managers. This particular notion of corporate governance via the financial sector is somewhat akin to the contemporary Japanese system, and it

135

is also similar to some current proposals for reforming the American mode of corporate governance.[16]

Finally, Wu and Jin recognized that, even with these measures, the demand for risk capital in a developing economy could be assuaged only with infusions of funding from society at large, particularly from international sources. Hence, the third step would be to allow large SOEs to issue shares on domestic and international stock exchanges. This would mark the complete shift to a stock system while presumably maintaining a semblance of state ownership through the specially designed state holding companies.

The Wu and Jin paper provoked a storm of reaction, much of it critical, within Chinese academic and policy circles.[17] At the time, profit contracting was the policy of choice in industrial reform circles and, in large part because of this, joint stock measures were effectively put on hold all the way through the late 1980s. Nevertheless, by the early 1990s, the Chinese policy community's romance with profit contracting was ebbing, and joint stock reforms rather quickly gained momentum. This movement was in part due to the mounting losses and increasing investment demands of firms managed through contract systems, and in part related to Deng Xiaoping's famous 1992 "Journey to the South." Internal sources within Chinese industry still cite Deng's southern trip – especially the leader's much-publicized calls for radical reform made during that trip – as the key factor that finally spurred the system into action.[18]

As early as February of 1992 – the same month as Deng's trip – the groundwork for joint stock restructuring in heavy industrial enterprises was already being set. From February 29 to March 4, 1992, the State Commission for Economic Structure Reform and the State Council's Office of Productivity (*Guowuyuan Shengchanban*) convened a work conference to discuss stock measures for state enterprises. The sheer number of governmental agencies represented at the meeting suggests the complexity of interests involved in such reform measures. Present were officials from thirteen different central ministries, plus officials from the economic structure reform commissions, planning commissions, financial departments, and state asset management commissions of fourteen provinces.[19] The result of that meeting was a series of rules and standards to be followed in the pending joint stock experiments. In September 1992 – well after the conclusion of Deng's turn through the South – the State Commission for Economic Structure Reform, acting under the authority of the State Council, named nine large-scale, heavy industrial state enterprises to undergo joint stock restructuring.[20] The largest among the firms chosen was Magang.

Over the next two years, Magang would pioneer stock reforms along a path nearly identical to that laid out by Wu and Jin ten years earlier. What Wu and Jin did not quite estimate, though, was the tenacity with which the old system would cling to power and the intractability of the soft-budget problems that joint stock reforms sought to address. In a sense, the young economists' theory was on target – they clearly understood the basic problems of state ownership – but they underestimated the difficulty of translating theory into practice. In a deeper sense, however, they underestimated just how intensely deferred reforms in the firm's external environment would affect even the most progressive reforms in the firm's internal environment.

MAGANG UNDER CONTRACT: THE PRESTOCK YEARS

Prior to its reorganization in 1992, Magang was in many ways a typical large state enterprise, albeit with certain unique advantages of its own. Built primarily from 1958 to 1961, the firm rapidly grew to become a fully integrated iron and steel producer, complete with mining, smelting, and steel rolling operations. Indeed, all the way through the 1970s, Magang served as a sort of political and economic model under the slogan, "In the North there's Daqing, and in the South, Magang!"[21] Magang is considerably newer than firms like Anshan or Shougang – firms that were operating prior to 1920 – so it faces fewer crises with regard to a deteriorating capital plant or desperately obsolete facilities. Similarly, Magang in 1962 established a train-wheel production facility, the only such plant in China and one of the few in the world. Magang train wheels have been exported throughout Asia and remain a major source of profit for the company. In short, even before stock reforms were undertaken at Ma'anshan Iron and Steel, the firm was in better shape, and had more potential, than the vast majority of large-scale state enterprises in China.

Nevertheless, Magang was also typical with respect to certain problems. It had always been burdened by a labor force far larger than needed, a force that on the eve of stock reforms stood at over 82,000 workers.[22] Furthermore, like any other large SOE in China, Magang must provide housing, full medical care, pensions, and a variety of other social services to those employees and their families. Ma'anshan Iron and Steel consists not only of factories and mines but also of hospitals, schools, day-care centers, and canteens. Officials at Magang note that for years they have been under considerable pressure not only to shed workers from the steel operation and create employment for them elsewhere, but also to provide employment for family members of workers.[23] The same managers complain that one of their biggest concerns in recent years has been to start up collective enterprises (small-scale food processing operations, textile companies, service organizations) for the sole purpose of employing Magang personnel, even if those collectives must operate at a loss.

This matter of finding employment for surplus workers arises at most large Chinese SOEs as they try to streamline. In order to improve efficiency in the firm's main operations, excess workers need to be moved into sideline areas, but neither the workers nor their families can simply be told to leave the company. This is precisely due to the SOE's conflicting role as production unit, employment agency, and provider of state social welfare benefits. In this respect Magang, like Angang, is at a geographical disadvantage, since it is not located in a major urban center. The city of Ma'anshan, like Anshan, exists only because of the steel mill, and hence the city does not present much of a market for consumer goods or services. Setting up collective factories or service organizations to absorb surplus labor in such an environment is no easy task. Cities like Ma'anshan or Anshan are totally different from Beijing or Shanghai, where the collective enterprises of a large SOE might hope to make money, or at least break even. For Magang, subsidiary collectives are strictly employment agencies, and usually loss-making ones at that.

Given these circumstances, it is not surprising that Magang by its own admission suffered throughout the 1980s from a habitual shortage of investment funds, chronically low labor productivity, and extremely low returns on investment.[24] Contributing to this were the usual incentive problems associated with socialist production: the emphasis on output maximization, input accumulation, and physical expansion. Magang was by no means the worst of China's steel mills – it usually ranked second in the MMI (Ministry of Metallurgical Industry) efficiency studies – but it was certainly not in good shape. It shared all the characteristic illnesses of large SOE's in China, the very problems noted by Wu and Jin in 1983.

By the 1990s, Magang had grown to become a two-million-ton capacity steel operation, but expansion had come at great cost. From 1983 to 1992, the firm received just under RMB 1 billion in government funds for investment in production facilities alone, not to mention significant (though unspecified) loans and subsidies for housing and other "nonproductive" uses.[25] While receiving major infusions of state resources, Magang – again, typically for a state firm – served simultaneously as a primary source of tax revenue for a variety of national and local state agencies. Through the late 1980s and early 1990s, Magang accounted annually for 85 percent of Ma'anshan City's tax revenue and for nearly 20 percent of Anhui Province's total revenue from industrial units.[26] In 1992, a rather typical year, Magang retained only 8 percent of its pretax revenues – a rather paltry sum, but about average among large steel producers in China. Magang, despite its advantages of relative newness and a good output mix, was hemorrhaging money just like other large SOEs. It had the usual insatiable appetite for investment as well as the usual problems of profits disappearing via governmental extraction or managerial inefficiency.

No doubt, as at Angang, poorly defined property rights played into this situation. Prior to the stock experiment, Magang – like any other large SOE in China – was subject to supervision and financial extraction by a complex layering of state agencies. Such a situation precluded a clear definition of lines of authority or accountability over the firm. The Anhui steel producer, like other major steel operations, was shifted in the mid-1970s from central ministerial to provincial jurisdiction. Meanwhile, however, Magang's output levels and product mix were still being determined by the central Ministry of Metallurgical Industry, even though taxation was usually handled at the provincial level. Magang's efforts to import equipment from abroad had to be channeled through the central State Planning Commission, and all major investment projects had to be approved at the central level. In short, officials within Ma'anshan Iron and Steel faced a complex, changeable, and frequently unpredictable outside chain of command.

Officials at the firm acknowledged that, by the mid-1980s, the ownership situation had become quite confused.[27] Looking back, senior managers noted that with the decreasing importance of the state plan in output allocation, the MMI ceased to have much authority over Magang. However, as in the situation of Liaoning Province and Angang, provincial officials in Anhui had neither the means nor the expertise to manage or monitor such a large firm as Magang.

In China, attempts to describe "who has authority over what" are inevitably hampered by the lack of generalizable rules. This is as true in steel as in any other key industry. Some large steel mills appear to be under central supervision, whereas others appear to be more under local control. Magang seems to come out closer on the provincial side of the balance, but authority relations right across the industrial sector tend to be rather hazy. The interwoven, cross-cutting lines of authority regarding personnel appointments are but one indicator of the situation. Prior to 1992, Magang's general manager and eight to ten vice-managers were all appointed by the provincial government, with the apparent approval of the MMI, while the party secretary and vice-secretary were appointed by the organization department of the provincial party committee.[28]

Far more clear, however, is that a number of governmental levels saw fit to extract from Magang. Both central and provincial tax agencies levied a range of circulation, sales, and natural resources taxes upon Magang and its mining subsidiaries. Furthermore, the municipal government over the years has also collected from Magang a wide range of fees to cover such things as infrastructure improvements, utilities usage, and public services. These fees were often levied ad hoc upon Magang, the municipal government's rationale being that the vast majority of beneficiaries for municipal projects would be Magang employees anyway. Ma'anshan Iron and Steel, as the single large state enterprise in the area, served as the same kind of cash cow for its city government that Angang did (and does) for Anshan City.

At the same time, just as at Angang, Magang had such a poorly defined governance structure that blame for poor performance could never be pinned on any single individual or agency. Errors could always be attributed to "objective conditions" or "historical factors," and performance data could always be adjusted to compensate. The nested problems dynamic operated at Magang just as at other large-scale Chinese SOEs. Not surprisingly, then, Magang suffered from the typical SOE ailments of low efficiency, low profitability, and a constant hunger for investment.

An initial attempt was made to clear up these problems in the latter half of the 1980s as Magang was shifted to the enterprise contracting system, a system then in its heyday as China's own home-grown brand of industrial reform. The notion was that the SOE could be reinvigorated if its relationship with the state, particularly the fiscal aspect of that relationship, were set down in contractual terms. Again, since contracts varied greatly from firm to firm, it is hard to generalize about the efficacy of contracting as a whole. Nevertheless, the contract embodied certain common themes in Chinese industrial reform. There was considerable attention paid toward separating the functions of firm and state and toward carving out autonomy for managers, but very little attention was directed toward corporate governance. The implications are twofold. First, no mechanisms were set up to guarantee that the firm appropriately used the funds it could now retain. Second, consistent reporting standards – standards that could reveal violations of the contract – were never established. "Profit maximization" was certainly hammered in as the goal, but nothing guaranteed that asset-enhancing strategies would actually be employed by managers. Actors both within and outside the firm could still engage in asset stripping, while managers could still blame poor performance on objective circumstances. Indeed, opportunities for both forms of behavior actually multiplied.

The actual terms of Magang's contract are instructive in this respect. The arrangement was initially set to last for five years, from 1988 to 1992, and set out a number of responsibilities on the part of both firm and state.[29] First, the enterprise guaranteed that it would annually submit a flat rate of RMB 130 million in profit to the state, a revenue transfer that in the West would be considered income tax. In addition, taking the firm's 1987 level of RMB 158 million in submitted circulation taxes as a base, Magang for the next five years would contribute circulation taxes at an increasing rate of 6 percent annually. In total, the company was slated to pay RMB 1.6 billion to the state over the five-year duration of the contract. The arrangement was a bit unusual in that it held income taxes constant while stressing increases in what were basically sales taxes. Instead of encouraging the firm to maximize net income, the resulting incentive structure seemed to push the firm to maximize sales revenues (essentially, output) in order to hit the increasing sales tax targets. Nevertheless, the underlying principle of the contract remained fairly typical: anything earned above the contracted submission targets was to be retained by the firm. If state investment were truly cut off, the firm might then have a substantial interest in trying to surpass the profit targets in order to maximize retained earnings. After all, the firm was (at least formally) being given a right to residual returns.

The state's responsibilities under the contract were twofold. First, the state had to guarantee Magang the "basic conditions" under which the production aspects of the contract could be fulfilled: a steady supply of raw materials and energy, and sufficient transportation facilities. Second, the state also had to provide the "basic conditions" – namely, bank loans – by which Magang could fund its modernization projects.

That this particular form of contract did not ease Magang's low productivity and high investment demand is understandable. In the first place, as just noted, the incentive structure was still skewed toward output rather than profitability. In the second place, by stipulating a constant flow of state bank loans and direct investment, the contract did not press the firm to rely on retained profit for modernization projects. Particularly because state bank loans tend to be "soft" – short-term loans can be rolled over year after year, and long-term loans can be converted into equity – Magang was never forced to adopt the kind of financial discipline that might lead to more commercially oriented behavior.

Moreover, instead of clarifying a confused property-rights situation, the contract simply duplicated it. The clauses referring to state responsibilities never actually specified who or what represents the state. The oddest thing is that the actual contracting agency was the Ma'anshan City government, the lowest possible rung on the state bureaucratic ladder and one that historically had little if any authority over Ma'anshan Iron and Steel. This, in a sense, was like asking a mouse to guard an elephant. Ma'anshan City is but an outgrowth of the steel plant itself. Indeed, when interviewed, the head of the city metallurgical bureau insisted that his office does not and never did have any authority over Magang, a statement that is not surprising given Magang's status as a major national firm.[30] In effect, the contracting party on the state side had no authority to fulfill the responsibilities outlined in the document.

In addition, Ma'anshan City was too low on the bureaucratic totem pole to offer Magang any protection from intervention by higher state agencies. The city, in fact, still had an interest in collecting ad hoc fees from Magang in order to fund urban development projects. Whether under the contract or not, Magang faced a situation in which a variety of uncoordinated state agencies intervened in the firm's management and made claims upon the firm's assets. Many agencies interfered, but none accepted responsibility for the consequences of its actions or for any other aspects of firm-level performance.

Finally, the contract's duration of only five years provided insufficient time for the firm to amass its own investment capital through profit retention. As mentioned earlier, Magang in the final contract year was still able to retain only 8 percent of its pretax income. Given the high tax targets and short duration of the contract, it was perhaps inevitable that the firm remain dependent on vast infusions of state bank loans. According to Magang's own accounting estimates, by the end of the contract the firm had submitted RMB 1.7 billion to the state and had received from the state over RMB 500 million in investment funding for modernization projects.[31] What that latter number does not include are the hefty loans generally received by large SOEs for nonproductive investments in housing or social welfare.[32] Nor does it include "commercial" loans extended by state banks on their own behalf.

By the end of this first five-year contract, none of the parties was satisfied, and the nested problems dynamic seemed to be grinding away just as it had before. In a way, the contract measures at Magang fit broader, nationwide patterns of reform. Policy makers at the center are eager to correct incentive problems within the firm, but are reluctant to do so in ways that involve tackling fundamental systemic factors. Stepping on the interests of managers is one thing, but stepping on the interests of local governments or state agencies is another. Similarly, the repercussions of telling managers to focus on profitability are minor, but the repercussions of rationalizing the fiscal system, commercializing the banking sector, and implementing bankruptcy regulations are substantial. The political costs of tinkering with managerial incentives on the margin are minimal. However, real changes in managerial incentives require the imposition of financial discipline, and the imposition of financial discipline requires major changes in economic institutions and elevated levels of unemployment. Unfortunately, the latter set of changes are terribly expensive politically.

The result, at least in the case of profit contracting, has been an unfortunate mix of cross-cutting policy measures. Managerial discipline is supposed to be encouraged through the establishment of profit targets and retention incentives, but excessive governmental extraction goes unpunished. Instead, banks are told to lend to insolvent firms. Management then faces soft budgets, and becomes increasingly inclined to pursue value-subtracting business strategies. Profit contracts are subsequently discredited for not effectively orienting the firm toward commercial operations. New measures, such as corporatization, are then attempted, but the same pattern persists. No enterprise-level measures – whether delivered in the form of profit contracts, responsibility systems, tax reductions, or joint stock restructuring – will work if financial discipline is not imposed. Because it is not the policy measures per se that fail, there is little point in pursuing new ones year after year. Rather, it is the fact that policy measures are so narrowly circumscribed, and that malfunctioning regulatory institutions so insulated from challenge, that real shifts toward commercially oriented behavior prove so elusive.

Nevertheless, this was clearly not the lesson Chinese policy makers drew from the failure of contracting at Magang, Angang, or any other firm. Instead, what was apparently learned was that firms needed even more radical internal restructuring. Not coincidentally, policy makers also recognized that such firms needed new infusions of capital, precisely at a time when the state was running out of money. Joint stock reforms, then, offered a convenient solution to both problems. Managerial arrangements would be substantially overhauled and, in the process, investment capital from both home and abroad would flow in. What was needed in 1992 to test the program were relatively young firms in high-profile, potentially high-growth sectors. Ma'anshan Iron and Steel fit the bill.

MAGANG UNDER JOINT STOCK OWNERSHIP: REFORM IN PRACTICE

When a large SOE in China undergoes managerial restructuring, bureaucratic interests are invariably affected and bureaucratic obstacles invariably emerge. The one thing driving reforms forward, though, is the firm's hunger for investment. Chinese firms – if they are to keep workers employed, housed, and paid – need money; more often than not, money from retained profits is simply insufficient to maintain enterprise operations. Moreover, if the state can no longer afford to channel investment funds into the firm then money must come from somewhere else, and that "somewhere else" in the early 1990s became international securities markets.

When asked the major purpose of joint stock reforms, Chinese officials at the enterprise and the ministerial level alike consistently point to a basic financial issue: such reforms offer the hope of raising large amounts of money in a short period of time, thus easing the funding shortages threatening SOE survival.[33] For the industry-level people, the issue is money and little else. There is no deep contemplation of property-rights reform or incentive restructuring for the world of tomorrow, but instead a basic quest to come up with enough funds to keep plants operating today. Even in official documents, "improving managerial autonomy" or "reinvigorating the firm" are placed low on the list of objectives in the stock reforms.[34] To this day, many policy makers and enterprise-level officials fail to distinguish between a stock and a bond, seeing both as just a form of loan or as a convenient means of capital enrichment. However, even though stock issues aim primarily to raise money, they do in fact also change the property-rights situation, managerial autonomy, and governance mechanisms. It is in these changes, many of them unpredicted, that Magang's problems after joint stock restructuring would lie.

Soon after Magang was chosen for joint stock experimentation in late 1992, a conference was convened to determine how to parcel out the firm's shares.[35] Even the experiment's initial approval – "approved by the State Commission on Economic Structure Reform under the leadership of the State Council, based on an [initial] combined report by Anhui Province and the MMI" – hints at the multiple layers of interests involved.[36] The initial planning conference was actually intended to pursue the first step in joint stock reforms described by Wu and Jin a decade earlier: the evaluation of the firm's net worth, and the divvying up of ownership shares among all agencies traditionally claiming authority over the firm.

According to at least one participant in that conference, trouble began immediately because of the sheer number of agencies making claims to Magang stock.[37] There was simply no means of adjudicating between those claims. Agencies ranging from the Ma'anshan City government to the provincial and central levels all made justifiable claims over Magang based upon existing lines of authority. That Ma'anshan City, and even in most cases Anhui Province, never possessed the means to supervise or monitor Magang was irrelevant. Again, the important issue here was money. Local agencies, throughout the various decentralization campaigns of the reform period, had been saddled by the center with increasing budgetary responsibilities.[38] Faced with major infrastructure projects, not to mention their own social welfare responsibilities, the localities – from the province on down – were not willing to give up control over revenue flows from a large SOE like Magang. Furthermore, central agencies –

some struggling simply to perpetuate themselves after planning roles had been reformed out of existence – clung tenaciously to stakes in Magang. The logic was simple. Magang would be receiving huge amounts of money from foreign stock issues and furthermore, as a major SOE, would never be allowed by the central government to go bankrupt. Since money would always be available for extraction, shares in Magang were too precious to be given up without a struggle.

It should be noted that a remarkably similar set of disputes arose at Wuhan Iron and Steel when that major producer first explored joint stock issues in 1993 and 1994.[39] There was the exact same scrambling for shares among a multitude of state claimants, and the same postponement of "step 1" in the joint stock process.

Because of these previous problems, a decision was made in the case of Magang to jump straight to Wu and Jin's "step 2": placing the firm under a state holding company before actually allowing stock to debut on the international market. Once again, reformers proved either unwilling or unable to challenge interests beyond the firm. As a result, critical structural issues were sidestepped, while major reforms within the firm were permitted to proceed.

In actual policy terms, Magang was divided into two parts, one of which became a state holding company and the other a stock company. Originally, the 82,000-employee firm consisted of fifty-three "units" spanning everything from the mining and steel operations to support services, housing bureaus, health-care facilities, and educational institutions.[40] On June 1, 1993, a formal division was made creating the Ma'anshan Magang Holding Company (hereafter referred to as "Magang Holding") and the Ma'anshan Iron and Steel Company (hereafter "Magang Steel"). Magang Steel consisted of the original Magang's thirty main production units – essentially the whole iron and steel operation, from the sintering plants all the way to steel casting and rolling facilities. Basically, anything directly related to steel production from the original Magang, including 53,000 employees, ended up concentrated in Magang Steel.[41] Magang Holding was left with the remaining twenty-three "ancillary" units of the original Magang – the entire mining operation, construction companies, housing agencies, health-care facilities, schools – and approximately 30,000 workers.

The motivating principle behind the division was to have Magang Holding retain a controlling share of Magang Steel and thus act as an agent of the state in "owning" the stock company. The method attempted, in a sense, to make a virtue out of a necessity. Since it was unlikely that the conflicting property-rights claims over the original Magang would ever be settled, the problem was simply obviated by making Magang Holding the sole representative of an undefined "state." Magang Steel, owned by an agent of the state, could itself still be considered state-owned, and Chinese reformers would thus not be perceived as backsliding on the maintenance of the socialist system. Magang Holding, throughout this whole process, would have the same status as any other Chinese SOE: it would be under the traditional hierarchical web of supervisory agencies. Furthermore, since all the potentially money-making portions of the original Magang would be concentrated in the public stock company, the shares of that company would conceivably appear more attractive – especially on the Hong Kong market, where over a quarter of all shares would be issued. Because Magang Steel would not be burdened by unseemly, nonproductive social service operations and bloated staffs, it would appear to casual investors as something resembling a modern Western firm. Only by this structural division could the stock firm hope to show some sort of profit, the kind of results that might attract desperately needed investment capital.

A less cynical view is that separating productive from nonproductive aspects of a large SOE actually constitutes real reform, since at least half of the firm, the "profit-center" half, could then stand a chance of pursuing commercially oriented production. Because social welfare functions had been removed from the firm, credible threats of bankruptcy could be wielded against managers. Steps were being taken that would at least make the imposition of financial discipline possible, if not probable. For World Bank observers, Magang's style of corporate reorganization represented a first step toward clarifying the ownership situation in state firms, and perhaps a first step toward ultimate privatization.[42]

In the case of Magang Steel, a total equity issue of 6.45 billion shares was undertaken. Before any shares even hit the market, Magang Holding was given a 62.5-percent ownership block, or approximately 4 billion shares. In November of 1993, 26.85 percent of the stock – 1.7 billion shares – was issued in the form of "H" shares on the Hong Kong market; then 9.29 percent was sold as "A" shares (stock available for purchase within China by Chinese citizens) on the Shanghai stock exchange. An additional 87.8 million shares, 1.36 percent of the total, were termed "corporate shares" and were retained by Magang Steel.[43] Ultimately, the issue of both "H" and "A" shares raised over RMB 6.6 billion, much of which came from Hong Kong. In terms of attracting investment, the equity issue was a boon to Magang.

The Magang Holding–Magang Steel Contractual Relationship

The actual relationships between Magang Holding and Magang Steel, and between the firms and the state, were far more complicated than the stock

Table 5.3. *Contractual relationship between Magang Holding and Magang Steel*

	Pricing basis	Total value (RMB)
Principal services rendered by Holding to Steel		
Primary, secondary, and kindergarten education	Actual costs	4,500,400
Canteens, baths, nurseries	Actual costs	4,725,833
Renting of housing by staff	Actual costs	5,945,150
Landscaping, sanitation, road maintenance	State prices	3,539,333
Renting of hotels and guest houses	Market prices	634,000
Others	Market prices	1,793,524
Total		21,138,240
Principal services rendered by Steel to Holding		
Water supply	Market prices	41,600
Electricity supply	Market prices	433,733
Oxygen supply	Market prices	19,800
Telephone services	Market prices	669,384
Total		1,164,517

Source: Ma'anshan Iron and Steel Company Limited (1994, p. 21).

distributions suggested. First, the firms themselves were wedded together by a series of contractual relationships. Superficially, Magang Steel, as a modern "public" company, was permitted to shed many of the worker housing and social service responsibilities of a traditional Chinese SOE. Nevertheless, in reality, the 53,000 employees of Magang Steel still had to receive these benefits. The central government may have been willing to streamline a company, particularly when the potential reward entailed capital inflows from abroad, but the government was not willing to cut workers off from the old system of cradle-to-grave benefits. As a result, the employees of Magang Steel were provided housing and social services through a series of contractual arrangements with Magang Holding. Table 5.3 describes the extent of these contractual relationships, as well as the value of services rendered in 1993.

The term "actual" costs used in these contracts was somewhat vague, particularly with respect to housing rents. How should rents have been determined in the absence of a housing market? Did Magang Holding's housing costs include only expenditures on upkeep, or were initial investments also reimbursed? None of these questions was clearly answered in the contract, but a hint that prices were somewhat skewed is that housing costs for over 50,000 workers in 1993 were not appreciably larger than the educational or child-care costs provided by Magang Holding.

It is hard to escape the conclusion, one confirmed by Magang officials, that Steel was getting the better end of the bargain in these contracts. Many of the services provided by Holding were extremely undervalued. In essence, Steel was receiving high market prices for the services it rendered to Holding – namely, those related to energy supply – whereas Holding was stuck with the one service that tends to cripple SOEs both administratively and economically: housing provision. The contract system fits the general pattern of bolstering the stock company as an investment opportunity while at the same time shifting the darker aspects of SOE operations over to the nonpublic holding company.

The bulk of Magang Steel's worker pension responsibilities – another traditionally huge drain on SOE coffers, and a perennial source of accumulated liabilities – was also shifted over to Magang Holding. Here, the actual arrangement was again murky, particularly since the rules were set out by Ma'anshan City and generally received little attention in central documents. Why Ma'anshan City had jurisdiction over this issue is unclear, but it demonstrates the ability of even low-level government agencies to retain regulatory powers after property-rights reform. In any case, under the Ma'anshan scheme, all employees of Magang Holding and Steel were entitled to pensions upon retirement, and each employee was obliged to contribute 2 percent of his or her salary annually to the pension fund. In addition, the Magang Group, the combination of Holding and Steel, was obliged to contribute 21 percent of the aggregate salaries of all employees to the pension plan. Magang Holding was then assigned the task of managing that plan.[44] Although the contributions of the group as a whole were specified, the scheme apparently did not delineate how Holding and Steel should determine their individual contributions. In other words, the contract was vague enough to make it difficult to pinpoint the exact responsibilities – particularly the exact financial obligations – of the stock firm.

Furthermore, the contract dealt only with the pensions of currently employed workers and did not address the issue of previously accumulated unfunded pension liabilities, a problem plaguing most large SOEs. Prior to reorganization, Magang – like any other large SOE – was paying pensions to a large group of retired employees: 16,000 individuals in the case of the Anhui steel producer.[45] With the reorganization, a decision was made simply to transfer this burden in its entirety to Magang Holding. Again, the idea seemed to be that the stock company should be shielded from any "historical problems" related to SOEs, regardless of the fact that the bulk of those retirees had been employed on the shop floors now classified as part of Magang Steel.

A final component of the Magang Holding–Magang Steel contract involved annual transfers of iron ore and limestone. The exact stipulation was that Holding, which was saddled with a traditionally unprofitable mining operation, would annually supply 2.3 million tons of iron ore and 70,000 tons of limestone to Steel for ten years. Prices of those raw materials were not to be higher than "domestic market price" – whatever that meant in a country where ore prices are, for the most part, administratively controlled – though the exact price in any given year was left for future "supplemental agreements." In short, while Magang Holding was guaranteed a purchaser for its ore, no clear pricing scheme was set out, nor was any enforcement mechanism established in the event that transactions failed to go as planned.

Whether considering this particular materials transfer arrangement or any other aspect of the contract between Steel and Holding, one gets the sense that significant issues were simply left open to interpretation by the parties involved. The notion of allowing a traditional Chinese SOE to sell shares – and sell them abroad, no less – appeared to be revolutionary, but a series of "hedges" would ultimately undermine the establishment of commercially oriented managerial incentives. These very same hedges would offer considerable opportunity for abuse, opportunities that were ultimately exploited by a wide variety of economic and political actors.

Personnel Appointments under the New System

One particular area of hedging involved the system of managerial appointment at Magang. Wu and Jin stressed early on that stock reforms would lead to a less politicized and more performance-oriented system of managerial appointment in the Chinese firm. In theory, the managers of a public firm, whether Chinese or foreign, should be chosen by a board of directors, a board that would itself be chosen through shareholder voting. For China, however, control over appointments – whether to the firm, to local agencies, or to central ministries – has been the most enduring and effective means by which central leaders retain control over the entire political and economic system. The personnel appointments process is, in a sense, the backbone of the Chinese party-state, and it is one of the few remaining sources of systemic coherence.[46] Under such circumstances, it is difficult to imagine that the Chinese government would surrender its right to control managerial assignments in major SOEs. It is particularly inconceivable – at least at the present time – that the state would sacrifice this right to foreign investor-owners.

Wu and Jin, and many other reformers, seem to have recognized this, but they still hoped that stock reforms would lead to a more objective system of appointments. The thrust of the 1983 argument was that state holding companies – preferably originating from the banking sector – would name managers according to strict and objective standards of financial performance. The state would retain nominal control, but the political aspects of the process would be diminished and the more commercially oriented aspects strengthened.

In the case of Magang, the personnel system has defied reform. Even when Magang Steel's equity issues first entered the planning stages, central authorities made it absolutely clear, at least within party circles, that managerial appointments would not be left up to shareholders. The Ministry of Metallurgical Industry emphasized in a 1993 internal document that strict party rule would be maintained at Magang, despite public share offerings.[47] This really was not even an issue at Magang Holding, since that company would still be a traditional SOE staffed by appointees from higher agencies. With Magang Steel, though, the initial MMI plan was to have the general manager of Holding serve simultaneously as the vice–party secretary of the stock company. Similarly, the party secretary of the parent company would serve as the vice–chairman of the board of the stock company, thus extending the state's authority down through the holding company and into the joint stock firm.

In addition, the MMI document emphasized that, while the stock company would have a corporate board (in theory representing shareholder interests), the company would also have a party committee. The responsibilities of the board and the party committee would be nearly identical. The MMI did note, however, that the corporate board would focus on more specifically "economic" issues whereas the party committee would have a more "political" function. Nevertheless, in this version of what the MMI termed a "socialist stock company," it seems ludicrous to debate whether the functions of the boards differ when their personnel, most notably at the leadership level, are all the same.[48]

In reality, what happened at Magang was that the general manager of Holding, Hang Yongyi, was also appointed chairman of the board of Steel.[49] Wang Wanbin, the senior vice–general manager of Holding and also the party secretary of Holding, was simultaneously named vice–chairman of the board of Magang Steel. What that meant was that the top two officials at Magang Holding also happened to hold the top two positions on the board of directors of the stock company, Magang Steel (see Table 5.4). Day-to-day operations at Steel, though, were to be handled by a separate appointee, the general manager. As an

Table 5.4. *Magang senior managerial personnel*

Magang Holding		Magang Steel	
Title	Appointee	Title	Appointee
General Manager	Hang Yongyi	Chairman of the Board	Hang Yongyi
First Vice-Manager	Wang Wanbin	Vice–Chairman of the Board	Wang Wanbin
Party Secretary	Wang Wanbin	Vice–Chairman of the Board	Li Zongbi
		General Manager	Li Zongbi

aside, it is interesting to note that Magang's Hong Kong publications – its stock prospectus and annual reports – scrupulously avoided mention of the communist party and party affiliation when referring to appointments. Yet Magang's domestic publications, including its stock prospectus aimed at the Shanghai market, referred openly to party operations and the party committee.[50]

Two important points are worth emphasizing with regard to the personnel situation at Magang. The first is that state agencies have essentially retained all their former rights of appointment. This issue was emphasized in the MMI's preparatory policy statements, and has been confirmed by the intermingling of senior positions at Magang Holding and Magang Steel. Officials at both portions of the company confirmed that all senior managerial positions – including all the vice-managers and vice–party secretaries – are still determined from above by Anhui Province, the Anhui party committee, and the MMI in Beijing.[51] Company officials noted dryly that state authorities would never leave something as important as senior personnel decisions in the hands of enterprise managers, let alone in the hands of stockholders.

This leads to the second, more complex point. The general manager and party secretary of the holding company shared senior positions in the stock company, but they did not control the appointments of their subordinates in the stock company. In other words, they could neither appoint nor fire the general manager of the stock company, the numerous vice-managers, and so on down the list. All those appointments were (and presumably still are) made by outside government agencies – namely, Anhui Province for most of the midlevel positions.[52]

This situation offered a new twist on traditional Chinese corporate governance, though not necessarily a positive one. As the agent of the "state," Magang Holding was supposed to be the prime monitor of Magang Steel, thus replacing the traditional plethora of outside supervisory agencies. Despite this, officials at Magang Holding did not have the kind of control over senior and midlevel managerial appointments that would permit effective enforcement or monitoring. The same was true with regard to Magang Steel's contractual obligations to Magang Holding. Except for the fact that the very top officials at Holding happened also to be senior officials at Steel, the parent company had none of the authority necessary to enforce contracts within the Magang Group. The "owner," after all, could not fire the managers of its publicly listed subsidiary. In short, the holding company was thrown into the supervisory role formerly held by government agencies, yet it was provided none of the powers needed to perform this function.

Additional Sources of Bureaucratic Intervention

Although control over personnel decisions may have been the clearest vestige of the old system, traditional bureaucratic intervention in the reorganized joint stock SOE was perpetuated by other means as well. A case in point was the extension of enterprise–government profit contracting at Magang even after the stock reforms. As mentioned earlier in this chapter, Magang from 1988 to 1992 operated under a tax contract signed with Ma'anshan City. The original idea was that, once joint stock reforms began at Magang, the contract would be replaced by a standard 15-percent corporate income tax and a national value-added tax. Actually, tax contracting was supposed to end – not just at Magang but throughout China – with the introduction of a federated tax system in January 1994. Yet, during 1992 and 1993, as Magang underwent reorganization, the original tax contract was simply extended to 1995. More important, the Anhui provincial government announced in March 1993 that profit contracting would continue indefinitely at Magang Holding after 1995.[53] The general pattern of poor coordination across various levels of government is typical of contemporary Chinese industrial regulation. Even after the promulgation of a standardized national tax law in 1994, provincial governments still stepped in and imposed totally different tax systems on individual firms.

The continuation of tax contracting at Magang Holding led to a number of odd situations. First, the provincial government was pursuing a tax policy that was inconsistent with national fiscal reforms. Even though the province had the power to enforce its tax policy on the firm, it did not have the power to prevent higher central agencies (e.g., the Ministry of Finance) from also stepping in and imposing their own tax policies. Second, Ma'anshan City was still the formal contracting party with Magang. Yet Ma'anshan City, as the lowest entity on the bureaucratic totem pole, had no means of protecting Magang from above-contract extraction; in fact, Ma'anshan City's actual interests were to exact fees from Magang for urban infrastructure projects.

When joint stock reforms began at Magang, the assumption of many people involved was first that Magang Steel would be receiving huge infusions of foreign capital, and second that Magang Holding would reap major financial rewards through the stock dividends paid out by Magang Steel. Governmental agencies, Anhui Province and Ma'anshan Municipality included, certainly would not easily surrender claims to those revenues. Although hesitant to go after the stock company itself, the supervisory agencies seemed eager to intercept the cash flow at the level of the holding company. It is partially for this reason that the system of tax contracting was extended indefinitely.

It is worth noting that Magang's stock prospectus for the Hong Kong market, issued in October 1993, described the original tax contract but then went on to state that, after joint stock restructuring, "it is not expected that the Group [Magang Holding and Magang Steel] will enter into any arrangement in relation to its operation, such as the five-year contract mentioned above, with either the Anhui Provincial Government or the Ma'anshan Municipal Government."[54] Yet Magang's own internal documents describe Anhui's decision in March 1993 to extend tax contracting indefinitely after 1995.[55] What appears to have happened is that Magang's Hong Kong publicists knew that tax contracting did not fit the image of a radically reformed, Western-style public company, so they just glossed over the issue. While in reality the old system remained quite robust, Magang's Hong Kong stock prospectus simply attempted to write it out of existence.

PROBLEMS REALIZED: MAGANG'S JOINT STOCK SYSTEM IN OPERATION

Within one year of Magang's reorganization, a series of problems began to emerge at both the holding and stock companies. First, the holding company ran into immediate financial troubles, since its primary sources of income were the unprofitable operations left over from the original Magang. The iron ore mines proved to be the heart of the problem. Mines in China habitually lose money for several reasons. Chinese ore tends to be of low grade: only 28 to 29 percent iron as compared to the 64- or 65-percent iron content found in Australian or South American ore. Furthermore, Chinese ore tends to be situated anywhere from 50 to 300 meters beneath the surface, precluding the less costly open-pit mining prevalent outside China. In general, iron ore processing tends to be more drawn out and expensive in China than in many other nations. Many

Chinese steel firms, though they own their own mines, still seek to import ore from Australia or Latin America, since the higher-grade ore lowers overall steel production costs. From the start, therefore, Magang Holding faced a challenge in trying to eke out profit from its primary production facilities, the mines.

This predicament was exacerbated by the tax situation. While Magang Holding was obligated to meet the annual tax submission targets set out in its contract with Ma'anshan City, the central Ministry of Finance also stepped in and imposed significant increases in the company's product taxes. Prior to 1994, a 3-percent product tax, paid by producers, was applied to ore sales. With the new 1994 federated tax system, that product tax was raised to 17 percent, severely eating into Magang Holding's profits. Furthermore, a new natural resources tax of approximately RMB 15 per ton was imposed on ore, again to be paid by producers. It should be noted that these new taxes levied by the Ministry of Finance were completely divorced from Magang's tax contract. In other words, despite the changing tax structure, Magang Holding still had to meet the annual flat-fee tax submission target set down by Ma'anshan City and Anhui Province.

In 1994, Magang Holding had eleven production facilities attempting to meet the tax submission targets, and extensive efforts were made to expand output while simultaneously undergoing technological modernization. In the first nine months of 1994, the holding company faced losses of RMB 197 million, a deficit made up in part by RMB 59 million in bank loans.[56] Magang accountants noted that the only way of meeting company financial obligations was to go to the banks for loans. Certainly one aspect of the pre-1994 system was alive and well: uncoordinated tax policies were forcing a firm to rely on bank loans in order to maintain basic production.

One might argue that, as an essentially unreformed SOE, Magang Holding should have been expected to run into financial problems. The real test, after all, was in the performance of Magang Steel. In actuality, however, Magang Holding's problems were directly related to a series of questionable financial practices by the stock company. The joint stock company was softening its own budget constraint by forcing loans from the financially troubled holding company. In the fall of 1994, senior officials of Magang Holding detailed the nature of the situation.[57] Through the first three quarters of 1994, a period of recession in the Chinese steel industry, Magang Steel elected not to honor many of its service contracts and purchasing deals with the parent company. In other words, as noted earlier, Steel was on the one hand supposed to pay Holding for worker housing and social services and on the other hand expected to pay for a steady stream of iron ore supplies. In the first nine months of the year, Steel was supposed to pay just over RMB 797 million to Holding. Yet the stock company elected to pay only RMB 298 million for its ore shipments (52 percent of the contracted amount) and only RMB 22.5 million for services (12.3 percent of the contracted price).[58] Even after deducting all the energy costs owed by Holding to Steel, the stock company still had paid only 63.7 percent of the amount actually owed to the parent holding company.

Even more significant, Magang Steel through much of 1994 announced dividend figures but elected not to pay out those dividends to Magang Holding.[59] In other words, the 62.5-percent majority owner was denied its profit dividends, though money was paid out to Hong Kong and Chinese individual investors. Apparently, Magang Steel informed its parent company that the dividend withholdings, in addition to the unpaid portions of the ore and services contracts, should really be considered (interest-free) "loans" being taken from the parent company.[60] Steel was essentially forcing credit from its nominal owner. This strategy allowed Magang Steel to artificially inflate its declared dividends, since dividends were being paid out on less than 40 percent of outstanding shares. Furthermore, the stock firm could artificially deflate its costs by reneging on contracts with Holding. As indicated by Figure 5.1, this behavior was occurring at precisely the time that Magang stock prices were declining precipitously in Hong Kong. As reports of Magang's wilting profits spread, investors began abandoning the stock. It is conceivable that Magang Steel's attempts to inflate dividend and profit declarations were part of a broader effort to stabilize share prices in Hong Kong and protect the firm's overall value.

A reasonable question is why the holding company did not simply force the stock company to turn over dividends and fees owed. After all, the holding company was, and still is, the majority owner of the stock firm. The answer lies in large part in China's unreformed personnel system. The general manager of Holding was indeed the chairman of the board of Steel, but he had no power to appoint or fire the senior management of the stock company. In other words, the general manager of the stock company – the person in charge of day-to-day operations – was in no real sense subordinate to the chairman of the board. Instead, the general manager was appointed by outside governmental agencies and was responsive to the perceived expectations of those outside agencies. The same was true for the vice managers of the stock company. They were responsible neither to Holding nor to any other shareholders. Instead, managers acted so as to maximize their firm's share price on the open market, regardless of how those actions impinged upon either the holding company or the long-term productivity of the stock company itself. Steel managers appeared to calculate that the one thing most necessary to avoid would be a further crash in the firm's

Hong Kong stock prices. After all, policy makers, domestic observers, and the international media were all paying attention to this experimental "public" SOE, and particularly to its share prices in Hong Kong. Presumably, as long as the stock price remained relatively stable, management could avoid any serious censure regardless of the actual financial condition of the firm. The situation is analogous to more traditional SOEs trying to maintain output and "paper profits" even by means of value-subtracting strategies. Cash-flow problems can always be explained away as a technicality, but overt loss making invariably draws unwanted attention.

What is interesting is that officials at Magang Holding could not fire the senior management of Magang Steel, and neither could they bring suit in Chinese courts. Again, the personnel system was the source of the problem. At least as interpreted by officials of Holding, China's nascent corporate code considered the legal representative of a joint stock firm to be the chairman of the board and the legal representative of a traditional SOE to be the general manager. Yet, as noted before, the general manager of Holding served concurrently as chairman of the board of Steel. If the funding dispute within the Magang Group were brought before a court then the senior executive at Magang Holding, the aggrieved party, would under Chinese law also happen to be the accused party. He would, in effect, have been forced to sue himself. Officials at Magang Holding expressed great reluctance to pursue these matters in court, since they feared any liability rulings against Steel could eventually be held against the accounts of the holding company. The boundaries of the parent and subsidiary companies were simply too intertwined and too convoluted to allow for adjudication by China's relatively undeveloped legal system.[61]

The stock company's soft budget constraint was also perpetuated in a general sense by outside bureaucratic actors. Government agencies have preserved their ability to intervene in restructured enterprises, but they tend to intervene selectively. The type of corporate division pursued at Magang ended up skewing that selection process. Magang Steel was accorded a degree of insulation, in large part because of its high-profile status as a national experiment. Therefore, the bulk of local state intervention fell upon Holding. Again, the logic was fairly clear. Magang Steel's debut on the Hong Kong and Shanghai markets led to a windfall in short-term investment. As long as the value of those Magang shares could be maintained, the Chinese state, as the prime owner of company assets, would benefit. In more general terms, Magang Steel was the flagship operation in a reform effort engineered by central leaders in Beijing. It was one of the first large Chinese SOEs to issue stock internationally, and presumably all of the bureaucratic personnel involved knew that the experiment had to be made to work. Even so, all the involved parties had their own interests, primarily financial ones, to protect. The easiest way to pursue those interests and tap into the capital inflows was to focus all claims on Magang Holding, a company that remained conveniently in the shadows while the spotlights were aimed at Magang Steel.

The previously mentioned behavior of the tax authorities is a case in point. The Ministry of Finance imposed steep tax hikes on Magang Holding's mining operations yet for the most part left Magang Steel alone. Similarly, Anhui Province and Ma'anshan Municipality insisted that Magang Holding pay its pre-arranged profit submission rate, even though a prime source of the holding company's revenue, dividends from its Steel shares, never materialized. Apparently, the solution was to permit Holding to borrow from state banks to make up the deficit rather than pressuring Steel to pay its obligations. Certainly the view of enterprise officials, and one tacitly confirmed by local officials, was that the province and municipality were wary of interfering in the stock company, given its special status and all the publicity attending its reorganization.[62]

Similarly, Ma'anshan City looked upon the whole Magang Group as a prime source of revenue for municipal infrastructure projects, but targeted Magang Holding when it came actually to collecting money. For example, since the Magang reorganization, Ma'anshan City has embarked on a RMB 60-million road-building project. Surmising that the steel conglomerate would be the primary user of those roads, Ma'anshan Municipality financed the project by imposing an ad hoc RMB 48-million fee on Magang Holding. The stock company, though, was spared any specific road-building fee.[63] Similar patterns appeared to obtain for local land use fees, transport fees, and environmental protection fees.[64] Such local levies in general are considered distinct from tax accounts – they do not fall under tax contracts – yet they are still imposed rather heavily, and seemingly indiscriminately, on the state enterprise. In the case of the Magang Group, the city elected to extract these fees almost exclusively from the holding company while leaving the stock company untouched.

All of these factors – the distorted financial flows, the personnel problems, the soft budgets – ultimately added up. Just a few years after restructuring, Magang Holding was short of cash and dependent on state bank loans to stay afloat. Magang Steel, despite siphoning money from the holding company, was also short of cash, for it had engaged in considerable fixed asset expansion and had extended large amounts of credit to customers. In effect, the firm was inducing demand, and it was trying aggressively to boost its sagging profits, but it certainly was not bringing in much cash. Although joint stock restructuring may not have fundamentally changed managerial incentives – output and sales maximization were still the order of the day – the reforms did indeed provide some of the capital infusions needed to keep the firm afloat. In essence, the reforms ended up providing both the capital and autonomy necessary to perpetuate value-subtracting production strategies.

Though the Magang joint stock experiment was in many ways quite radical, the net result was not so different from what obtains at "unreformed" firms such as Angang. Inefficient enterprises and asset-destoying managerial behavior are perpetuated by a political system unwilling or unable to effect real systemic change. Indeed, many bureaucratic interests actively attempt to thwart real reform in the modern industrial sector. Ultimately, the fallback is always to keep transfusing stagnant state enterprises with investment resources, thus trading off the long-term economic health of the nation for the short-term perpetuation of a broken system.

CONCLUSION

For firms like Ma'anshan Iron and Steel, joint stock restructuring does constitute radical change. Ten years ago, few people would have believed a Chinese SOE could successfully issue shares on a foreign stock exchange. However, the outcomes of these changes have been anything but stellar. The important lesson – an obvious one, perhaps, but one worth stressing – is that policies bearing a certain economic logic in theory lead to unpredicted outcomes when passed through an existing political system, particularly a system characterized by malfunctioning market governance mechanisms. When the state regulatory bureaucracy, the banking system, and the legal system are all deeply politicized and decidedly non–market-oriented, policy makers can certainly *try* to induce commercial behavior among enterprise managers. Those efforts, however, are almost guaranteed to fail. Those efforts – whether in the form of profit contracts or joint stock reforms or tax incentives – will indeed cause changes, but not the ones policy designers likely desire, and not the ones that lead to overall economic growth.

In theory, corporatization should have worked at Magang. The allocation of ownership shares to specific state actors should have stopped the predation problem, while at the same time giving these actors incentives to monitor firm-level management. That foreign investors were involved, and that the international business media was watching, should have further induced state actors to curtail predatory behavior. Furthermore, as funds from public stock offerings replaced soft loans from the state banking system, managers should have become motivated to achieve real returns on capital. After all, the budget constraint in theory should have been tightening.

The problem, however, was that these theoretically promising moves bucked up against partially reformed and deeply malfunctioning market institutions that did not simply go away once joint stock restructuring took place. The division of Magang, combined with the various contractual ties between the resulting two firms, simply aggravated the situation. The Magang Group would still have access to soft loans, and the state would still have access to group assets. At the same time, managers could still run up inventories, receivables, and other credit sales without suffering any apparent penalty. Because the institutional environment around the firm remained essentially unreformed, soft budgets within the firm also remained unreformed. What had expanded, however, was the autonomy with which managers and state bureaucrats alike could pursue value-destroying strategies.

This division of Magang, rather than solving the nested problems situation, simply aggravated both legs of the dynamic. On one hand, the property-rights problem was never resolved, since any number of state agencies could still claim control over Magang Holding. On the other hand, corporate governance became only more complex and dysfunctional once Magang Steel was placed under the "control" of a powerless owner. In other words, all the property-rights problems related to undefined state ownership were dumped in the lap of the holding company, while most of the corporate governance lapses were shifted over to the stock company. Because ownership over the holding company was left unspecified, any number of state agencies could come in and extract. Indeed, the allure of extraction became even greater since the holding company was presumed to have access to the joint stock firm's foreign funds. At the same time, the stock firm could also beat up on its holding company "owner," since the owner was essentially powerless. In effect, nobody ended up governing Magang Steel. The division resulted in a highly concentrated form of state predation on one side and a highly concentrated form of corporate nongovernance on the other.

In a similar sense, the division encouraged a further splitting of control over assets and responsibility for liabilities. Control over assets devolved to the parties on either side of Magang Holding. On the one hand, there was the stock firm, which at least over the short term had unlimited and unsupervised access to productive assets and Hong Kong–based investment. On the other side were the state agencies attempting to grab these assets secondarily by extracting from the holding company. Liabilities, however, were dumped by both sides into the lap of Magang Holding. The stock company extracted indirectly by taking interest-free loans; the state agencies extracted directly through taxes and fees. Meanwhile, the holding company had little choice but to pass its own liabilities onward to the state banking system. Instead of destroying the nested problems dynamic, corporatization simply facilitated and concentrated that destructive cycle. Assets remained split from liabilities, and managers were never forced to bear any costs for capital. Not surprisingly, managerial incentives failed to reflect any dramatic shift toward market-oriented standards.

What corporatization did do, however, was to create a perplexing, hybrid property-rights form, the "public" SOE. What exactly is this new hybrid? The acclaimed Chinese economist Wu Jinglian, writing before any empirical evidence was available, speculated on what might happen if joint stock reforms were undertaken in Chinese SOEs.[65] He predicted two possible scenarios. In the first, nothing would be changed. The joint stock SOE would be no different from the traditional state firm, totally controlled by layers of state agencies. Managers would still be appointed by the state, and basic managerial decisions would be carried out by the state. The state would exert that control simply by dominating the enterprise board of directors. In the second scenario, everything would change. The enterprise would be under nobody's control and nobody's supervision, for either the state "owners" would have no representatives on the board of directors, or the representatives that they did have would be so deprived of information as to be rendered ineffectual.

The lesson of Magang is that in reality both outcomes are produced, and in the same firm. At Magang Steel, managers are still appointed from above, and there is still bureaucratic control over basic investment and production decisions. Yet, especially with the creation of a new bureaucratic layer – the powerless holding-company "owner" – the stock firm runs wild. It is presented with extraordinary opportunities to capture rents and misapply funds and is simultaneously free of the kind of outside supervision that might prevent such behavior. The Chinese "public" SOE is a true hybrid, a new property-rights form, sitting somewhere in the middle between the traditional state firm and the Western public corporation. Unfortunately, the Chinese hybrid captures many negative aspects of both worlds – and painfully few positive aspects of either.[66]

Meanwhile, true restructuring does not take place. Oddly enough, the stock firm is given the freedom to capture rents and pad its accounts, yet it is not given what in the West would be considered basic managerial autonomy. The "public" SOE cannot determine its own staffing levels, it cannot set its own investment projects, and in many respects it cannot shift its product mix. All of these decisions require approval by one state agency or another. Most important, the public SOE is never in any real sense forced to bear any cost for the capital it uses, whether that capital comes from within China or without. Under such circumstances, one would be hard-pressed to see how managerial incentives could point toward efficiency maximization or productivity enhancement.

Nevertheless, among all the disparate supporters of joint stock measures in China – from policy makers in China to economists in the West – there is still a tendency to view the Magang experience through rose-tinted, albeit contradictory, lenses. Each group, measuring Magang in terms of how closely it approaches an ideal theoretical form (either state socialism or market capitalism), neglects some parts of the story, accepts other parts, but inevitably loses sight of the whole.

For example, the position of some observers has been that, despite the troubles observed at Magang, corporatization constitutes a major advance if only because of the division of firms into productive and nonproductive components.[67] This argument asserts that, in traditional SOEs like Angang, any profitable or efficient shop floors are smothered in the general mess of a bloated, overstaffed conglomerate. The traditional SOE is so drained financially by its social service obligations that even its most efficient productive elements have no hope of competing on an open market. Insulating Magang's steel operation from its housing and social service bureaus is therefore seen as a giant step forward toward allowing the firm to compete on an equal footing in global markets. Magang Steel is viewed not as a perfect entity but rather as one on its way to becoming a textbook modern corporation – a professionally managed organization responding to clear market incentives.

However, this argument confuses potential with actual behavior and, in ignoring the latter, misses the real nature of China's joint stock reforms. Magang Steel, despite its organizational streamlining, displays all the ills of soft budgets and nonproductive rent seeking. It makes money by sucking resources out of a state-financed owner and by "borrowing" money from materials suppliers, all the while juggling its accounts to disguise its true financial situation. Such behavior can hardly be considered a mere passage through a brief transitional phase, a minor glitch on the way to becoming a powerful market competitor. The stock company has no reason – and under the present system will never have any reason – to tighten its production practices when it can more easily subsist on soft money flowing in from its owners, investors, and state banks. The rents a firm like Magang Steel can capture are made possible precisely because it is not a public company in the Western sense but is instead a bureaucratic agency in a deeply confused bureaucratic hierarchy.

Magang Steel behaves the way it does for systemic reasons: it responds rationally to the incentives and capabilities provided by the nested problems dynamic. Magang Steel runs roughshod over its "owner" because state agencies have refused to give that owner power over personnel appointments. Furthermore, state agencies (the banks) continue to infuse the "owner" with funds that the stock company will ultimately exploit. Hence, the holding company is deprived of its last weapon against the subsidiary, poverty. Finally, the highest-level state agencies have made Magang Steel a publicized model, a model that must at least appear to be successful. Firm managers – as much players in a high-level political game as in an enterprise-level economic game – therefore resist making the long-term investments in productivity that might result in success a decade down the line. Instead, they do what is far easier and far less risky: they "create" success by refusing to pay bills, shirking dividend distributions, and manipulating accounts. Magang is as unlikely to become a modern corporation as any of its unreformed counterparts in the Chinese steel industry. Traditional Chinese steel mills run up triangular debt with suppliers and purchasers, while Magang Steel runs up debt with its holding-company owner. The only difference between the two debt situations is that the latter seems even more poorly regulated than the former.

From a totally different perspective, supporters of state ownership in China – especially government ministries – herald the Magang experiment as an indicator of the vitality of Chinese SOEs. The MMI's internal descriptions of Magang nicely convey the flavor of this view. They enumerate all the ways the state and party still maintain control over the stock company, as if to say that not an inch of ground has been given on the ownership issue; at the same time, they point to the vast sums of money that have flooded in from Hong Kong. The rather smug view seems to be that, since foreign investors have faith in the state firm and are willing to pump in money, all is well. Because investors (at least for the short term) are willing to infuse SOEs with money, costly systemic reforms – ones usually involving unpleasant sacrifices of state power – need not be pursued.

How accurate is this view? It is ironic that Hang Yongyi, the general manager of Holding and the chairman of the board of Steel, has proudly noted in recent years that in Hong Kong, Magang is the "king of the 'red chip' stocks" (*hong chou gu wang*).[68] The phrase is often repeated with much fanfare in company and ministerial documents. The term is indeed used in Hong Kong, with a much different meaning from what Mainland officials seem to understand, and explains to some extent why Magang shares sold at all on the international market.

In Hong Kong usage, the phrase "red-chip firm" has a decidedly political flavor, the notion being that a firm backed by the Chinese state will never be allowed to go under no matter how bad its performance. A Chinese SOE appearing on a foreign stock exchange will never be allowed fail, for that would be a colossal embarrassment to the government. The firm will always be bailed out, and will always be able to come up with some dividends. Therefore, it is a "red chip" not because of its economic potential, which is essentially ignored, but because of its political status. In an odd way, the Hong Kong investors see the situation more clearly than either Chinese government propagandists or World Bank optimists. The World Bank thinks firms like Magang will one day become "blue chips": the Chinese government confuses red chip for blue chip entirely, thinking they are the same; and only the Hong Kong investors see Magang for what it really is – a chip that will always be red, never blue.

Of course, Magang is not the only red chip that has run into major problems over the past years. During 1995, a year in which the Hong Kong market climbed 21 percent overall, stock values for the seventeen mainland SOEs listed at the time dropped 32 percent.[69] Cases of mismanagement developed at a number of firms, including the relatively famous beer producer Tsingtao Brewery. After listing at 36 cents per share in the summer of 1993, Tsingtao stock surged to U.S. $1.40 by 1994. At the same time, despite explosive growth in the Chinese beer market, Tsingtao's profits fell by 49 percent, and the U.S. $190 million raised from the initial public offering seemed to disappear into thin air.[70] In 1995, it became clear that company managers had taken at least U.S. $71.2 million of the funds and simply loaned it out – in a fashion not so different from the state banking system – to other firms.[71] Portions of the proceeds from the initial public offering found their way into Chinese bank accounts, where the funds could be channeled away from planned expansion projects and toward new business ventures. The irregularities were serious enough for the Hong Kong stock exchange in April 1995 to suspend trading of the firm's stock. Meanwhile, the company's plans for physical expansion had to be postponed, and projected production increases were halved. Not surprisingly, as news of these developments spread by the end of 1995, the brewery's stock price in Hong Kong dropped some 57 percent after the resumption of trading. Even in a thriving beer market, the company was foundering.

In terms of the plight of Chinese SOEs, red-chip status – whether in the case of Magang or Tsingtao – is unfortunately more a reflection of the problem than the solution. The Chinese government cannot continue to bail out joint stock SOEs indefinitely, particularly as more and more firms become involved. From the macroeconomic perspective, the government's funding of inefficient stock firms like Magang Steel is no different from the government's funding of traditional money losers like Angang. The end results are still low productivity and misallocated resources. Even worse, in the case of joint stock reforms the fickle confidence of foreign investors has now become part of the equation. The Chinese government gambles that infusions of foreign capital can compensate for the absence of real enterprise reform. But how long will that money keep flowing in? How long will even Hong Kong investors keep faith in the red chips?

In the meantime, Chinese SOEs continue to increase output levels, sink resources into fixed asset expansion, and accumulate liabilities. At some point down the line, as some proponents hope, firms like Magang Steel may indeed be auctioned off to the highest private bidder. One wonders, though, whether there will be anything of value left to sell.

6

Shougang: The Rise and Fall of an Industrial Giant

INTRODUCTION

THE preceding case studies have described how partial reforms in China's economic system inhibit market-oriented behavior in large industrial producers. Managers have certainly been encouraged to maximize profits, but in an environment of soft budgets, profit maximization has often translated into asset destruction. In such a setting, property rights, ownership, and corporate governance essentially fail to function. Initial indications from firms like Magang and Tsingtao Brewery suggest that, under such circumstances, internal restructuring – the issuance of stock, expansion of managerial autonomy, and exposure to foreign capital flows – simply expands the opportunities for value-subtracting business strategies. Policy makers have aggressively attempted to reform the firm from within, but they have been far less successful and enthusiastic in reforming the firm from without. In short, they have never fully tackled the regulatory environment. The unfortunate lesson of firms like Angang and Magang is that when external regulatory institutions remain at best partially reformed, even the most progressive internal restructuring efforts lead to chaos. It is one thing in such an environment to encourage commercial behavior in peasant producers or small industrial firms. It is another thing entirely to encourage such behavior in complex production organizations that by definition feature complicated relationships between ownership and control.

Certainly one broad lesson from the Chinese experience is that institutional forms from one type of socioeconomic system cannot be casually picked up piecemeal and transplanted onto another. Firms like Magang or Tsingtao Brewery can be made to look like public corporations in developed market economies, but making them actually behave like market-oriented corporations is more difficult. Indeed, when such attempts are made, undesirable outcomes frequently obtain. Yet China's decade-and-a-half experience in enterprise reform has been neither devoid of success nor lacking in variation. Indeed, it is in the cases of variation – cases of firm-level turnarounds, both positive and negative – that the most can be learned. It is in this context that the experience of the Capital Iron and Steel Company ("Shougang") becomes so interesting.

Shougang is a firm that, over the course of the reform era, has successively served as a symbol of great accomplishment and a symbol of abject failure. It is a firm that in the 1980s actually did adopt commercially viable growth strategies, actually did appear to operate in a hard-budget environment, and did achieve financial self-sufficiency. Yet, it is also a firm that in the 1990s plunged into extraordinary financial problems, problems far surpassing anything observed at Angang, Magang, or any other major Chinese SOE. Shougang, from its high points to its low, reflected not only varying *degrees* of autonomy from state control but also, and more important, two markedly different *types* of producer autonomy. The first type led to value-enhancing business behavior, while the second led clearly to value destruction. Both involved profit maximization and both involved nominal "market" orientation. The history of Shougang is so interesting because it illuminates the circumstances under which one form of behavior transforms into the other, as well as the means by which incentives for commercial behavior devolve into incentives for outright rent seeking.

Shougang, even in its heyday in the late 1980s, was by no means a world-class steel operation. Its production costs were high, its profits overstated, and its output figures somewhat inflated. Nevertheless, the firm achieved something few other Chinese SOEs had: it attained financial self-sufficiency. Through a series of externally imposed reforms, the firm was cut off from outside sources of funding and was forced to face what amounted to a draconian budget constraint. The company was effectively cut off from the system of state subsidies and loans that guaranteed the survival of competing firms like Angang or Magang. As compensation, the Beijing steel firm was granted greater access to retained earnings, greater control over investment decisions, and superior protection from the normal bureaucratic morass affecting Chinese SOEs. In effect, firm-level managers were accorded a particular form of autonomy, one that was severely bounded by a hard budget constraint. Managers were granted unprecedented freedom of action. The outside enforcement of the hard budget constraint, however, guaranteed that any managerial actions taken would affect – for better or worse – the bottom line of the firm. Autonomy and accountability were essentially coupled in the hands of enterprise managers. As a result, managerial behavior took on a decidedly commercial tone. Cash flow was maintained, retained profits were carefully reinvested, and efficiency-enhancing modernizations were steadily pursued. Whether or not Shougang was a world-class steel firm and whether or not China even today should maintain a steel industry that cannot compete at world prices are legitimate questions, but ones beyond the scope of this study. What counts from the perspective of enterprise reform and with respect to the relationship between incentives and behavior is that Shougang, through the 1980s, avoided the hemorrhaging of money so characteristic of many Chinese state firms.

Shougang's successes were directly attributable to the particular form of profit contract shared between the firm and supervisory government agencies. As indicated by the earlier case studies, profit contracts were neither unique to Shougang nor generally very effective in China. Indeed, no matter where applied, enterprise performance contracts always have major drawbacks. For reasons that will be discussed later, they tend to be short-term measures at best and, even then, potentially destructive in terms of the incentives they create. Nevertheless, the Shougang case was remarkable in that the contract was actually enforced against all parties involved, the state and the firm. In other words, the firm truly was cut off from the partially reformed, budget-softening institutional environment that undermined the performance of so many SOEs. Once the firm was insulated from the malfunctioning external environment, internal reform mechanisms – in this case, profit retention arrangements – could be allowed to have their impact on managerial incentives. So often in China, internal restructuring efforts are undercut by external countermeasures – cushioning devices that permit funds to flow back into the firm when managerial errors become too costly or state tax extractions too onerous. In essence, restructuring efforts are never allowed to proceed, for they consistently fall prey to a malfunctioning regulatory environment. In the case of Shougang, contracting may not have been the best choice of restructuring method, but at least it was permitted to function as planned. At least the firm truly was insulated from outside contamination, while internal measures were given a chance to take effect. In a broad sense, the contract provided an arena in which Shougang would either sink or swim based on its own business decisions. The creation of that environment alone constituted a rare and significant step forward in Chinese enterprise reform efforts.

The point here is to suggest neither that profit contracts are ideal policy measures nor that Shougang's lofty performance figures from the 1980s are entirely reliable. Profit contracts, like the performance data, embody serious shortcomings. The more important general conclusion is that managerial incentives *can* be shifted through certain types of policy packages, whether those packages are framed in terms of enterprise contracts, systemwide tax reforms, or even joint stock restructuring. The key, however, is that those policy packages can work only if the firm is insulated from malfunctioning regulatory institutions. The lesson over the short term, of course, is that the firm needs to be cut off from external funding sources. Yet, as will be discussed later, this is not a viable solution for most firms over the long term. Rather, the broader lesson is that *the reform agenda must focus on rationalizing the firm's external environment before zeroing in on the internal environment.* For internal incentives to change, hard budgets must be enforced, and for hard budgets to be enforced, malfunctioning regulatory mechanisms – whether in the form of noncommercial bank lending, predatory taxation, or nonenforcement of bankruptcy – must be curtailed.

The point is actually reinforced by Shougang's stupendous financial collapse in the mid-1990s. Often the best way to understand what makes a reform package work is to see what ultimately causes it to fall apart. After nearly twelve years of impressive performance, Shougang's economic house in the early 1990s came crashing down. Over a two-year period beginning in 1993, the firm, through a series of rather inane investment decisions and financial miscues, managed to drive itself into insolvency. Zhou Guanwu, Shougang's long-time head and the man who personified both the firm's achievements and its well-known arrogance, was ignominiously forced into retirement while his son, a Shougang executive, was imprisoned on corruption charges.

What is so interesting is not just the gory details of the collapse but also the circumstances under which managerial behavior changed so drastically. In the early 1990s, for a variety of reasons that will be discussed in this chapter, Shougang's insulation from soft credit ended. Once management gained unprecedented access to credit, the hard-budget terms under which autonomy had been exercised essentially dissolved. A worst-case situation developed in which managers already accorded with high degrees of autonomy were also permitted access to decidedly noncommercial forms of financing. The firm, in effect, was given its own bank. Asset-destroying strategies of monumental scale – well beyond anything undertaken at comparable firms – became not only feasible but frankly quite attractive to Shougang leaders. Moreover, given the malleability of accounting standards, the damage wrought by value-destroying strategies went unnoticed for years as the firm continued to sink deeper into insolvency. Once Shougang's insulation from malfunctioning external governance mechanisms ended, the internal reform package that had worked fairly well in the past thoroughly collapsed. The flaws which that reform package had always contained now became crucial, thoroughly undermining market-based incentives. Contracts that force firms to hit profit targets are fraught with problems, but contracts that force firms to hit profit targets in an environment of limitless subsidies are recipes for financial disaster. Once the budget constraint was softened, Shougang's profit contract enabled managers to engage in reckless investment, unfettered expansion of capacity and output, and firm-level asset destruction.

Unfortunately, many Western and Chinese observers conflate the two aspects of the Shougang story, the relatively successful period of growth and the utterly disastrous period of financial collapse. During its years of success, Shougang drew many detractors and for many different reasons. The firm's achievements were viewed with suspicion in Chinese bureaucratic, academic, and industrial circles. Many of these attitudes then resonated in Western academic and policy circles and, when Zhou Guanwu was ousted in 1995, rumors abounded that Shougang had for years squandered investment funds. Because it was simply assumed both by Western observers and many Chinese analysts that Shougang's past successes had been trumped up, the firm's financial collapse was of only secondary interest. The real story, it was believed, had to do with the firm's apparent fall from grace in the midst of a central leadership succession struggle. In other words, it was assumed that Shougang's previous economic record had been a propaganda fable, a product of Shougang's close connections to Deng Xiaoping. The only real issue in early 1995 then involved figuring out why this relationship seemed to have soured. Shougang was viewed almost exclusively from the perspective of an ongoing succession crisis at the very highest ranks of the Chinese state.

This approach misses the crux of the Shougang story. The firm's successes in the 1980s were indeed valid, and they were directly related to the reform package embodied by the profit contract. The collapse starting in late 1992 and culminating in late 1994 was also quite real and was also related to the profit contract. The true story, though, is to be found not in elite succession politics but rather in the economics of the case itself and in the changing circumstances under which the contract was applied. The Shougang experience illustrates what can be achieved through property-rights and enterprise governance reform, and also what sorts of new problems are unleashed by those reforms.

The major thrust of this chapter will be to explain in detail both Shougang's successes in the 1980s and its financial distress of the mid-1990s. Over the years, there have been a number of allegations leveled at the Beijing steel company, allegations that when taken together constitute a sort of "myth of Shougang." The overriding element of this myth is that Shougang's achievements throughout the 1980s and early 1990s were the product of a "sweetheart" deal with Beijing in the sense that the firm's profit contract granted a position in which failure would be absolutely impossible. The notion is that Shougang's profits derived almost exclusively from the firm's ability to extract rents from the Chinese pricing system while simultaneously avoiding normal tax burdens. In this view, Shougang is of no economic interest because it was never anything more than an artificially propped-up model enterprise in a malfunctioning transitional economy.

A further element of the myth focuses on Shougang's exclusivity, the notion that the company's profit contract somehow came at the expense of other firms and so constituted an unfair competitive advantage. It is assumed that, from the start, Shougang was granted the kind of privileges that every other firm wanted but no other firm could ever hope to receive. Indeed, it was granted preferential treatment while others were excluded precisely so that it could rise above the rest and be guaranteed success. In this view, such special treatment was accorded because Shougang's leader was so tied to Deng Xiaoping personally, and the firm's contract so tied to Deng's goals politically, that the firm could not be allowed to fail. Nobody dared let it fail. In this sense, it was a sort of Potemkin Village or (perhaps more accurately in the Chinese context) the reform era's version of Dazhai, a "pie in the sky" model with no basis in reality.[1] Frankly, it was this view that made Shougang's 1995 apparent fall from grace so interesting. The question became one of determining what could have changed in leadership circles that permitted Deng's showcase for industrial reform finally to be exposed after all these years.

The "myth of Shougang," like any other myth, gains currency by being grounded at least partly in fact. Every one of the critical views just outlined contains elements of truth, albeit truth that has been somewhat distorted and pulled out of context. Shougang itself has made the situation worse over the years by churning out its own public relations hyperbole and statistical obfuscation, at times proclaiming itself one of the most (if not *the* most) profitable and efficient steel operations worldwide. By any objective measures, these claims are utter nonsense. In addition, the Beijing steel producer has attempted to portray itself as a model for worker democracy, progressive boardroom–shop-floor relations, and "scientific" personnel management. Again, these are claims that have little grounding in fact. Finally, Shougang in the early 1990s did make gross investment errors that led to very real and serious financial problems. A major purpose of this chapter will be to sift fact from fiction in an effort to present a more accurate understanding of Shougang's past economic achievements and present economic troubles.

SHOUGANG: AN OVERVIEW

Although Shougang outperformed its competitors through the 1980s, the firm entered the reform period with all the ills typical of large Chinese SOEs. With respect to size, scope, levels of technology, and social welfare burdens, Shougang was (and indeed still is) quite similar to firms like Angang or Magang. Capital Iron and Steel, founded originally as the Shijingshan Iron Factory in the western suburbs of Beijing, started operating in 1919, the same year as Angang. Following the establishment of the People's Republic, Shougang was expanded into an integrated iron and steel producer, with facilities ranging from iron ore mines to steel rolling mills. By the 1970s, Shougang, much like other contemporary state steel mills, suffered from all the usual problems of outdated equipment, uncertain supplies, and declining efficiency. By the end of the Cultural Revolution, the Beijing company was producing only 400,000 tons of steel annually, the lowest output among China's eight major steel companies.[2] Like Angang, Shougang at the time was also a "living museum of steel technology," still using steam turbines and Bessemer converters from the days of the Empress Dowager, Ford-style boilers from the turn of the century, and waste-heat coke ovens from the 1920s.[3] Needless to say, the modernization tasks facing firms in this situation are tremendous.

Through the present day, Shougang has also faced the typical personnel problems affecting large SOEs in China. By the early 1990s, the firm's payroll included over 220,000 workers.[4] In accordance with the system of state benefits, the firm is required to provide workers and their families with housing, medical care, and full pensions upon retirement. As a result, Shougang, much like Angang or Magang, has been forced to develop its own dormitory and apartment complexes, hospitals, schools, and child-care facilities. Finding employment for surplus workers and their assorted dependents has been a constant source of concern. Simply dismissing workers and paring down the payroll has not been, and is not today, a managerial option. Canceling benefits is also not an option. In part because of this, Shougang has attempted to move workers out of the steel operation by setting up a vast network of smaller subsidiary enterprises and service companies. In recent years, Shougang has expanded into shipping, construction, electronics, machinery manufacturing, and to some extent automobile and truck production. In typical fashion for large Chinese SOEs, Shougang has become a huge conglomerate extending well beyond its original site in Beijing.

The Beijing steel enterprise has also been fairly typical with respect to the sort of bureaucratic environment within which it operates. Just like Magang and Angang, Shougang has found itself at the bottom of multiple, upside-down pyramids of supervisory governmental agencies, the matrix of overlapping regional and ministerial supervision that is known in China as the *tiao-kuai* system. Control over the enterprise operates horizontally through local agencies and vertically through the central ministries. Supervisory responsibilities – again, at least on paper – become dispersed among a multitude of agencies, while the only clear point is that the firm is subordinated to all. Not surprisingly,

Shougang officials have continually complained that their firm has too many "mothers-in-law," too many state agencies all claiming some sort of authority over the steel firm.[5] The complaints have been understandable. In formal terms, Shougang on the administrative side has been subordinated to the Ministry of Metallurgical Industry, the State Council, the Ministry of Finance, and several other central bureaus. Meanwhile, the Shougang party organization, itself intertwined with the firm's administrative apparatus, is subordinated to the Beijing municipal party organization. To some extent, the Beijing municipal government has also attempted to assert its authority over the firm, a major employer for Beijing and a major source of tax revenue for municipal agencies.[6]

Even today, this complex bureaucratic environment still leads to confusion and outright disputes between the firm and various government agencies. The most obvious sources of contention relate to money – namely, tax payments by the firm. As will be discussed in subsequent sections, Shougang's tax arrangement with the state through the 1980s and early 1990s was set by a fifteen-year profit contract. Nevertheless, government agencies at both the central and local level repeatedly attempted to intercede at the fringes of the contract in efforts to extract more money from the firm. As Shougang became increasingly profitable, state claimants to its funds grew proportionally. During the implementation phase of the national "tax for profit" (*ligaishui*) policy, for example, the Ministry of Finance (MOF) attempted to apply a new 6-percent value-added tax (VAT) to Shougang. The MOF, after initially supporting Shougang-style profit contracting, rapidly became a major opponent after the firm's retained earnings began to grow.[7] A new VAT, while technically exogenous to the Shougang contract, would eat into the firm's sales revenue, decrease the firm's operating funds, and thus make it more difficult for the firm to meet its contractually determined profit targets. In the view of both Shougang and MMI officials, this whole episode reflected an effort by the MOF to shift the goalposts half-way into the game.[8]

Similarly, the Beijing city government repeatedly attempted to extract profits from Shougang on an ad hoc basis. Even with regard to basic tax payments, the bureaucratic situation was complicated, and policies were always subject to interpretation. Shougang's tax payments were regulated by a contract with the central government, yet the firm actually submitted its income taxes to the Beijing municipal government. Meanwhile, sales taxes went directly to the central tax bureau of the MOF. At least until 1994, Beijing Municipality was bound – via a tax-sharing contract – to turn over a portion of local tax revenues to the center on an annual basis. What seems to have happened on occasion was that the municipality had trouble meeting its tax quota to the center and thus had to scramble for funds at the last minute. Shougang, as the largest enterprise in Beijing and a profitable one at that, became a prime target for eleventh-hour tax extraction. In 1992, Beijing mayor Chen Xitong approached Shougang's management and demanded a tax payment of RMB 200 million, a payment completely removed from Shougang's normal tax contract with the central government. Though in most respects Shougang (except for the firm's party organization) could no longer be considered a locally owned firm, the municipal government still attempted the ad hoc extraction, apparently under the principle of "you are a state firm and we represent the state."[9] This is all quite reminiscent of tax problems at comparable firms like Angang or Magang.

As in other firms, the boundaries of Capital Iron and Steel were manipulated – at times arbitrarily – by outside agencies. In January of 1988, for example, Shougang acquired the Beijing Number Eighteen Wireless Components Plant, a collective formerly under municipal control. Yet, when it became clear that the collective would become part of a centrally controlled SOE, problems developed. Under the Chinese tax code at the time, the municipality could claim in entirety the tax submissions of a collective firm. For tax submissions from a traditional "state firm" like Shougang, however, the municipality could at best only share proceeds with the center and in some cases could make no claim at all. The Beijing municipal government, therefore, decided summarily to reclaim the Number Eighteen Plant in April 1989.[10] Similarly, in November 1988, Shougang signed an agreement with the municipal government of Zhenjiang City in Jiangsu Province, allowing the steel company to take over the Zhenjiang Boat Plant. That agreement was later abrogated by the locality. By the end of 1990, Shougang had lost the Shougang Qinhuangdao Machinery Plant, the Shougang Agricultural Services Company, and the Shougang Zhenjiang Shipping Company; in each case, the local governments presiding over those firms terminated existing agreements.

Again like other firms, Shougang faced (and still faces) a certain amount of bureaucratic confusion regarding personnel appointments. As noted previously, both central and local agencies have had certain formal powers in the appointments process. The top three officials at Shougang – the party secretary, the general manager, and the chairman of the board (*dongshizhang*) – are all appointed directly by the central State Council, the highest administrative agency in the nation.[11] It seems that the provincial government (the Beijing municipal government has provincial status) and the MMI are granted only nominal power in approving these appointments. Meanwhile, the enterprise party organization, including the party secretary, is supposed to be under the formal control of the Beijing municipal party organization, even though the municipality

173

does not appoint the secretary. In reality, it might have been difficult by the early 1990s for the municipal party organization to exert authority over Shougang party secretary Zhou Guanwu, since by that point he was also holding the rank of vice-minister of metallurgy, a rank equivalent or superior to that of most municipal party officials. Understandably, such environments can be confusing to participants and observers alike. Both formal and informal lines of authority intermingle, sometimes operate in opposite directions, and in all cases leave much to interpretation.

Perhaps more important from the personnel perspective, midlevel managerial appointments were formally made from outside the firm. Just as at Angang and Magang, vice-managers were appointed by the MMI with a certain amount of local approval. In theory, outside agencies had the power to reach into the firm, circumvent senior management, and make key personnel appointments in the inner reaches of the firm.

Finally, in the broadest sense, Shougang's officials seemed motivated by the same managerial goals that prevailed industrywide: in essence, managers sought to maximize output. As one former MMI cadre explained, the tried-and-true measure of performance for managers in Chinese industry – whether at Angang, Magang, Shougang, or any other large firm – is output growth.[12] Despite fifteen years of enterprise reform efforts and increasing levels of marketization, certain remnants of command-era thinking still survive. Politically, managers gain recognition for output and capacity expansion. As the plant grows, so too does the manager's political power.[13] Though disgusted by this condition, long-term planners and economists at Shougang readily acknowledged its existence. One senior engineer, attempting to explain Shougang's triangular debt problems, noted that cutting production when the market for steel slackens is simply not an option for Shougang or for any other major steel producer.[14] The engineer explained that a steel enterprise leader, whether a party secretary or general manager, would run into career problems if production were cut; he would not dare make such reductions if he wanted to advance professionally.

In the case of Shougang in the early 1990s, there were constant profit and efficiency targets, but Zhou Guanwu made it known to employees that one goal was paramount: becoming the first plant in China to achieve an annual output capacity of ten million tons or more.[15] Unfortunately, this sort of goal even today reflects a political reality that under certain circumstances can lead to extremely destructive business strategies. As suggested in the case of Angang, output maximization when combined with a soft budget constraint – unlimited bailout funds from state banks – frequently leads to value-subtracting business behavior.

174

Yet at Shougang, at least through 1992, financial losses were avoided. The firm had no access to state investments or loans and hence operated on what effectively constituted a hard budget. Furthermore, though facing the same bureaucratic morass as other firms, the Beijing steel producer was far more successful in negotiating its way through the mess. Just as they did at other firms, a variety of state agencies attempted to interfere in Shougang, but Shougang fought back, at times successfully. The MOF's efforts to apply a new value-added tax in 1984 were rebuffed. Beijing's 1992 effort at ad hoc profit extraction was challenged by Shougang and brought to the State Council for adjudication.[16] Even in the area of midlevel managerial appointments, Shougang officials (namely, Zhou Guanwu) fought to maintain control, often by bending the rules or simply skirting the formal supervisory system. Like other state firms, Shougang continually ran head-on into an uncooperative system; unlike other firms, Shougang challenged that system and occasionally won. Given that the state firm in China is still but the bottom element of an extensive state bureaucracy – a bureaucracy basically immune to legal sanction – such behavior is extraordinary. In turn, Shougang achieved impressive economic results. If nothing else, it was self-sustaining through the early 1990s, did not in any appreciable sense act as a drain on Chinese state coffers, and paid its taxes in the meantime. For Chinese SOEs, this represented quite an accomplishment.

THE PROFIT CONTRACT

For both supporters and detractors alike, a central aspect of the Shougang story involves the firm's formal profit contract with the state. Although Shougang had been the subject of several profit retention experiments since 1979, the actual profit contract familiar to observers today dated back to 1982, when the State Council granted formal approval. The contract operated under the aegis of the State Council and basically functioned as an arrangement exclusively between that body and Shougang.

The arrangement had several key stipulations, the most important of which dealt with tax submission and profit retention.[17] After paying all its sales and circulation taxes, Shougang was obliged to submit a certain level of profit to the state each year, the equivalent of income tax; this level increased annually at a set rate. The original profit submission level for 1982 was determined by taking the firm's 1981 profit submissions of RMB 270 million and adding a 6-percent increase. The notion was that the firm would then hand over profits to the state at an increasing rate of 6 percent each year for the next fifteen years. Because in the first year of the contract Shougang surpassed its profit target by a larger margin than expected, the State Council raised the annual increase rate to 7.2 percent, where it remained for the next thirteen years.

A key stipulation of the contract was that Shougang would retain all profits earned in excess of contracted submission levels. In other words, any above-contract earnings were to be retained in entirety by the firm. If Shougang did not meet its profit submission targets in any given year then the firm still had to pay – using its retained funds, wage allotments, or any other money that was available. That is, Shougang was obliged to pay regardless of how much profit it realized in any given year. The contracted profit submission level was not subject to negotiation: the state claimed this money unconditionally. Similarly, the firm's right to retain any surplus profits was also not subject to negotiation.

Perhaps most important to the arrangement's incentive effects, Shougang was removed from the system of state subsidies. After 1982, Shougang was not to receive any subsidies, loans, or any other form of outside state investment – a policy that even Shougang's detractors generally acknowledge was strictly enforced at least until 1993. The point of these initial stipulations was to guarantee a steady flow of income to the state, relieve the burden on state coffers, and establish a set of financial inducements and penalties to shape enterprise behavior.

A second set of stipulations set up strict distribution requirements for any above-contract profits retained by the firm. Sixty percent of all retained earnings were to be devoted to technological modernization and development of production capabilities. Twenty percent would go toward worker welfare and housing. The remaining 20 percent would be earmarked for worker bonuses. The point here was to avoid the phenomenon of enterprises using retained funds exclusively for consumption-oriented activities: bonus payments, new housing construction, or enhanced worker benefits. The Chinese were familiar with such patterns from their own limited reform experiences, as well as from stalled reform efforts during the 1960s in the Soviet Union and Yugoslavia.[18]

A third stipulation linked the firm's wage bill to annual profit levels. Though this aspect of the contract changed a bit during the first few years, after 1985 the relationship between profits and wages was set at a fixed ratio of 1 to 0.8. What this meant was that, as annual profits either rose or fell by one percentage point, the company's wage bill also had to rise and fall accordingly by 0.8 percent. The aim here was again to avoid the phenomenon of firms driving up their costs by constantly increasing worker wages. Just as with the stipulations setting up distribution requirements for retained earnings, the goal of the wage ceilings was to push the firm into capping costs and devoting as many resources as possible to technological modernization and revenue generation.

A fourth set of stipulations involved the firm's right to market its own output. At the time the contract was established, Chinese industrial firms were assigned certain output levels in accordance with the state plan, a practice that to some extent still occurs today.[19] As part of early efforts to encourage marketization, or at least reduce the scope of the plan, firms were instructed to sell 2 percent of their planned output on what would constitute the "open market." Though planned output levels would occupy the vast bulk of a firm's production, surplus output – or at least a part of that surplus – could also be sold by the firm on the open market. In the case of Shougang, the profit contract permitted the firm to sell not 2 percent but as much as 15 percent of its output on the open market. Furthermore, all above-plan output could be marketed by the firm. As will be discussed later, this measure did not appear particularly important when the contract was signed, since at that point China did not yet have a two-track pricing system distinguishing between "plan" and "market" goods.[20] Instead, the 15-percent "self-sale" measure was aimed mainly at scaling back the scope of the state plan. Nevertheless, a few years later, this measure attracted great attention – and became a major source for the myth of Shougang – when two-track pricing provided great benefits to those who could market their own goods outside the state plan.

A fifth and rather critical aspect of the contract involved its fifteen-year duration.[21] Ever since the early 1980s, Chinese reformers had experimented with a variety of enterprise contracts, but none of these arrangements had been as long in duration as the Shougang example. There are of course many reasons why most Chinese contracts remained restricted to just one or two years in duration. Supervisory agencies were usually not willing to cede power for an extended period, and even the firms themselves were often unwilling to accept responsibility over the long term. Nevertheless, duration is absolutely critical in the functioning of the profit contract. A firm can be presented with all sorts of performance incentives, but troubles inevitably arise if those incentives are set to last for only two or three years. A short time horizon leads to inadequate investment in the long-term productive capabilities of the firm, a phenomenon as familiar to American industry as it is to Chinese.

Finally, a sixth element of the contract involved a particular definition of just who constituted parties to the arrangement. With most versions of managerial responsibility systems or profit contracting in China, agreements were between state agencies on the one hand and top management of the firm on the other. In the case of Shougang, the contract was said to extend down to each and every worker, not merely to the general manager or the party secretary. Just as the firm as a whole would join the contract, so would each worker. Just as the firm as a whole would operate under the principle of "the base target is nonnegotiable, and the more you earn the more you keep" (*bao si jishu, chao bao quan liu*), so would each worker. The Shougang contract was heralded as a new experiment in worker democracy. Ironically, while this form of worker democracy was continually trumpeted by Shougang's own public relations material, it served perhaps as the least important stipulation of the contract and the least honored in practice.

Taken as a whole, however, the six main elements of the contract followed a common theme. They attempted to force the enterprise both to generate increasing levels of income and to devote the bulk of that income toward productive investment. The normal siphons of enterprise funds (wage increases, bonus payments, housing construction) were effectively shut down, or at least restricted, and any cushion for mistakes was eliminated by cutting off state investment and other direct subsidies to the firm. Certainly the long-term hope of state authorities was that the contractually obligated firm would, over time, become a major generator of state revenue. In other words, by priming the pump a bit and allowing the firm to retain some profits initially, reformers hoped to realize even greater increases in state revenue while at the same time expanding production and increasing industrial efficiency. Shougang, in a sense, represented the Chinese version of supply-side economics.

From the perspective of the firm, the contract just described did not – at least on the surface – appear to be a "sweetheart" deal. The firm was obligated to turn over a set amount of money to the state (the profit submission) at an annual increasing rate of 7.2 percent. In order to meet that increasing level of submitted profits, the firm each year would have to either expand production or cut costs. Both avenues contained initial costs, for they required investments in technological modernization and new production facilities. Yet, because the firm's access to state investment funds had been severed, all modernization projects would have to be financed through retained earnings, the portion of profit not turned over to the state. As a result, the firm in any given year had to realize profits considerably beyond the targeted submission levels just to have enough retained earnings to maintain adequate investment for the future. Particularly at the beginning of the contract, when initial investment requirements were heavy, overall profits would have to accumulate at a rate much faster than the 7.2-percent annual rise in submitted profit. Furthermore, if the firm were to falter in any given year, its ability to meet the contractual targets in future years would be seriously jeopardized. In other words, mistakes, particularly in the beginning, would reverberate throughout the contracted period. This is because, in order to meet the profit submission target during a "bad" year (a year of low profitability), the firm would have to redirect funds from its own investment projects toward paying the state. Down the road, then, because investment would be lacking, the firm would face increasing difficulties meeting the necessary surplus between total realized profit and submitted profit. This particular form of contract is extremely unforgiving – mistakes early on snowball through the years.

Shougang party secretary Zhou Guanwu, by actively seeking the fifteen-year profit contract for his firm, engaged in a high-risk gamble. From the start, Zhou ensured that his name would become synonymous with Shougang and with the Shougang contract. He openly advocated this particular brand of reform in the years leading up to 1982 and, in a sense, staked his reputation and his career on its success. The potential rewards were unprecedented access to, and control over, investment funds – funds that could transform Shougang into the largest steel producer in China and catapult Zhou Guanwu into the national political arena. The risks, however, were also substantial. Failure to meet the contract would in the short term cripple Shougang and in all probability ensure that it remained the smallest among China's major steel firms. The state would hardly allow Shougang to go bankrupt or cease operations, but infusions of state bailout funds – a signal that the contract had failed – would certainly discredit Zhou Guanwu and the whole concept of long-term enterprise contracting. This did finally occur in 1995.

An important point that casts further doubt on the sweetheart nature of the deal is that the profit contract ultimately accepted by Zhou Guanwu was offered not only to Shougang.[22] Prior to 1982, other steel firms – including the somewhat newer and more efficient Magang – were offered the same sort of long-term profit contracts, but none of their managers accepted. As one Magang official involved in early reform efforts recalled, nobody dared guarantee the kind of growth rates that could support a 7.2-percent annual increase in submitted profits. Only Zhou was willing to take the gamble, displaying considerable daring at the time by accepting the contract.[23] Such growth rates were unheard of in the Chinese steel industry in the late 1970s and early 1980s. Even Zhou himself, when promoting the concept in an April 1982 report to the Beijing party committee, sought an increase rate of only 5 percent.[24] Later that year, apparently under pressure from the MOF, the State Council raised the rate first to 6 percent and then to 7.2 percent the following year.

The irony is that, at the beginning of the contract, the MOF was supportive (it obviously sensed the potential of increased revenues) whereas steel managers, fearing ruin, shrank from the offer. By the early 1990s, the positions had reversed. After Shougang's successful expansion and increasing levels of profit

Table 6.1. *Shougang retained earnings, 1981–92*
(RMB 100 million)

Year	Enterprise retained profit	Annual increase
1981	0.57	
1982	1.15	102%
1983	1.52	32%
1984	2.42	59%
1985	3.33	38%
1986	4.55	37%
1987	6.11	34%
1988	8.01	31%
1989	8.84	10%
1990	11.39	29%
1991	11.11	−2%
1992	19.58	76%

Sources: For 1981–90, Shougang internal data from Hao (1992, vol. 2, p. 27). For 1991–92, Chinese Academy of Social Sciences Institute of Economics (1993, p. 38).

retention, MOF officials became vocal opponents of the contract while competing steel managers claimed that Shougang was receiving preferential treatment to which they should all be entitled. Not surprisingly, it was at this point that the accusations of a sweetheart deal for Shougang began to gain currency.

Shougang's record throughout the 1980s and early 1990s indicates that Zhou Guanwu made the correct gamble. Company publications repeatedly assert that, from 1978 to 1990, total output on average increased 7.7 percent annually, three percentage points higher than the average among large-scale Chinese steel producers.[25] Similarly, Shougang's "realized profit and tax" (*shixian lishui*) – akin to gross profits in the West – increased on average by 17.5 percent annually, seven and a half percentage points higher than the average for other large steel firms in China.[26] As Table 6.1 indicates, Shougang was able to achieve the increases in above-contract retained earnings needed to sustain a 7.2-percent annual increase in income-tax payments to the state.

Table 6.2 shows the level of steel output growth sustained by Shougang as part of the effort to achieve its increasing profit and investment levels. As will be explained later, even as Shougang pursued diversification through the late 1980s and early 1990s, the steel operation remained the firm's major source of income and its primary focus of activity. Hence Table 6.2 does not describe Shougang's

Table 6.2. *Shougang finished steel output,*
1981–92 (10,000 tons)

Year	Output of finished rolled steel	Annual increase
1981	150	
1982	160	7%
1983	178	11%
1984	200	12%
1985	221	11%
1986	255	15%
1987	283	11%
1988	314	11%
1989	326	4%
1990	374	15%
1991	402	7%
1992	436	8%

Sources: Ministry of Metallurgical Industry (1985–93); Chinese Academy of Social Sciences Institute of Economics (1993, p. 29).

expansion in entirety, but the data give an impression of the underlying production increases leading to (and at the same time funded by) greater profit levels.

With regard to the data, a number of questions have been raised regarding the veracity of Shougang's claims that output increases in the 1980s were financed solely through retained earnings. The issue is not so much whether Shougang actually received covert subsidization as whether the firm boosted output levels simply through mergers and acquisitions with a series of previously independent steel producers. There is no doubt that some such behavior did occur. Through the 1980s, Shougang essentially subsumed Beijing Municipality's Metallurgy Bureau and its affiliated firms. Data are sketchy, but it does seem that the firm boosted output levels on the margins through such mergers. Nevertheless, throughout this period the vast bulk of the firm's output was still being produced by its main Beijing steel facilities.

The Pricing Issue

A more serious reason for doubting Shougang's profit figures concerns pricing. Most of the firm's detractors have suggested, with good reason, that Shougang's financial success was due not to commercially oriented behavior but rather to implicit subsidies contained within the steel market's pricing mechanisms. In other words, the issue is whether Shougang's gains were the result of straight-forward productivity increases or instead the result of successful efforts on the firm's part to capture rents in the Chinese price structure. A Hong Kong ana-lyst neatly mirrored the view of skeptics when in 1995 he declared, "Shougang was always made to be a big success story . . . but it was a lot of baloney. If you allow one company to sell steel at market prices while others have to sell below cost, of course that company's going to be able to reap big profits."[27]

By the time Shougang's profit contract was signed in 1982, Chinese reform-ers were attempting to wean industrial firms from the state plan while continu-ing to guarantee state control over minimum production levels. In other words, the goals were to ensure certain production levels by assigning firms output tar-gets and simultaneously to encourage firms to respond to demand signals from the open market. Hence, in the early 1980s, all steel firms were responsible for directly marketing 2 percent of their within-plan output; presumably, they would directly market any above-plan output.[28] Shougang was responsible for directly marketing 15 percent of its within-plan output and then all the rest of its above-quota production. At first this was more of a burden than a privilege because significant price differentials had by 1983 not yet developed between "plan" and "market" output. The measure was intended primarily to aid the state by reducing the responsibility of the plan for allocating all goods.

This situation changed dramatically with the introduction of two-track pric-ing for industrial goods in 1984. Following similar developments in the agri-cultural sector, Chinese industrial products would now command low prices when sold to state agencies on the plan but much higher prices when sold on the open market. In 1985, China's open-market price for a ton of rolled steel was nearly twice that of the state-plan price.[29] Obviously, any firm that could sell a disproportionate level of output on the open market could capture huge rents contained within the two-tiered system, a system that persisted until steel prices were fully decontrolled in early 1993.

Because Shougang had been granted precisely this opportunity by the con-tract, it is understandable that the firm's profits in subsequent years were held suspect by many observers. That Shougang could sell 15 percent of its planned output at open-market prices versus the 2 percent accorded to other firms consti-tuted, at least in theory, a significant financial advantage having nothing really to do with Shougang's efficiency, productivity, or managerial strategy. Crit-ics also suggested that Shougang's planned output levels assigned by the state were abnormally low. The implication is that state authorities were coddling

Table 6.3. *Plan and market shares in Shougang's*
output of rolled steel, 1983–92

Year	Percent for plan	Percent for market[a]
1983	61	39
1984	56	44
1985	54	46
1986	54	46
1987	59	41
1988	55	45
1989	58	42
1990	54	46
1991	46	54[b]
1992[c]	26	68

[a] Company data for the share of directly marketed steel from 1983 to 1991 also include output withheld by the firm for its own uses. Therefore, not all the directly marketed share was necessarily marketed.
[b] Ministry of Metallurgy data for this year place the figure at 59.1 percent.
[c] MMI data do not account for the additional 6 percent of output in 1992, though presumably this share was retained by the firm for its own use.
Sources: For 1983–91 data, Shougang company data presented in Chinese Academy of Social Sciences Institute of Economics (1993, p. 167); for 1992 data, Ministry of Metallurgical Industry (1993, p. 338).

Shougang, providing it with low planned output levels so that the firm could achieve greater above-quota production – production that commanded premium open-market prices.

Although such accusations are not entirely unfounded, the situation in reality was quite complex. Table 6.3, displaying Shougang's output mix between plan and market during the 1980s and early 1990s, does appear at first glance to indicate that the firm was granted low levels of within-plan production. This seems particularly apparent when Shougang's total output share devoted to the state plan is compared with that of Angang during the mid-1980s (see Table 6.4).[30] Nevertheless, such comparisons are deceptive. Across the steel industry, within-plan output targets, even for rolled steel products, were set according to the individual firm's capacity to produce pig iron.[31] This latter

Table 6.4. *Angang, Magang, Shougang: Performance under the contract,*
1986–90 (RMB 10,000)

	1986	1987	1988	1989	1990
Angang					
Sales revenue	551,562	616,121	712,021	795,230	774,465
Sales tax	72,502	80,785	81,930	107,971	104,223
Gross profit	126,779	136,683	153,383	130,404	76,136
Retained profit	38,539	44,072	60,059	40,000	−15,181
Modernization funds mobilized	98,379	120,167	167,408	158,747	114,514
Modernization funds used	88,028	134,556	199,165	162,325	229,414
Magang					
Sales revenue	127,103	141,553	171,732	205,162	245,158
Sales tax	15,434	17,564	20,410	26,510	32,442
Gross profit	26,663	27,706	26,812	21,879	20,479
Retained profit	8,285	9,189	6,351	6,425	6,192
Modernization funds mobilized	27,697	30,179	34,971	30,997	51,088
Modernization funds used	32,085	27,902	36,502	32,880	48,780
Shougang					
Sales revenue	312,306	368,222	438,010	512,313	690,300
Sales tax	36,282	42,362	46,779	63,978	89,451
Gross profit	100,465	114,391	138,745	155,103	160,415
Retained profit	61,594	76,233	99,368	122,715	499,516
Modernization funds mobilized	42,757	92,138	114,553	116,916	115,292
Modernization funds used	60,355	85,787	64,936	71,750	110,993

Source: Ministry of Metallurgical Industry, *Caiwu chengben tongji ziliao* (Beijing: Yejin Gongye Chubanshe, 1993), pp. 996–9 (Angang data), pp. 994–7 (Magang data), pp. 982–5 (Shougang data).

figure depended on blast furnace capacity and a particular furnace utilization coefficient. The capacity figures and utilization coefficients differed widely among firms owing to wide variations in facilities. In turn, the share of within-plan production also differed from firm to firm. Angang, in a sense to its misfortune, had always been a major pig iron producer; as a result, its within-plan output targets for rolled steel were also high. Other firms, though, had much lower planned output levels, some actually far lower than Shougang's. If the comparison is extended beyond just Angang, Shougang's plan share was not conspicuously low among major Chinese steel producers.

Table 6.5. *Plan versus market output among
major steel producers, 1992*

Firm	Plan share	Market share
Shougang	26.2	67.7
Baotou	34.9	58.9
Angang	50	45.9
Taigang	9.8	75.5
Bengang	22.1	85.6
Baoshan	54.5	45.5
Magang	49.6	32.9
Wugang	46.9	40.2
Pangang	40.4	31.4

Source: Ministry of Metallurgical Industry (1993, pp. 338–9).

Table 6.5 presents only a snapshot for 1992, but the general distribution among firms remained similar back through the 1980s. In earlier years, however, the share of planned output for all firms tended to be higher. As Shougang officials have been eager to point out, the Beijing company's absolute tonnage of steel allotted to the state plan increased at an average annual level of 9.3 percent during the 1980s, a higher rate of increase than for any other major steel firm in China.[32] Interestingly, the share of a firm's output devoted to self-marketing in general tends to be a poor predictor of profitability or other performance indicators. Some of the firms with the highest percentages of directly marketed steel also happened to be the poorest performers nationally.[33]

In theory at least, great rent-seeking opportunities existed in the two-tiered system, but capitalizing on such opportunities proved to be difficult or even destructive from the perspective of long-term growth. First, during recessionary periods of the 1980s, it was not always easy for firms to market their steel. In other words, in the but partially marketized Chinese system, "market" prices for steel were high but actual purchasers nonexistent. In a way, this is similar to the situation Chinese steel companies faced in the early 1990s: market prices for steel were high so long as transactions moved forward on a noncash basis. The point is that while in theory vast rents were opened in the Chinese system, in reality they were not always open to capture – particularly when the seller had to maintain cash flow. Given the hard budget constraint set by the contract, maintenance of cash flow became essential to Shougang. In addition, because the firm faced great pressure to expand output and increase profits over the long term, there was a continual need for technological modernization and renovation. During the mid-1980s, regardless of the market price for steel, Shougang frequently needed to use surplus output for its own construction and modernization efforts. It became a matter of strategic choice: capture rents in the current price structure or devote output toward the enterprise expansion needed to maintain the contract.

Shougang in reality pursued both strategies over time, a point borne out by a 1992 MMI study. The actual benefits reaped from pricing advantages were minimal, however. Shougang official records assert that, between 1984 and 1987, the firm devoted nearly all of its above-plan output to its own modernization and expansion projects.[34] The explanation is that Shougang was at that time just beginning a series of projects to expand capacity, update equipment, and build new housing. Like other steel firms, Shougang had no access to state steel allocations, so it could not sell its own steel at high market prices and then turn around and buy back steel at low state-plan prices. Meanwhile, there was great pressure to expand capacity given the long-term increase in rates stipulated by the profit contract. As a result, within the firm itself there was significant demand for construction-grade steel. The MMI has confirmed that, during this initial phase of rapid expansion, Shougang did indeed devote practically all surplus output to in-house uses.[35]

It was from 1988 to 1990 that Shougang reaped the benefits of its pricing advantage, capitalizing during those years on the rents contained within the two-track system. In attempting to measure these gains, the MMI has estimated that Shougang was able to earn during those three years an additional RMB 680 million from privileged open-market sales.[36] However, the ministry points out that, throughout this period, the prices Shougang received for sales to the state plan were lower than those received by any other major steel firm.[37] In other words, Shougang received lower rates for its within-plan output than did other companies. Ministry of Metallurgical Industry economists estimate that Shougang's RMB 680-million windfall from market pricing was offset by an RMB 812-million loss from sales to the state plan.[38]

Admittedly, these figures are inexact, given that they are measuring hypothetical situations in an extremely murky price structure. Nevertheless, they cast doubt on the assertion that Shougang's success was based solely on rent seeking. Those opportunities were certainly present, but all available evidence suggests that they were not used in the way that Shougang's detractors have claimed. Hence, although this aspect of the myth of Shougang is grounded in reality – the price differentials existed, and Shougang did indeed have unusual direct marketing privileges – it is in essence wrong. It neglects the firm's costs, it neglects the firm's raw material demands, and ultimately it mistakes what could have happened for what actually did happen.

The "Shougang as Dazhai" Perspective

Even if the rent-seeking explanation for Shougang's success is shown to be incorrect, there is still a pervasive belief that Shougang's profits were somehow ill-gotten, that Shougang was a Potemkin Village, a "Dazhai" built on fraudulent data. The notion is that Shougang from the beginning was a showcase for Deng Xiaoping's reform policies and, as such, had to be proven a success over the years. It could not be allowed to fail – it was a national model, after all.[39] Hence, the Beijing company is dismissed as a case unworthy of study from the economic perspective. It was too special, too privileged, too political – in short, too closely linked with Deng.

This perspective has several flaws, the first of which is that it grossly overestimates the extent to which profit contracting embodied Deng Xiaoping's vision of industrial reform. An important point is that when China began experimenting with economic reform in the late 1970s, impetus for policy innovation frequently came via bottom-up rather than top-down processes.[40] In many cases, the provinces themselves served as important launching pads for reform experiments. Shougang's initial profit retention arrangement to an extent followed this pattern. By 1978, Wan Li, the party secretary of Anhui Province, had already encouraged local experimentation with household responsibility systems – profit retention, in a sense, for the agricultural producer. The Anhui leader was beginning to promote the use of similar methods to stimulate China's moribund state enterprises. At the same time, Sichuan party secretary Zhao Ziyang was pursuing a similar strategy through his own local agricultural and industrial experiments. Initially, the center remained quiet, yet as these experiments achieved early successes, both the ideas and the men behind them were elevated to the national level. Deng Xiaoping signaled the start of national reform efforts with the Third Plenum of the Eleventh Party Congress at the end of 1978; by 1979, both Zhao Ziyang and Wan Li had been brought into the Politiburo. By 1980, Zhao was China's premier and Wan Li vice-premier. Also by this time, profit contracting had come to Shougang.

From 1979 to 1981, Shougang had a series of one-year profit contracts, the first two allowing the firm to retain a percentage of total profits and the third allowing full retention of all profits above a certain base level. The one name that continually kept cropping up in association with Shougang during these years was that of Wan Li. It is fairly clear that profit contracting had become Wan Li's personal project and that Shougang had become a vehicle for his ideas. The Shougang company chronology indicates that, in August 1981, the vice-premier convened a "profit contracting responsibility system" discussion meeting at Shougang where he urged the firm onward in its efforts.[41] Then, in January of 1982, Wan Li again extolled the virtues of Shougang's early profit retention schemes at a national conference on metallurgical production. In May of that year, the vice-premier reappeared at Shougang publicly to urge the firm on, declaring that under the "responsibility" system Shougang had become a center for efficiency and each of its workers a veritable "minister of finance."[42] The interesting thing is that, during these early years, other leaders – particularly Deng Xiaoping, but also Zhao Ziyang – were notable for their absence from Shougang's records. Other than Wan Li, senior officials were apparently avoiding Shougang, neither visiting the firm nor extolling it in their speeches. It was not until 1984, after Shougang's long-term contract had commenced, that another senior leader (party secretary Hu Yaobang) started making appearances at Shougang. Still, Zhao Ziyang and Deng Xiaoping remained on the sidelines with respect to Shougang. Deng actually did not grace the firm with a visit until 1992.

Meanwhile, though it is hard to discern what might be considered a "national" policy for industrial reform during the 1980s, there were some rather clear turns in the road. Enterprise profit contracting, the system in which individual firms would sign contracts with specific state agencies, gained initial popularity from around 1981 to 1983. By 1983, and certainly by 1984, profit contracting seemed to give way to the national "tax for profit" (*ligaishui*) effort in which individual enterprise profit retention contracts were replaced by a standardized, national income-tax system. After the tax-for-profit system proved unworkable, profit contracting returned again in force – this time becoming widely disseminated among industrial firms – from around 1987 to 1989.[43] After this point, though, and particularly by 1992, national policy had shifted away from contracting and moved toward corporatization and joint stock reforms. Ironically, it was only after this point that Shougang received its greatest national political attention.

During this process of policy evolution, Shougang was associated more with Vice-Premier Wan Li than with Deng Xiaoping. Furthermore, there is no evidence to suggest that profit contracting per se embodied Deng's vision of industrial reform. After all, the first wave of contracting nationwide was soon superseded by the tax-for-profit reforms. It makes no more sense to say tax-for-profit was Deng's policy vision than it does to say that contracting was.

Instead it may be surmised that, during the early 1980s, China's leadership circle was divided over industrial policy – understandably so, given the intractability of the problems at hand.[44] After initially supporting profit retention contracts in Sichuan, premier Zhao Ziyang apparently switched his allegiances and began spearheading the nationwide tax-for-profit system. Meanwhile, Wan Li and party secretary Hu Yaobang still championed contract solutions, a position that explains their continued appearances at Shougang. Zhao seemed to prevail briefly in 1984, just as Hu Yaobang started to jump on the pro-Shougang bandwagon, only to have his national tax policies once again replaced by contracting two to three years later. And where was Deng during this split? It seems fair to assume that Deng acted as a balancing force, initially throwing his weight behind contracting and then allowing tax-for-profit to move to the fore. If Deng indeed had been so closely tied to profit contracting of the Shougang variety, then why would he have let it recede from national attention? The simple answer is that he was not – at least through the 1980s – closely linked to contracting in industry, but instead shifted back and forth as the entire nation searched for a solution to its industrial ills. Deng was, to use the Chinese expression, "crossing the river by feeling for the stones"; he was groping around for a workable policy.

In a sense, this interpretation stems from a particular view of the post-Mao policy process that emphasizes the pragmatic and (to some extent) pluralistic nature of economic policy making during the 1980s. For China at the time, the problems facing both industry and agriculture were huge, and the solutions were anything but clear. As a result, a period of true experimentation ensued. As noted previously, the center often remained quiet as a variety of experiments were pursued at the local level. Those experiments that showed promise in local trials were then extended on a national level under the auspices of central agencies. Central elites, often divided amongst themselves over policy options, encouraged their own local pilot programs. The result was that even as national policy in the abstract seemed to shift from one style to the next, in fact there were always a variety of experiments going on simultaneously. Shougang was but one of those experiments. So, when tax-for-profit became national policy, many enterprises nationwide were still being governed by contract. When contracting reappeared as national policy in the late 1980s, tax-for-profit still remained in effect, a fact that explains in part the confusion attending this second round of profit contracting.

During this period, because so many different policies were being tested, it is extremely difficult to conceive of the existence of a "Dazhai," a single unit embodying the vision of a single paramount leader. Deng Xiaoping seemed

189

consciously to avoid the creation of such models, an effort reflected in his absence from Shougang during the 1980s. To suggest that Shougang during the 1980s was *the* national model – and thus a model that would never be allowed to fail – simply does not fit with the degree of policy variation that we know existed at the time.

Furthermore, if Shougang had been the preferred model, why then were there so many cases of bureaucratic interference in the firm? That the Ministry of Finance has continually (and quite publicly) protested Shougang's relatively low tax burden suggests that the tax bureaucracy for one was unwilling to play its part in the Shougang-as-national-showcase scenario. The same is true for Beijing Municipality's efforts to reassert claims on Shougang earnings. If Shougang was so clearly "Deng's firm," why would Beijing mayor Chen Xitong repeatedly quarrel with the enterprise over tax payments? Were all these bureaucratic actors simply not getting the message? In some of these cases, the supervisory authorities were successful and in others not, but the point is that they were willing publicly to criticize Shougang and its profit contract; such bureaucratic interference is the norm in Chinese industry. It would be ludicrous to suggest that Shougang was a special project – a showcase for the elites – somehow immune from the normal bureaucratic problems facing large SOEs.

It is equally ludicrous to suggest that Zhou Guanwu was always a special favorite of Deng's and hence that Shougang benefited as a result. Zhou's background simply does not suggest a particularly close link to Deng. According to his official biography, Zhou was born in 1918 in Shandong Province and joined the communist party at age nineteen in 1937.[45] That same year, Zhou joined the communist Eighth Route Army, where he served over the next twelve years in a series of positions from the platoon up to the regimental level. Ultimately, he served as vice–chief of staff at the division level.[46] This position, though not undistinguished, certainly does not put Zhou among the more senior or well-known military leaders of the time.

After the founding of the People's Republic, Zhou followed the career path of many other officers – he was sent to serve in a civilian production unit. During this initial period after "liberation," the communist party faced the tasks of running a nation far earlier than expected. As a result, they suffered a severe shortage of cadres, particularly of those with technical or managerial backgrounds. By 1950, a vast demobilization of military units was under way to provide personnel for civilian managerial roles. As part of this national trend, Zhou Guanwu was sent to Shougang – then still known as the Shijingshan Iron and Steel Company – serving first as head of the personnel office. Again, although the position itself is not unimportant, neither is it conspicuous.

One might imagine that, if Zhou had truly been some sort of brilliant favorite of Deng Xiaoping's, the young military officer would have been posted to a position somewhat higher up the political ladder than the enterprise level. A position in local or provincial government would have been more appropriate, perhaps. Even at the enterprise level, Zhou was not posted to a senior managerial position. Over the next nine years, however, Zhou Guanwu worked his way up through a series of midlevel managerial positions, including vice–factory chief and factory chief. By 1959, he had successfully worked his way up to the senior level, attaining the position of manager of the Shougang Company and party secretary of the firm.[47] From 1979 to 1983, Zhou served as one of the vice-ministers of metallurgy as well as vice–party secretary of the MMI, all the while retaining his position as Shougang party chief. From 1983 to 1995, Zhou devoted his time fully to Shougang, serving as party secretary and "chairman of the board," a title that had grown out of the reform period.

Once again, Zhou's biography, while not unimpressive, fails to confirm any particularly close connection with Deng or any other major political leader. Zhou's career advancement could certainly be termed successful, but his rise was by no means meteoric by industry standards. His staying power at Shougang through decades of political turbulence obviously suggests a certain degree of savvy and craftiness. Nevertheless, until well into the reform era, Zhou Guanwu was a minor personage, a "player" at neither the national nor local level.

In all likelihood, this whole matter of Zhou Guanwu's close connection with Deng Xiaoping was as much a creation of Shougang's public relations efforts as anything else. In China, as in most countries, political connections count in business. Firms know this and generally publicize, glamorize, and embellish their connections whenever possible. They encourage political figures to make "inspection tours" of the firm, they seek to have national leaders script personal calligraphy on company entrance gates, and they continually release photos of their management with political luminaries. It is a constant game in China, and for good reason. In a system in which the bureaucracy is so overbearing, arbitrary, and omnipresent, a survival strategy for the firm is to create the impression that it has personal patrons. Shougang (like every other enterprise) engages in this practice, and because the firm is so big and is located in Beijing, it does have the opportunity to come into contact with major political personages. However, given the kind of public relations material that flows out of companies in China, an observer could be forgiven for thinking that all firms, not just Shougang, are somehow favorites of Deng Xiaoping.

Zhou Guanwu was, indeed, a deeply political figure, yet in a somewhat different respect from what is commonly understood. Zhou was not impressive for his political connections but rather for his political ambition and outright arrogance. The connections themselves are even today rather difficult to assess. On the one hand, Zhou did serve under Deng prior to the founding of the People's Republic. On the other hand, Zhou never climbed beyond the enterprise level – a rather minor position from the national political perspective. As one Shougang economist privately surmised, Zhou probably felt cheated in being relegated to the enterprise level, basically left out of the elite power game.[48] His cohorts from the war years had long ago moved onto more high-profile positions, while Zhou was but a company official.

Yet Zhou Guanwu seems to have been able to manipulate his connections in one important respect. Unlike other enterprise-level officials, he was permitted to stay in his position well beyond retirement age. Across the steel industry during the reform era, retirement rules have been strictly enforced; as a result, managers and party secretaries, after climbing their way up the seniority system, generally serve only a few years before being forced out. Zhou, on the other hand, was already sixty years old when serving as Shougang party secretary in 1979. He remained at that post until his resignation seventeen years later in 1995. Somehow, Zhou was granted immunity from forced retirement, immunity that some Shougang employees suggested came from Deng himself.[49] Why might immunity have been granted? Unlike most other enterprise-level officials, Zhou had publicly linked himself with a particular reform experiment – he had essentially stuck his neck out and become personally tied to a test case. It is conceivable that the political leaders linked to profit contracting, most likely Hu Yaobang or Wan Li, would have preferred not to remove Zhou and risk shaking up a major national test case just when contracting itself was being challenged by the tax-for-profit reforms. The important point is that this immunity, combined with his already long-term service at Shougang, allowed Zhou to build up the company as his own power base, his own fiefdom – in a sense, his own launching pad to national recognition.

Again, aside from the retirement issue, Zhou was notable politically more for his ambition than his connections. He clearly was less risk-averse than his counterparts at other firms, and he was far more eager to have his own name associated with a particular brand of enterprise reform. Furthermore, he enjoyed unparalleled longevity at a single firm, longevity which allowed him to turn that firm into his own "mountain top." In line with this, he was willing to confront the bureaucracy while his counterparts at other firms remained silent. Throughout this process, the profit contract served as a vehicle for Zhou's ambition, a means by which he could fight off interference in his firm and achieve the breathing room needed for iconoclastic development strategies. In a sense, for better or worse, Zhou Guanwu became one of the few true entrepreneurs in Chinese state industry. As a result, he was probably the only enterprise-level official who through his own efforts became a household name in China.[50]

The Contract as Property Right and Governance Mechanism

Shougang's long-term profit contract essentially secured for the recipient a de facto property right vis-à-vis the state. Yet, this property right did not simply signify "autonomy" or "freedom from constraint," the kind of license that can lead to either value destruction or value enhancement. Rather, by strictly enforcing a hard budget constraint, the contract brought about a merger of autonomy and accountability, precisely the kind of merger needed to encourage value-enhancing strategies in complex market producers. The irony is that, in the poorly institutionalized legal environment of China during the 1980s, the firm had to be tied closer to the state in order to achieve more market-oriented incentives. In other words, a closer, clearer tie to specific state agencies had to be established so that renegade state agencies could not – in the haze of confused authority relations – tax the firm into insolvency. The state, ironically, had to be brought in so that it could ultimately be forced out. Only once a clearer tie between firm and state was established could the firm begin to operate on anything resembling a hard budget.

For this reason, a key feature of the Shougang contract was its specificity with regard to just which agencies represented the state. As pointed out earlier in reference to contracting at Angang and Magang, it was often the case that profit contracts failed to single out a specific agency to represent the state's side of the bargain. Instead, several agencies were named, none took responsibility, and in the end, the inefficient supervisory system that the contract was supposed to replace was merely duplicated in the agreement itself. The Shougang case was different, though. Formally, there were still many agencies claiming some sort of supervisory role over Shougang, and the profit contract itself had to receive official approval from the State Commission on Economic Structure Reform, the State Economic Commission, the State Planning Commission, and the Ministry of Finance. Nevertheless, it was clear from the start that the Shougang contract operated exclusively under the aegis of the State Council, the paramount administrative agency in the Chinese government. The contract, in effect, was between the company and the State Council only.

Whether or not the "state" was defined formally in the Shougang contract, the definition was certainly clear in practice. The "state" meant the State Council, and nothing more. While Shougang officials may not have been able to name their supervisory agency among all the competing "mothers-in-law," those officials knew exactly where to go in the event of a dispute: the State Council. When the Beijing municipal government attempted to extract extra profit from the firm in 1992, Shougang took the case to the State Council. When the Ministry of Finance tried to change Shougang's tax status, it was the State Council that resolved the conflict. The point is not that the State Council always decided in favor of Shougang. In the 1992 dispute with Beijing, for example, Shougang still was forced to acquiesce in part to the municipality's financial demands.[51] Rather, the point is simply that an arbiter existed, an arbiter that accepted responsibility and enforced its decisions. The result was that, while it still operated in the same bureaucratic morass that affected other firms, Shougang had a means of asserting its interests through appeals to the State Council. By hearing the disputes, the State Council served as a protector, fending off the more egregious attempts at interference by other agencies.

At the same time, it was also clear to the firm and all other parties involved that there was a single, identifiable agency capable of monitoring noncompliance with the agreement. In Angang's case, the firm consistently failed to meet contractual obligations, yet no single state agency stepped forward to impose sanctions or accept responsibility. In Shougang's case, it was perfectly clear that this particular profit contract was to be enforced by the State Council. At the same time, agencies (e.g., the Ministry of Finance) that had been deprived of their "rightful" claims to Shougang revenue also served an important de facto governance role. They constantly audited the firm in an effort to catch misappropriation of funds and thereby claim firm-level revenues as their own. The contract, by shutting out state claimants to firm-level funds, actually motivated these agencies to provide constant monitoring.

The most interesting aspect of Shougang's financial debacle in the mid-1990s was its demonstration of precisely how this sort of system breaks down. As soon as the firm was actually granted special political status and was at least perceived to be a favorite of the national leader – as happened with Shougang in 1992 –competing state agencies backed off and ceased their monitoring efforts. The firm still retained its autonomy and certainly its claims to revenue flows, but it could no longer be held responsible for losses. Enjoying what amounted to boundless financial liberty, the firm was easily able to divide assets from liabilities, claiming the former while thoroughly skirting the latter.

The point becomes somewhat clearer if viewed from the nested problems perspective introduced in Chapter 3. According to that model, firms – owing to the legacy of command planning and the resulting inherited burdens – always have excuses to demand capital from the central government. Capital flows in but, because property rights remain ill-defined and the state bureaucracy highly fragmented, governmental agencies extract significant portions of that capital. Firms, however, do not resist, for the more agencies extract, the more the firms have reason to demand more investment and blame poor performance on exogenous factors. Performance information becomes increasingly cloudy, but in truth *all* the players benefit over the short term. Assets are divvied up between actors in the state agencies and in the firm itself, while liabilities are passed on to the central budget and ultimately to "the people." Individual interests are rewarded while costs are passed on to the macroeconomy as a whole. Authority becomes separated from accountability, just as assets are split from liabilities.

The Shougang contract actually reversed this situation by restoring the links between authority and accountability on one side and between assets and liabilities on the other. The two key facts here are that (1) the firm was tied to a single administrative agency and (2) outside investments into the firm were summarily cut off. This combination served at once to stop bureaucratic predation upon the firm and to deprive the firm of the usual excuses for subpar performance. The nested problems dynamic was effectively broken. The firm would have the right to retain its earnings, but it would also lose the privilege of relying on the usual excuses for bank loans. Handicaps inherited from the command era no longer counted, for the firm would simply have to deal with those on its own.[52] State predation no longer counted, for it was effectively curtailed. Finally, the fudging of profit levels also no longer counted. The firm could manipulate its books all it wanted, but it would still have to fund its own operations and pay its annually rising fees to the government. Blame for poor performance was no longer to be spread across a multitude of actors but was instead made traceable directly to the firm. The firm would keep the fruits of its success and would be held accountable for the costs of its failures, regardless of whether those costs were linked to inherited problems. Whether justly or not, accountability was being pinned at the level of the firm. Importantly, however, accountability was being matched by authority. Outside actors – nonparties to the contract – were being held at bay by the State Council.

In a sense, the contract represented a serious effort at imposing market selection and the beginnings of real corporate governance. In the nested problems dynamic, because it can never be determined what exactly is causing poor performance in any given firm, all firms get subsidized. No consistent selection takes place. The Shougang contract basically created a "time zero" from which to begin evaluating firm-level performance. Handicaps inherited from the previous era, whether justly or unjustly, would become the responsibility of the firm rather than an excuse for subsidization. Predation would also be stopped.

195

The idea here was that exogenous influences on firm performance – whether from improper bank lending, subsidization, or bureaucratic predation – would be curtailed as much as possible. Once that was achieved, performance could be linked analytically to managerial strategy and firm-level productivity. That is, the major sources of firm-level outcomes could now realistically be seen as coming from within the firm rather than from without. In effect, the onus of responsibility for outcomes, positive or negative, could be shifted back to the firm.

This shifting of responsibility marked a key first step in establishing effective enterprise governance. In the case of Shougang, if Zhou Guanwu did not meet his annual profit targets then his own career would certainly be threatened. Admittedly, few mechanisms existed to ensure that Zhou used the money at his disposal properly, and it is far from clear how effective the auditing by supervisory agencies really was. Nevertheless, the cutting of outside investment flows served as an important governance mechanism in itself. Firm-level management was severely constrained in terms of the amount of funds with which it could play. Zhou Guanwu could in fact have done whatever he wanted with the firm's earnings, but if requisite amounts were not pumped back into technology upgrades and operations then performance would surely slacken. In other words, the cutting of outside funding, when coupled with the relinking of firm-level performance to internal earnings and managerial strategy, limited the scope of managerial misbehavior that could actually occur. Zhou could squander funds, but ultimately he would stand to blame if the firm faltered. In a sense, the restoration of accountability meant that, at least tacitly, something akin to a threat of bankruptcy was always lurking in the background. Whether the state could have credibly threatened to bankrupt Shougang is an open question, but it could certainly have credibly threatened to terminate Zhou Guanwu.[53] This may have been a rather bare-bones method of governance, but it marked a tremendous improvement over what has gone on at comparable firms in the transitional environment.

By setting and actually enforcing Shougang's contract, the State Council, rather than abdicating on its responsibilities by allowing banks to keep pumping in the loans, acted decisively to perform a basic selection function. Perhaps more accurately, it created a basis upon which market selection could operate. In other words, the government was not picking winners and losers. It was not determining that "Firm A" was to live while "Firm B" was to die. Instead, by cutting Shougang off – from both loans and predation – the State Council was exposing the firm to the market and holding out hope that the market itself could serve as an effective selection mechanism. Even though it involved only one firm, the experiment achieved what few other reform efforts have. It effectively exposed the firm to the market, eliminated the "noise" usually surrounding SOE performance in a transitional environment, and created a basis for market selection.

The general point is that few governments, and certainly not the government in such a large and disaggregated country as China, have the information needed efficiently to pick winners and losers among industrial firms. Particularly in the transitional context, simply providing the means for the market to perform this function represents a monumental task. The experience of the Shougang contract suggests, though, that there is hope on this front. If determined, government actors can create the basis for market selection even in the modern industrial sector. They may not be able to pick who wins and who loses, but they can certainly create the basic arena in which firms can *become* winners. Moreover, the government can at least stabilize financial flows enough so that winners can be distinguished from losers. Finally, it can avoid the ultimate outcome of the nested problems dynamic, in which good firms are dragged down with the bad and all become losers.

Even just in the case of Shougang, however, the government had to go to great lengths to ensure that the firm actually did get exposed to the market. Particularly in the area of state predation, measures had to be taken that went well beyond the limited stipulations of the contract. Officially, Shougang turned over a fixed amount of profit to the state annually. Anything earned above that level (residual profit) was retained by the firm. Yet the formal contract alone was not sufficient to guarantee these rights. The problem was that the contract came into play only after sales taxes, value-added taxes, and circulation taxes were deducted from the firm's sales revenue. Only after all these primary taxes were deducted could the firm assess its total profit and then submit a portion of that profit to the state as income tax or profit remission. In formal terms, then, the contract was incapable of preventing situations in which government agencies would increase the tax burden on the firm as soon as profitability began to rise, the phenomenon known in Chinese as *bian da kuai niu* ("whipping the fast ox"). That is, nothing in the contract officially prevented either local agencies or the central tax bureau of the Ministry of Finance from increasing Shougang's sales taxes, circulation taxes, or other nontax fees every time Shougang started to show greater profits. Only the income tax, the profit remission to the state, was protected by contract.

The contractually granted right to residual returns would actually be rendered meaningless if tax agencies were able to raise the firm's sales-tax burden at will – there would never be any profits to retain, no matter how successful or efficient the firm.[54] Unfortunately, this is a common phenomenon in China, and it nearly occurred at Shougang. As previously described, soon after Shougang started to show high retained earnings under the contract, the MOF tried to reclaim those earnings by applying a 6-percent increase in Shougang's VAT. Throughout the 1980s and early 1990s, as will be discussed later, the MOF actively and publicly complained that Shougang's profit contract threatened the revenue collecting capabilities of the state. There was considerable interest in clawing back the increasing levels of financial resources accumulating in the firm. At Shougang, though, the State Council enforced not just the letter but also the spirit of the contract. In other words, the basic pre–profit remission tax burden was held constant, despite efforts of certain agencies to the contrary, while profit remissions to the state rose annually at the agreed-upon fixed rate of 7.2 percent. In short, Shougang was granted a right to residual returns and, just as important, a stable tax environment in which achieving returns became a real possibility.

How then did Shougang's incentive structure shift in response to this long-term grant of property rights? It should first be noted that in the deepest sense, for better or worse, ultimate incentives remained essentially constant. Large SOEs in China are inherently political organizations, and despite increasing degrees of marketization, the firms are still arms of the state. What this means is that, for Shougang and most other large state firms in China, the ultimate goal of enterprise management has always remained output maximization. The more a firm produces, the more attention an enterprise leader receives. With attention comes influence, power, and career mobility. For Zhou Guanwu, the ambition to climb politically and become a major figure in reform circles only increased the appetite for output growth. As Shougang's own economists admit, Zhou's overriding goal was to shape his firm into the largest steel producer in China, surpassing Angang in total output.[55]

What the contract did do, however, was create a secondary set of incentives, parameters in a sense that shaped the means by which the company could pursue output growth. First, because Shougang was cut off from state subsidies, the firm could finance expansion only through retained earnings. Instead of simply relying on massive infusions of state funds to fuel growth, the firm was suddenly thrown into a hard-budget situation. Hence for Shougang the vital issue became not just the absolute level of investment within the firm but also, and more significantly, the rate of return on that investment. All of a sudden, efficiency of investment became critical, a situation that produces far different behavior from what is observed in much of Chinese state industry. Second, because of the ever-increasing profit submission levels set by the contract, the firm had no choice but to devote retained earnings to carefully coordinated investment projects rather than to short-term quick fixes. During the initial years of the contract, investment funds were scarce, so efforts had to be devoted to increasing efficiency as the sole means of eking out more profit from existing facilities. Low-cost but intensive growth would have to be pursued. In order to meet increasing profit submission rates over the long term, careful plans were needed for extensive investment in the physical growth of the company. In short, the contract made profitability and long-term investment the sole means by which output expansion could be pursued. The time horizon of the enterprise leader was effectively forced outward, and his only hope of success was to engage in a long-term development strategy. The contractually induced incentives pushed the enterprise leader to maximize efficiency, profitability, and long-term investment, all within the general SOE constraints of maintaining full employment and paying out the full range of social welfare benefits to workers.

In summary, the profit contract did not guarantee success for the firm, but it did create an operational environment and a set of incentives under which success could be possible. It eliminated many of the most serious problems exogenous to the firm – namely, bureaucratic predation coupled with constant subsidization – and then shifted basic performance incentives within the firm. The contract granted the firm a property right, but property rights alone do not guarantee success in China any more than they do in the West. In simple terms, the contract leveled the playing field between firm and state. Once this was accomplished, it became the responsibility of enterprise management to chart its own course for success or failure.

ENTERPRISE STRATEGY UNDER THE CONTRACT

As noted previously, the profit contract is only half of the Shougang success story. The other half pertains to enterprise strategy, the choices Shougang made to capitalize on the opportunities created by the contract. In this area of enterprise strategy, there are two main areas worth exploring: (1) the actual investment plan undertaken during the 1980s and early 1990s; and (2) the company culture shaping the workplace environment during this period. The first area is relatively straightforward, and the facts are not disputed by opponents of Shougang. The second area is far more subtle, wrapped up in the whole enigma of Zhou Guanwu. A definite Shougang company culture was created by Zhou – an effective means of instilling discipline and esprit de corps – but there are widely differing accounts of just what that company culture actually entailed.

199

Investment Strategy

In the area of investment, Shougang followed a relatively simple progression from small, short-duration, high-return investments to larger and more comprehensive longer-term projects.[56] In 1979, as Shougang operated under its first profit retention plan, the average investment project hovered around RMB 17,000. During the period from 1981 to 1985, the first few years of the long-term profit contract, average investment projects had expanded to RMB 572,000. From 1986 to 1990, the scope had increased to RMB 2.5 million, more in line with what would be expected from a capital-intensive industry like steel.[57] On the one hand, this was a course dictated by the financial restraints set by the contract. Shougang had to rely on its own retained earnings to fund investment, retained earnings that were naturally scarce during the first years of the contract. On the other hand, that Shougang actually followed this logical strategy is impressive from the perspective of the traditional socialist firm.

Whether in China, in the former Soviet Union, or in Eastern Europe, the large SOE has historically opted for massive, single-shot investment projects. The reasons are simple. In all of these systems there exists a pervasive sense of having fallen behind the developed world; as a result, there is an incessant desire to catch up in a hurry.[58] This sentiment is then compounded at the enterprise level by the soft budget constraint. Liquidation of assets is never a threat, no matter how bad the investment decision, so risk fails to act as a restraint.[59] Finally, in part because of the resulting inefficiencies and in part because investment funds are allocated by the state, the firm always needs investment but never knows when the next allocation will arrive. Hence, there are clear incentives to grab as much investment as possible with one-shot, sweeping modernization projects, no matter how wasteful or inappropriate given the conditions of the particular firm. Shougang, particularly during the 1980s, clearly avoided this path. Its leaders sought expansion, but they were forced to proceed with a more calculated, longer-term effort.

During the first years of the contract, in the early 1980s, the firm focused on low-cost investments that would increase efficiency and pay for themselves within a matter of weeks or months. For example, RMB 270,000 was used to make relatively simple adjustments in Shougang's converters, adjustments that would permit increased use of scrap steel and other waste products from the rolling process.[60] The full investment was recovered within one and a half months. Similarly, RMB 400,000 was devoted to improving the No. 1 Smelting Plant, an investment that was recovered within two months. Shougang seems to have made a virtue of financial necessity by retaining old equipment as a base and slowly adding newer components instead of merely scrapping obsolete facilities. Shougang simply did not have the resources to engage in wholesale modernization of equipment. Furthermore, the ever-increasing profit quotas to the state forced Shougang to avoid the kind of production stoppages that come with major construction projects. The production facilities had to be kept up and running as much as possible, a reality that allowed little more than incremental, piecemeal modernization efforts. The strategy, which Shougang officials termed "sparing the hen that still lays eggs," led to the retention of early-model oxygen-blown converters, which were then slowly upgraded through ten years and RMB 7.5 million of investment. The capacity of these converters, built in 1962 as the first of their kind in China, was expanded four times beyond their initial level. Shougang, like any other Chinese steel firm, was determined to expand both capacity and actual output. However, financial limitations prevented the firm from simply pouring money into fixed asset expansion.

The issue is not that Shougang's strategy was necessarily impressive by world steel standards. Rather, the point is simply that Shougang stretched to the limit the few resources it actually had. Shougang's method of stretching the life-span of outdated equipment basically reflected the firm's new hard budget constraint and the resulting focus on cutting waste and increasing efficiency. These behavioral patterns would carry over into the larger investment projects that would follow by the middle to late 1980s.

When these larger projects did arrive, Shougang displayed a certain amount of craftiness both by importing low-cost second-hand equipment and also by spacing investments out over time. By the mid-1980s, Shougang was under increasing pressure from the state to build, from scratch, a rolling facility for steel sheet. The capital costs for such a facility would conceivably run in the RMB billions, money that Shougang simply did not have. The company, however, took advantage of the downturn in the American steel industry by importing from the United States second-hand rolling machines. The machines dated from the 1950s, but again Shougang proved willing to build up on a base of old equipment. After a total investment of just under RMB 50 million, the firm had a sheet-metal rolling operation that by the late 1980s was realizing RMB 135 million annually in sales. A similar process was followed with the construction of the No. 2 Steel Smelting Plant. Second-hand, essentially obsolete machinery was imported from Belgium and then, over a period of several years, updated through a four-stage investment process. Again, while Shougang's investment choices may not have been ideal from the perspective of world steel standards – the firm clearly was not on the cutting edge of technological modernization – the Beijing firm was showing a degree of flexibility, frugality, and efficiency unprecedented for Chinese SOEs. Its investments were showing positive returns, and it was basically supporting itself.

Beginning around 1985, Shougang also embarked on a policy of diversification beyond steel production.[61] The firm established a series of small plants producing an assortment of goods including home appliances, foodstuffs, wood products, textiles, and furniture. On a larger scale, Shougang established a major electronics operation, several local joint-venture chemical and mining facilities, and international joint ventures with both Sweden and Japan. There were several reasons behind this expansion. First, like other large SOEs in China, Shougang continually sought employment for its surplus workers. Second, the firm hoped that the returns from relatively small investments in other sectors (not nearly as capital-intensive as steel) could then fund modernization projects in the Shougang steel operation. This second issue forced the firm to be somewhat more careful than other SOEs in the type of diversification pursued. In other words, Shougang needed not only to create jobs but also to ensure that those jobs produced some profit for the company. In a sense, "careful" might not be the appropriate adjective to describe Shougang's efforts. After all, the firm took risks by investing heavily in industries (such as electronics) that had no proven record at the time in China. Shougang's strategy might better be described as "entrepreneurial" – risks were taken, and sometimes for reasons no better than employment creation, yet the constraining factor was the need always to ensure profitability. It is this last aspect, rather than the vertical and horizontal expansion itself, that has distinguished Shougang from other state steel firms in China. Nevertheless, Shougang is still mainly a steel plant. Even by the mid-1980s, more than 80 percent of company profits were coming from its Beijing steel operations.[62]

Company Culture

Shougang's investment strategy in the 1980s and early 1990s was coupled with a particular kind of shop floor culture, a culture that many employees traced directly to Zhou Guanwu. This company culture, however, had two sides – the one that the firm's public relations bureaus attempted to project to the outside world, and the one understood by Shougang employees themselves.

As for the public image fostered by Shougang, there was a continual emphasis on worker democracy, participation, and self-management. Shougang spokespeople frequently noted that senior managers, including Zhou Guanwu, were elected by workers, and that workers themselves were given a major voice in how the shop floor should be run.[63] Shougang publications regaled the reader with stories of company employees selflessly working overtime to meet production quotas and willingly forgoing bonuses for the sake of the company.[64] As the brochures noted, "the workers and staff are masters of their own factory." Much of this, unfortunately, had little basis in reality.

In more serious terms, Shougang publicists made a point of stressing that the profit contract governing enterprise performance actually extended down to each worker. Every unit of the Shougang Company – whether a factory, or a research institute, or a mine, or anything else – was handed down a contract from management, and the contracts were then disseminated down to the individual worker. These agreements specified tasks to be completed, time frames, resource allocations, and penalties for noncompliance (penalties generally involved the withholding of bonuses or other benefits). These contracts did indeed exist, but their voluntary nature was greatly overstated. They were as much commands between superior and subordinate as contractual arrangements between equals. Employees certainly acknowledged in private that the performance targets were always quite ambitious and the work environment stressful by Chinese standards.[65]

Even so, there is still the lurking question of just how management avoided the "ratchet effect." Why did workers surpass their performance targets when they knew that doing so would only raise the standard for the next time around, thereby making their own lives more difficult? Why did employees not seem to do only the minimum amount required? Furthermore, why was there not more free-riding? In such a labor-intensive environment as a steel operation, why should any single worker really worry about being caught shirking? Shougang seems to have dealt with these problems to a greater degree than other Chinese firms, yet all the flowery Shougang literature pointing to worker democracy offered few explanations as to how this was achieved.

The answer is actually quite far removed from any notions of democracy and voluntarism. In essence, Zhou Guanwu ran Shougang by *dictat*. The system, if anything, was autocratic rather than democratic. Zhou personally controlled appointments of senior managers and in the process carried out frequent and public demotions. He created an atmosphere of intimidation and, to some extent, fear – an atmosphere that ultimately worked its way down to the shop floor. The result was a degree of discipline not usually found in state firms. For better or worse, Zhou turned around the sort of work ethic, or nonwork ethic, usually pervading Chinese SOEs.

A major component of Zhou's power was his grip over key personnel decisions. On the organizational charts of most steel firms, a series of vice–general managers are situated just below the general manager and party secretary. Those vice–general managers are usually appointed by outside agencies and are therefore not directly accountable to the leaders of the firm itself. At the same time, there might be one or two "assistants to the general manager" who are appointed from within the firm. At Shougang, the system was reversed. Zhou decreased the number of vice-managers and simultaneously increased the number of assistants.[66] By this means, Zhou effectively circumvented the supervisory agencies and kept key personnel decisions in his own hands. In part because of Zhou's prestige, and in part because Shougang was recognized as an experimental firm, supervisory agencies in both the party and government seemed to have condoned this breach of normal personnel management at Shougang.

Most significant is what the party secretary ultimately did with his power. At most large state firms, demotions are rare, particularly at the senior level. Officials displaying the most extraordinary ineptitude are simply shuffled horizontally, moving from position to position until they are effectively sidelined from the main operations of the firm.[67] Outright firings or demotions are generally avoided, since nobody wants to accept responsibility for the mistaken appointment in the first place. The result is a rather relaxed and risk-free environment, one which might reward success with a promotion but which holds out few forms of punishment for failure. At Shougang, the situation was quite different. Zhou not only appointed his senior managers, he routinely fired them as well. More accurately (since actual firings were virtually impossible at a state firm), the officials were ignominiously dropped to the very bottom rungs of the organizational chart. As one Shougang employee recounted, these sorts of demotions happened every year and were much publicized within the company.[68] The senior official who performed poorly would be demoted right down to the shop floor and, in being so shamed, served as a warning to managers and workers alike, a tactic reminiscent of Mao Zedong's "killing the chicken to scare the monkeys."

The fear that poor performance would be punished ran throughout the company. One employee explained only half-jokingly that, at Shougang, "big brother is always watching."[69] Within the enterprise, there was an autonomous, roaming "disciplinary committee" whose prime function was to investigate lagging performance or violations of company policy. Apparently, in any branch of the company, if complaints started mounting (either officially or unofficially) then the disciplinary committee was likely to make an appearance. When the committee showed up, employees knew that trouble would not be far behind; demotions or other penalties were likely to follow. The disciplinary committee built up enough of a reputation that at least some company employees casually referred to it as the "Gestapo."[70] No matter how crass, this sort of mocking expression suggests the extent to which employees received the message that slacking would not be tolerated at either the highest or lowest levels of the company.

Company records actually acknowledge that the firm's personnel policy led to what became known industrywide as the "Shougang phenomenon."[71] The "phenomenon" was that factory-level cadres, general factory managers or senior engineers, were frequently dismissed – not because of traditional "political" problems but rather because of failure to fulfill managerial responsibilities and performance targets. Shougang records note that, each year, approximately 9 percent of all factory-level managerial cadres suffered demotions, a fantastic number for a Chinese state firm.[72] Apparently, 90 percent of those cadres were relieved of their positions for performance-related problems (as opposed to what is termed "political" or "lifestyle" errors). In terms of actual numbers, the company during the first decade of the contract promoted 1,424 factory-level managerial cadres while demoting 678. Of those 678, 38 were dismissed outright, an extreme measure given the lifetime employment usually accorded employees of state firms.

The irony is that even in 1994, well before Zhou Guanwu came under any sort of public scrutiny, some employees were already grumbling about the senior leader's failure to abide by his own rules. It was common knowledge in the company that Zhou owned four cars, including a Cadillac and a Mercedes. Furthermore, it was understood that Zhou had set up his own son in an important Shougang managerial position, a sort of nepotism not uncommon in China but hardly in line with Shougang's strict merit system.

Zhou's behavior was neither surprising nor particularly outrageous, except that it was coming from an enterprise leader instead of a major political figure. Zhou created at the enterprise level the sort of paternalistic, Confucian brand of autocratic rule that characterizes China's political system as a whole. Shougang employees occasionally joked that Zhou was Shougang's Deng Xiaoping, and in a sense they were absolutely right. The steel director created a form of personal rule at Shougang that demanded strict compliance with a set of regulations and at least outward loyalty on the part of employees. Strict hierarchies were maintained and orders flowed from the top down, not from the bottom up. In his own writings, Zhou asserted that the keys to success for a nation, a people, or an enterprise are all the same, and that they all concern leadership.[73] The leader must be a master of organization, ensuring that all serving below him know their place in the hierarchy and work according to the rules and responsibilities of their position. It is up to the leader to make his charges obey willingly and accept the organizational structure that he has designed. According to Zhou, it is upon this leadership ability that the fate of the enterprise turns. Certainly at Shougang, such discipline seemed to be an overriding goal. In return, workers who performed up to basic standards and followed this discipline could expect to be taken care of by Zhou. They received wages, bonuses, benefits, and housing all better than the average in Beijing. At the same time, employees – particularly cadres – who failed to play by the rules or failed to perform up to standards would be swatted down and humiliated publicly. Finally, disloyalty would not be tolerated. Cadres who sought to go to other firms or study abroad, or who attempted to leave, would in general run into big problems and significant barriers.[74] In a sense, Zhou cast Shougang in the image of a big family: responsible for its charges, meting out punishment when necessary, and intolerant of disloyalty. In part as a result, employees displayed a certain ambivalence toward their employer. Many were proud of its accomplishments, and senior cadres in particular tended to be genuine believers in the profit contract system. On the other hand, there was a certain degree of fear and intimidation, an atmosphere that they admitted made life difficult. Not all employees wanted to be a part of the Shougang "family," and not all wanted to live by rules that they had no part in creating. Last, although grateful to the senior leader for his stewardship of Shougang and the resulting benefits that had trickled down to the shop floor, many employees resented Zhou's exalted status beyond the reach of his company's own rigid rules.

The company culture that Zhou Guanwu created was not the most progressive by Western standards, nor did it prove to be extraordinarily effective over the long term. As a tactic of increasing labor productivity, intimidation has its limits. Nevertheless, this style of management was an important component of Shougang's success story under the profit contract, and it should be recognized as such. In the positive sense, the management style accomplished something rather unusual for China. It shook workers and cadres alike out of the complacency and indolence usually found in the Chinese state-owned enterprise. It gave a needed stimulus to a workplace environment previously characterized by slacking, absenteeism, and inefficiency. Unfortunately, replacing the corrosive egalitarianism of the old managerial system with its polar opposite – extreme hierarchy and one-man rule – created new problems that would flare into the open by 1995.

SHOUGANG'S 1995 COLLAPSE

By the end of the 1980s, the Shougang success story was receiving rather frequent attention in the Chinese media.[75] The state press – eager to report

Table 6.6. *Shougang revenue, profit, and fixed asset growth, 1990–95*
(RMB 100 million)

	1990	1991	1992	1993	1994	1995
Sales revenue	69.03	79.39	112.42	150.25	193.64	208.45
[increase from previous year]		15%	42%	34%	29%	8%
Gross profit	16.04	17.41	22.79	29.54	43.58	30.99
[increase from previous year]		9%	31%	30%	48%	−29%
Net value of fixed assets	32.08	35.59	39.23	79.43	118.8	201.81
[increase from previous year]		11%	10%	102%	50%	70%

Source: Ministry of Metallurgical Industry (1991, pp. 319, 331 [1990 data]; 1992, pp. 98, 110 [1991 data]; 1993, pp. 100, 106 [1992 data]; 1995, pp. 380, 382, 385 [1993–94 data]; 1996, pp. 346, 348, 351 [1995 data]).

something positive about the socialist workplace – latched onto the Shougang experience, producing a number of articles filled with hyperbole, exclamation points, and mind-numbing statistics. Meanwhile, the Western press remained aloof – a steel firm *not* plagued by problems hardly makes for gripping copy. By March 1995, however, Shougang suddenly found itself splayed over the pages of every major newspaper in the West, not as a success story but instead as a scandalous failure. On February 13, 1995, Zhou Beifang – the son of Zhou Guanwu and an important figure in Shougang's overseas operations – was detained in Beijing pending an official corruption investigation. The following day, Zhou Guanwu abruptly retired from his post as party secretary and chairman of the board of Shougang, a move that came as a total shock to observers both inside and outside the company. Clearly, something strange had happened at the venerable Beijing steel plant, but journalists seemed unable to decide quite what the story was.[76] Did the Zhous' downfall suggest that Shougang was a financial wreck, and perhaps that its prior achievements were all a big lie? Even more interesting, was this whole episode an opening salvo in the post-Deng succession crisis, a preemptive strike by Jiang Zemin on one of Deng's cronies in industry? Question marks were the order of the day.

Financial Collapse

That Shougang through the early to mid-1990s suffered a financial collapse is beyond dispute. Tables 6.6, 6.7, and 6.8 together provide an idea of what

Table 6.7. *Shougang balance sheet, 1993–95*[a]
(RMB 100 million)

	1993	1994	1995
Assets			
Current assets	110.67	88.3	90.74
Long-term investments	14.62	30.06	29.84
Fixed assets			
Fixed assets at cost	104	147.75	301.06
Net fixed assets	79.43	118.8	201.81
Ongoing construction	40.15	61.45	47.94
Total fixed assets	119.98	180.75	249.75
Intangible assets	−0.45	0.99	0.88
Total assets	244.82	300.1	371.11
Liabilities and owner equity			
Current liabilities	113.6	138.36	138.32
Long-term liabilities	62.44	62.29	60.02
Owner equity	68.78	99.45	172.77
Total liabilities and owner equity	244.82	300.1	371.11
Current ratio (current assets : current liabilities)	0.97	0.64	0.66

[a] Because of rounding errors, columns in some cases do not sum perfectly.
Source: Ministry of Metallurgical Industry (1994 [1993 data]; 1995 [1994 data]; 1996 [1995 data]).

exactly went wrong.[77] As indicated by Table 6.6, Shougang in the first half of the 1990s began to experience reduced profit growth even as it was aggressively expanding fixed assets. In a manner not so different from Angang, Shougang essentially decapitalized itself by permitting long-term investment thoroughly to crowd out working capital. As the balance sheet in Table 6.7 illustrates, Shougang's current ratio dipped seriously between 1993 and 1994 and remained below the 1.0 level throughout the entire 1993–95 period. The firm, like Angang, was operating with negative net working capital, and it could maintain production only through infusions of short-term loans. Needless to say, the Beijing steel producer was thrown into tremendous liquidity problems, and on several occasions had difficulty issuing wages. Even worse, infusions of short-term liquidity were frequently diverted to fixed asset investment. It was not until late 1994, however, that these patterns became apparent to outsiders,

Table 6.8. *Shougang, statement of changes in financial position,*
1993–94[a] *(RMB 100 million)*

	1993	1994	Total
Souces of circulating funds			
Increased owner equity	10.68	30.66	41.34
Withdrawn depreciation funds	2.20	4.38	6.58
Increased long-term debt	5.85	−0.15	5.70
Total	18.73	34.89	53.63
Uses of circulating funds			
Increased fixed assets	42.19	43.75	85.94
Increased ongoing construction	9.71	11.94	21.65
Increased long-term investment	10.37	15.44	25.81
Other increased assets	−0.36	1.52	1.16
Total	61.91	72.66	134.57
Net change in working capital	−43.17	−37.77	−80.94

[a] This is a partial statement showing changes in working capital accounts. Data trace changes from end of 1992 through end of 1994.
Source: Ministry of Metallurgical Industry (1995a, pp. 2–4; 1995d, p. 10).

when the firm began defaulting on loans that many policy makers did not even know Shougang was carrying. By that point, the firm had not only dragged itself to the verge of insolvency but had also effectively undermined a major national bank, one rather closely affiliated with the steel firm. It was at this point that Zhou Guanwu was dismissed and MMI investigators were sent in to piece together the recent history of financial irregularities. Major infusions of state equity were needed simply to keep the firm and its primary lender afloat.

Table 6.8, derived from MMI investigation reports, provides a sense of what Shougang was doing in the early 1990s. From the end of 1992 to the end of 1994, Shougang poured approximately RMB 13.5 billion into fixed assets, on-going construction, and long-term investment. Meanwhile, increases to operating funds from retained profits, retained depreciation funds, and long-term loans amounted to only RMB 5.36 billion. The RMB 8.1-billion difference is reflected in the net decrease in Shougang's working capital described in Table 6.8. As the MMI discovered, not surprisingly, the firm during this period expanded its short-term borrowings by approximately RMB 8.26 billion.[78]

Clearly, short-term loans were being used to finance long-term investment and ongoing construction. Such behavior fits the general pattern in China of enterprises treating short-term credits as prime sources for long-term finance, the idea being that loans can simply be rolled over in lieu of repayment.

Funds ultimately found their way into several major projects, including RMB 445 million for the Qilu iron and steel works in Shandong, RMB 714 million for diesel oil projects in Jilin, RMB 900 million for propane processing facilities, and RMB 186 million for the Liuzhou iron and steel works. In the midst of all this expansion, expenses unrelated to production also shot upward. In 1994, managerial expenses stood at RMB 620 million, a 121-percent increase over the figures for 1992. In Shougang's electronics company alone, nonoperating expenses were up 299 percent. Although statistics were incomplete at the time of the MMI's investigation, it appeared that managers spent RMB 180 million on cars, cellular phones, and pagers alone. Clearly, the discipline of the early contract years had totally collapsed.

The Prelude to Collapse

Shougang's financial undoing, and the firm's whole turnaround from economic model to economic disaster, resulted from the confluence of several disparate trends. First, toward the final years of the profit contract, basic laws of diminishing returns on investment were starting to impinge on firm-level operations. In objective terms, it was becoming increasingly difficult and increasingly expensive for the firm to meet its rising profit quotas. Second, on a decidedly more subjective note, Zhou Guanwu's overweening ambition to turn Shougang into China's largest steel producer increasingly began to influence firm-level strategy. The director, in essence, became determined to expand output not incrementally but exponentially. Third, Shougang became increasingly involved in Chinese elite political machinations. Political involvement by the firm, and political interference in the firm, then undermined many of the strictures related to the original profit contract. Not only did outside monitoring essentially stop, but the firm was at the same time accorded privileged access to credit. The firm that for a decade had been insulated from malfunctioning regulatory and financing mechanisms was suddenly given privileged entree to those very mechanisms.

When taken together, the three trends produced tremendous managerial autonomy, unprecedented access to soft credit, and an increasingly tenuous investment environment. The collapse of monitoring, together with access to the state banking system, provided Shougang with a decidedly soft budget constraint.

Zhou Guanwu could then apply virtually unlimited funding to whatever expansion programs he envisioned. It was precisely at this stage in Shougang's development, however, that diminishing marginal returns were making expansion increasingly expensive and unfeasible. The manager, in effect, was given unlimited funds to fuel his increasingly unrealistic ambitions. The outcome was a situation even worse than Angang's. The incentives for output and capacity expansion may have been the same, but in Shougang's case the managerial ambitions were greater, the available funds more substantial, and the possibility of governance even more remote.

Enterprise Expansion Efforts

As early as 1988, Capital Iron and Steel began to prepare for a massive expansion effort, part of Zhou Guanwu's vision for building Shougang into China's first ten-million-ton capacity steel operation. In one sense, Shougang had to keep expanding capacity and output in order to meet escalating profit targets. In another sense, Zhou was determined to build the firm into China's largest steel producer. This drive for expansion was reflective of the profit contract's incentive structure but at the same time was held in check by the contract's financial strictures. As soon as those strictures were relaxed and ambition permitted to reign unabated, problems developed.

By 1994, Shougang had indeed become the largest steel producer in China, surpassing Angang. In doing so, however, the Beijing steel producer had undermined its own future viability. Shougang in the early 1990s was devoting 70 percent of its technical modernization funds to steel smelting or presmelting processes alone. Only 15 percent of the modernization budget ended up in the firm's steel rolling operations. The motivation for this was clear – the firm was trying to maximize its output of raw steel, even at the expense of being unable to process that raw steel once produced. Because so much money was invested in upstream production processes and so little downstream, the whole production system became bottlenecked and thrown out of balance. By 1994, inventories of steel ingot and semifinished steel products had climbed by over a million tons, thus squeezing enterprise accounts by approximately RMB 1.2 billion.[79] The firm had no facilities to process the excess unfinished steel, and given the slow market, no other firm was interested in processing the mounting inventories either.

While aggressively expanding capacity in its Beijing facilities, Shougang also commenced construction of an entirely new steel operation on a greenfield site in Shandong Province.[80] Unfortunately, the new "Qilu" iron and steel works was ill-fated from the start. The basic idea was to build a totally modern, fully integrated iron and steel facility right on the Shandong coast, a project that – in combination with Shougang's existing facilities in Beijing – would make the firm the undisputed giant of the Chinese steel industry. One problem was that the greenfield site chosen for Qilu had no access to domestic ore mines. The overall notion of using imported ore at Qilu was not extraordinary, particularly since Chinese mills were increasingly relying on higher-grade ores available only from outside the country. A more serious problem concerned the nature of demand in the Chinese steel market. It was by no means clear at the time that the Chinese market could sustain the increased output to be produced by Qilu. For most Chinese steel operations, output could be moved off the premises only if credit sales were permitted. Whenever strictures against triangular lending were applied, demand would sink precipitously. Certainly the implication was that demand might not have been nearly as robust as many in the Chinese steel industry believed. Finally, the desirability of the actual Shandong site was highly questionable.

In general, Shougang had achieved success previously by focusing not so much on expansion of scale as on efforts to increase efficiency and lower costs. Now, with this huge Shandong plan, the company was taking a great leap into the unknown. However, given the managerial latitude accorded to Shougang by the profit contract, and given that the Qilu project would be funded by Shougang's retained earnings rather than state funds, the project was permitted to proceed. Shougang went ahead and acquired the land, and initial construction efforts commenced.

By the early 1990s, though, it became clear to the Ministry of Metallurgical Industry that the project was unfeasible. An investigative team of the MMI's Iron and Steel Division (*Gangtie Si*) concluded that the harbor at Qilu was incapable of handling the large container ships needed to bring in imported iron ore.[81] It was simply too shallow. As a result, Shougang over the long term would need not only to build port facilities at Qilu, as expected earlier, but also to dredge the harbor – a task that was by no means guaranteed success. In fact, the only harbor on the East China coast capable of handling large ore-carrying vessels was Ningbo, hundreds of miles to the south in Zhejiang Province. At least during Qilu's first years of operation, Shougang would need to have all its ore shipped first to Ningbo and then moved up to Shandong either by small ship or rail. It was a crippling problem that should have put an early end to the project. Unbelievably, Zhou Guanwu remained determined to press ahead with Qilu, in part because of his overall desire to expand production and in part, perhaps, because of his wish to direct massive capital investments toward his home province. Shougang set off to build a steel mill that would be thoroughly dependent on shipped-in ore, but on a site that was thoroughly incapable of handling ore-bearing ships! It is absolutely mind-boggling that such plans were allowed to continue.

In 1992, Shougang acquired the iron ore mines of the Peruvian state steel industry, thus securing the future source for Qilu production needs. In line with this development, the firm started its own shipping firm, acquiring twelve large-scale container vessels for transporting ore from Peru to China. Capital construction proceeded at the Qilu site, while the company purchased a second-hand cold rolling mill from Kaiser Steel in the United States. The mill was to be disassembled and shipped to China for use in Shandong. During this period, the firm was also aggressively seeking to expand its Beijing facilities in the quest to become China's largest steel producer. Output levels were continually being raised, even in the face of the Chinese steel market's downturn in 1993 and 1994. With each investment and output decision, Shougang seemed to be digging itself deeper and deeper into future financial troubles.

It should be noted that none of this was done in secret. Visitors to Shougang were as late as 1994 still being regaled with stories of the company's expansion into Shandong and its path-breaking efforts in Peru. Company public relations officials were not at all embarrassed to describe the firm's ambitious expansion projects or to show models of the elaborate beachside recreational facilities that were to be built for workers. Not quite explained were the means by which Shougang was financing this whole venture. Not surprisingly, it was in the financial area that a major disaster was brewing.

That Shougang operated through the mid-1990s with negative net levels of working capital alone suggests that the terms of the profit contract were no longer being enforced (see Table 6.7). The firm was clearly maintaining day-to-day operations by amassing liabilities rather than relying on its own retained earnings. No longer was this a firm cut off from outside sources of credit. In one sense, it can be argued that much of this borrowing went on unbeknownst to industrial regulators. Many MMI officials were truly taken by surprise when news of Shougang's dire financial situation began to leak out of the firm. In a more important sense, however, state regulators bear responsibility for providing the conditions under which such value-subtracting firm-level behavior could take place. Shougang in the early 1990s was granted privileges that essentially constituted open invitations to financial malfeasance.

The clearest case of inappropriate privileges extended to Shougang involves the 1992 establishment of Huaxia Bank. The Beijing steel producer was basically granted the right to start and own its own bank, one of only five new

213

commercial banks permitted to emerge in the reform era.[82] Huaxia Bank grew extremely rapidly in its first few years, a period (not surprisingly) coincident with its owner's rapid expansion and financial undoing.[83] Controlling its own bank, Shougang was able to gain direct access to Chinese household savings, for the bank – like any other in the state system – could accept household deposits and then extend commercial loans. As indicated earlier, it was precisely during this period that Shougang managed to outspend its own internal resources by some RMB 8.1 billion. Circumstantial evidence suggests that Huaxia Bank was extending loans to its parent in order to make up the difference. Indeed, once news of Shougang's financial misbehavior broke in 1995, the state immediately terminated Shougang's sole ownership over Huaxia. Moreover, the new owners (three major industrial groups), rather than purchasing the bank from Shougang, simply injected funds directly into the bank, increasing the bank's registered capital from RMB 1 billion to RMB 2.5 billion.[84] At the same time, the state also seems to have injected capital directly into Shougang, bailing the moribund steel operation out of insolvency.[85]

It is almost incomprehensible that, given all the problems associated with financial institutions in China, Chinese officialdom could have granted an industrial producer like Shougang the right to own a bank. That single act virtually guaranteed that Shougang would no longer face a hard budget constraint. Regulatory officials may not have known that irregular lending activities were taking place, but it is hard to imagine that they could have expected otherwise.

The Huaxia Bank, however, was neither Shougang's only vehicle for amassing capital nor the steel producer's only newfound privilege. About the same time as Huaxia Bank was created, Shougang began pursuing so-called backdoor listings in Hong Kong. The steel conglomerate would purchase dormant companies in Hong Kong, inject capital, and then issue equity shares on the Hong Kong stock exchange. These issues produced an inflow of foreign capital that ended up, at least in part, funding the parent company's expansion. The back-door listings also produced a complex set of financial interactions ripe for abuse by officials associated with the business. Zhou Beifang, the son of Zhou Guanwu, served as chairman of one such Shougang-owned Hong Kong corporation, Shougang Concord. It was because of his activities at Shougang Concord that the younger Zhou was detained on corruption charges. In 1996, Zhou Beifang was convicted of "economic" crimes and sentenced to death.[86] Whether or not Zhou Beifang actually engaged in inappropriate activities, rumors of his corrupt behavior and playboy lifestyle abounded among Shougang employees in Beijing, and well before the firm's problems became public in 1995.[87] More important, back-door listings, although technically not illegal in

China, were a benefit accorded only to select firms and as such served as a privileged source of "easy" money for grand investment plans. The previously tight Shougang budget constraint was slowly being eroded just as Zhou Guanwu's appetite for output growth was expanding.

The Politics of Collapse

As noted earlier, the softening of Shougang's budget constraint came in the midst of three related developments in the enterprise: declining returns on investment, expanding managerial ambitions, and an official visit by Deng Xiaoping. In 1992, Deng made a highly publicized visit to Shougang, a visit that seems to have whetted Zhou Guanwu's already considerable appetite for expansion and encouraged the Shougang boss to push for an extension of contracting beyond the slated termination date in 1995. At the same time, the last few years of Shougang's fifteen-year contract marked a period in which the steel firm was facing the bitter reality of diminishing marginal returns. The fifteen-year profit contract demanded a constant rate of increase in submitted profits, a condition that was acceptable during the first ten years, but increasingly difficult to meet by the early 1990s. The firm was forced to expend more and more resources simply to maintain a constant rate of growth. In any industrial endeavor, a point is reached at which the marginal cost of expanding simply exceeds any marginal gains that may accrue as a result. This was Shougang's situation in the early 1990s.

Unfortunately, Deng's 1992 visit, suddenly thrusting Shougang and Zhou Guanwu into the political limelight, came just at this time. Zhou Guanwu was receiving extraordinary political attention and was more eager than ever to promote the one reform, profit contracting, to which he was so personally linked. Yet, just as he was seeking to do this, the utility of contracting for his own firm was running out. Zhou's interests vis-à-vis his own personal power game were starting to run counter to the interests of the firm; not surprisingly, the Shougang party secretary chose to maximize the former rather than the latter.

The politics of this whole affair is admittedly turbid, but probably not quite as wrapped up in high-level succession battles as is frequently asserted. Soon after completing his famous reform-spurring "Journey to the South" (*nanxun*) in the spring of 1992, Deng Xiaoping made a high-profile appearance at Shougang, an inspection tour that was publicized throughout the Chinese media. This marked the first time that the senior leader had personally associated himself with Shougang, thus injecting a rather unfortunate element of politics into the Shougang experiment. The problem was not that Shougang suddenly became a favorite of Deng's and thus no longer had to abide by any budgetary constraints. Rather, the impact was more subtle. During the *nanxun,* Deng reiterated his support for reform in general and, in so doing, single-handedly incited a huge speculative boom in the economy. In specific terms, Deng lent his support to corporatization efforts in heavy industry. It was not profit contracting that was urged but rather joint stock efforts in line with the Western model of corporate governance. Stock reforms became all the rage after the trip, and it was precisely because of this that firms like Magang, Tsingtao Brewery, and China Huaneng would within a few years be issuing stock in Hong Kong and New York.

Nevertheless, as he tried to stimulate industrial reform in general in 1992, Deng perhaps felt the need to associate himself with some successful enterprise, regardless of whether its success grew out of an "outdated" reform. What resulted was the national leader's appearance at Shougang. Profit contracting was by no means suddenly brought back into fashion, and certainly Deng did not associate himself with this reform style per se. In this sense, it would probably be an exaggeration to say that Shougang even in 1992 had become a "showcase" for Deng's reform strategy, an experiment that had to be made to work. Instead, it was an experiment that had already worked without the senior leader's overt interference, but one that served conveniently as an example of what sort of potential existed in state industry as a whole. Deng may have been pushing corporatization, a reform anathema to Shougang managers, but he needed also to promote the continued viability of state ownership – one of the few remaining pillars of socialism in China.[88] It was in this last area that Shougang came in handy.

The irony is that in finally promoting Shougang even to such a limited extent, Deng undermined the system of enterprise governance embodied by the contract. Once Shougang was viewed as a favorite of Deng, no state agencies would throw up any obstacles before the firm. More precisely, the firm would no longer be prohibited from tapping into the state banking system. Once the budget constraint was softened in this manner, the long-term viability of the firm no longer hinged on the efficiency of current investment. The lines of accountability once clarified by the contract suddenly blurred again, thus fanning the flames of Zhou Guanwu's personal ambition. Company publications began featuring photos of Zhou Guanwu fawning on Deng Xiaoping. By 1994, visitors to Shougang would begin their tour by viewing a spectacular room-sized mural depicting Deng's visit to the company. Clearly, the steel firm was trying to convey the message that it was the anointed favorite. Meanwhile, Zhou Guanwu increasingly used the firm as a vehicle for his self-aggrandizement.

Company employees claim that one single goal – that of surpassing Angang as China's largest producer of steel – began to consume all company planning efforts. As MMI investigators later noted, the company's finance departments became subordinated to the planning bureaus. The firm ceased to worry about their bottom line. Accordingly, a series of extravagant investment projects ensued, including the infamous Qilu mill.

That the Qilu project was ever allowed to proceed suggests that, after Deng's visit in 1992, the supervisory agencies that had previously been so tough on Shougang – constantly attempting to rein in the firm – were now keeping a more respectful distance. The State Council during the 1980s provided important insulation to Shougang in an essentially hostile bureaucratic environment. After 1992, though, because politics was overtly injected into the picture, the bureaucratic environment became less hostile and the insulation too extreme. At least within the MMI, it was felt that nobody could stand in the way of Zhou Guanwu, no matter how inane his investment plans.[89] Nobody was quite willing to step forward and perform the necessary supervision.

The unbridling of Zhou Guanwu could not have come at a worse time from the perspective of Shougang's objective economic situation. As noted before, companies cannot expand indefinitely because of the diminishing incremental returns on investment. Shougang clearly was confronting this problem in the early 1990s, during the waning years of the contract. By mid-1994, the feeling of Shougang's in-house economists was that the contract had served the firm well: good managerial habits had been developed, the company had funded its own substantial modernization efforts, and unprecedented growth had been achieved. However, now that the contract was nearing its end, the time had come to move on.[90] For these economists, contracting was not an end in itself but rather an effective means of negotiating the firm's transition to the market. They recognized that a firm cannot keep expanding forever, and nor should it try. Instead, they hoped that Shougang could just eke out the one remaining year of contractually mandated growth and then perhaps shift to a more standardized tax system – albeit one with far lower rates than were currently prevailing in China.

Apparently, Zhou Guanwu was utterly unwilling to heed suggestions that Shougang begin preparing for the next step beyond contracting. Indeed, more than one Shougang economist in 1994 complained bitterly to this author that Zhou Guanwu had become the biggest threat to the future well-being of the firm. Just as the utility of contracting was waning for Shougang, in-house economists were mortified to find out that Zhou Guanwu was actually pressing central agencies to have Shougang's profit contract extended beyond 1995.

Undoubtedly, Deng's 1992 visit emboldened Zhou. Furthermore, Zhou had his own reputation and status to consider: as the firm moved beyond contracting, so too might it move beyond Zhou himself.

Zhou's policies ended up being the exact antithesis of what the firm needed. In order to bolster the claim that Shougang still could expand and maintain the profit contract, the party secretary was sinking vast amounts of money into long-term and ultimately futile expansion. Meanwhile, as Shougang's economists well knew, the bottom had fallen out of the Chinese steel market by 1994. On the one hand, cheap imported steel was flooding into China only to be snapped up by purchasers with cash. On the other hand, traditional purchasers of Shougang steel – namely, other state firms – had their own cash-flow problems and could not pay for steel purchases outright. By 1994, Shougang could dispose of its output only by joining in the triangular debt game. This was hardly the time for Shougang to be expanding or to be pushing for an extended profit contract. Rather, it was a time to buckle down and weather the storm, tactics for which Shougang was probably better suited than other firms in the Chinese steel industry. At least its production costs were relatively low, its major modernization efforts already well under way and funded, and its overall debts negligible.

Zhou Guanwu was not, however, willing to ride out the storm. Instead, more money was pumped into expansion. Well into 1994, Zhou was still goading employees to increase output and surpass Angang. Yet during that same year, Shougang economists in their internal reports were continually scaling back the company's estimated profits. For the first time, it looked as if Shougang would not be able to meet its mandated profit submission (for 1994).[91]

By late November of 1994, Zhou Guanwu made a last-ditch effort to improve company performance by personally exhorting employees to work harder. In a tactic reminiscent of Maoist political campaigns, Zhou reinstated mandatory "political study" sessions within the company; perhaps not surprisingly, the study materials were Zhou's old speeches.[92] For many Shougang planners and economists, this last development signaled that the firm could be saved only by the resignation of its party secretary. In mid-1994, the likelihood of such a resignation seemed nil.

The Downfall of Zhou Guanwu

Zhou Guanwu's resignation in February 1995 came as quite a shock; as noted previously, it provoked all manner of rumor and speculation. Nevertheless, the reasons for that resignation were fairly simple. Shougang's ill-advised investments in the early 1990s were hardly kept under wraps, but far more secret were the financing strategies pursued by the firm. As already indicated, in 1994 the company began to accumulate large amounts of short-term debt. It was only when Shougang began defaulting on those loans, one to two years later, that the true extent of the firm's financial distress became publicly evident; it was precisely at this point that Zhou was forced to step down. The downfall of Zhou was related less to political intrigue than to straightforward managerial bungling.

Nevertheless, the damage had been done. Shougang's impressive ten-year record of achievements has been eclipsed by the firm's spectacular collapse. Zhou Guanwu left a legacy not of managerial élan but instead of hubris and managerial incompetence. Shougang has been bailed out by the state, and its investment projects, for the most part, have been summarily halted. "Qilu" is dead. That the firm is surviving in the near term is clear. What is far less certain, though, is the type of long-term lessons that will be drawn from the entire Shougang experience. Shougang throughout the reform period has been continually dismissed as an anomaly, and the sensational events of 1995 have served to further that trend. But it would be a shame simply to ignore Shougang. The firm's impressive rise and its equally impressive fall offer a complete perspective on the changing nature of incentives and autonomy in the enterprise reform process.

THE BROADER LESSONS OF THE SHOUGANG EXPERIENCE

Chinese policy makers over the past decade have understood in the abstract that property-rights reform is needed at the enterprise level. They have also understood, at least in theory, that enterprise–government relations must be rationalized, that government agencies must be prevented from micromanaging the firm, and that incentives must be shifted at the managerial level. The problem, however, is that for large industrial producers, these goals cannot be achieved simply through policy measures targeted within the firm. For large industrial organizations, property-rights reform by definition involves changes not only in the firm's internal managerial environment but also in its external institutional environment. Only through a simultaneous pursuit of *both* types of change can firm-level autonomy and accountability be linked and managerial incentives actually shifted. Unfortunately, such boundary-crossing reforms have rarely emerged over the past few years.

Part of the problem is that policy makers, by focusing on ownership "clarification" or managerial "autonomy," have not always asked the right questions. They have not generally considered what property-rights reform actually means for organizations – namely, large industrial firms – whose ownership is inherently unclear. Both with past profit contracting and with present corporatization, similar mistakes are repeated. Efforts are made to clarify power and incentives inside the firm, but key incentive-setting external issues remain unresolved. Policy makers then wonder why value-subtracting business behavior persists even after managerial autonomy and apparent property rights have been extended to the firm. In reality, however, as long as the external environment remains at best partially reformed, property rights will not function as intended in large industrial producers.

The Shougang experience, in a sense, shows both sides of the coin. Of course, the lesson of the firm's success is not that profit contracts are ideal policy instruments. In the broadest sense, enterprise-by-enterprise contracting entails tremendous transaction costs from the policy perspective and frequently leads to accusations of unequal treatment. Furthermore, by forcing the firm to meet performance targets, contracts run the risk of subverting market signals for changing demand conditions. Contracts are by no means ideal, but what the Shougang case shows is that internal reform measures – when appropriately coupled with changes in the institutional environment – can change managerial behavior for the better. Managers can be pushed to pursue value-enhancing strategies, whether through contracting, corporatization, or any other restructuring technique. The choice of which technique to use becomes important in the future, but of immediate concern is how to set the appropriate circumstances under which *any* technique can have a chance of working. In Shougang, because the firm was protected from state extraction and insulated from the state banking system, hard budgets were enforced; this provided fair ground for testing an internal reform measure. The contract did encourage efficiency maximization, but it also promoted undue emphasis on capacity expansion. Perhaps the lesson is that more standardized techniques than individual enterprise contracts need to be pursued, but at least lessons *can* be drawn. The Shougang profit contract reflects one of the few instances in which a reform measure was actually permitted to work its effect upon the firm without being either diluted by subsidy countermeasures or undermined by state predation. The simple lesson is that, under such circumstances, incentives really can shift.

Of course, Shougang's collapse testifies to the fragility of these arrangements. Once the firm is exposed to soft credit, the window of opportunity for market-oriented restructuring slams shut. In other words, once a malfunctioning regulatory environment is reintroduced, internal reform mechanisms become vitiated and ultimately fruitless. Even worse, managerial autonomy under such circumstances frequently expresses itself through value-destroying business strategies.

Table 6.9. *Taxes and profits for all firms in the Chinese*
metallurgical industry

Category	1985	1986	1987	1988	1989	1990	1991	1992	1985–92
Gross surplus[a]	12.8	14.2	15.8	18.1	19.3	16.8	20.5	27.1	144.7
Submission[b]	9.1	10.2	11.4	12.7	14.1	13.4	17.3	21.2	109.4
Gross retained[c]	3.8	4.0	4.4	5.5	5.2	3.3	3.3	5.8	35.3
Two charges[d]	0.9	1.0	1.1	1.4	1.3	0.8	0.8	1.5	8.8
Net retained[e]	2.8	3.0	3.3	4.1	3.9	2.5	2.5	4.4	26.4
% Submitted[f]	78	79	79	77	80	85	88	83	81
% Retained[g]	22	21	21	23	20	15	11	16	18

Note: Aside from percentages, units in RMB million.
[a] Gross surplus = gross profits before all submissions of taxes and profits.
[b] Submission = submission to the government treasury in the name of taxes and profits.
[c] Gross retained = gross surplus − submission.
[d] Two charges = 25% of gross retainment submitted to the government in the name of "charges for the development of energy and transportation projects."
[e] Net retained = gross retainment − two charges.
[f] % Submitted = (submission + two charges)/(gross surplus).
[g] % Retained = (net retained)/(gross surplus).
Source: Ministry of Metallurgical Industry internal records (data from a sample ranging from 1,318 production units in 1985 to 1,744 firms in 1992).

Unfortunately, as the Shougang experience also suggests, the problem is not only that policy makers at times ask the wrong questions. Rather, the more significant issue is that key bureaucratic actors frequently resist the more comprehensive enterprise reform packages. The MOF's hostility to Shougang's profit contract, and the attempts by various agencies to tap into the firm's revenue flows, attest to the sort of resistance that comprehensive restructuring efforts face.

For all the reform measures employed over the past fifteen years, and for all the rhetoric concerning property-rights reform, firms have never been able to achieve any appreciable degree of profit retention. As indicated by Table 6.9, Chinese steel firms throughout much of the reform period retained very little income in general but also retained less and less income over time. Regardless of which variety of reform happened to be popular at any given moment, industrial producers were never able to access their own financial returns. Instead, they were forced almost a priori to turn back to the state for even the most basic operating funds. It is no wonder, then, that incentives have been

221

slow to respond to market signals. Because firms do not retain financial returns, incentives for asset-enhancing strategies fail to develop. Incentives are then further distorted as the firm is forced to rely on soft loans in order to maintain production. Little reason exists for the firm to protect even the paltry assets it can retain.

The Ministry of Finance, in particular, seems to have trouble internalizing this point, and in fact has proven quite hostile to the argument. An article written from the MOF's perspective in 1982 expresses sentiments that were just as prevalent in the mid-1990s:

> The delegation of authority to enterprises now means, after all, the use of state funds to fatten enterprises. If state funds are exhausted and the enterprises have more funds than they know how to use, does this mean any advancement of social welfare? I don't think so. It may even turn out to be a social evil, because the state will be powerless to do anything for the good of the people.[93]

The MOF was consistently hostile to the Shougang profit contract and the whole idea of increasing enterprise profit retention for two reasons. The first involved pragmatic issues relating to the ministry's own increasingly heavy financial burdens. By the late 1980s, China's tax revenues were failing to keep pace with the nation's rising GNP (gross national product). Given all the infrastructure and developmental needs of the country, the MOF was facing ever-increasing demands on state expenditures. Local governments found themselves in a similar position. The short-term financial needs of many government agencies militated against any easing of tax extraction, even if lower rates of enterprise taxation would lead to higher revenues over the long term. The understandable view of some in the MOF was that China did not have the luxury to wait for the long term when short-term needs were so great.

Furthermore, China suffered – and indeed still suffers – from a rather poorly developed, poorly coordinated, and poorly staffed tax-collection apparatus. For most agencies, it is generally easier to focus collection efforts on single large firms rather than a multitude of smaller firms. Hence, when revenues are needed, it is state-owned heavy industry that bears the brunt of collection efforts and ends up paying a disproportionate share.

The second and more clearly expressed reason for the MOF's hostility toward the kind of protections accorded by the Shougang contract concerns political power. For many officials in the MOF, the issue of whether lower taxes might lead to better enterprise performance or higher revenues over the long term is simply immaterial. In their view, it is simply wrong for enterprises to retain

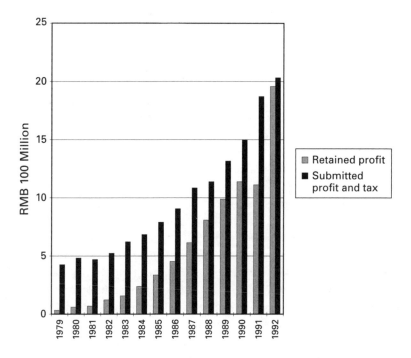

Figure 6.1. Shougang's Retained Profit versus Submitted Profit and Tax,
1979–92

funds that more appropriately belong to the nation – or, more specifically, to the MOF. The issue is one of principle, not pragmatism.

For central finance officials, the trend outlined in Figure 6.1 constituted a veritable affront to governmental authority. Revenue submissions from Shougang were increasing in absolute terms, but at a slower rate than the enterprise's own retained profits. The pie was expanding in absolute terms for everybody, but the MOF's slice was shrinking in relation to the firm's slice. The MOF and its counterparts at the local level end up in a self-defeating position. By maintaining that "surplus" profits should be allocated by the state rather than the firm itself, they focused on the division of the pie at the expense of the size of the pie. In doing so, these fiscal actors ensured (1) that firms would not be able to fund internal operations; (2) that firms would have to turn to the state for subsidies; and (3) that firm-level incentives would continue to be shaped by soft budget constraints. Unfortunately, until these attitudes change (or are forced to change), effective enterprise restructuring will not take place in China.

Ironically, as the Shougang case suggests, to give the firm breathing room from the state frequently entails tying the firm closer to particular state agencies. In a poorly institutionalized environment, where law has no bite against governmental actors, only state agencies themselves can protect the firm and enforce financial discipline. The state, in effect, must insulate the firm from the state. Properly motivated central agencies must act decisively to cut off lending to the firm and at the same time protect the firm from predatory extraction. Only once this happens can the firm truly be exposed to the efficiency-rewarding incentives of the market. This is the basic lesson of Shougang. The long-term profit contract happens to be the one reform in recent Chinese experience that was actually able to achieve this goal. If a standardized tax system operating across all firms could produce the same effect, so much the better. The point is simply that something resembling an enterprise right to residual returns must be maintained and appropriately coupled with a hard budget constraint. Regardless of how clarified ownership may become, *only when firms retain resources and face hard budgets can managerial autonomy ever truly be coupled with accountability.* Only under such circumstances – whether in China, the United States, or anywhere else – can policy makers hope to encourage asset-expanding behavior in large industrial producers. Shougang illustrates the potential for achieving these objectives in China as well as the substantial obstacles that must be overcome in the process. Chinese policy makers face monumental challenges – indeed, challenges for which there are neither simple models to follow, easy paths to take, nor half-way measures to pursue.

224

Part III

REASSESSING CHINESE PATTERNS OF ECONOMIC DEVELOPMENT

7

Extending the Argument: Budget Constraints and Patterns of Growth in China

IN previous chapters, a constraints-based approach – the nested problems dynamic – was used to explain the particular problem of urban SOE restructuring. In this chapter, we will explore the broader implications of the nested problems dynamic. What can the constraints-based approach tell us about reform beyond the SOE sector? Can the same concepts used to illuminate patterns of urban industrial stagnation also help us understand the phenomenal growth of Chinese rural industry? More broadly, to what extent can a constraints-based approach change our perspective on the overall drivers of growth in postcommand economies? How might our sense of the "appropriate" package of reform policies to adopt change as a result?

TRADITIONAL APPROACHES TO CHINESE REFORM

Like China itself, Western sinology over the past fifteen years has undergone an extraordinary transformation. Long-held perspectives have given way to novel approaches, approaches themselves made possible by unprecedented research opportunities. China's "opening" to the West, although focused mainly on foreign trade and business, has certainly had its academic research component as well. Scholars both within China and abroad have moved aggressively to grasp these new opportunities and to develop new modes for understanding an ever-changing social, political, and economic landscape.

Nevertheless, for all its variety and creativity, recent work on China has been rather circumscribed – somewhat confined within narrow intellectual parameters. Despite their differences and disagreements, scholars of reform generally speak the same language of "property rights," "decentralization," "liberalization," and "autonomy." There is an almost universally held assumption that productive economic behavior is somehow innate, something natural that can be freed up through the dissemination of power and rights. Reform, therefore, becomes viewed as the process by which this unleashing of economic dynamism occurs. What drives changes in behavior are new freedoms from constraint and new powers of independent decision making for economic actors. Reform is understood as an "opening," a dismantling of old strictures and a dissemination of new freedoms. It is defined, in effect, as a blossoming forth.

Of course, there is nothing intrinsically wrong with this view. Anybody who has spent time in China over the past decade knows perfectly well that the country truly has changed, that living standards have improved dramatically, and that all sorts of unprecedented freedoms and opportunities now exist in society. Nevertheless, by viewing reform almost exclusively as a blossoming forth, and by viewing economic behavior as driven almost exclusively by freedom from constraint, scholars end up focusing on only particular kinds of questions. In other words, scholars tend to assume that economic reform – and, by extension, economic growth – entails the dissemination of rights and autonomy to key actors in the system. The significance of rights or of freedom from constraint as the driver of economic behavior is accepted a priori. The main academic arguments then revolve primarily around determining who possesses these rights and where power actually resides in the system.

Of course, plenty of disagreement exists even within these established parameters. Some scholars underscore the importance of provincial power.[1] Other scholars assert that the real change lies in the rights accorded village-level governments.[2] Still others assert that, in fact, the center actually continues to hold key rights and that maintenance of central control actually furthers reform.[3] Finally, there are those who focus on the ability of basic economic producers to achieve freedom by operating outside the existing system.[4]

Does the center rule, or do the provinces? Are village-level governments or rather individual firms the key actors? Is it centrally mandated policy that sets economic actors free, or are those actors simply moving beyond the system and gaining freedom on their own? Is it perhaps a combination of the two? Has entrepreneurship really developed in the reform era, and if it has then who are the entrepreneurs? Who are the market actors and why?

Almost inextricably linked with these descriptive questions of "who actually does rule" are more normative questions of "who should rule." What is the optimal distribution of rights for achieving economic growth? How can entrepreneurial behavior be promoted? Should property rights be granted wholesale to private owners, or can those rights reside in the hands of state actors? Which level of the state should be empowered? Is it the center or instead the grass-roots level that should maintain control rights?

That China scholars tend to confine themselves to these types of questions, and to rights-based analyses in general, is in part reflective of broader developments outside the China field. Much scholarship on China takes on a rather reactive and derivative quality. Always lurking in the background is the neoclassical assertion that growth requires private property rights and that effective postcommunist reform requires "big-bang" privatization.[5] Just as the collapse of the Soviet bloc pushed China off the front pages of the popular media, neoclassical policy programs in Eastern Europe captured the academic limelight once associated with Chinese-style reform. Chinese reform went from being viewed as impressively progressive to suspiciously conservative or even downright recalcitrant. Why bother studying China when the real action, and the economically significant change, is in Eastern Europe and the Soviet Union?

The "China side," scholars whose careers are deeply invested in the relevance of Chinese reform, gamely counters by showing not only that growth is possible without privatization but also that gradualism is actually an optimal policy for a variety of social, political, and economic reasons. In effect, much academic literature on China either explicitly or implicitly attempts to weigh in on the "gradualism versus shock therapy" question. The problem, however, is that by letting other people set the terms of debate, China scholars have been steered down only the most well-trod paths of explanation and analysis. They argue assiduously that property-rights reform can substitute for outright privatization, or that governmental decentralization can substitute for nonintervention in the economy, yet nobody challenges the fundamental neoclassical notions of causation and behavior.[6] Few scholars seriously entertain the possibility that rights, freedom, and autonomy are *not* the driving forces behind successful postsocialist reform or economic behavior in general. Few scholars challenge the dominant view of reform as a dismantling of constraints, an opening of new opportunities, and an unleashing of innate energies. The "China side," by trying so hard to counter the "big bang," has in a broader sense been co-opted by it.

The preceding chapters on SOE reform have attempted to explore reform through a decidedly different lens – one that is different from that adopted by advocates of gradualism and shock therapy alike. This work has attempted to move away from rights-based frameworks by focusing instead on the significance of *constraint* in shaping economic change. Reform is defined not so much as an opening up but rather as a tightening up or even a clamping down. Behavioral change is viewed not as a spontaneous response to new freedom but rather as a forced response to new pressures and strictures. Indeed, autonomy is viewed as somewhat of a constant, something that existed as much in the command economy as in the reform era. However, autonomy was in the past expressed through rent seeking or other nonproductive behavior. Industrial managers used their power to hoard inputs. Commune officials manipulated harvest estimates.[7] Farmers hid rice.[8] Factory workers shirked labor. The list goes on and on. "Eating from the big pot" or skimming off "iron rice bowl" systems of lifetime employment are just as much expressions of producer autonomy and entrepreneurial behavior as are more productive, market-oriented activities. One focus of the constraints-based approach, though, is to ask how autonomy in any system is channeled toward either asset-expanding or asset-squandering behavior. The approach assumes that, from the producer's or entrepreneur's perspective, neither form of behavior is necessarily optimal and neither is simply chosen spontaneously. Rather, changes are made in the face of pressure. It is not choice but rather lack of choice that brings about change. The engine of causation is constraint, not opportunity or "rights."

Of course, the argument here is not over truth per se. In a sense, the constraints-based approach is to the rights-based perspective what the Copernican view of planetary motion was to the Ptolemaic. "Rights" can be viewed as the focus of reform, just as Earth can be viewed as the center of the solar system. In both cases, though, the calculations become decidedly more complicated and the explanations more convoluted. The real question is which analytical framework – which representation of reality and causation – carries us further in understanding the phenomena at hand. Which offers us the better vantage point for understanding observed past outcomes and potential future ones? Which can explain variations across time and geographical space? Postcommand reform undoubtedly involves simultaneous and deeply interwoven shifts in autonomy and constraint, freedom and responsibility, and power and authority. The facts themselves can support a variety of analytical frameworks. The issue at hand is which analytical approach gives us more explanatory power, more analytical bang for the buck.

The constraints-based perspective clearly shows that, in the SOE sector, the "rights" associated with reform have led to a whole range of possible economic behaviors, both positive and negative. Under certain institutional circumstances in the reform environment, power and rights translate into more rent-seeking opportunities and further rent-seeking behavior. In the urban industrial sector, access to soft lending from the banking system vitiates budget constraints for enterprises and governmental agencies alike. In such a situation, rent seeking clearly pays for a number of economic actors, while incentives for value-expanding economic behavior are few and far between. The increasing autonomy afforded by reform simply allows more rent seeking, on a grander scale, and with less immediate risk of getting caught. In essence, what develops are rights without accountability and freedom without responsibility. Reform becomes indeed a process of opening up, but opening up to behavior that is anything but growth-promoting. As the cases of Angang, Magang, and even Shougang suggest, the economic outcomes can be dismal indeed.

Alternatively, even within the state sector, positive outcomes are possible and market-oriented behavior has been observed. But as suggested by Shougang's decade of success, the key is not the dissemination of rights but rather the establishment of strict and clearly defined constraints. Of course, not all forms of constraint are useful. The command system was full of constraints and targets, particularly constraints upon managerial authority and targets for material output. Ironically, one problem with those constraints was that they did not effectively impinge on key aspects of producer autonomy. The command economy's restrictions on producers were both misdirected and fairly weak. Producers were left myriad opportunities, mostly through their control over information, to squirrel away assets and capture rents in the economy.

What counts in SOE reform is not the imposition of just any constraint at all, but rather the imposition of a hard budget constraint. Producers, to some extent, can elect to behave as they wish in any economy. They can behave in accordance with the law, or they can behave in egregious violation. Similarly, entrepreneurial actors can seek financial gain through value-expanding or value-subtracting activities. From the policy perspective, the key is to ensure that clear costs apply to value-subtracting behavior. It is precisely these costs that hard budget constraints impose.

In a sense, the key to growth-promoting reform is not the dissemination of freedom to do anything but rather the imposition of constraints against doing many things. When policy makers are committed to *not* bailing out unproductive, money-losing firms, managers are forced for their own survival to seek growth-promoting strategies. Similarly, when bailout financing no longer cascades upon the firm, local governments are forced to curtail predatory taxation. Excessive taxation in the absence of bailout loans undermines the firm, and once the firm is gone, so too is the locality's tax base.

The imposition of hard budgets does not mean that every economic actor will behave intelligently or appropriately. Some Chinese managers, like their counterparts everywhere else in the world, will still adopt inappropriate strategies, even when the viability of their firm is at stake. Similarly, some governmental actors, even when their long-term revenue base hangs in the balance, will still tax firms to death. Information is never perfect, those interpreting information are never perfect, and mistakes are inevitably made. Reform that truly clamps down, however, ensures at the very least that those who make the mistakes are identified and perhaps even weeded out. Poorly managed firms go out of business. Poorly managed localities run out of money, fail to attract additional business, and (it is hoped) have their leadership replaced. At least accountability in such circumstances can be traced. More important, at least the basis is provided upon which efficient allocation of scarce societal capital can be achieved. The basis is created upon which financial institutions can channel investment into firms that are well run. By extension, then, wealth will flow toward regions or localities whose governments promote business rather than prey upon it. Scarce resources, in effect, end up moving toward those who can expand those resources and make them less scarce.

The point here is not to suggest what might occur in a hypothetical, ideal situation. Rather, this is what *does* occur in the Chinese SOE sector. Where reform has taken on the quality of a clamping down, and where decision makers have made the extremely difficult choice of restricting firm-level access to resources, managerial behavior has shown signs of shifting toward growth promotion. Alternatively, for cases in which reform has involved solely an "opening up," a "spreading of power," and an "expansion of freedom," behavior has often tended toward rent seeking – not necessarily in a criminal sense, but as a purely rational strategy for coping with chaotic economic circumstances. In essence, pursuing reform solely via "liberalization" is the easiest step decision makers can take. The far harder step, but the one upon which successful SOE restructuring depends, involves the pursuit of reform as the imposition of costs and constraints, the kind of constraints that push actors to adopt market-oriented, value-expanding strategies for their very survival.

An interesting question, however, is the extent to which this notion of reform as a "clamping down" can explain patterns outside the state sector. How does the constraints-based view stack up against the rights-based view in explaining phenomena such as TVE growth or broad regional income disparities in China? Can either view single-handedly, with one unified explanation, illuminate both why urban SOEs have stagnated and why rural TVEs have boomed? Can either view explain why rapid rural industrialization has been a primarily regional phenomenon, one certainly more associated with the coastal South than the North and one virtually absent in the industrial Northeast? Why do some local governments promote business while others do not?

In essence, what we are looking for is a "Copernican" framework for reform. We have one approach, the constraints-based view, that seems to explain phenomena in the urban sector. We have an entirely different approach, the rights-based view, which (as will be shown in what follows) supplies a sophisticated explanation for rural growth. As with the Ptolemaic notion of Earth's position in the universe, each view can explain one thing and explain it well.

Which, however, can explain many things? Which can be the equivalent in reform studies to an idea that explains not only the Earth's motion vis-à-vis the Sun but also the motion of all the planets?

EXTENDING THE ARGUMENT: THE FACTUAL TERRAIN OF
CHINESE REFORM

Any broad explanation of Chinese reform, particularly the kind of explanations that result in sweeping policy recommendations, must avoid focusing on only specific, disaggregated elements of the reform experience. In other words, it is not enough to explain only the rapid expansion of rural enterprises, or just the growth of exports as a portion of GNP, or only the relative stagnation of urban industry. These specific phenomena must be seen as part of some broader whole, a broader web of connections constituting the entire rich tapestry of Chinese reform.

What, exactly, are the main attributes of this tapestry? Unquestionably, a prime attribute involves impressive macroeconomic growth. From 1979 to 1991, China's GNP grew 8.6 percent annually, or 7.2 percent on a per-capita basis.[9] In 1992, GNP growth shot up to 12.8 percent.[10] Meanwhile, exports as a portion of GNP rose from around 5 percent in 1978 to nearly 20 percent in 1991.[11] Clearly, China was getting considerably richer than in the past, considerably quicker, and with far more reliance on exports. China, in its own way and whether intentionally or not, was shifting from extreme strategies of import substitution to the sort of export-promoting strategies pursued in the rest of East Asia.

Within this broad pattern of growth, several interesting things were happening. First, the nonstate sector (perhaps "nontraditional" would be more accurate) began to outstrip the state sector in terms of total contribution to national industrial growth.[12] Whereas in 1978 the nonstate sector accounted for only 22 percent of China's total industrial output value, that share had risen to well over 50 percent by the mid-1990s. Between 1978 and 1991, not only had employment grown much faster in the nonstate sector than in the state sector, but also total factor productivity (TFP) growth remained consistently higher in the former than in the latter.[13] China's economy was undergoing tremendous transformations in the area of ownership. The absolute number of nonstate firms was shooting upward, and the firms themselves were producing far more efficiently than their state-owned counterparts. As indicated throughout the earlier chapters of this study, the urban state sector, though enjoying some productivity gains of its own, was sinking deeper and deeper into financial distress.

The nonstate sector had, in effect, become the locomotive of China's export-oriented growth, slowly but surely dragging the urban industrial sector along with it.

The second interesting fact is that, within this overall pattern of nontraditional sector growth, the most impressive gains were made in the countryside. Between 1978 and 1990, the total output value of China's locally owned rural collective enterprises grew at a spectacular annual rate of 26.7 percent.[14] That the national average for all firms during the period was somewhere around 13 percent shows just how significant the contribution was from rural industry. From 1978 to 1991, the sheer number of people employed in rural industry shot upward from 28.3 million people to 96.1 million.[15] Meanwhile, between 1986 and 1990, exports from the TVE sector expanded 65.6 percent annually. China's countryside during the reform era has been engaged in an extraordinary transformation, a veritable industrial revolution as peasants leave the land for jobs in industry.

The third interesting feature is that the pace of reform has varied not only by sector but also geographically. It is not that rural collective industry has surged past the urban SOE sector in every province and autonomous region, but rather that the phenomenon has been concentrated in only certain areas. This is a critical point for understanding both the specific causes of rural industrialization and the more general drivers of economic growth in transitional systems.

Even a quick survey of the data serves to illustrate this point.[16] The stark income disparities between China's coastal East and inland West are well known, and they are as old perhaps as Chinese history itself. Far more variable and less understood, however, are the economic disparities within China's coastal provinces. Clearly, important shifts have taken place over the past two decades. From 1953 to 1978, China's era of command planning, the basic trend was that the industrial North and Shanghai grew relatively rapidly, while the rural South grew relatively slowly. During that period, areas like Shanghai, Beijing, Liaoning, and Heilongjiang – centers of heavy industry – experienced annual GNP growth rates at or above 9 percent. At the bottom of the list, at 5.2 percent, was the primarily rural (or, at most, light industrial) Guangdong. Absolute income disparities during this period simply mirrored the growth trends. In 1978, at the very start of reform, rural southern provinces like Fujian and Guangdong were ranked as low-income and lower-middle-income areas (respectively), while northeastern industrial giants like Jilin, Heilongjiang, and Liaoning ranked among China's highest-income areas.

However, during the first decade and a half of post-Mao reforms, the trends reversed in important ways. The high-growth areas shifted to the South, with

Guangdong leading the pack with 13.3 percent annual growth and with Zhe-jiang at 12.5 percent, Hainan at 12 percent, and Fujian at 11.6 percent. These were precisely the areas that had, in a sense, been marginalized during the com-mand era, for they simply were not major centers of heavy industry and thus were not big targets for central investment. Ironically, the areas once privileged during that earlier era, the northeastern industrial centers, have experienced the slowest growth levels nationwide during the reform years. Heilongjiang sits at the bottom of the list with a 6-percent growth rate, while Liaoning and Jilin are close behind at 7.8 percent and 8.2 percent, respectively.

Meanwhile, significant shifts have also occurred in absolute levels of wealth. Guangdong, previously ranked among the lower-middle-income areas, is now among China's five wealthiest provinces. Fujian has followed close behind, moving from the absolute bottom low-income category before reform to the upper-middle-income group by the 1990s. Conversely, Jilin has dropped from the upper-middle to the lower-middle group, and Heilongjiang has dropped from the high-income classification to the upper-middle group.

The point is simply that rural-led industrialization and TVE-led economic growth cannot properly be cast as "national" phenomena in China. It is some-what of a distortion to suggest that China's story writ large has been one of the growth in the countryside surrounding and ultimately bolstering the cities. Rather, the story has been one of a particular sort of rural-led growth – growth not in every rural area of China, but rather rapid development in areas neglected during the command period. The Chinese experience has been one not so much of growth in the countryside surrounding the cities as of growth in the South sur-rounding, and ultimately stimulating, the North. Today, however, while north-ern areas like Shandong finally boom, industrial northeastern provinces – even the large rural expanses of the Manchurian plain – remain relatively dormant.

Any comprehensive analysis of reform must account for these patterns. It is not enough just to explain successful TVE growth. Nor is it enough just to ex-plain SOE stagnation. Rather, explanations for one must be reconcilable with explanations for the other, and all must account for the regional disparities evi-dent to even the most casual observer of China.

LOCAL STATE CORPORATISM: A RIGHTS-BASED APPROACH
TO TVE GROWTH

In this section we will examine how one particular property-rights–based ap-proach – the "local state corporatism" perspective – copes with the patterns of reform just described.[17] The local state corporatism view is chosen not in the

Figure 7.1. The Local–State Corporatism Argument

hope that it can serve as a straw man but rather because it reflects – through its linking of property-rights analyses with notions of state-led development – a set of ideas that have gained tremendous currency both within China and abroad. Furthermore, as will be discussed later, the local state corporatism view has significantly different policy implications from the constraints-based approach.

The local state corporatism (LSC) view sets out broadly to explain China's economic growth during the reform era and, more specifically, the tremendous growth of collective enterprises in the Chinese countryside.[18] The argument suggests that China's system of fiscal contracting, by granting local governments the right to collect and keep tax revenue, motivated these local governments to promote business.[19] In other words, reform – defined in this case as fiscal reform – reassigned property rights, or "control over assets," downward to local governments.[20] Village-level governments, the theory asserts, were given unprecedented rights to engage in economic activity – rights, essentially, to be free from outside intervention and control. What they did with those rights was to pursue industrial development, and the more secure the rights they enjoyed, the more aggressively they pursued growth. In other words, because local governments enjoyed control and cash-flow rights over local assets, officials had a clear incentive to seek long-term expansion of those assets by starting new firms. The local government, in the LSC view, served as a sort of company headquarters, coordinating the various component firms of what, in essence, became a diversified business corporation.[21]

The causal argument is illustrated in Figure 7.1. Fiscal reform leads to local governmental property rights, which in turn lead governments to promote business, which in turn leads to economic growth. Furthermore, the closer the ties between government and business, and the more nearly unilateral governmental decision-making power actually is, the more local business will develop.[22] Local state intervention is seen as a positive force for the efficient allocation of resources, where efficiency is defined in economic rather than social welfare terms. The key to TVE success is considered to be state control over assets – state control that mirrors, in a sense, the behavior once attributed on a grander scale to Japan's Ministry of International Trade and Industry.[23] The evidence

236

cited to support this point is the fact that TVEs, which are owned by specific localities, perform better than larger SOEs, which are "owned" by the undifferentiated population as a whole.[24] Again, the closer the tie to the state – a state that can control assets, move those assets between its various enterprise holdings, and thereby pick winners and losers in the local business environment – the more robust the observed economic growth.

Of course, lurking behind this argument is a fundamental assumption that fiscal reform has not only granted localities the power to retain revenue, but has also cut localities off from central subsidies. In other words, there is a key assumption that hard budget constraints actually apply to the local governments involved. Only if hard budget constraints actually apply to local governments does it become imperative for these governments to seek expansion of the local tax base. Otherwise, these governments could accrue wealth simply by encouraging more central subsidization. Proponents of the LSC view mention this condition only in passing, assume that it applies to rural local governments nationwide, and then move on to underscore state intervention (made possible by property rights) as the key to successful economic growth.[25] Local governmental property rights to allocate resources and intervene in firms are pinpointed not only as the drivers of growth but also as the means by which states can potentially transcend markets in the developmental process.[26] Only with the hard budget assumption, then, does it make sense to say that the closer the ties between local state and firm, the higher the realized growth levels.

THE CONSTRAINTS-BASED RESPONSE

Constraints-based approaches are decidedly skeptical of the LSC explanation for TVE growth. First, they do not understand how any conclusions at all can be drawn from the study of only successful cases of development. By examining only situations in which TVEs have thrived, LSC approaches commit the error of selecting on the dependent variable, to use social science terminology. By trying to explain what they themselves define as a constant (TVE growth) and then by selecting only successful TVEs, LSC proponents have no way of proving that state intervention is the key. After all, the key might just as well be in other factors found across successful TVE environments: functioning labor markets, foreign investment, export orientation, or a host of other variables. There is just no way to produce anything beyond bare assertions if one's cases all include state intervention and all include successful TVE promotion.

Even worse, by restricting their study to only successful cases, LSC advocates run the risk of drawing spurious correlations between state intervention

237

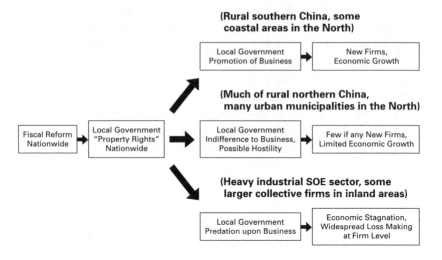

Figure 7.2. The Constraints-Based Perspective

and growth. Indeed, if they extended the study to rural areas in which TVEs have *not* been successful (i.e., the Northeast), then they would likely find plenty of state intervention but not much growth. More generally, LSC theory cannot explain why fiscal reform and the resulting reassignment of property rights to local governments, essentially national phenomena, have failed to bring about a proliferation of successful firms in most of northern and northeastern China. Why are positive economic outcomes restricted to the South and selected northern provinces like Shandong? Why have municipal governments in urban areas, governments with full rights to start their own firms, been slow to take advantage of these powers, particularly in the Northeast? Why do they seem to behave differently from certain grass-roots agencies in rural areas?

As indicated by Figure 7.1, LSC looks out at the Chinese reform experience and observes fiscal reform leading to local promotion of business. The constraints-based approach takes a distinctly different view. It sees a fiscal contracting system applied – at least until 1994 – nationwide, but with a range of observed economic outcomes (see Figure 7.2). Rights are reassigned to local governments throughout the land, but those governments do not all use their rights in the same way. Some areas, no doubt, do promote business and successfully manage a number of enterprises. Other areas, however, appear somewhat indifferent to business. Time and again one observes municipal or even rural governments that have been less than responsive to the needs of local business.[27] Indeed, in some northern locales, small firms have simply picked up and moved to more hospitable environments in the South. Finally, there is the heavy industrial SOE sector, one in which local governments have acquired property rights yet seem to use those rights to prey upon the firm. These microeconomic patterns are then reflected in the regional income disparities and differential rates of regional growth cited earlier. In both absolute and relative terms, the Northeast is growing far more slowly than the coastal South. Clearly something beyond the constants of fiscal reform and governmental decentralization is driving the observed patterns of variation. A constant simply cannot explain the varying outcomes described in Figure 7.2.

Nonetheless, what can explain the variation in a unified manner is the degree to which hard or soft budget constraints obtain at the local level. Rights devolve to every locality, but what differs across localities is access to soft lending and subsidization. In other words, what differs is the hardness of the budget constraint, and these differences then explain the range of observed behavioral outcomes. The constraints-based approach zeros in on a variable that LSC assumed away as already resolved – the flexibility or "softness" of local governmental budget constraints – and in so doing develops a unified explanation for a range of reform outcomes.

The hypothesis is that fiscal reform imposed severe restrictions and financial constraints on certain localities while leaving others essentially untouched. The areas most affected in the constraints-based sense were those (in the rural South) that had been essentially neglected during the command era. With the onset of reform, these areas, like every other in the country, lost the bulk of their direct fiscal subsidies from the center. Like every other region, they were told, in effect, to fend for themselves. What was different about these areas, though, was that they were not blessed with any existing large industrial firms, the kind of firms that would continue to receive subsidies and soft loans from the state banking system. Most southern areas, simply because of historical fate and their second-tier role in the earlier command era, did not have the option of using existing traditional industrial firms as conduits for central subsidies. Southern governments were instead faced with a situation of "reform or die," "promote business or go hungry," or at least "engage in entrepreneurship or stay poor."[28] If they wanted to climb out of poverty, they had little choice but to start their own firms or, at the very least, create environments conducive for other people to come in and start firms. In essence, selected areas in the South enjoyed the benefits of backwardness.

At least as important, firms in these areas also faced hard budget constraints. Particularly for smaller firms, there were no easy "policy loans" from the central banking system, no soft subsidies to fund inefficient operations. Again, the situation was one of "produce efficiently or go out of business." Not surprisingly, tremendous levels of market exit have gone hand-in-hand with like levels of market entry for firms in the TVE sector. It is also possible to observe that, for those few TVEs that actually grow large enough to attract central bank loans, performance often declines and the firms then start to look decidedly like traditional SOEs.[29] Local state intervention persists, but in an environment of softened budget constraints. The pressure for growth promotion evaporates as the opportunities for rent seeking materialize. The point is that, for firms and local governments alike, the key to behavioral change – and the key to understanding a range of performance outcomes – is not the dissemination of rights or freedom per se but rather the exact opposite: the degree to which unyielding budget constraints are actually imposed.

The point is more than a semantic one, as becomes clear when behavior is observed in newly empowered localities that do not face the burden of hard budget constraints. Consider counties in the industrial Northeast that happen to have major large-scale factories within their boundaries. Why should the local governments in these areas promote new business? Direct fiscal subsidies from the center may have dried up, but the locality can still extract from existing traditional firms. Those firms, because they are repeatedly bailed out by the banking system and thus face no real threat of bankruptcy, make a prime target for income extraction. Local governments have every incentive to use their newly acquired autonomy to prey upon the firm. More subtly, these governments are under no pressure to adopt entrepreneurial attitudes, and can instead afford to maintain perspectives associated with the old system. It is hardly surprising that urban officials in cities like Anshan or Harbin consider it "beneath their positions" to involve themselves in promoting collective firms.[30] It is hardly surprising that Harbin Municipality essentially drove important collectives to relocate in the South, and is only now trying to lure them back – in part, perhaps, because SOEs are in such distress that they no longer serve as effective conduits of central funds. The fundamental empirical fact is that many municipal and rural governments in China have been empowered with all sorts of new rights, but these bureaucracies, even the very lowest grass-roots ones, frequently resist expressing these rights via business promotion.

In the industrial Northeast and in many other parts of China, soft money remains available and budget constraints remain flexible. Growth remains slow at the regional level precisely because there is no tremendous pressure to change, no bitter financial constraints that necessitate behavioral adaptation. Over the past years, there has been no "reform or die" set of strictures, and – again, not surprisingly – there have been no corresponding "reform or die" attitudes at the local level. Only now that localities can see the impressive growth achieved in the South (and their own relative poverty) are attitudes changing. More important, only now that the SOEs really appear to be collapsing, and only now that indirect subsidies from the center really might disappear, are northeastern localities seeming to become even remotely interested in small-scale business promotion. Unfortunately, they now face a long march up the learning curve in an increasingly competitive domestic and international environment.

The general point for transitional economies is that, where there exist considerable amounts of "traditional" industry (big state firms), there also exist plenty of opportunities to soften budget constraints. Incentives for economic actors up and down the line – from enterprise managers to top government officials – suffer as a result. Rights, power, and authority spread down the line, but what does not necessarily spread is any corresponding pressure to engage in asset-expanding behavior. Where such pressures do exist – where hard budgets have been imposed, either by design or default – market-oriented, growth-promoting behavior can indeed be observed. As noted earlier, not all actors respond positively; at least some do, though, and the rest are ultimately weeded out. The rights, however, remain constant. It is the degree of restraint that varies, and it is the degree of restraint that explains varying outcomes. By implication, successful reform must be viewed not as a freeing up but instead, at least in the economic sense, as a clamping down.

WHY DOES THE DISTINCTION MATTER?

Beyond the rather important issue of analytical coherence, why should we really care whether local growth is explained negatively in terms of budget constraints or positively in terms of state intervention? What if we simply acknowledge that both are involved? After all, both are clearly observed to some degree. Why not compromise and say that the LSC view is correct, state intervention *is* the key to growth, but only in those areas where hard budget constraints already apply?

Unfortunately, the differences between the two approaches cannot be finessed so easily. Indeed, they are more nearly mutually exclusive than one might think, for they embody vastly different analytical views of what drives growth as well as vastly different normative recommendations for which policies should be adopted to achieve such growth.

Through their identification of local state intervention as the driver of Chinese growth, LSC advocates end up backing the general notion that states can

241

transcend markets. In other words, LSC focuses on the question of "who should own," and the answer it provides is "the local state." The theory, through its description of local governments as "corporate headquarters" and firms as "corporate divisions," implies the superiority of local ownership not only to central ownership but also to private ownership.[31] After all, if one accepts the government–enterprise corporation analogy, then it makes no more sense to say that individual firms should be privatized than it does to say that the constituent divisions of an integrated corporation should be spun off and forced to operate independently. Certainly in the business world, the notion of "corporation" implies some distinct advantage over dispersal of the constituent parts. Otherwise, there would be no point in having a corporation. Similarly, the notion of "local state corporatism" as an engine of growth implies that state organization of firms is somehow superior to the dispersal of firms to separate owners. This notion is reinforced by the LSC assertion that the more centralized and tightly integrated the local corporation, the better.[32] Local control is good, and tighter local control is better. The basic idea is that the corporate headquarters, the local government, knows better than the constituent divisions what entails an efficient (from the growth perspective) allocation of resources. There is no point letting the "divisions" battle out their respective notions of efficient allocation through intense free-market competition. Instead, the local government, the "board of directors," can move assets from bad firms to good, pick winners and losers, and avoid the duplication and waste of resources brought on by cutthroat competition. The local state becomes the engine for change and development, transcending the market by achieving growth faster and more efficiently.[33]

The policy implications of these assertions are clear. Any policy maker who believes the logic behind LSC should do everything in his or her power to reassign ownership rights to local governments. Local governments should be empowered in every way possible to intervene in firms and promote growth. Emphasis should be placed on disseminating rights, freedom, and authority, especially to local governments. Meanwhile, proper skepticism should be maintained toward competitive markets, and privatization should be avoided. Because corporate systems are better than competitive systems, every effort should be made to create business–government partnerships for growth. The state should be organized to take advantage of its ability to transcend markets, and the way to do this is to empower local governments.

The constraints-based approach, by focusing on the systemic conditions under which ownership is exercised rather than on the specific issue of "who owns," unequivocally rejects the logic of LSC. Even at the purely abstract level, it finds LSC's equating of state intervention with corporate business management highly problematic. In general, internalizing the activities of many business units into one single corporate enterprise makes sense if the additional costs incurred are outweighed by higher realized profits.[34] In other words, by merging disparate businesses into one single corporation, one creates added administrative costs and all sorts of organizational costs. Purely in administrative terms, managing a large corporation is far more costly than managing a small firm. At least in theory, it makes sense to tolerate these costs only if they are outweighed by gains from the increasing volume of business activity.[35] That is, firms should group together if there are economies of scale and scope to be realized. Perhaps by producing in great quantities, the firms together can save money. Alternatively, by specializing in specific aspects of the production process, the firms when grouped together can realize greater efficiency and productivity. Corporatization should lead to some sort of observable vertical or horizontal integration of business operations. The point is that, unless these benefits from integration clearly exist and are utilized, it makes no sense to replace market coordination of independent firms with corporate coordination of linked firms.

In the case of Chinese TVEs, it is hard to see how government control over firms is actually achieving any benefits of integration. Certainly, LSC advocates have yet to show that locally controlled TVEs actually group their production in such a way as to achieve economies of scale or scope. Indeed, it has yet to be shown that these firms actually group or coordinate their productive activities at all. Can vertical integration be observed? Is there horizontal integration? It hardly seems so. The only clear thing is that the government controls both personnel appointments and the flow of assets between firms. Yet, if control over personnel and assets is all that is involved, why should local government officials be able to make better decisions than firm-level managers? If anything, because they are more distant from the locus of production, political officials have even less of the information necessary to assign the disposition of firm-level assets. All sorts of transaction costs and administrative complexities are added by allowing governments to determine the disposition of assets, but none of the coordinated production that might lead to higher profitability seems evident.

Under such circumstances, the absolute best that local state corporatism could hope to achieve are outcomes equal to what the competitive market would produce. In other words, the best that can be expected from this sort of intervention is an outcome no worse than if the government just stayed out and left the firms alone. This is a fairly low payoff, and hardly the sort of thing that one would want to underscore as an engine of growth.

243

The policy implication, however, is not that Chinese firms should be privatized. Rather, the constraints-based approach asserts that concern over "who owns" – whether private individuals, the central government, or local agencies – is at most a second-order issue. The approach moves away from issues of ownership and instead hypothesizes (1) that productivity is low in transitional economies because budget constraints are soft, and (2) that productivity varies with the increasing hardness of the constraint. When budget constraints are absent, no owners of any kind have incentives to engage in asset-expanding activity; there is simply no pressure to do so. Indeed, immediate survival and enrichment is secured by pulling assets out of productive use and expending them. Alternatively, growth-promoting behavior – whether by governments, firms, or individuals – develops regardless of ownership in response to new financial pressures: the cutting of externally provided subsidies. Behavioral change is forced through the imposition of extremely tough, unyielding financial pressures.

If this perspective is accurate, policy makers should concentrate first and foremost on imposing hard budget constraints upon firms and localities alike. "Who owns" the assets is far less important than the circumstances under which ownership of any kind is exercised. While the government should certainly get out of the business of allocating resources, it should also cease viewing its own activities in terms of the reassignment of rights, freedoms, and autonomy. Indeed, expanding freedom under soft-budget conditions, particularly to lower-level governmental agencies, actually threatens to impede economic growth. Similarly, privatization in an environment of readily available soft credit can also increase rent seeking and hence impede growth.

Government policy should instead focus on issues like commercializing the banking sector and regaining control over central–local financial transfers. Either lending should be cut off entirely, or banks should be made truly responsible for their balance sheets. If the government feels the need to issue subsidies, it should certainly avoid doing so through the ostensibly commercial banks. Banks could then reasonably be held responsible for their losses and ultimately be forced to exit the market if losses became habitual. Similarly with central–local financial transfers, business loans should be permitted only on a commercial basis. If the center itself does not have the ability to make commercial lending decisions, then let foreign investors fund local business development. The center absolutely should fund social welfare and education, and should do whatever is necessary to encourage local saving. Yet, if it wants to spur local business growth, the way to do this is not simply to dole out authority coupled with subsidies. Money intended for business growth should be supplied only on hard-budget, commercial conditions. Only when an environment embodying those conditions has been established does it make sense to begin worrying about who owns, who has rights, and who has freedom. Furthermore, even at that point, it hardly makes sense to be concerned about transcending the market. Policy makers undertake a Herculean task in simply trying to achieve basic market conditions, let alone transcending them.

The constraints-based versus rights-based debate raises one final issue regarding the role of investment in China's development. Advocates of LSC could conceivably argue that TVE development has occurred mainly in the South because that is where investment is available. Because of sheer geographical proximity, these are the areas that have enjoyed the bulk of overseas Chinese investment from Hong Kong, Taiwan, and Southeast Asia. Fiscal reform and local state property rights would still stand as the drivers of growth, but outside investment would be recognized for its role in fueling and enabling the process. If only investment would flow into the rest of rural China, where local state property rights also hold, growth would be achieved.

Ironically, this view melds with another school of thought prevalent in China today, the "neoauthoritarian" perspective on development. Neoauthoritarians assiduously oppose the sort of local autonomy measures advocated by LSC theory.[36] Nevertheless, both approaches dovetail along the idea that state intervention can transcend market forces. Neoauthoritarians place their hopes on the central state while local state corporatists focus on grass-roots activity, but the schools are linked by their faith in the potentially salutary nature of state intervention in the economy. Neoauthoritarians, though, place particular emphasis on the role of investment, especially state-controlled investment, in spurring economic growth. The central government should do all it can, in this perspective, to redistribute wealth in China and overcome the regional disparities that have become prevalent under reform. In other words, investment is the key to even the market-oriented growth promoted by local governments. Regional disparities exist precisely because many localities have had no access to investment resources. It should be a prime objective of the center, therefore, to transfer resources from richer areas to poorer in an overall effort to spur nationwide growth.

The constraints-based perspective takes a decidedly different view of the role of investment. Instead of focusing on levels of investment, it focuses on the differential conditions under which investment is made. As it does with regard to "autonomy," the constraints-based approach hypothesizes that investment can be viewed as a relative constant in China. Certainly the South during the reform era has enjoyed a disproportionate share of overseas – mostly "overseas

245

Chinese" – investment. The North and Northeast, however, have also enjoyed tremendous amounts of investment in the form of central subsidies to heavy industrial SOEs. Over 70 percent of domestic lending in China goes to the state sector. The rural collective sector, particularly in Guangdong and Fujian, enjoys investment from abroad; the state sector enjoys tremendous investment from the central government. The former develops rapidly, though, while the latter stagnates. Of interest then is not the level of investment but rather the conditions under which investment is made. In the state sector, soft budgets for firm and bank alike mean that no clear return is demanded on investment. Future investment can be obtained by the recipient regardless of how efficiently current investment is used. Even if lenders realize no returns at all, funds continue to flow. In the rural sector, however, hard-budget conditions exist. Foreigners, or even local governments, have no compunction about pulling investment out of firms that achieve no returns, and such firms ultimately must exit the market. In one way or another, investment migrates toward those who use it efficiently. Not surprisingly, the returns in this sector are far higher than in the state sector.

The lesson is actually the same as that learned during the command era. Growth is only partially driven by levels of investment. Ultimately, what counts more are the conditions that can increase the efficiency and productivity of investment. The problem with the command system was that it failed on precisely this score. More and more investment was required over time to achieve the same levels of output. An analogous problem exists in the state sector today. The broader lesson, one consistent with the constraints-based approach, is that simply throwing money at the problem of low growth will not make the problem go away. Simply pumping in more investment will not solve anything. Rather, the real issue of concern is what type of investment is pumped in, from what source, and under what conditions.

Similarly, it is hard to see how transferring resources from high-productivity regions to low-productivity regions will lead to overall gains in national wealth. Rather, such action is likely to result in depressed rates of growth. From the policy perspective, the key is to change not the level of investment but rather the conditions under which investment is used. Hard budget constraints must be imposed and commercial standards established. If such constraints are not imposed then those who use investment will face no pressure to realize returns. Under such conditions, foreigners will eventually leave the market, for although such investors have acknowledged an impressively long time horizon with regard to China, they are not in the business of dispensing either subsidies or charity. The government will then be left with the task of funding investment, albeit investment that carries no likelihood of achieving positive returns.

Regardless of the origin or level of investment, growth depends on an efficient allocation of resources, and an efficient allocation of resources requires investment under hard-budget conditions. *The imposition of hard budget constraints should be the prime goal of transitional reform.*

SUMMARY

This chapter has attempted to reinterpret transitional reform in terms of the specific propositions that emerged from our study of SOE performance. The same variables that explain SOE stagnation – soft budget constraints and access to soft lending – serve by their very absence to explain successful TVE development. A unified explanation was put forward to explain the complex and highly interrelated patterns of Chinese development. Reform was recast as a process of clamping down rather than loosening up, and significant policy implications were drawn out.

The point of this analysis is not to suggest that property rights are necessarily a bad way to understand the incentives of economic actors. Rather, the point is that only in the presence of appropriate constraints – hard budget constraints – do the property rights accorded through reform even begin to resemble "rights" as described by economic theory. This is all the more true in complex production organizations, organizations in which property rights are (by definition) dispersed.

In general, true property rights in the economic sense imply not only the freedom to use assets and the power to enjoy the benefits accruing from that use, but also responsibility to absorb any losses that result. When power devolves to lower governmental levels or individual economic producers through reform, that change does not, at least in any formal sense, constitute a reassignment of "rights." The real reassignment of rights takes place only when devolution of financial power is matched by devolution of financial responsibility. Only at that point can the recipients of these powers be considered to hold property "rights." Moreover, only at that point do incentives against value-subtracting, rent-seeking behavior truly develop. It is for this reason that the constraints outlined in this chapter, at least with regard to understanding behavioral outcomes, take causal precedence over the dissemination of "freedom" or "power."

Through the reform process, many actors have acquired power, but only some have actually acquired property rights in any real sense of the term. Some rural governments operate with these rights, as do some large state firms. Many do not, however, and incentives become skewed as a result. The key causal variable is the nature of constraint, the degree to which reform has been able to impose the kind of financial accountability that leads to value-enhancing behavior.

Although the causal variable may be clear in the constraints-based approach, other issues may appear somewhat opaque. The analysis has simultaneously advocated some forms of state intervention and condemned others; there has likewise been support for some forms of unfettered market activity but skepticism toward others. There has been discussion of state agencies stepping in and "carving out" property rights, yet dismissal of the local state's role in co-ordinating business. What then should be the proper role of the state in transitional systems? That the state plays a crucial role in such systems is indisputable. The question, however, is: What types of state action lead to growth, and what types impede growth? What should the proper role for the state be in what is not so much a developing market economy as an economy attempting to develop a market?

8

Conclusion

T HE preceding chapters have been motivated by two rather different objectives. In one sense, they have sought – particularly through the case studies – to further our understanding of a major policy issue facing contemporary China: the reform of the state industrial sector. By illustrating the depth and complexity of the problem, the analysis has attempted to present a somewhat different face of China – neither the rising economic giant nor potential economic competitor often portrayed in the West, but rather a troubled transitional nation confronting absolutely awesome obstacles in its path to development. In a second sense, these chapters have sought to provide an alternative conceptual framework for understanding postsocialist reform in general, an approach that challenges popular notions of privatization and property-rights restructuring. Yet, what really are the implications of the theoretical and descriptive threads of the study? How do they change our broader understanding of East Asian development, and our specific image of China?

THE CONSTRAINTS-BASED APPROACH

This study has made some general assumptions about economic behavior; it has assumed that, given the certain degree of freedom and autonomy that exists in any system, entrepreneurs will always rise up to capture opportunities to amass wealth and benefits. The interesting question, however, involves determining how the combination of constraints and incentives in any given system influences the form that this entrepreneurial behavior takes. Do economic producers, particularly the most entrepreneurial ones, seek personal gain through value-enhancing or, alternatively, value-subtracting means? What is the nature of constraint that inclines producers to follow one strategy instead of the other?

What has changed with the collapse of command planning in countries like China is not the degree of individual economic autonomy or "rights" per se. What has changed are the ways that autonomy or noncompliance is expressed and the types of economic activity over which autonomy can be exercised.

These changes, as the case studies of Chapters 4–6 have illustrated, take their most complicated form in large industrial producers, complex production organizations that by definition involve ambiguous property-rights arrangements. The constraints-based approach provides a sense of why these large firms do not naturally respond to the market even after planning is lifted, and why they do not behave as predicted when confronted with ownership restructuring efforts. Indeed, the new approach allows us to understand why ownership itself fails to function in the transitional context. Finally, the constraints-based approach outlines a series of roles that the state plays in shaping producer behavior, roles that range from being decidedly positive to decidedly negative with regard to encouraging economic growth. In transitional, marketizing economies, only some economic producers behave as they are "supposed to"; many do not. To a great extent, the actual behavior of producers reflects incentive structures that have been established (wittingly or unwittingly) by the state.

But what really is the role of the state in transitional systems, and what *should* that role be? In discussions of the sources of economic growth, the state frequently takes on an almost mystical quality, demonized by some and lionized by others. At different times and in different contexts, the state has been identified both as the source for all economic disaster and as the wellspring for all economic salvation. However, the constraints-based approach attempts to explore a middle ground. Earlier chapters have suggested that, in China's SOE sector, renegade state agencies contribute to the softening of firm-level budget constraints. Yet at the same time, the constraints-based view asserts that, in an environment of malfunctioning regulatory institutions, the state itself becomes the only organization capable of insulating large industrial producers and establishing hard budget constraints.

Between advocating intervention in some sectors and retreat in others, can the constraints-based approach be considered consistent in its view of the state's role in postsocialist reform? The approach clearly links a particular variable (hard budget constraints) to the success or failure of transitional reform, but does the theory provide us with any consistent notion of the state's role in these systems?

Perhaps the best way to begin understanding what a theory *is* is to understand expressly what it is *not*. The constraints-based approach is not another model of the state-centric variety used to explain growth in the newly industrializing countries of East Asia. This work's advocacy for limited intervention in the postcommand SOE sector is decidedly different from the "developmental state" notions associated with Japan, Korea, and Taiwan.[1] Explanations of East Asian growth often begin from the premise that successful development in the twentieth century – whether in Europe, China, or anywhere else – entails a process by which state actors strategically and aggressively manipulate domestic and international markets to serve national interests.[2] The state is described as a unitary force, a unidimensional actor that can either help or hinder development. In its most positive light, the state – through its massive concentration of power and human capital – is the only body capable of pushing modernization through in a competitive and potentially hostile world.[3] By directly intervening at both the macro and micro levels, state actors are presumed to achieve economic growth beyond what the market alone could produce.

The means by which the state actually achieves these outcomes is subject to some dispute among scholars. For some observers of East Asian patterns, developmentally minded state actors are important to the extent that they concentrate and direct capital into areas where private investors are unwilling to venture.[4] In other words, the state, by deliberately raising incentives and lowering risks for investors, encourages capital flow into economically transformative projects from which private entrepreneurs would normally shy away.[5]

Other scholars have suggested that, in successful late developers, the state acts more directly by deliberately attempting to distort relative market prices in order to stimulate economic growth.[6] The state uses subsidies to directly discipline large industrial firms and to encourage those firms to pursue outward-looking, export-oriented patterns of growth. In the case of South Korea, Alice Amsden asserts that the state intentionally "got prices wrong" by using a combination of selective tariffs, quotas, export subsidies, and subsidized credit.[7] Infant industries were protected from foreign competition and were simultaneously provided clear financial incentives to export.[8] Conversely, firms that performed poorly in healthy industries were deliberately penalized by the government, deprived of bailout loans, and often allowed to founder. In a general sense, the state is portrayed as the great mediator, transcending the market in order to achieve growth of unprecedented magnitude with unprecedented speed.

Perhaps the most popularized embodiment of the developmental state concept is Japan's Ministry of International Trade and Industry (MITI), a model that has clearly influenced interpreters of Chinese rural development.[9] This ministry was described in its peak years as meticulously using powers over credit provision and taxation to select key industries as the locomotives of national, export-oriented growth. The agency was the ultimate autonomous bureaucracy, the "greatest concentration of brainpower in Japan," and the mechanism by which Japan achieved an ultra-efficient, growth-oriented mode of economic coordination unimaginable on the free market.[10] According to this view, objective and highly skilled government bureaucrats were in charge, working directly with individual firms in order to plot a course of national development.[11] Whether or not MITI actually lived up to its legendary status, the ministry has become a powerful role model internationally, leading to similar organizations in nations as diverse as Korea and Hungary.

Indeed, the idea has spawned powerful imitators not only in the academic world, and not only among China's local rural cadres, but also at the very centers of power in Beijing. That alone is reason enough to focus on just how the role of the state should be interpreted in conceptual terms. One need not probe deeply in Beijing to come across central policy makers feverishly "picking" the key industry that will serve as the locomotive of Chinese growth for the twenty-first century. Yesterday it was steel, today automobiles, and tomorrow perhaps aerospace. Whether analytically supported or not, the developmental state idea attracts politicians like spotlights attract moths.

Even in the most sober academic circles, the East Asian "developmental state" notion has been kept alive – albeit in a somewhat understated fashion – by the influential World Bank publication, *The East Asian Miracle*.[12] The view presented in *The East Asian Miracle* builds upon the neoclassical emphasis on markets for guiding efficient resource allocation, but acknowledges that state intervention may be needed in cases of market failure. The basic idea is that successful developers pursue "market-friendly" strategies of maintaining macroeconomic stability, investing appropriately in human capital, ensuring a competitive climate for private enterprise, and promoting openness to international trade.[13] Interventions beyond these fundamental market-facilitating measures – in other words, interventions that attempt to go one step further by directly guiding resource allocation – are viewed with suspicion.

Certainly, most of the East Asian developmental states did make some effort to guide resource allocation directly, primarily through policies that targeted specific industries for growth. Nevertheless, the World Bank report finds little evidence that these interventions produced anything beyond market-conforming results.[14] In short, the direct interventions produced outcomes that markets would likely have produced on their own.

However, the World Bank showers praise on East Asian governments for actively intervening to keep markets open, inflation under control, and currencies properly valued – all in the context of privatized, nonsocialist systems. Clearly, the more conservative World Bank view emphasizes the facilitation of markets rather than the transcendence of markets, but the state is still portrayed as a key actor. The basic notion of a developmental state is left untrammeled.

On the surface, the developmental state idea bears a certain resemblance to the forms of SOE intervention advocated by the nested problems approach. After all, in both cases the state becomes an agent for promoting positive economic outcomes. In both, the state deals directly with the firm, intervening (for better or worse) in the micro economy. That, though, is the extent of the similarity. In reality, it is hard to imagine two models that could be more dissimilar. In the developmental state model, the government is seen as a unitary actor, somehow facilitating or transcending markets in a fashion that promotes growth and industrialization. The state is the solution, and the market is the vehicle. In transitional systems, however, particularly with respect to large SOEs, the state constitutes a large part of the problem, and there is no functioning market to serve as a vehicle. There is no functioning market at least in part because the state fails to act in a unitary fashion. The state, rather than being an "it," is more aptly described as a "they," and "they" already intervene extensively at the firm level. "They" are not the brilliant constellations of talent attributed by Chalmers Johnson to MITI but are instead massive bureaucracies devoid of any clear mission or coordinating mechanism. They are the banks, the local governments, the central tax agencies, the every other agency searching for a mission after the collapse of command planning. When opportunities arise – namely, when soft budget constraints prevail – plenty of these state actors opt for rent seeking over growth promotion. The transitional agencies are barely capable of getting prices right or keeping their hands off the items being sold, much less of taking a giant step further and deliberately getting prices wrong for the good of the national economy.

Furthermore, that transitional systems face an SOE restructuring problem of greater magnitude than anything found in the rest of the developing world cannot be overstated. *Transitional systems are not developing market economies; they are economies trying to develop markets.* Moreover, they are industrialized economies built atop (and structured by) a system that for several decades operated as the complete antithesis of free markets. The result is a collection of the most complex economic actors possible: highly integrated companies with a host of potential agency problems but no market selection mechanisms for governing those actors. Under these circumstances, the immediate task in post-socialist transitions is not to do better than the market, or somehow to correct the market, but rather to create the bare essentials for a market.

As the constraints-based approach suggests, it hardly makes sense to worry about who owns these economic actors when ownership itself does not function. Until governance over complex economic actors has been established – in other words, until credit is tightened and market selection processes made to work – ownership, in any meaningful sense of the term, will fail to function. In a situation of nonfunctioning ownership, it makes little sense to worry about who holds the nonfunctioning ownership rights.

In concrete terms, the constraints-based approach does say something very specific with regard to policy sequencing. For large industrial producers, ownership restructuring within the firm cannot precede reform in external regulatory mechanisms. Privatization, corporatization, and other property-rights restructuring efforts will be to no avail in large firms if governance cannot function. Unless financial markets, accounting standards, and other key institutions of governance are made to operate on a commercially oriented basis, market reforms at the producer level will not result in value-enhancing behavior. Over the long term, real reform must occur in the regulatory environment, reform that has never quite materialized in contemporary China. Over the short term, policy makers must act decisively to insulate the firm from its external environment, which includes a malfunctioning banking system and a poorly coordinated fiscal system.

In a more general sense, however, the state cannot be viewed as some sort of magic bullet. Quite to the contrary, state intervention in transitional systems is for the most part counterproductive and, unfortunately, rampant. However, truly reform-minded state actors in such an environment will focus on devoting all their energies toward creating absolute baseline market conditions, the kind of market conditions that offer the possibility of sustained future growth. A key prerequisite for market ownership is the establishment of a functioning system of property rights – rights not in a "producer empowerment" sense but rights in the sense of linked power and accountability. The point is not that private ownership must be created, but rather that the basic grounds for ownership *itself* must be established. Economic producers must be required to face hard budgets. They must be permitted to reap the benefits of asset-expanding activity and be forced to absorb the costs of asset-destroying activity. In other words, the bare essentials for market-oriented interaction must be established where they have not arisen naturally or historically. In China's rural sectors, market conditions obtain today for a number of reasons relating to both history and the nature and size of the economic producers involved. In the urban state sector, populated primarily by complex industrial producers, barriers toward market operations are both substantially different and tremendously higher.

It is precisely in the SOE sector where state intervention is required. This is not market-facilitating intervention but rather market-creating intervention – intervention against fundamental obstacles to market activity. Until soft lending is curtailed and renegade agencies of the state are driven off, hard-budget conditions cannot prevail over the complex producers that constitute the urban industrial sector. Unless hard budget constraints prevail, corporate governance will fail to function, thus undermining ownership of any kind, public or private.

254

As long as ownership is undermined, value-enhancing behavior at the firm level will fail to evolve. In short, key actors in the central state must identify the problem and bring all their power to bear against a host of societal interests – interests that have been empowered by reform and have been presented with a host of rent-seeking opportunities. Intervention is needed neither to supersede the market nor to expand economic autonomy, but rather to impose the fundamental marketlike constraints that promote growth and establish "rights" in any economically meaningful sense of the term. Positive, growth-promoting state intervention must be directed against pervasive negative state intervention. In the SOE sector, the state must be brought in for the short term so that it can ultimately be moved out in the long term. There are no lofty goals here other than the most basic goal of all, the creation of a functioning market economy.

However, where basic marketlike constraints already exist, state intervention – particularly in the area of resource allocation – becomes either superfluous or patently destructive. In the Chinese TVE sector, economic producers and governments alike face hard-budget conditions, essentially by default. Because soft credit is generally unavailable, market selection operates. Those firms that perform well attract capital, and those that do not are driven from the market. There is no magical state intervention driving these processes forward. Indeed, predatory extraction is punished through the decapitalization and ultimate insolvency of the firm. Ownership works because most producers themselves are small. Agency problems are therefore either barely extant or decidedly minor, and market selection is allowed to function. Just as plenty of new entrants hit the market each year, plenty exit through bankruptcy. Given that markets essentially function and ownership essentially works in these rural environments, the likelihood of state intervention or ownership bringing added benefits becomes highly dubious. Hence the constraints-based approach, for the same minimalist reasons it advocates intervention in the SOE sector, assiduously rejects intervention in the TVE sector.

THE CONSTRAINTS-BASED APPROACH AND NEOCLASSICAL NOTIONS OF THE STATE

Oddly enough, the bare-bones objectives for intervention just described suggest that, if anything, the constraints-based approach should be equated with neoclassical perspectives on growth. The neoclassical view of development stresses "getting the basics right."[15] In order for sustained growth to occur, in this view, markets must be permitted to function – nothing more, and nothing less. For markets to function, there must be macroeconomic stability and a consistent legal code to guide economic transactions. There must be extensive domestic and international competition, unhampered by price controls or relative price distortions. Governments must get out of the business of directly running firms and instead focus on providing a stable environment for investment.

The constraints-based model subscribes unconditionally to these broad goals, but objects strenuously to the neoclassical emphasis on private ownership as both a vehicle for and measure of economic success. Neoclassical perspectives identify markets as the drivers of growth and private ownership as the driver of markets.[16] This connection between the question of "who owns" and the viability of growth may be pertinent to developed market economies or even to developing market economies (though even there, room for argument exists). What cannot be emphasized enough, however, is that transitional systems are *not* developing market economies. Again, they are economies, and often already industrialized economies, trying desperately to develop markets. In other words, they are – at least with regard to the modern industrial sector – pre-existing systems, on pre-existing trajectories, facing the historically unprecedented task of reversing course and shifting over to an entirely new mode of economic allocation.

Certainly, it would be nice if politicians could be summarily chased out of the firm in transitional environments. It would be nice if all the problems of SOE reform could be wished away through rapid privatization. The problem, though, is that the anti–state-ownership, pro-privatization views of the neoclassical school actually assume a level of coherent state intervention well beyond what currently exists in countries like China. As a result, these scholars focus on the question of "who owns" before the institution of ownership itself has been established. Advocates of privatization seem to take for granted the existence of governments that can provide laws to protect property rights, rules to regulate property transfers, and mechanisms to ensure proper effective corporate governance in complex producers. In modern capitalist systems, such institutions and mechanisms flow virtually unnoticed from the state. A basic but actually quite complex degree of governmental intervention is tolerated – indeed, taken for granted – simply to make the market economy function.

Unfortunately, even this minimalist degree of *regulatory* intervention is well beyond what transitional countries like China currently enjoy. It is well beyond what transitional governments in general are capable of providing. Of course, in transitional systems there is no lack of state intervention, but there is precious little of the coherent, subtle, coordinated government action that makes a modern industrial economy work. With so many renegade agencies and so little coordinated government regulation, the Chinese state industrial sector takes on something of a "Dodge City" atmosphere. There are few rules, few responsibilities, many cases of the strong preying upon the weak, and a tremendous amount of waste. You can privatize under these circumstances, but doing so will neither get the government out of the firm nor yield a functioning market.

The purpose of relinking the complex urban firm to the state under these circumstances is neither to move backward toward the old system nor to leap forward toward some highly interventionist model characteristic of Japan or Korea. Rather, the goal is to move the Chinese state sector from Dodge City to the bare-bones market that neoclassical approaches advocate. To reach the neoclassical objective, direct state intervention into individual SOEs is needed, and is needed quickly.[17] To meet the challenge of SOE reform in transitional systems, one must bring the state in to get the state out.

In effect, the real question involves determining how to create market outcomes in systems that have neither the institutional nor legal mechanisms essential for market operations in a developed economy. What advocates of rapid privatization end up doing is simply wishing the problem away. They hope that, by passing a few regulations and declaring firms "private," state intervention will disappear and firms will behave just as textbook capitalist businesses do. As the cases of China's corporatized SOEs suggest, the real world unfortunately does not work this way. Neither state intervention nor producer rent seeking goes away simply because one wants them to or because laws are passed against them. Particularly in a pre-existing complex industrial economy – as opposed to an industrializing rural environment – markets and market-oriented behavior do not arise spontaneously but instead must be actively created, and created against stiff opposition. The complex, urban industrial sector must be made, through state intervention, to face the same budget constraints that bear down almost naturally (or at least by historical accident) on many rural industrializing areas. In transitional systems, there is only one organization with enough power to undertake this task: the very state that was causing so much trouble in the first place.

Yet, even the limited type of intervention advocated by the constraints-based approach can serve only as a temporary measure. It is a stop-gap attempt to restore hard budgets and the basic preconditions for market selection to the urban industrialized sector, those portions of the economy inherited from the days of command planning. In the long run, though, countries like China will struggle to develop the institutional, regulatory, and legal mechanisms that make markets functions in a stable and standardized fashion. As the recent financial debacle at Shougang suggests, China, even in its more progressive experiments, has yet to realize fully the corporate governance mechanisms – particularly with regard to functioning financial markets – that are needed to regulate large enterprises in an industrial economy. The country still has many obstacles to overcome in its transition to the market.

SOE RESTRUCTURING AND IMAGES OF CHINA

The preceding chapters on SOE reform, while partly attempting to address the-oretical debates, have also attempted to speak to popular images of China, par-ticularly images held in the West. Increasingly through the 1990s, China has come to be viewed as both a wonderful economic prize and a rising interna-tional menace, a country that offers tremendous markets for foreign business but one that also refuses to play by commonly accepted rules of the game. On almost every front – human rights, trade policy, arms control, intellectual property-rights protection, birth-control policies, environmental protection – China is portrayed as a country that not only flouts the rules, but flouts them with unbridled malevolence. Perhaps clearest of all, as China grows phenome-nally rich it forbids foreign competitors from enjoying the fruits of its market. Horror stories abound from foreigners doing business in China. That foreign business concerns repeatedly lose money in an environment of impressive na-tional growth is seen as another indicator of China's intrinsic recalcitrance.

The growing hostility toward China is not entirely without reason, nor has China always adopted the most cooperative of stances with regard to the out-side world. Like many countries, China has a host of problems in many of the areas most frequently cited, including human rights, political expression, environmental protection, and market access. Furthermore, extremely sensi-tive to intrusions upon national sovereignty, Chinese leaders have frequently met foreign criticism with either stony silence or utter denial. China does have problems, and many of those problems are legitimately the concern of the in-ternational community.

However, the preceding chapters on China's collapsing SOE sector should inject, at the very least, a note of caution. China is a growing nation but one beset by colossal economic problems. It is a country whose banking system and modern industrial sector are on the verge of collapse, and one that is con-templating the ever-growing possibility of widespread urban unemployment and industrial stagnation. Meanwhile, it is a country whose government is less and less equipped to cope with these mounting problems. Revenues have be-come increasingly difficult to collect, economic information has become in-creasingly distorted, and the state bureaucracy has become increasingly dis-united. Although the integrity of the nation is not in doubt, the ability of the government to cope with its mounting economic troubles definitely is. China today is a country whose biggest problems, in some respects, stem more from *lack* of regulation than from excessive regulation.

In such an environment, it is not entirely surprising that foreigners have had trouble making money in China. As the preceding case studies have illustrated, many of the problems about which foreigners complain – and frequently attribute to unfair rules of the game – also afflict Chinese domestic producers. The rules continually change, state agencies frequently place themselves above the rules, and many economic actors simply ignore the rules altogether. When major SOEs like Angang can force neither creditors to pay nor local agencies to obey firm-level boundaries nor distributors to deliver goods, it is no wonder that foreign firms attempting to operate in China's modern industrial sector face the same problems. Interestingly, the one area that has grown substantially, the rural industrial sector, avoids most of these problems entirely by exporting a large share of its output. As best as it can, it avoids the problems of the domestic market by locating near the coast and simply shipping its goods out to foreign markets. In fact, China's prime export sector happens to be its least regulated, least subsidized, and least politically connected; it is precisely the sector that has been cut off from a banking system preoccupied with supporting state industry.

There are numerous lessons to be learned from this situation, not the least of which is that China may be a tremendously overrated market for Western industrial goods. When Western firms fail to earn money in China, perhaps the first assumption should not be that the cause involves Chinese malevolence and market protection. Protectionism obviously exists, but perhaps the first area to which we should turn for understanding is the experience of Chinese domestic firms. There is no reason to believe that outsiders should be any more successful negotiating the Chinese market than their counterparts in Chinese domestic industry (e.g., Shougang, Angang, Magang). The situation in China today is chaotic for a whole range of economic producers, foreign and domestic. As this study has tried to suggest, the problems stem as much from lack of control as from excessive control, and as much from governmental incapacity as from malevolence. Foreign business seems to operate under the assumption that, because China has experienced economic growth, the nation's domestic market must be raring to absorb almost every good imaginable, from consumer products to capital machinery. When problems arise, the first reaction is to blame trade barriers. Interestingly, foreign business concerns rarely seem to step back and reconsider whether their initial assessment of the Chinese market was accurate. Perhaps a more realistic view would be that China's market is intrinsically uncertain, extremely undeveloped, and possibly ill-equipped to absorb the capital-intensive goods and services offered by many foreign concerns. Perhaps this is not a country that can or should be purchasing airplanes, automobiles, power plants, and heavy machinery in great quantity. Given the financial morass surrounding the prime purchasers of these goods – state-owned firms and state agencies – how long should we expect the buying to continue, and how wronged should we feel when the buying tails off?

Certainly the most immediate lesson of this study is that, when confronting China and its national policy makers, the outside world should be willing to accept a dose of humility. China is a nation with monumental economic problems, problems for which nobody has clear solutions. As the history of SOE reform suggests, Chinese policy makers in the reform era have made serious mistakes, but they have also shown extraordinary flexibility, pragmatism, and ingenuity. Many Chinese policy makers, for all the newfound wealth of their nation, still perceive the country as teetering on the edge of catastrophic poverty. In some respects, their perception is correct. As they wrestle with unprecedented problems, many policy makers truly do seek to improve the lot of the average Chinese citizen. If nothing else, this period of great uncertainty and looming economic crisis warrants from outsiders a stance more of cooperation and caution than outright confrontation. It warrants cooperation not because China's emergence as a great power is in the world's interest but rather because China's utter collapse, and all the problems associated with that collapse – widespread urban poverty, potential social unrest, and increased environmental depredation – is decidedly not.

Notes

CHAPTER 1

1. For a detailed discussion of growth data, see World Bank (1996a).
2. This was singled out as the key issue at the Fifteenth Party Congress, and was subject of Jiang Zemin's keynote address.
3. For a discussion of firm-level behavior in socialist command economies, see Kornai (1980, 1992).
4. State enterprise restructuring, particularly the opening up of 10,000 of the largest SOEs to joint stock ownership, was a major focus of China's Fifteenth Party Congress in September of 1997. See Jiang Zemin, "Holding High the Great Banner of Deng Xiaoping Theory, Carrying the Cause of Building Socialism With Chinese Characteristics to the 21st Century," Report to the Fifteenth CPC National Congress (12 September 1997), Xinhua Domestic Service (21 September 1997), in FBIS document no. CHI-97-264.
5. For a comprehensive account of the whole process of "growing beyond the plan," see Naughton (1995).
6. For a more detailed discussion of the costs of deferring state-sector reform, see Lardy (forthcoming).
7. The notion of a "hard" versus a "soft" budget constraint was developed by János Kornai; see Kornai (1980; 1992, pp. 140–5). A firm's budget constraint is said to be "soft" when the long-term viability of the firm becomes unrelated to the firm's profitability or liquidity. In other words, no matter how much money the firm loses, it can continue to count on subsidies or credit to maintain operations.
8. See Broadman (1995), World Bank (1997), and Lardy (forthcoming, Chapters 1 and 3).
9. Corporatization refers to the transformation of the firm into a modern joint stock corporation, with shares issued to a wide range of public and private holders.
10. Market behavior in this sense implies efforts by actors to expand the value of their assets by responding to market forces of supply and demand. Market-oriented firms attempt to produce goods whose value exceeds that of the inputs needed to make those goods. Of course, associated with this are efforts to increase profits by cutting costs or increasing sales, as well as meeting financial obligations – to creditors, investors, workers, and other stakeholders – within an assigned period.
11. Chandler (1977, pp. 9–10). See also Berle and Means (1968, pp. 112–16).

261

12. In the socialist command economy, they can rest assured that the firm will be kept afloat through government investment.
13. For a brief summary of these internal and external mechanisms, see World Bank (1997, p. 12).
14. Perkins (1994, pp. 27–8) describes five generally accepted steps a command economy must take to evolve into a functioning market economy: (1) macro stability must be achieved, (2) inputs and outputs must be made available for sale and purchase on the open market, (3) prices must be freed up to reflect relative scarcities, (4) barriers to market entry must be lifted and competition achieved, and (5) decision makers in production units must have an incentive to maximize profits by cutting costs or raising sales. China has been quite effective in negotiating steps (1)–(4) but far less effective with step (5), particularly with regard to the modern industrial sector.
15. For an historical overview of these policy measures, see Naughton (1995), Shirk (1993), and Byrd (1992).
16. At the end of 1995, it was estimated that some nine million workers in the industrial Northeast were failing to receive regular paychecks; see Chen (1996). State-owned enterprises serve as havens for surplus labor in urban industrial areas, essentially disbursing through wages what in most systems would be considered unemployment benefits.
17. It is ironic to see how similar complaints by Chinese central officials about local noncompliance with national regulations mirror the complaints made by Liu Shaoqi in the early 1960s regarding local and firm-level noncompliance with the plan (see Liu 1991). Similarly, a perfectly reasonable explanation of the economic disaster surrounding the Great Leap Forward is that localities failed to comply, yet this time in the direction of *over*compliance. They were simply too enthusiastic in the starting of "backyard" steel furnaces, too eager to outstrip assigned agricultural and industrial quotas, and too willing to implement ill-advised production techniques (see Bernstein 1984).
18. State Statistical Bureau (1996, p. 401).
19. Qian and Xu (1993, p. 138). The authors provide an excellent general summary of the categories (pp. 138–40).
20. Qian and Xu (1993, p. 138).
21. Some of the case studies explored in later chapters fall under this category, but even those firms have at various times and under various circumstances been placed under the authority of local agencies.
22. Many of the benefits distributed by the state firm have come to be considered *rights* by Chinese workers – that is, rights to which the citizens of a socialist country are entitled. Particularly for workers old enough to recall the prereform era, the withdrawal of these rights by the state would be considered a grievous offense, much worse than any abstract restrictions on freedom of speech, religion, or belief, and much more worthy of mass protest.
23. Unquestionably, the property-rights arrangement of these generally small firms is far clearer than that of large SOEs – but also, for that matter, of any modern industrial firm. As the following chapters will argue, property rights in any large firm (whether a Chinese SOE or a public corporation in the United States) are by

definition complicated and unclear. It is therefore highly questionable to suggest that the *reason* why collectives "work" while SOEs do not is because property rights over the former are clearer than those over the latter. Unclear property rights in large industrial producers is a constant, whether or not those firms are successful, and whether they exist in China or the West.

24. For a variety of views, see Walder (1994), Oi (1992), World Bank (1996a, p. 66), Lardy (forthcoming, Chapter 1), and Perkins (1994).
25. See William A. Byrd, "Entrepreneurship, Capital, and Ownership," in Byrd and Lin (1990, pp. 189–207).
26. For an interesting discussion of this topic, see Naughton (1992). The article correctly shows that collectives grew initially in the postreform era by capturing monopoly rents from SOEs. The small size of collectives also reduces the saliency of governance issues for these firms.
27. Qian and Xu (1993, p. 139).
28. China's gross value of industrial output in nominal terms by 1995 was over twenty times that of 1978 (see State Statistical Bureau, *China Statistical Yearbook*, various years). In 1993, the growth rate of SOEs was 6.4 percent, whereas that of the TVE component of collectives was 41.3 percent (Broadman 1995, p. 7).
29. "Large-scale" in this sense pertains to firms with over 500 employees (*dazhongxing qiye*); see Naughton (1995, p. 164).
30. This is in part because Chinese policy makers have been loath to cede control over what are viewed as "pillar" national industries, and in part because the kinds of reforms that would bring greater competition in the sector – through either increased entry by nonstate firms or exit by failing state concerns – have simply been deferred.
31. State Statistical Bureau (1996, p. 90).
32. State Statistical Bureau (1996, p. 87). In 1995, there were 112.6 million urban workers in SOEs. Ninety-seven percent of those employees were classified as "formal employees," presumably eligible for the full range of social welfare benefits accorded workers in the state sector.
33. Broadman (1995, p. 8).
34. State Statistical Bureau (1996, p. 221).
35. Naughton (1992, pp. 15–16).
36. Lardy (forthcoming, Table 2.3). "Within budget" refers to industrial SOEs that are classified by the state as independent accounting units and that have received direct subsidies from the central government. See also Broadman (1995, note, p. 12).
37. Lardy (forthcoming, Table 2.3). However, it could be argued that these aggregate losses were shrinking relative to GDP.
38. Acknowledgment was made by the State Statistical Bureau. See Wang Yong, "Key State Firms Set to Revive," *China Daily (Business Weekly)* (15 September 1997), in FBIS document no. CHI-97-258.
39. Lardy (forthcoming, Chapter 1).
40. For an excellent discussion of this topic see Broadman (1995, pp. 13–15). Explicit subsidies are direct allocations to unprofitable firms, whereas implicit subsidies are directed investment for fixed assets and for funding the recipient firm's operating expenses. They are all, in effect, bailout loans to keep the firm running.

41. In 1985, government revenue was 22.4 percent of GDP. By 1990 the percentage had dropped to 15.8, and by 1995 it was down to 10.7 percent (State Statistical Bureau 1996, pp. 22–3). A sort of feedback loop has developed. The state in recent years has been capturing less and less of GDP, in large part because its prime source of revenue, state industry, is stagnating. Hence the state has fewer resources at its disposal for bailing out unprofitable SOEs and is unwilling to run up large fiscal deficits; instead, it shifts SOE funding over to the state banking sector.
42. Lardy (forthcoming, Chapter 1). See also Broadman (1995, p. 15).
43. Lardy (forthcoming, Table 3.1).
44. Lardy (forthcoming, Chapter 3).
45. Naughton (1995, p. 264). Book value is defined by Naughton as the depreciated value of fixed assets plus the value of accumulated inventory.
46. Lardy (forthcoming, Table 2.5).
47. As will be illustrated in the case studies, firms overstate the value of their inventories, overstate the value of their receivables (firms are frequently unwilling to write off "nonperforming loans" to purchasers), and underestimate or thoroughly neglect depreciation.
48. Statement attributed to Qiu Xiaohua, chief economist of China's State Statistical Bureau (see Chen 1996).
49. Ministry of Metallurgical Industry (1995b, p. 4).
50. This author routinely heard complaints by Ministry of Metallurgical Industry officials during the same period that workers at several major national steel conglomerates were going unpaid. The percentage cited is from Chen (1996).
51. The case of Capital Iron and Steel (Shougang), described in detail in Chapter 6, is a good example.
52. Lardy (forthcoming, Chapter 3). See also "Small Change, China's Banks Labour with the Baggage of Their Past," *Far Eastern Economic Review* (8 August 1996), p. 62, and "China Scrambles to Avert Banking Crisis," *Wall Street Journal* (6 August 1996).
53. "Small Change, China's Banks Labour with the Baggage of Their Past," *Far Eastern Economic Review* (8 August 1996), p. 62. Estimates are based on a study reportedly undertaken by Liu Yucao of Nankai University in Tianjin.
54. Broadman (1995, note, p. 15). The central bank's capacity to extend these loans is actually supported by lending quotas that are distributed to banks nationwide. Banks in regions of the country with high levels of household savings deposits but low levels of state industry (i.e., the South) are bound by low lending ceilings. These banks have little choice but to place their deposits into the interest-bearing accounts of the PBC. Alternatively, banks in regions with low deposits but high levels of state industry (e.g., the industrial Northeast) are granted high lending levels, levels ultimately supported by PBC funds. The net effect in the most general sense works out to a redistribution of funds from high-growth to low-growth areas and from households in the South to SOEs in the Northeast. See Lardy (forthcoming, Chapter 3).
55. One example is the Huaxia Bank, initially an arm of the Capital Iron and Steel Group. This bank will be discussed in greater detail in Chapter 6.

56. World Bank (1997, p. xi).
57. See Seth Faison, "In Major Shift, China Will Sell State Industries," *New York Times* (12 September 1997), and "Zhu Rongji Addresses World Bank Meeting," Xinhua Domestic Service (24 Sepember 1997), in FBIS document no. CHI-97-267. See also Jiang Zemin's 1997 Report to Fifteenth Party Congress, in FBIS document no. CHI-97-264.

CHAPTER 2

1. See Adam Smith (reprinted 1986) and Coase (1959). For the perspective translated into the contemporary transitional context, see Boycko, Shleifer, and Vishny (1995) and Frydman and Rapaczynski (1994).
2. For clear statements of the privatization perspective, see Boycko et al. (1995), Frydman and Rapaczynski (1994), and Sachs (1993).
3. Coase (1959, p. 14).
4. Note the similarity to the property-rights perspective afforded by local state corporatism in the Chinese context. There the idea is also that if property rights are clearly and coherently allocated to the correct actors – in this case, local governments – then efficient, market-oriented behavior will result.
5. Milgrom and Roberts (1992, p. 288).
6. Pryor (1973, pp. 7–8); Milgrom and Roberts (1992, p. 289).
7. Pryor (1973, p. 2).
8. For a detailed explanation, see Grossman and Hart (1986).
9. Milgrom and Roberts (1992, p. 289).
10. Milgrom and Roberts (1992, p. 291).
11. As will be noted later, the property-rights perspective does not, however, simply assume that all producers will be effective in realizing their productivity-maximizing goals. The market itself is needed to sort out the successful from the unsuccessful.
12. Milgrom and Roberts (1992, p. 288).
13. For a more detailed discussion, see R. H. Coase, "Notes on the Problem of Social Cost," in Coase (1988).
14. Coase (1959, p. 25).
15. Jones (1982, p. 5). For a more detailed discussion, see Aharoni (1986).
16. Yair Aharoni, "State-Owned Enterprise: An Agent without a Principal," in Jones (1982, p. 69).
17. In this view, privatization is considered to be essentially the same whether pursued in the most developed of market economies or in the most troubled of postcommunist systems. For example, depoliticization of the SOE was clearly a major objective of the U.K. privatization efforts associated with "Thatcherism." See Lawson (1992; cited also in Boycko et al. 1995, p. 11) and Stiglitz (1994, p. 1).
18. For an intelligent explication of the privatization argument for Eastern Europe, see Sachs (1993). Sachs notes on p. 2 the "uncharted territory" nature of sweeping privatization.
19. Earle, Estrin, and Leschenko (1995, p. 1).
20. Economist Intelligence Unit (1996b, p. 14).

21. Czech Statistical Office figure, cited in Economist Intelligence Unit (1996a, p. 15).
22. Economist Intelligence Unit (1996c, p. 15).
23. Corporatization refers to the valuation of SOE assets and subsequent distribution of equity shares to specific owners, either inside the state bureaucracy or in the private sector. This is a key step before any formerly socialist SOE can be privatized through sale of shares on securities markets. By the early 1990s, China had corporatized approximately 3,000 SOEs. See Wu (1993, p. 210). See also State Statistical Bureau (1994, p. 378).
24. For example, see Li (1992, pp. 12–13).
25. See especially Boycko et al. (1995, pp. 121–3).
26. Earle et al. (1995, p. 25). In this study of 439 Russian companies, the authors found surprisingly little variation in incentives and performance between old state-owned enterprises and newly privatized firms. Newer firms started after the end of communism did show better performance outcomes, but old firms that had undergone privatization appeared far less able to shed habits of the past.
27. Sachs (1993, p. 2).
28. Frydman and Rapaczynski (1994, p. 51).
29. Czech Statistical Office figure, cited in Economist Intelligence Unit (1996a, p. 15).
30. As indicated earlier, widespread shutdowns are dangerous under such circumstances because the standards for evaluating performance and for distinguishing "good," efficient, viable firms from "bad," inefficient, nonviable ones become so unclear. Destruction of the entire industrial sector runs the risk of pulling down the good with the bad, thus destroying what few economic assets the nation possesses.
31. At times this has undoubtedly been caused by policy disputes at the elite level and the resulting lack of any sort of consensus on reform strategy. More typically, though, the experimental attitude seems to grow out of a generally agreed upon attitude of caution. In its attempts to reform socialism, China is in many cases moving down an unknown path. Given the absence of historical precedents, individual reform measures often have unknown consequences. Hence, policy makers are reluctant to subject the entire system to any single measure. Specific reforms are attempted on a small scale and, if successful, are then gradually disseminated nationwide.
32. Oddly enough, as the case studies will make clear, those large-scale SOEs that have been drawn in closer to *local* governments tend to perform miserably. In other words, the local state corporatism (LSC) variant of property-rights theory – the notion that granting property rights to local governments solves firm-level incentive problems – fails to hold for the SOE. Neither the privatization nor the LSC view accurately describes the problems of the urban SOE; see also Chapter 7.
33. See especially Boycko et al. (1995, pp. 10–11, 30–3).
34. Privatization advocates are not the only ones who describe the reform process as one of transferring property rights. Similar modes of analysis are often used to describe effective local–state ownership in China; see Walder (1994).
35. Coase (1959, p. 15).
36. Frydman and Rapaczynski (1994) also make this point and confront it in their work.
37. Boycko et al. (1995, p. 9) make precisely this assertion in their description of the fundamental beliefs underpinning Russian privatization.

38. See Chandler (1977).
39. Of course, this broad generalization should be qualified. The requirements of the steel industry in the early part of the century, requirements that focused on scale economies in a relatively stable technological environment, clearly differ from those of a biotech firm today trying to engineer new cures for disease. Nevertheless, the common features concern the significant capital requirements – either to build production facilities in the former case or to conduct research and development in the latter – and the monumental challenges involved in managing complex information and operations in both cases.
40. Milgrom and Roberts (1992, p. 314).
41. Milgrom and Roberts (1992, p. 315).
42. Williamson (1985, p. 19).
43. Alchian and Demsetz (1972).
44. Aoki and Kim (1995, p. xi).

CHAPTER 3

1. In a sense, the equivalent in a property-rights–based system would be predatory governmental taxation upon private owners. The owners still hold residual rights to cash flow, but the government imposes taxes at such high levels that nothing is left to constitute the residual. Such extraction is performed on the basis not of ownership but of the raw power of state authority.
2. *Rent seeking* refers to efforts to realize earnings without actually contributing to production.
3. As will be discussed in Chapter 7, this is a key difference between urban SOEs and rural TVEs in China. The urban SOE has access to the state banking system and also has no real risk of liquidation. Big SOEs do not go bankrupt in China. However, TVEs are quite different. They generally do not have access to state lending, which is underscored by the fact that 70 percent of bank lending in China still goes to the state sector. Partially as a result, there is not only tremendous entry into the TVE sector but also tremendous exit from it: thousands of TVEs go bankrupt every year. That these firms do have an ultimate budget constraint – the fact that many actually do go under – severely constrains rent-seeking behavior by government officials and managers alike.
4. The point is not that market-oriented behavior necessarily guarantees firm-level success. What it does, however, is create the possibility for success. It signals the decline of institutional barriers to success, and it shifts responsibility back to firm-level variables such as managerial ability, product differentiation, and strategy.
5. For important differences between the Chinese and Soviet models, see Qian and Xu (1993).
6. For a more thorough description, see Naughton (1995, pp. 26–33).
7. This was in part due to necessity – the Chinese desperately lacked trained bureaucrats to coordinate planning – and in part a reflection of Mao Zedong's emphasis on local self-reliance and disdain for bureaucratic stagnation.
8. Interview, former planner, Ministry of Machine Tools.

9. This, in essence, is the "ratchet effect."
10. See Kornai (1992, pp. 160–3).
11. In other words, the pattern of managers overstating needs and planners systematically deflating those firm-level requests undoubtedly led to many allocative errors and production bottlenecks. Similarly, the pattern of allocating to high-priority firms and withholding from other firms, regardless of their respective needs, also led to misallocation and inefficiency. This is indisputable. What is also indisputable, however, is that these planning mechanisms did cap the extent to which soft-budget demands for inputs were actually met. For a more detailed discussion of these patterns, see Chapter 4.
12. The notion of *moral hazard* applies to situations in which types of insurance encourage the very forms of behavior that are intended to be insured against. For example, having fire insurance may disincline a property owner to invest in sprinkler systems or other fire-preventing mechanisms. The fire insurance encourages behavior more likely to result in dangerous fires. With regard to the financial sector, knowledge that the government will insure deposits and provide bailout funds may encourage high-risk lending among bankers.
13. Undoubtedly, a certain amount of corruption attends some of these transactions. In return for steering centrally funded high-risk loans, the banker receives a side payment from the borrower.
14. Much of this general comparison between market and planned systems comes from Kornai (1992, pp. 97–103, 447–50).
15. Frydman and Rapaczynski (1994, p. 10).
16. Pryor (1973, pp. 40–1).
17. Kornai (1992, p. 53).
18. The implication here is not necessarily that local officials are engaged in corruption, though opportunities for corruption undoubtedly exist. Often, such ad hoc revenue collection serves to fund completely legitimate government activities. The problem involves more the rationality of the system than the criminality of the personnel involved.
19. Stiglitz (1994, p. 182).
20. Stiglitz (1994, p. 183). As Stiglitz notes, with so much "noise" – exogenous distortions in firm-level performance data – any government threat to cut off firm-level subsidies becomes highly noncredible.
21. Taxation here refers not only to formal taxes but also to informal fees and levies imposed upon the firm.
22. Naughton (1995, pp. 254–5).
23. Banks monitored only to the extent that they were in charge of keeping separate investment and operating accounts for the individual firm. Firm-level profits as well as allocated investments were kept in these accounts, which essentially belonged to central planners rather than to the firm itself. In other words, banks permitted firms access to these accounts only in accordance with orders flowing down from the planners. The banks, however, were not charged with actually monitoring investments once the funds left the accounts. Again, the banks were simply the cashiers, making sure the cash drawer opened only when dictated by higher-level state officials.

24. Lardy (1992, pp. 32–3). Lardy notes that, between the 1950s and early 1970s, the ICOR (ratio of gross investment to absolute increase in output) figures for Chinese industry rose by more than 80 percent, from 3.0 to 5.5. This occurred even though, by the 1970s, Chinese planners were allocating less and less capital to housing and other "nonproductive" investments.
25. Stiglitz (1994, p. 211).
26. Stiglitz (1994, p. 209).
27. Naughton (1995, p. 255).
28. Stark (1996, p. 1012).
29. Perkins (1994, note, p. 39).
30. Perkins (1994, p. 38).
31. Stark (1996, p. 1014).
32. Stark (1996, p. 1014).
33. Stark (1996, p. 1015) makes a similar (albeit more extensive) list of potential firm-level claims for bailout funds in transitional systems.

CHAPTER 4

1. This chapter is based in part on a series of interviews conducted at the Anshan Iron and Steel Company in November 1994, as well as interviews at the Wuhan Iron and Steel Company in August 1994. I am also indebted to Mr. Ken-ichi Imai of the Institute of Developing Economies in Tokyo for providing me with records of his own interviews conducted at Angang in October 1994.
2. Anshan Iron and Steel has been in operation since 1919; Wuhan Iron and Steel has been in operation since 1958. See Ministry of Metallurgical Industry (1993). A comprehensive account of Angang's history prior to the founding of the People's Republic in 1949 can be found in Xie and Zhang (1984).
3. China was, and still is, a country in which capital is scarce and labor plentiful. Because of these factor endowments, real interest rates (the price of capital) have always tended to be high, prohibitively high for the development of heavy industry. Under such conditions, normal market forces favor the development of light, non–capital-intensive industry. To develop heavy industry under such circumstances, market forces must be directly challenged and factor prices intentionally distorted. Capital must be made inexpensive through forcefully constrained interest rates. Once interest rates are forced downward, however, *everybody* wants capital. Command planning – which in effect substitutes direct allocation for market allocation – becomes necessary to ensure that, once factor prices are intentionally distorted, scarce capital actually moves toward heavy industry. Command planning, whether effective or not, does have a logic. It allows poor, agricultural countries in a relatively short period of time to marshal societal resources and channel them to firms like Angang. For a complete discussion of the logic of the plan, see Lin, Cai, and Li (1996, pp. 19–90).
4. As will be shown, Angang's assets have become increasingly composed of relatively unmarketable inventories and nonperforming loans extended to steel consumers.
5. Interviews, Anshan Iron and Steel.

6. Data on firm-level liabilities became available only after accounting standards were shifted in 1993.
7. Angang's current ratio (current assets divided by current liabilities) moved from 0.76 in 1993 to 0.96 in 1994, and then back down to 0.80 in 1995. See Ministry of Metallurgical Industry (1995, p. 355; 1996, p. 389). Although neither "published" in any commercial sense nor available for purchase, these detailed statistical volumes are made available to domestic and foreign personnel involved in Chinese steel industry projects.
8. Ministry of Metallurgical Industry (1995d, p. 3). The extent to which firms accurately account for unpaid pension liabilities is the subject of considerable dispute in China today. Many industry experts within China feel that firms underestimate such liabilities.
9. Because so much bank lending in China amounts to little more than subsidization – interest rates are charged, but infrequently collected – the central government cannot simply manipulate the interest rate in order to cut back lending. Instead, credit is suspended.
10. Ministry of Metallurgical Industry (1995d, p. 3).
11. "Angang qing qian xiang chu xin zhe" [Angang's New Track in Debt Clearing], *Gongshang shibao* (31 October 1994). The article quotes a series of figures presented by Angang's chief economist at a Beijing conference on enterprise debt management.
12. Company figures from interviews.
13. Sales taxes in Chinese industry are levied primarily on the producer rather than the consumer.
14. Ministry of Metallurgical Industry (1995d, p. 3).
15. Ministry of Metallurgical Industry (1995, p. 355; 1996, p. 389).
16. Ministry of Metallurgical Industry (1995b, pp. 8–9).
17. Technically, the MMI data for Wuhan Iron and Steel is presented in the form of a "statement of changes in financial position" that shows both changes in working capital balances during a given period and changes in the working capital accounts themselves. See Stickney and Weil (1994, p. G-85). These statements are still used in China today, but have generally been replaced in the West by the standard "statement of cash flows."
18. Ministry of Metallurgical Industry (1995b, pp. 8–9).
19. Interviews, Angang Institute of Management and Angang Economics Institute.
20. Interview, retired planner, Shougang Economics and Technology Development Company.
21. A comprehensive discussion of this history of administrative reorganization is presented in Byrd (1992, pp. 309–16).
22. Byrd (1992, p. 310).
23. Byrd (1992, p. 310).
24. Interview, Angang manager.
25. Byrd (1992, p. 312).
26. For a detailed analysis of contract responsibility systems in Chinese industry, see Chen (1995). For a more political analysis, see Shirk (1993).

27. Details on the exact stipulations of the contract were provided by the Angang Economics Institute.
28. The profit submissions for 1986 were used as a base level.
29. Wages were supposed to rise with pretax income at a rate not exceeding 0.8 to 1.
30. According to company records, this sum of RMB 33 million was devoted entirely to employee welfare. See Anshan Iron and Steel Company (1993, p. 327).
31. Interview, senior Angang economist. The figure is perhaps accurate, at least in the sense that Angang's total tax bill is greater than the sum of money transferred by Guangdong to central coffers. Yet the figure does not consider the flow of bank loans directed by the center into Angang. Interestingly, many of these bank loans are made possible by bank lending quotas that transfer deposits of household savings from the South (places like Guangdong) to the industrial Northeast.
32. In 1992, Angang's payables amounted to RMB 30.35 billion, while formal loans to the firm amounted to RMB 62.19 billion. See Anshan Iron and Steel Company (1993, p. 318).
33. For an excellent analysis of this process, see Lardy (forthcoming, Chapter 3).
34. The government encourages these regional transfers by providing banks in some areas with low lending ceilings and by providing banks in other areas – namely, those with high concentrations of heavy industry and state ownership – with high lending quotas. For a detailed description of this process, see Lardy (forthcoming, Chapter 3).
35. In some cases, firms do not have the authority to defy local agencies. In other cases, firms are willing to contribute since in doing so they can claim that, despite poor productivity, they are "sacrificing" for the country.
36. The formation of subsidiary chains, enterprise groups, and affiliated operations fulfills a number of other needs, not the least of which is providing employment for dependents of workers in the core enterprises. Horizontal and vertical integration also becomes useful given the rather undeveloped and highly uncertain state of markets for basic industrial inputs.
37. Anshan Iron and Steel Company (1993, pp. 33, 319). The MMI in its 1993 yearbook elected to list the larger figure (Ministry of Metallurgical Industry 1993, p. 98).
38. Byrd (1992, p. 339). The phenomenon is well documented in the Byrd study, conducted mainly in the late 1980s.
39. Byrd (1992, pp. 332–3).
40. Byrd (1992, p. 334).
41. Byrd (1992, p. 336).
42. Byrd (1992, p. 336).
43. Interviews at Angang, Shougang, Magang, and Wugang all produced the same sorts of views toward the affiliated collectives. They are seen as a headache, but as necessary to absorb excess labor and move unneeded workers and their dependents out of the main steel operations.
44. In general, it should be noted that Chinese SOEs are extremely limited in their abilities to expand their geographical scope. The firm is administratively tied to the locality, and it cannot casually expand to other regions of the country. However, some of the more dynamic SOEs and collective firms are skirting this constraint by

271

merging with (or otherwise buying) geographically distant firms. In other words, Chinese firms are diversifying beyond their narrow geographical boundaries via complex mergers, acquisitions, and asset transfers.

45. Anshan Iron and Steel Company (1993, p. 257).
46. Anshan Iron and Steel Company (1993, p. 257).
47. Anshan Iron and Steel Company (1993, pp. 148–50). The yearbook presents a three-page chart to detail the number of chickens, eggs, pigs, and fish raised by each factory within Angang on an annual basis.
48. This essentially fits the answers provided to Byrd several years earlier, though Byrd reports that the top three appointments are made by the Central Committee of the CCP. The general idea is that the top three officials are appointed by central authorities in Beijing. At least one other large steel mill in China, Capital Iron and Steel (Shougang), also has top management appointed by the State Council.
49. "Liu Qi buzhang zuo zhongyao jianghua" [Minister Liu Qi Makes an Important Speech], *Yejin bao* [*Metallurgy News*] (23 August 1994).
50. This managerial shake-up was the subject of considerable attention throughout the steel industry in late 1994. The reasons for the firing and reshuffling of top Angang officials were not announced publicly, but were known throughout the industry and were a frequent topic of open discussion. Unless otherwise noted, the information presented here was gleaned in conversations with MMI, Capital Iron and Steel, and Ma'anshan Iron and Steel officials. Understandably, Angang officials were not willing to discuss the case.
51. "Liu Qi buzhang zuo zhongyao jianghua," *Yejin bao* (23 August 1994).
52. In interviews, Angang officials were not willing to specify the exact process for the appointment of vice-managers, but they did suggest that it was primarily the task of the provincial government and the MMI. This would fit the pattern prevailing at other large steel mills.
53. The situation described here is rather typical of large Chinese SOEs, but there is some variation even among steel companies. In select cases, such as Capital Iron and Steel, the general manager or party secretary has been able to capture much of the power of personnel appointments and seed midlevel managerial positions with his own people. See Chapter 6 for further details.
54. Ministry of Metallurgical Industry (1995b, p. 3).
55. Ministry of Metallurgical Industry (1995b, p. 3). See also World Bank (1997, p. 70). The World Bank team seems to have observed similar behavior in a variety of medium-sized Chinese SOEs located in a number of cities.
56. Ministry of Metallurgical Industry (1995c, p. 5).
57. Ministry of Metallurgical Industry (1995c, p. 5). Of the twelve major firms studied by the group, four became net loss makers during this period.
58. To say that firms were required to sell on a cash basis is a bit too strong. Rather, they were required to limit sales for which there would be no payment during the normal accounting cycle. In other words, firms were not supposed to extend credit by simply rolling over loans (receivables) from one annual cycle to the next.
59. See Ministry of Metallurgical Industry (1995c).
60. Ministry of Metallurgical Industry (1995c, p. 4).

61. Other studies of smaller SOEs observe this same pattern of short-term loans being used as long-term finance under the tacit agreement that the loans will be rolled over indefinitely. See World Bank (1997, p. 70).
62. In the first three quarters of 1997, the state sector achieved a 10.1-percent increase in output over the same period of 1996. See "Industry Posts 10 Percent Increase," *China Daily* (10 October 1997).
63. For an excellent description of the philosophy behind the pre-1993 and post-1993 accounting systems, see Ministry of Metallurgical Industry (1995b).
64. The balance sheet was actually still a statement of changes in financial position rather than the more internationally accepted cash-flow statement. See Ministry of Metallurgical Industry (1995b, pp. 7–8) and World Bank (1997, p. 65).
65. World Bank (1997, p. 65).
66. Ministry of Metallurgical Industry (1995b, pp. 3–4).
67. Many of these factors evident in the Chinese steel industry were also observed in wider World Bank studies. See World Bank (1997, p. 70).
68. The conversion of nonperforming loans into equity will be documented in the case of Capital Iron and Steel (Shougang); see Chapter 6. The new accounting standards have also been criticized for using the direct method of cash-flow accounting instead of the more internationally recognized indirect method. The indirect method adjusts for revenues (such as payables and receivables) that do not generate cash.
69. Interview, former senior accountant, Ministry of Metallurgical Industry.
70. Anshan Iron and Steel Company (1993, p. 318).
71. Anshan Iron and Steel Company (1993, p. 319).
72. Ministry of Metallurgical Industry (1993, pp. 98, 106).
73. This has clearly been recognized by policy makers in Beijing. See Ministry of Metallurgical Industry (1995b, p. 3).
74. Broadman (1995, p. 16); estimates are from the World Bank Resident Mission in China and China's State Statistical Bureau.
75. Angang company figures; interviews, Angang Economic Institute. See also "Angang qing qian xiang chu xin zhe," *Gongshang shibao* (31 October 1994).
76. Ministry of Metallurgical Industry (1995c, p. 2).
77. I am indebted to a Cambridge University Press reviewer for a series of penetrating comments on this subject.
78. Data come from Ministry of Metallurgical Industry (1995c).
79. Major firms like Angang, Wugang, Shougang, Baogang, and Magang are all officially listed as net creditors. Baogang and Magang were both part of the twelve-firm MMI study noted earlier; the other firms were not included.
80. Ministry of Metallurgical Industry (1995c, p. 3).
81. "Angang qing qian xiang chu xin zhe," *Gongshang shibao* (31 October 1994).
82. For example, see Jefferson and Rawski (1994b, p. 53). As Jefferson and Rawski note, "There is little room to doubt that profit has become the dominant objective of managers in China's state industries." See also Dong (1992a; also cited in Jefferson and Rawski 1994b, p. 55). Dong notes that "enterprises arrange production plans according to market conditions, with the objective of increasing profit."

83. Sicular (1994). See also Shaoguang Wang, "The Rise of the Regions: Fiscal Reform and the Decline of Central State Capacity in China," in Walder (1995, pp. 87–113) as well as Wang and Hu (1993).
84. Sicular (1994).
85. This was true even at Angang, where there were so many financial problems.
86. Interview, Angang.
87. This point was made quite eloquently by the general manager of a state appliance factory in Baotou, Inner Mongolia (interview, October 1994).
88. The one exception is Shanghai's Baoshan Iron and Steel Company, which went on line in 1985 with completely modern equipment. Having started so late in the game, it is blessed with far lower staff levels than any other major firm in the industry.
89. A reasonable question is why any manager in such circumstances would declare losses. In some cases, firms face such dire situations that even paper profits cannot be declared. In other cases, losses are declared when newly appointed managers seek to lower the standards of evaluation for their own future performance. In other words, new managers frequently come in and revise downward the inflated profit declarations of previous management teams. For a description of this behavior, see "Wang Mingzao shijian shi ouran de ma?" [Is the Matter of Wang Mingzao Entirely Unexpected?], *Jingji ribao* (5 October 1995).

CHAPTER 5

1. See Ma'anshan Iron and Steel Company Limited (1994, p. 14). Tsingtao Brewery actually became the first Chinese SOE to list in Hong Kong with its July 1993 initial public offer. As of mid-1996, twenty mainland SOEs had listed shares on either the Hong Kong or New York stock exchanges, in total raising just under U.S. $4 billion in capital. See "Foreign Listing of State Enterprises to Continue," *Zhongguo tongxun she* (6 February 1996), in FBIS document no. CHI-96-034 (21 February 1996).
2. By mid-1997, thirty-two Chinese state firms were listed on the Hong Kong stock exchange and eight were listed on the New York stock exchange.
3. "Securities Official on Firms Listed Overseas," *Renmin ribao* (overseas edition) (24 July 1995), in FBIS document no. CHI-95-187 (7 November 1995).
4. Much of this chapter is based on a series of interviews conducted at Ma'anshan Iron and Steel during October of 1994.
5. Ministry of Metallurgical Industry (1995c, p. 2).
6. Magang receivables declined 5.8 percent after the dissemination of MMI directives prohibiting such sales. Other firms like Sugang and Baogang reduced their levels of receivables by 48 and 21.3 percent, respectively. Magang had the eighth slowest rate of decline among the twelve major firms studied (Ministry of Metallurgical Industry 1995c, p. 2).
7. Magang's inventories of steel products rose from 14,400 tons in 1993 to 24,700 tons in 1994. Inventories were up at a number of major producers in this year, including Shougang, Wugang (Wuhan Iron and Steel), and Angang. See Ministry of Metallurgical Industry (1995, pp. 100–1; 1996, pp. 110–11).

8. Eight of the twelve firms studied by the MMI exhibited declining inventory levels (Ministry of Metallurgical Industry 1995c, p. 1).

9. By mid-1994, similar patterns were being observed at other Hong Kong–listed Chinese SOEs, including Beiren Printing, Kunming Machinery, and Tsingtao Brewery. See Holberton and Lucas (1994).

10. The decline was apparent even in mid-1994. Through the spring of that year, Hong Kong's Hang Seng Index declined 31 percent but Magang shares declined 45 percent, so the firm was underperforming the market. See Holberton and Lucas (1994).

11. See World Bank (1996b, pp. 44–65). It should be noted, however, that the World Bank has been quite realistic in acknowledging that property-rights reform measures of any kind – whether gradual corporatization or outright privatization – are unlikely to be effective if financial discipline is not imposed on the firm. This becomes an important point in understanding the problems Magang has faced in its own restructuring efforts.

12. This notion of divided assets and liabilities reflects the analysis used by Stark (1996) for Hungary.

13. The paper appeared publicly in 1985 as: Wu Jiaxiang and Jin Lizuo, "Gufenhua: Jin yi bu gaige de yi zhong silu," *Jingji ribao* (3 August 1985).

14. See especially Kornai (1980).

15. For an alternative view, see Shirk (1993).

16. For example, see Hideaki Miyajima, "The Privatization of Ex-Zaibatsu Holding Stocks and the Emergence of Bank-Centered Corporate Groups in Japan," in Aoki and Kim (1995).

17. Wu (1993, pp. 211–15) provides an interesting account of this debate and a guide to many of the primary sources involved. For actual responses to the Wu and Jin article, see Wang Xiaoqiang, "Qiye fei gufenhua de sikao," *Jingji ribao* (13 July 1985) and Chen (1986).

18. Hang (1994, p. 4).

19. Wu (1993, p. 232).

20. Li (1994a, p. 15).

21. Interview, chief economist, Magang.

22. Ministry of Metallurgical Industry (1993, p. 99).

23. Interviews, Magang.

24. Hang (1994, p. 4).

25. Ma'anshan Iron and Steel Company Limited (1993a, p. 49).

26. Feng (1994, p. 2).

27. Interviews, chief economist and chief accountant, section heads.

28. Interview, chief economist.

29. Details of the contract are provided in Feng (1994, pp. 2–6).

30. Interview, bureau chief, Ma'anshan City Metallurgical Bureau. The bureau chief had a difficult time explaining what (if any) authority his position entailed. Both he and Magang officials noted that the city has nothing to do with managing the firm, though it certainly relies on Magang's revenue contributions.

31. Feng (1994, p. 4); Ma'anshan Iron and Steel Company Limited (1993a, p. 49).

32. Magang officials openly stated that Magang, like every other large firm, received large amounts of state funding for social service needs, but declined to produce exact figures.

33. See Li (1994a, p. 15). Similar comments were made to me by officials at Magang and Wugang – the other firm in the steel sector undergoing stock reforms – as well as by officials at Angang, who saw joint stock reforms as one last-ditch way they could raise money to pay their workers.

34. Li (1994a, p. 15).

35. Information regarding this conference comes exclusively from interviews, most notably with the chief economist at the Magang General Company (Holding) and section heads at the Magang Stock Company.

36. Hang (1994, p. 4).

37. Interview, Magang.

38. Just as the center has decreased financial transfers to localities in many cases, it has also increased the number of unfunded mandates for investment that it sends to the localities. In other words, the center has been telling localities to engage in increasing amounts of financially draining projects but has not matched those requests with fiscal transfers.

39. Interviews, officials in the Office for Joint Stock System Reform, Wuhan Iron and Steel Company (Wugang).

40. For details on the division of the firm, see Li (1994b, p. 4).

41. Magang Steel originally started with 51,000 workers, but by the time of its formal commissioning on September 1, 1993, boasted 53,000 workers. For exact breakdowns of staff distribution, see Ma'anshan Iron and Steel Company Limited (1993a, p. 62).

42. For a more detailed discussion of this perspective, see World Bank (1997, pp. 33–47).

43. Additional details can be found in Hang (1994, p. 6) and Li (1994b, p. 5).

44. Ma'anshan Iron and Steel Company Limited (1993a, pp. 62–3).

45. Interviews with Magang Holding accounting officials, economists, and Magang Steel accountants.

46. It can be argued that central control over personnel decisions even today remains the single most important source of coherence in the Chinese system. For a sophisticated analysis on this subject, see Huang (1996).

47. Li (1994b, p. 5).

48. Li (1994b, p. 5).

49. Li (1994b, p. 5).

50. Note that page 4 of the Magang 1993 Annual Report issued in Hong Kong makes no mention of Wang Wanbin's status as party secretary, whereas a nearly identical biography in Magang's "A" share stock prospectus for the Shanghai market includes a reference on page 48 to Wang's status as the senior party official in Magang Holding. See Ma'anshan Iron and Steel Company Limited (1993b, p. 48).

51. Interviews, Magang.

52. Interviews, Magang.

53. Feng (1994, p. 6).
54. Ma'anshan Iron and Steel Company Limited (1993a, p. 57).
55. Feng (1994, p. 6).
56. Internal figures supplied by Magang.
57. Interviews, Magang Group, October 1994.
58. Magang Holding chief accountant. Internal figures supplied by Magang Holding.
59. Interviews, Magang Holding chief accountant, Magang Steel accountants.
60. Interviews, Magang Holding.
61. The validity of Magang Holding's interpretation of the law is somewhat immaterial. Rather, what is important to recognize is the great reluctance of officials to pursue any of these extremely serious matters through the courts.
62. Interviews, Magang, Ma'anshan City Tax Bureau, Ma'anshan City State Asset Management Commission.
63. Interview, chief economist.
64. Interview, Ma'anshan City Tax Bureau director.
65. Wu (1993, p. 226).
66. It is interesting to note that the phenomenon is hardly unique to China. Hybrid property-rights forms – "public" SOEs, multilayered state holding companies, interenterprise ownership, and all the accompanying soft budgetary behavior – have been observed in contemporary Hungary by Stark (1996).
67. The World Bank and the International Monetary Fund have made a series of sophisticated arguments on this front. See, for example, World Bank (1996b, pp. 44–65). The World Bank correctly asserts, however, that financial discipline must be imposed if joint stock efforts are to function. In discussions with this author, Gary Jefferson has also argued – in a far more eloquent fashion than is being given justice in this passage – for the benefits of separating manufacturing from social welfare functions.
68. Hang (1994, p. 4).
69. "A Surprisingly Bitter Brew," *New York Times* (27 December 1995).
70. "A Surprisingly Bitter Brew," *New York Times* (27 December 1995).
71. "Chinese Brewer's Stock Is Suspended," *Wall Street Journal* (12 April 1995).

CHAPTER 6

1. The Dazhai production brigade served as a national model for Maoist agricultural policy and egalitarianism from the mid-1960s through the mid-1970s. Immediately before and during the Cultural Revolution, a series of "In Agriculture, Learn from Dazhai" campaigns swept across China, influencing everything from grass-roots political goals to actual agronomy techniques that often bordered on the absurd. In subsequent years, the spectacular grain yields once reported by Dazhai have been thoroughly discredited, and the once model production brigade has been reduced to little more than a symbol of the failure of revolutionary Maoism.
2. Zhou (1992, p. 3).
3. Zhou (1992, p. 16).
4. Ministry of Metallurgical Industry (1993, p. 98).

5. Interviews, Shougang Research and Development Corporation.
6. The municipality's claims of authority over Shougang have some validity. During the Cultural Revolution, control over even huge firms like Angang or Shougang was formally shifted down to the local level, even if in practice local government had neither the expertise nor the manpower to oversee companies engaged in heavy industry. During the late 1970s and early 1980s, the Beijing city government continued to exert direct authority over Shougang, though that authority has declined in recent years.
7. The "tax for profit" policy attempted to replace the firm's traditional practice of submitting profit quotas to the government with a more standardized system of income and value-added taxes. Numerous problems developed with the policy, not the least of which was the fact that the Chinese state pricing system made certain industries particularly profitable while others – especially producers of raw materials – were almost inescapably put in a losing position. Hence, a standardized income tax was seen as patently unfair to those industries suffering losses due to fixed state prices. The effort was essentially abandoned in 1986 in favor of contracting, though it has reappeared in a somewhat more advanced form with the 1994 federated tax system.
8. Interviews, Shougang Research and Development Corporation. The episode is also recounted in Ministry of Metallurgical Industry, "Shougang jingying jizhi de gaige zhanxianle gongyouzhi jingji de shengji yu huoli," in Hao (1992, vol. 1, p. 75).
9. The story was related by several senior engineers at Shougang.
10. Chinese Academy of Social Sciences Institute of Economics (1993, p. 140).
11. Interview, senior economist and senior engineer, Shougang. It should be noted that, in the case of Shougang, until 1995 the party secretary and the chairman of the board were the same person – Zhou Guanwu.
12. Interview, retired MMI official.
13. Interview, retired MMI official.
14. Interview, senior engineer, Shougang Research and Development Company.
15. Interviews, Shougang. This problematic goal is confirmed in the internal MMI investigation report on Shougang's problems in 1995. See Ministry of Metallurgical Industry (1995a, p. 5).
16. Shougang officials suggested that some funds were ultimately turned over to Beijing in this case, but far less than the initial demands of Chen Xitong.
17. The stipulations are presented in detail in Hao (1992, vol. 1, pp. 309–11).
18. The latter two cases, as well as Chinese awareness of those cases, are covered in detail in Wu (1993).
19. Steel prices were deregulated in January 1993, but firms still have arrangements whereby industrial ministries guarantee purchases of portions of output.
20. Ministry of Metallurgical Industry Economic Development Institute (1992, p. 73).
21. Though the contract was established in 1982, the 1981 base year for setting subsequent profit submissions was included in the fifteen-year duration. Therefore, the contract officially ran from 1981 to 1995.
22. Interview, senior official, Ma'anshan Iron and Steel Company (Holding); interview, retired official, Ministry of Metallurgical Industry.

23. It was particularly interesting to hear this account from a Magang official, in a sense a competitor of Shougang's, but an admirer nonetheless.

24. Zhang Chunsheng et al., "Shougang da shiji," in Hao (1992, vol. 1, pp. 280–1).

25. The company frequently uses 1978 as an endpoint, for it was in the next year that Shougang first became the subject of profit retention contracts. Although the long-term fifteen-year contract began in 1982, it had been preceded by several different one-year arrangements.

26. These statistics appear in a variety of Shougang publications, and can also be found in Chinese Academy of Social Sciences Institute of Economics (1993, pp. 19–20).

27. Quoted in Austin and Howell (1995).

28. In the early 1980s, above-plan output was not a particularly significant factor for most steel producers since the vast bulk of their output capacity was captured by the plan.

29. Interview, economist, Shougang.

30. The plan shares dropped precipitously by the early 1990s as the price differentials between plan and market goods receded and the marketing responsibilities increasingly devolved to the individual firms. Beginning in 1993, any differences were erased entirely as the state-plan price was set at market levels. Ironically, at this point it became advantageous for firms to have higher ratios of planned output, since at least this output was guaranteed a purchaser – the state. Firms like Shougang that had higher self-marketed levels were under greater pressure to find purchasers, particularly as demand for steel dropped during 1993 and 1994 while competition from imports increased.

31. Interviews, Shougang Research and Development Corporation. See also Chinese Academy of Social Sciences Institute of Economics (1993, p. 37).

32. Zhou (1992, p. 8).

33. For example, the Tangshan Iron and Steel Company by 1992 was directly marketing over 70 percent of its output but was still a loss-making firm. Except for Shougang, the firms with the lowest planned output levels generally have remained at the lower end of MMI performance studies for major state steel firms.

34. Zhou (1992, pp. 7–8).

35. The study was conducted by the Economic Development Institute of the MMI. The MMI's objectivity in matters relating to Shougang is a complex issue. On the one hand, MMI officials have been resentful of Shougang's financial autonomy and their own inability to intercede in Shougang production or investment decisions. The firm has no lack of detractors in the Metallurgy Ministry. On the other hand, within the Economic Development Institute, Shougang has had a number of supporters over the years, primarily industrial economists genuinely dedicated to finding solutions to China's SOE reform problems. Finally, 1992 marked the height of Shougang's political fortunes and, conceivably, the height of pressure on the MMI to produce pro-Shougang studies.

36. Ministry of Metallurgical Industry Economic Development Institute (1992, p. 74). The exact nature of this calculation is a bit murky. It seems the MMI based its calculation on the hypothetical situation in which Shougang would have sold only 2 percent of its output on the open market instead of the contractually allowed 15 percent.

37. Prices differed between firms first because the actual products being sold differed in quality and kind and second because state prices seemed subject to a certain degree of negotiation between the firm and state officials.
38. Ministry of Metallurgical Industry Economic Development Institute (1992, p. 74).
39. Such views are often expressed (though not, for obvious reasons, in written form) by Chinese economists, industrial managers, and even average workers. Most Beijing taxi drivers are happy to talk about Shougang's tight connections with China's political elite. Western journalists have picked up on this, particularly when Shougang became a major news story in 1995. For representative pieces, see Karl Huus with Z. X. Wang, "The Reckoning Begins: Corruption Case Puts Red-Chip Companies on Alert," *Far Eastern Economic Review* (2 March 1995), p. 16; Lincoln Kaye, "Goodbye to All That," *Far Eastern Economic Review* (23 March 1995), pp. 46–7.
40. Shirk (1993, pp. 199–202) illuminates this point in detail.
41. Zhang Chunsheng et al., "Shougang da shiji," in Hao (1992, vol. 1, p. 278).
42. Zhang Chunsheng et al., "Shougang da shiji," in Hao (1992, vol. 1, p. 282).
43. The periodization is approximate, but generally follows the analysis set out in Wu (1993); see also Shirk (1993).
44. See Shirk (1993, pp. 197–329) for a detailed account of the elite split over contracting and tax-for-profit.
45. Li (1991, p. 330).
46. Li (1989, p. 253).
47. Zhou apparently remained at Shougang during the Cultural Revolution, weathering out the various upheavals of that turbulent period.
48. Interview, Shougang economist.
49. Interviews, Shougang.
50. Zhou has been publicized enough in the Chinese press to be relatively well known among Chinese urban residents, even outside of Beijing.
51. Interviews, Shougang Research and Development Company.
52. This is an important aspect of Zhou Guanwu's daring in accepting the contract in the first place. He was agreeing to forgo loans, and he was promising growth in revenue submissions, all while continuing to carry the social welfare and technological renovation burdens inherited from the command era.
53. This, in a sense, is what happened in 1995. Zhou was terminated and the firm, essentially insolvent, was bailed out.
54. In some sectors – the coal industry is an example – it is not unusual for firms to be thrown into a loss-making situation just by the sales tax and natural resources tax.
55. Interviews, Shougang senior engineers, economists, former factory manager.
56. Hao (1992, vol. 2, p. 24).
57. Hao (1992, vol. 2, p. 24).
58. Kornai (1992, pp. 160–1).
59. Kornai (1992, p. 163).
60. Hao (1992, vol. 2, p. 24).
61. Chinese Academy of Social Sciences Institute of Economics (1993, p. 136).
62. Interview, Shougang economists, Shougang Research and Development Company. The point is important because some observers have suggested that Shougang is

profitable primarily because it channels resources into collective enterprises, which have over the years tended to be taxed less heavily than standard state firms. In other words, the accusation is that Shougang, and other state firms, decapitalize themselves by taking assets from the main operations and funneling them into private or collective firms where those resources can be sheltered from tax. In the process, a sort of unsanctioned privatization process occurs. While this may indeed happen in some firms, there is no evidence of such behavior at Shougang. Given the amount of both publicity and state auditing that Shougang has attracted over the years, such efforts on a large scale would probably be rather difficult.

63. The company has held elections for leaders since 1988, but (not surprisingly) Zhou Guanwu has won every time. It is never mentioned whether there were any other candidates. In 1988, 96 percent of the workers voted and Zhou received 99.14 percent of the votes cast. One wonders what happened to the other 0.86 percent. Shougang midlevel managers admit in private that the elections are simply for show.

64. Capital Iron and Steel Company (1993, p. 14).

65. Interviews, Shougang.

66. Interview, Shougang economist.

67. Interview, Shougang economist.

68. Interview, Shougang economist.

69. Interview, Shougang economist.

70. Interviews, Shougang.

71. Hao (1992, vol. 2, p. 472).

72. Hao (1992, vol. 2, p. 472).

73. Zhou Guanwu, "Geji lingdao ganbu dou yingdang shi chusi de zuzhijia," editorial, *Jingji ribao* (Shougang company reprint, 1994).

74. This is particularly true with the educated economists and planners in Shougang research institutes. Many describe how they are well taken care of, but they bristle at the fact that college classmates at other postings have been able to return to school for graduate degrees or, better yet, go abroad. At Shougang, applying to leave the firm usually brings trouble to the employee. Barriers to departure – often financial barriers – appear out of nowhere, and furthermore the employee is branded as disloyal.

75. For example, see Jiang Shijie, "Hu hu you sheng qi," *Renmin ribao* (13 February 1989); Li Jiajie et al., "Qiye keji jinbu de yangban," *Guangming ribao* (14 March 1991); Liu Lusha, "Rencai chicheng de da wutai," *Guangming ribao* (15 March 1991); and Cheng Yuan, "Shougang jingyan si bian lü," *Jingji ribao* (5, 6, 9, 11 September 1991).

76. For example, see Karl Huus with Z. X. Wang, "The Reckoning Begins: Corruption Case Puts Red-Chip Companies on Alert," *Far Eastern Economic Review* (2 March 1995), p. 16; Lincoln Kaye, "Goodbye to All That," *Far Eastern Economic Review* (23 March 1995), pp. 46–7; Austin and Howell (1995); and Steven Mufson, "Web of Intrigue in Chinese Steel Firm Probe," *Washington Post* (16 March 1995).

77. There are some inconsistencies across the tables in part because data are drawn from a range of Chinese sources, both public and classified. Table 6.6 is based on a combination of MMI public records and internal publications. Table 6.7 is drawn

from MMI internal publications. Table 6.8 is drawn from MMI internal investigatory reports.

78. Ministry of Metallurgical Industry (1995a, p. 2).
79. Ministry of Metallurgical Industry (1995a, p. 5).
80. The Qilu mill would be "greenfield" in the sense that it was to be constructed from scratch instead of being built from existing facilities on site. Qilu would be comparable to the Baoshan Iron and Steel Company in Shanghai, China's last greenfield steel plant.
81. Interview, retired MMI official.
82. Beginning in the mid-1980s, China permitted the emergence of two national comprehensive banks (the Bank of Communications and the CITIC Industrial Bank) as well as three smaller comprehensive banks (the Everbright Bank, the Minsheng Bank, and the Huaxia Bank). See Lardy (forthcoming, Chapter 3).
83. A detailed discussion of Huaxia Bank's financial irregularities can be found in Lardy (forthcoming, Chapter 3).
84. Lardy (forthcoming, Chapter 3).
85. As indicated by Table 6.7, owner equity spiked upward in Shougang in 1995. This seems to have been the result of a direct infusion of capital on an equity basis by the state.
86. The sentence was suspended for two years, and is likely to be commuted to life in prison. See "Zhou Beifang Reportedly Sentenced to Death with Reprieve," *Tung fang jih pao* (30 October 1996), in FBIS document no. CHI-96-211 (31 October 1996).
87. Several Shougang economists and retired advisors commented bitterly to this author in 1994 about Zhou Beifang's behavior and the fact that nothing was being done about it while other Shougang employees were held to such high standards.
88. Shougang managers and economists bristle at the notion of corporatization in China. Most are true believers in contracting, at least over the short term, and in a sense they see corporatization as a favorite of the state bureaucracy that seeks to retain its grip over the firm (interviews, Shougang).
89. Interview, retired MMI official.
90. Interviews, Shougang Research and Development Company.
91. Even in late 1994, Shougang economists were unaware that their company had already started to receive emergency bailout loans from the state banks. Apparently, those loans were done quietly – kept secret even from the company's internal think-tanks – and not revealed until 1995.
92. Interviews, Shougang economist.
93. Ma Daying, "On Unified Financial Authority and Concentrated Finance Resources," *Caijing wenti yanjiu* (January 1982), pp. 6–12; cited and translated in Shirk (1993, p. 237).

CHAPTER 7

1. For example, see Shirk (1993).
2. See Oi (1992).

3. See Huang (1996).
4. See Naughton (1995).
5. Though in fairness to the historical record, it should be noted that "big bang" or "shock therapy" reform packages in Eastern Europe applied primarily to the issue of monetary stabilization and only secondarily to firm-level privatization. Nevertheless, privatization was seen as a crucial (albeit second-order) component of the program.
6. For a clear presentation of the property-rights reform argument, see Walder (1994).
7. See Bernstein (1984).
8. See Oi (1989).
9. Qian and Xu (1993, p. 135); data from China Statistical Yearbooks.
10. Ibid.
11. Ibid.
12. The "state sector" applies to firms that are officially "owned by the people" (*quanmin suoyoude*) and supervised by either central, provincial, prefectural, or county governments. These were the firms that in the command era were basically "on the plan." They also include all of the major heavy industrial producers that form today's urban SOE sector. "Nonstate" or "nontraditional" firms include those that are privately owned or, more commonly, those that are owned directly by district or village-level governments. Such firms, which would include TVEs and urban collectives, are owned not by the "whole people of the nation" but rather by specific grass-roots–level governments representing specific local populations. For an excellent explanation, see Qian and Xu (1993, pp. 138–40).
13. Qian and Xu (1993, p. 140).
14. Oi (1992, p. 99).
15. Qian and Xu (1993, p. 141).
16. The following data on longitudinal and cross-sectional regional income disparities in China are taken from Hu and Wang (1996).
17. The term "local state corporatism" is used by Oi (1992). For similar statements of the view, see Walder (1994) and Nee (1992).
18. Oi (1992, pp. 99–100).
19. Oi (1992, p. 102).
20. Walder (1994, p. 53).
21. Oi (1992, pp. 100–1).
22. Walder (1994, p. 62).
23. Oi (1992, note, p. 119).
24. Of course, a better test of the hypothesis would be to compare a successful set of TVEs with an unsuccessful set. Is the government–enterprise tie closer in the former group than the latter? That this author doubts so is not really the point. Rather, the issue is that a comparison between TVEs and SOEs offers no real test of the hypothesis that state intervention is the key behind TVE growth.
25. Walder (1994, p. 62).
26. Walder (1994, p. 63); Oi (1992, pp. 121–5).
27. Stories like this abound with regard to the city of Nanjing. Researchers at the CASS Institute for Industrial Economics report the same phenomenon in Northeastern

municipalities like Harbin (interviews, Chinese Academy of Social Sciences Institute of Industrial Economics).

28. There is clearly an analog to this pattern in the story of rural decollectivization and the adoption of the responsibility system for peasant producers. Decollectivization began in some of the poorest areas of China – Anhui and Sichuan – and only then spread outward across the country. Granted, that the responsibility system was adopted depended on the existence of creative decision makers – namely, Wan Li in Anhui and Zhao Ziyang in Sichuan. But the more general point is that the impulse behind the adoption of responsibility systems in either the post–Great Leap Forward period or the early reform era was extreme poverty and economic collapse. Constraints limited freedom of choice and necessitated the encouragement of behavioral modes that ran counter to accepted ideology and practice.

29. This hypothesis is based solely on the author's own limited contact with larger rural collectives in China. A good example of a rural collective that got into big trouble through excessive lending is the Shangqiu Fuyuan Meatpacking Company, a 2,300-employee firm in rural Henan Province (author's visit).

30. Indeed, in Anshan City, the municipality has been so uninterested in promoting its own business that Southerners have moved in on their own to try to provide consumer goods and services to the population. Strolling the streets in these environments, one is hard-pressed to find the numerous restaurants, shops, or markets that proliferate in the South, or even now in cities like Beijing. This author in his own visits to Anshan encountered officials who proudly stated that they have no reason to engage in small-scale, export-oriented business: "Angang is one of the nation's largest and most important firms; we don't need to worry about the market, or attracting foreigners, or promoting exports" (author's interviews, November 1994).

31. Walder (1994, p. 62).

32. Walder (1994, p. 62).

33. Oi (1992, p. 119).

34. For a profound discussion of the phenomenon, see Chandler (1977, pp. 6–12).

35. Chandler (1977, p. 8).

36. For a clear statement of this perspective, particularly with regard to fiscal power, see Wang Shaoguang, "The Rise of the Regions: Fiscal Reform and the Decline of Central State Capacity in China," in Walder (1995, pp. 87–113); see also Wang and Hu (1993).

CHAPTER 8

1. Evans (1992, p. 151).

2. Gordon White and Robert Wade, "Developmental States and Markets in East Asia," in White (1988). For seminal works on the theory of "late" development, see Gerschenkron (1962) and Hirschman (1958).

3. Evans (1992, p. 142).

4. Hirschman (1958, p. 35); Evans (1992, pp. 147–8).

5. Evans (1992, p. 148).

6. Amsden (1989, p. 8). See also Wade (1990).

7. Amsden (1989, p. 10).
8. For example, Amsden points out that in the Korean cotton textiles industry during the 1960s, tariffs were waived on imported cotton for those textile manufacturers exporting finished goods.
9. See Johnson (1982).
10. Johnson (1982, p. 26); Evans (1992, p. 152).
11. Scholars have debated whether MITI was actually "autonomous" in the Weberian sense or rather "embedded" in the firm-level environment in which it was operating. Evans suggests that MITI's success was due to the fact that MITI officials, rather than being totally removed from industry, actually could use a series of informal connections with industry-level managers in order to implement policy. In other words, bonds between government agents and private power holders were reinforced by old school ties, industry associations, and a maze of quasigovernmental organizations. In this sense, MITI's success is attributed to its "embedded autonomy" (Evans 1992, pp. 153–4).
12. World Bank (1993).
13. World Bank (1993, p. 10).
14. World Bank (1993, p. 21).
15. World Bank (1993, p. 9).
16. Neoclassical recommendations for postsocialist transition are clearly stated in Sachs (1993) and Boycko et al. (1995).
17. The notion that some forms of direct government intervention are needed to restore markets is by no means an entirely original one. Frank, Kim, and Westphal (1975) have essentially described such a process, albeit at the macro level and involving currency valuation, with regard to the South Korean case.

Bibliography

BOOKS AND ARTICLES

Aharoni, Yair (1986). *The Evolution and Management of State Owned Enterprises*. Cambridge, MA: Ballinger.

Alchian, Armen A., and Harold Demsetz (1972). "Production, Information Costs and Economic Organization," *American Economic Review* 62: 777–95.

Alford, William P. (1995). *To Steal a Book is an Elegant Offense*. Stanford University Press.

Amsden, Alice H. (1989). *Asia's Next Giant: South Korea and Late Industrialization*. New York: Oxford University Press.

Anshan Iron and Steel Company (1993). *Angang nianjian 1993* [The Angang Yearbook 1993]. Beijing: Renmin Chubanshe.

Aoki, Masahiko, and Hyung-Ki Kim (1995). *Corporate Governance in Transitional Economies*. Washington, DC: World Bank.

Aslund, Anders (1991). *Gorbachev's Struggle for Economic Reform*. Ithaca, NY: Cornell University Press.

Austin, Bill, and Martin Howell (1995). "Asia Today: Rise and Fall of a Top Chinese Industrialist," *Bloomberg Business News* (6 March).

Bain, Joe S. (1959). *Industrial Organization*. New York: Wiley.

Berle, Adolf A., and Gardiner C. Means (1968). *The Modern Corporation and Private Property*. New York: Harcourt, Brace & World.

Bernstein, Thomas (1984). "Stalinism, Famine, and Chinese Peasants," *Theory and Society* 13(3): 339–77.

Boycko, Maxim, Andrei Shleifer, and Robert Vishny (1995). *Privatizing Russia*. Cambridge, MA: MIT Press.

Broadman, Harry G. (1995). "Meeting the Challenge of Enterprise Reform," World Bank Discussion Paper no. 283, International Bank for Reconstruction and Development / World Bank, Washington, DC.

(ed.) (1996). "Policy Options for Reform of Chinese State-Owned Enterprises," World Bank Discussion Paper no. 335, International Bank for Reconstruction and Development / World Bank, Washington, DC.

Byrd, William A. (1992). *Chinese Industrial Firms under Reform*. New York: Oxford University Press.

Bibliography

Byrd, William A., and Qingsong Lin (eds.) (1990). *China's Rural Industry*. New York: Oxford University Press.

Capital Iron and Steel Company (1993). "Capital Iron and Steel Corporation – An Archetype for Enterprise Reform in China" (pamphlet). Beijing: New Star Publishers.

Chandler, Alfred D. (1977). *The Visible Hand: The Managerial Revolution in American Business*. Cambridge, MA: Belknap Press.

(1990). *Scale and Scope: The Dynamics of Industrial Capitalism*. Cambridge, MA: Belknap Press.

Chen, Congxin (1986). "Shilun quanmin suoyouzhi qiye de gufenhua," *Guanli shijie*, no. 2.

Chen, Derong (1995). *Chinese Firms between Hierarchy and Market*. London: Macmillan.

Chen, Kang, Gary Jefferson, and Inderjit Singh (1992). "Lessons from China's Economic Reforms," *Journal of Comparative Economics* 16: 201–25.

Chen, Kathy (1996). "China's Economic Feats in '95 Hide Flaws," *Wall Street Journal* (2 January).

Chinese Academy of Social Sciences Institute of Economics (1993). "Jianshe shehui zhuyi xiandai qiye zhidu de youyi tansuo – Shougang gaige yu fazhan lilun sikao" (research report).

Clague, Christopher, and Gordon C. Rausser (1992). *The Emergence of Market Economies in Eastern Europe*. Cambridge, MA: Blackwell.

Coase, R. H. (1959). "The Federal Communications Commission," *Journal of Law and Economics* 2: 1–40.

(1988). *The Firm, the Market, and the Law*. University of Chicago Press.

Demsetz, Harold (1988). *Ownership, Control, and the Firm: The Organization of Economic Activity*, vol. I. Oxford: Blackwell.

(1989). *Efficiency, Competition, and Policy: The Organization of Economic Activity*, vol. II. Oxford: Blackwell.

Deyo, Frederic C. (ed.) (1987). *The Political Economy of the New East Asian Industrialization*. Ithaca, NY: Cornell University Press.

Dong, Furen (1992a). "Behavior of China's State-Owned Enterprises under the Dual System," *Caimao jingji* 12: 55–7.

(1992b). "Zhongguo guoyou qiye gaige: Zhidu, xingwei yu xiaolu," report presented by the Chinese Academy of Social Sciences Institute of Economics (July).

(1992c). *Zhongguo guoyou qiye gaige: Zhidu yu xiaolu*. Beijing: Zhongguo Jihua Chubanshe.

Earle, John S., Saul Estrin, and Larisa Leschenko (1995). "Ownership Structures, Patterns of Control and Enterprise Behavior in Russia," Discussion Paper no. 20, London Business School.

Economist Intelligence Unit (1996a). *Czech Republic/Slovakia: Country Report (3rd Quarter 1996)*. London: EIU.

Economist Intelligence Unit (1996b). *Poland: Country Profile 1995–96*. London: EIU.

Economist Intelligence Unit (1996c). *Ukraine: Country Profile 1996–97*. London: EIU.

Evans, Peter (1992). "The State as Problem and Solution: Predation, Embedded Autonomy, and Structural Change," in Haggard and Kaufman (1992).

288

Bibliography

Evans, Peter B., Dietrich Rueschemeyer, and Theda Skocpol (1985). *Bringing the State Back In*. Cambridge University Press.

Fang, Zun (1993). "Guoyou dazhongxing qiye huoli de zhicu," unpublished policy paper, Shougang Research and Development Corporation.

Feng, Baoxing (1991). "Cong Shougang chengbao de shijian tan caizheng yu shengchan de guanxi," *Jingji yanjiu* 10: 65–71.

Feng, Renshan (1994). " 'Bao gu jiehe' xian shou bing xu xiandai qiye zhidu maibu," internal Magang company report.

Ferris, Andrew (1984). *The Soviet Industrial Enterprise*. London: Croom Helm.

Frank, Charles R., Kwang Suk Kim, and Larry E. Westphal (1975). *Foreign Trade Regimes and Economic Development: South Korea*. New York: National Bureau of Economic Research.

Frydman, Roman, and Andrzej Rapaczynski (1994). *Privatization in Eastern Europe: Is the State Withering Away?* Budapest: Central European University Press.

Frydman, Roman, Andrzej Rapaczynski, John S. Earle, et al. (1993). *The Privatization Process in Central Europe*. Budapest: Central European University Press.

Gelb, Alan, Gary Jefferson, and Inderjit Singh (1993). "The Chinese and East European Routes to Reform," paper presented at Eighth Annual Macroeconomics Conference, National Bureau of Economic Research.

Gerschenkron, Alexander (1962). *Economic Backwardness in Historical Perspective*. Cambridge, MA: Belknap Press.

Gillis, Malcolm, Dwight H. Perkins, Michael Roemer, and Donald R. Snodgrass (1992). *Economics of Development*, 3rd. ed. New York: Norton.

Granick, David (1990). *Chinese State Enterprises: A Regional Property Rights Analysis*. University of Chicago Press.

Grossman, Sanford J., and Oliver D. Hart (1986). "The Costs and Benefits of Ownership: A Theory of Vertical and Lateral Integration," *Journal of Political Economy* 94(4): 691–719.

Haggard, Stephan, and Robert R. Kaufman (eds.) (1992). *The Politics of Economic Adjustment*. Princeton, NJ: Princeton University Press.

Hang, Yongyi (1994). "Shenhua gaige, zhuanhuan jizhi, chuangjian xiandai qiye zhidu: Magang gufenzhi gaizhi de shijian yu chubu renshi," *Yejin guanli*, no. 6.

Hao, Zhen (ed.) (1992). *Shougang gaige* [Shougang Reforms], 3 vols. Beijing Chubanshe.

Harding, Harry (1987). *China's Second Revolution*. Washington, DC: Brookings.

Hay, Donald A., Derek J. Morris, Guy Liu, and Shujie Yao (1994). *Economic Reform and State-Owned Enterprises in China 1979–1987*. Oxford: Clarendon.

Hirschman, Albert O. (1958). *The Strategy of Economic Development*. New Haven, CT: Yale University Press.

Holberton, Simon, and Louise Lucas (1994). "International Company News: Chinese Stocks Lose Their Shine," *Financial Times* (6 May).

Hu, Angang, and Shaoguang Wang (1996). "Changes in China's Regional Disparities," *WCCS Papers* (Washington Center for Chinese Studies), vol. 6, no. 9 (September).

Huang, Sujian, and Zhiyu Shen (1993). *Gongsi zhidu yu qiye gaige*. Beijing: Jingji Guanli Chubanshe.

289

Bibliography

Huang, Yasheng (1990). "Web of Interests and Patterns of Behaviour of Chinese Local Economic Bureaucracies and Enterprises During Reforms," *China Quarterly* 123: 431–58.

(1996). *Inflation and Investment Controls in China*. Cambridge University Press.

Jefferson, Gary (1990). "China's Iron and Steel Industry: Sources of Enterprise Efficiency and the Impact of Reform," *Journal of Development Economics* 33: 329–55.

Jefferson, Gary H., and Thomas G. Rawski (1994a). "How Industrial Reform Worked in China: The Role of Innovation, Competition, and Property Rights," paper prepared for the World Bank Annual Conference on Developmental Economics (April).

(1994b). "Enterprise Reform in Chinese Industry," *Journal of Economic Perspectives* 8(2): 47–70.

Jefferson, Gary H., Thomas G. Rawski, and Yuxin Zheng (1992). "Growth, Efficiency, and Convergence in China's State and Collective Industry," *Economic Development and Cultural Change* 40(2): 239–66.

Jefferson, Gary, and Inderjit Singh (1993). "China's State-Owned Industrial Enterprises: How Effective Have the Reforms Been?" Unpublished manuscript.

Johnson, Chalmers (1982). *MITI and the Japanese Miracle*. Stanford University Press.

Jones, Leroy P. (1975). *Public Enterprise and Economic Development: The Korean Case*. Seoul: Korea Development Institute.

(ed.) (1982). *Public Enterprise in Less-Developed Countries*. Cambridge University Press.

Kornai, János (1980). *Economics of Shortage*. Amsterdam: North-Holland.

(1990). *The Road to a Free Economy*. New York: Norton.

(1992). *The Socialist System: The Political Economy of Communism*. Princeton, NJ: Princeton University Press.

Lampton, David. M. (ed.) (1987). *Policy Implementation in Post-Mao China*. Berkeley: University of California Press.

LaPorte, Robert, Jr., and Muntazar Bashir Ahmed (1989). *Public Enterprises in Pakistan*. Boulder: Westview.

Lardy, Nicholas R. (1983). *Agriculture in China's Modern Economic Development*. Cambridge University Press.

(1992). *Foreign Trade and Economic Reform in China, 1978–1990*. Cambridge University Press.

(forthcoming). *China's Unfinished Economic Revolution*. Washington, DC: Brookings.

Lawson, Nigel (1992). *The View from No. 11: Memoirs of a Tory Radical*. London: Bantam.

Li, Fangdai (1989). *Zhongguo renwu nianjian 1989*. Beijing: Huayi Chubanshe.

(1991). *Zhongguo renwu nianjian 1991*. Beijing: Huayi Chubanshe.

Li, Kazhang (1994a). "Magang shixing gufenzhi zhanlue juece de fenxi," *Yejin guanli*, no. 3.

Li, Peilin (1994b). "Magang zhuangui gaizhi de you yi chang shi," *Yejin jingji yu guanli*, no. 2.

Li, Yining (1992). *Zhongguo jingji gaige yu gufenzhi*. Beijing University Press.

Bibliography

Li, Yining, Fengqi Cao, and Guoyou Zhang (1992). *Zeyang zujian gufenzhi qiye*. Beijing Daxue Chubanshe.

Lieberthal, Kenneth G. (1995). *Governing China: From Revolution through Reform.* New York: Norton.

Lieberthal, Kenneth G., and David M. Lampton (eds.) (1992). *Bureaucracy, Politics, and Decision Making in Post-Mao China*. Berkeley: University of California Press.

Lieberthal, Kenneth G., and Michel Oksenberg (1988). *Policy Making in China: Leaders, Structures, and Processes*. Princeton, NJ: Princeton University Press.

Lin, Justin Yifu, Fang Cai, and Zhou Li (1996). *The China Miracle*. Hong Kong: Chinese University Press.

Little, Ian (1982). *Economic Development: Theory, Policy, and International Relations.* New York: Basic Books.

Liu, Jun, and Lin Li (eds.) (1989). *Xin quanwei zhuyi*. Beijing Jingji Xueyuan Chubanshe.

Liu, Shaoqi (1991). *Selected Works of Liu Shaoqi,* vol. II. Beijing: Foreign Languages Press.

Ma'anshan Iron and Steel Company Limited (1993a). *New Issue and Placing (Prospectus).* Stock prospectus for Hong Kong stock market (20 October).

(1993b). *Zhaogu shuoming shu (A gu) 1993*. "A" share stock prospectus for Shanghai stock market (6 November).

(1994). *1993 Annual Report.*

McKinnon, Ronald I. (1991). *The Order of Economic Liberalization: Financial Control in the Transition to a Market Economy.* Baltimore: Johns Hopkins University Press.

Mann, Jim (1989). *Beijing Jeep.* New York: Simon and Schuster.

Milgrom, Paul, and John Roberts (1992). *Economics, Organization, and Management.* Englewood Cliffs, NJ: Prentice-Hall.

Milor, Vedat (ed.) (1994). *Changing Political Economies: Privatization in Post-Communist and Reforming Communist States.* Boulder: Lynne Rienner.

Ministry of Metallurgical Industry (annual volumes, 1985–1993). *Zhongguo gangtie gongye nianjian* [Yearbook of the Iron and Steel Industry of China]. Beijing: Zhonghua Renmin Gongheguo Yejin Gongyebu Chubanshe.

(annual volumes, 1994–1996). *Zhongguo gangtie tongji* [China Iron and Steel Statistics].

(1995a). "Shougang zijin yunying de xianzhuang yu duice," unpublished internal report (27 April).

(1995b). "Zijin liuliang yanjiu: Lilun fangfa he anli fenxi" [Capital Liquidity Research: Theory, Methods, and Case Analysis], unpublished report.

(1995c). "Huadong diaochazu huibao cailiao" [East China Investigatory Group Report], unpublished internal study.

(1995d). "A Simple Analysis of Steel Enterprise Funding Problems," unpublished internal report.

Ministry of Metallurgical Industry Economic Development Institute (1992). "Shougang jingying jizhi de gaige zhanxianle gongyouzhi jingji de shengji yu huoli," in Hao (1992, vol. 1, pp. 72–88).

Naughton, Barry (1992). "Implications of the State Monopoly over Industry and Its Relaxation," *Modern China* 18(1): 14–41.

291

(1995). *Growing Out of the Plan: Chinese Economic Reform, 1978–1993.* Cambridge University Press.

Nee, Victor (1992). "Organizational Dynamics of Market Transition: Hybrid Forms, Property Rights, and Mixed Economy in China," *Administrative Science Quarterly* 37: 1–27.

Nee, Victor, and David Stark (eds.) (1989). *Remaking the Economic Institutions of Socialism: China and Eastern Europe.* Stanford University Press.

North, Douglass C. (1990). *Institutions, Institutional Change and Economic Performance.* Cambridge University Press.

Oi, Jean C. (1989). *State and Peasant in Contemporary China.* Berkeley: University of California Press.

(1992). "Fiscal Reform and the Foundations of Local State Corporatism in China," *World Politics* 45: 99–126.

Oksenberg, Michel, and James Tong (1991). "The Evolution of Central–Provincial Fiscal Relations in China, 1971–1984," *China Quarterly* 125: 1–32.

Perkins, Dwight (1986). *China: Asia's Next Economic Giant?* Seattle: University of Washington Press.

(1994). "Completing China's Move to the Market," *Journal of Economic Perspectives* 8(2): 23–46.

Perry, Elizabeth J., and Christine Wong (eds.) (1985). *The Political Economy of Reform in Post-Mao China.* Cambridge, MA: Harvard University Press.

Preston, Richard (1991). *American Steel.* New York: Avon.

Pryor, Frederick L. (1973). *Property and Industrial Organization in Communist and Capitalist Nations.* Bloomington: Indiana University Press.

Qian, Yingyi, and Chenggang Xu (1993). "Why China's Economic Reforms Differ," *Economics of Transition* 1(2): 135–70.

Ramamurti, Ravi (1987). "Performance Evaluation of State-Owned Enterprises in Theory and Practice," *Management Science* 33(7): 876–93.

Ramamurti, Ravi, and Raymond Vernon (eds.) (1991). *Privatization and Control of State-Owned Enterprises.* Washington, DC: World Bank.

Sachs, Jeffrey (1993). *Poland's Jump to the Market Economy.* Cambridge, MA: MIT Press.

Sachs, Jeffrey, and Wing Thye Woo (1993). "Structural Factors in the Economic Reforms of China, Eastern Europe and the Former Soviet Union," paper presented at the Economic Policy Panel meeting in Brussels, Belgium (October).

Scherer, F. M. (1980). *Industrial Market Structure and Economic Performance,* 2nd ed. Chicago: Rand McNally.

Schurmann, Franz (1968). *Ideology and Organization in Communist China,* 2nd. ed. Berkeley: University of California Press.

Shirk, Susan L. (1993). *The Political Logic of Economic Reform in China.* Berkeley: University of California Press.

Shue, Vivienne (1988). *The Reach of the State.* Stanford University Press.

Sicular, Terry (1994). "Going on the Dole: Why China's State Enterprises Choose to Lose," conference paper, "Zhongguo jingji tizhi xiayibu gaige huiyi" [The Next Step in China's Economic Structure Reform Meeting] (23–26 August).

Bibliography

Smith, Adam (reprinted 1986). *The Wealth of Nations*. London: Penguin.

Stark, David (1996). "Recombinant Property in East European Capitalism," *American Journal of Sociology* 101(4): 993–1027.

State Statistical Bureau (1991). *Zhongguo tongji nianjian* [Statistical Yearbook of China]. Beijing: Zhongguo Tongji Chubanshe.

(1994). *Zhongguo tongji nianjian* [Statistical Yearbook of China]. Beijing: Zhongguo Tongji Chubanshe.

(1996). *Zhongguo tongji nianjian* [Statistical Yearbook of China]. Beijing: Zhongguo Tongji Chubanshe.

Stickney, Clyde P., and Roman L. Weil (1994). *Financial Accounting,* 7th ed. Fort Worth, TX: Dryden.

Stiglitz, Joseph E. (1994). *Whither Socialism?* Cambridge, MA: MIT Press.

Tyson, Laura D'Andrea (1977). "Liquidity Crises in the Yugoslav Economy: An Alternative to Bankruptcy?" *Soviet Studies* 29(2): 284–95.

Vickers, John, and George Yarrow (1988). *Privatization: An Economic Analysis*. Cambridge, MA: MIT Press.

Vogel, Ezra F. (1989). *One Step Ahead in China*. Cambridge, MA: Harvard University Press.

(1991). *The Four Little Dragons*. Cambridge, MA: Harvard University Press.

Wade, Robert (1990). *Governing the Market: Economic Theory and the Role of Government in East Asian Industrialization*. Princeton, NJ: Princeton University Press.

Walder, Andrew G. (1986). *Communist Neo-Traditionalism*. Berkeley: University of California Press.

(1989). "Factory and Manager in an Era of Reform," *China Quarterly* 118: 242–64.

(1994). "Corporate Organization and Local Government Property Rights in China," in Milor (1994, pp. 53–66).

(ed.) (1995). *The Waning of the Communist State: Economic Origins of Political Decline in China and Hungary*. Berkeley: University of California Press.

Wang, Hong, and Yuanjun Deng (eds.) (1994). *Zui xin gongshang shuizhi shiyong shouce*. Beijing: Zhongguo Shijieyu Chubanshe.

Wang, Shaoguang, and Angang Hu (1993). *Zhongguo guojia nengli baogao* [A Report on China's State Capacity]. Shenyang: Liaoning Renmin Chubanshe.

Waterbury, John (1993). *Exposed to Innumerable Delusions: Public Enterprise and State Power in Egypt, India, Mexico, and Turkey*. Cambridge University Press.

White, Gordon (ed.) (1988). *Developmental States in East Asia*. London: Macmillan.

Williamson, Oliver E. (1985). *The Economic Institutions of Capitalism*. New York: Free Press.

Williamson, Oliver E., and Sidney G. Winter (eds.) (1991). *The Nature of the Firm: Origins, Evolution, and Development*. New York: Oxford University Press.

Woo, Wing Thye (1993). "The Art of Reforming Centrally-Planned Economies: Comparing China, Poland, and Russia," paper presented at the annual meeting of the American Economics Association (February).

World Bank (1990). *China: Revenue Mobilization and Tax Policy*. International Bank for Reconstruction and Development, Washington, DC.

Bibliography

(1993). *The East Asian Miracle: Economic Growth and Public Policy.* New York: Oxford University Press.

(1995). *Bureaucrats in Business: The Economics and Politics of Government Ownership.* New York: Oxford University Press.

(1996a). *The Chinese Economy: Fighting Inflation, Deepening Reforms.* World Bank Country Study, Washington, DC.

(1996b). *From Plan to Market: World Development Report 1996.* International Bank for Reconstruction and Development, Washington, DC.

(1997). *China's Management of Enterprise Assets: The State as Shareholder.* International Bank for Reconstruction and Development, Washington, DC.

Wu, Jiajun, Chunqin Liu, and Shaoming Zhou (1993). *Zhongguo qiye zhidu gaige yanjiu.* Beijing: Jingji Guanli Chubanshe.

Wu, Jinglian (1992). *Jihua jingji haishi shichang jingji.* Beijing: Zhongguo Jingji Chubanshe.

(1993). *Da zhong xing qiye gaige* [Large and Medium Scale Enterprise Reform]. Tianjin Renmin Chubanshe.

Wu, Xiaoling, and Ping Xie (1994). "A Tentative Plan for the Restructuring of the Debts of State-Owned Banks and Enterprises in China," unpublished policy paper, Beijing (August).

Wu, Yuan-li (1965). *The Steel Industry in Communist China.* New York: Praeger.

Xie, Xueshi, and Zhang Keliang (eds.) (1984). *Angang shi, 1909–1948 nian* [The History of Angang, 1909–1948]. Beijing: Yejin Gongye Chubanshe.

Zhou, Guanwu (1992). "Shougang gaige de jiben jingyan," in Hao (1992, vol. 1, pp. 3–41).

Zhou, Xiaochuan, and Zhigang Yang (1994). "1994 Zhongguo shuizhi gaige: yi qude de chengji he chi jiejue de wenti," conference paper, "Zhongguo jingji tizhi xiayibu gaige huiyi" [The Next Step in China's Economic Structure Reform Meeting] (23–26 August).

NEWSPAPERS, NEWSMAGAZINES, AND WIRE SERVICES

Bloomberg Business News
Far Eastern Economic Review
Financial Times
Gongshang shibao
Guangming ribao
International Herald Tribune
Jingji ribao
New York Times
Renmin ribao
South China Morning Post
Wall Street Journal
Washington Post
Yejin bao

Index